INTERPRETING THE GOSPEL OF JOHN
IN ANTIOCH AND ALEXANDRIA

WRITINGS FROM THE GRECO-ROMAN WORLD
SUPPLEMENT SERIES

Clare K. Rothschild, General Editor

Number 17

INTERPRETING THE GOSPEL OF JOHN IN ANTIOCH AND ALEXANDRIA

Miriam DeCock

Atlanta

Copyright © 2020 by Miriam DeCock

All rights reserved. No part of this work may be reproduced or transmitted in any form or by any means, electronic or mechanical, including photocopying and recording, or by means of any information storage or retrieval system, except as may be expressly permitted by the 1976 Copyright Act or in writing from the publisher. Requests for permission should be addressed in writing to the Rights and Permissions Office, SBL Press, 825 Houston Mill Road, Atlanta, GA 30329 USA.

Library of Congress Cataloging-in-Publication Data

Names: DeCock, Miriam, author.
Title: Interpreting the gospel of John in Antioch and Alexandria / by Miriam DeCock.
Description: Atlanta : SBL Press, 2020. | Series: Writings from the Greco-Roman world supplement series ; 17 | Includes bibliographical references and index.
Identifiers: LCCN 2020012827 (print) | LCCN 2020012828 (ebook) | ISBN 9781628372786 (paperback) | ISBN 9780884144472 (hardback) | ISBN 9780884144489 (ebook)
Subjects: LCSH: Bible. John—Criticism, interpretation, etc.
Classification: LCC BS2615.52 .D45 2020 (print) | LCC BS2615.52 (ebook) | DDC 226.506—dc23
LC record available at https://lccn.loc.gov/2020012827
LC ebook record available at https://lccn.loc.gov/2020012828

Contents

Abbreviations vii

Introduction 1

1. John, His Gospel, and Its Interpretation in the
   Schools of Alexandria and Antioch 43

2. The Cleansing of the Temple of John 2 77

3. The Samaritan Woman at the Well of John 4 97

4. The Healing of the Man Born Blind of John 9 139

5. The Good Shepherd Parable of John 10 163

6. The Resurrection of Lazarus of John 11 191

7. Conclusion 215

Bibliography 219
Ancient Sources Index 229
General Index 243

Abbreviations

ACCS	Ancient Christian Commentary on Scripture
ACT	Ancient Christian Texts
ACW	Ancient Christian Writers
Adv. Jud.	Chrysostom, *Adversus Judaeos*
ANF	Roberts, Alexander, and James Donaldson, eds. *The Ante-Nicene Fathers: Translations of the Writings of the Fathers Down to A.D. 325.* 10 vols. Buffalo: Christian Literature, 1885–1887.
BAC	Bible in Ancient Christianity
Bapt.	Tertullian, *De baptismo*
BETL	Bibliotheca Ephemeridum Theologicarum Lovaniensium
BibInt	Biblical Interpretation Series
BLE	*Bulletin de littérature ecclésiastique*
C. Ar.	Athanasius, *Orationes contra Arianos*
CAnt	Christianisme antique
CBQ	*Catholic Biblical Quarterly*
CEAug.SA	Collection des études augustiniennes, Série Antiquité
Cels.	Origen, *Contra Celsum*
CG	Julian, *Oratorio contra Galilaeos*
CJAn	Christianity and Judaism in Antiquity
Comm. Agg.	Theodore, *Commentarius in Aggaeum*
Comm. Am.	Cyril, *Commentarius in Amos*
Comm. Cant.	Origen, *Commentarius in Canticum*
Comm. Gal.	Chrysostom, *Commentarium in Galatas*; Theodore, *Commentarius in epistulam ad Galatas*
Comm. Habac.	Cyril, *Commentarius in Habacuc*
Comm. Heb.	Cyril, *Commentarius in epistulam ad Hebraeos*

Comm. Isa.	Chrysostom, *Commentarius in Isaiam*; Cyril, *Commentarius in Isaiam*
Comm. Jo.	Origen, *Commentarii in evangelium Joannis*; Theodore, *Commentarii in evangelium Joannis*
Comm. Jon.	Theodore, *Commentarii in Jonam*
Comm. Joel.	Cyril, *Commentarius in Joelem*
Comm. Mal.	Theodore, *Commentarius in Malachiam*
Comm. Matt.	Origen, *Commentarius in evangelium Matthaei*
Comm. Mich.	Cyril, *Commentarius in Michaeam*; Theodore, *Commentarius in Michaeam*
Comm. Nah.	Theodore, *Commentarius in Nahum*
Comm. Os.	Theodore, *Commentarius in Osee*
Comm. Phil.	Theodore, *Commentarius in epistulam ad Philippenses*
Comm. Ps.	Chrysostom, *Commentarius in Psalmos*; Diodore, *Commentarii in Psalmos*; Theodore, *Commentarius in Psalmos*
Comm. Rom.	Origen, *Commentarius in Romanos*
Comm. Zach.	Cyril, *Commentarius in Zachariam*; Theodore, *Commentarius in Zachariam*
CSCO	Corpus Scriptorum Christianorum Orientalium
d.	died
Dem. ev.	Eusebius, *Demonstratio evangelica*
ECF	Early Church Fathers
ECS	Early Christian Studies
Ep.	Cyril, *Epistulae*; Cyprian, *Epistulae*
Ep. Calos.	Cyril, *Epistula ad Calosyrium*
Ep. Greg.	Origen, *Epistula ad Gregorium Thaumaturgum*
Ep. Val.	Cyril, *Epistula ad Valerian*
ETL	*Ephimerides Theologicae Lovanienses*
FC	Fathers of the Church
frag.	fragment
GCS	Die griechischen christlichen Schriftsteller der ersten [drei] Jahrhunderte
Haer.	Irenaeus, *Adversus haereses (Elenchos)*
Hist. eccl.	Eusebius, *Historia ecclesiastica*; Socrates, *Historia ecclesiastica*; Theodoret, *Historia ecclesiastica*
Hom.	Severian of Gabala, *Homilae*
Hom. 1 Cor.	Chryosostom, *Homiliae in epistulam I ad Corinthios*

	Abbreviations
Hom. 1 Thess.	Chryosostom, *Homiliae in epistulam i ad Thessalonicenses*
Hom. Act.	Chrysostom, *Homiliae in Acta apostolorum*
Hom Cant.	Origen, *Homiliae in Canticum*
Hom. cat.	Theodore, *Homiliae ad catechumenos*
Hom. Exod.	Origen, *Homiliae in Exodum*
Hom. Ezech.	Origen, *Homiliae in Ezechielem*
Hom. Gen.	Chrysostom, *Homiliae in Genesim*
Hom. Heb.	Chrysostom, *Homiliae in epistulam ad Hebraeos*
Hom. Isa.	Chrysostom, *Homiliae in Isaiam*; Origen, *Homiliae in Isaiam*
Hom. Jer.	Origen, *Homiliae in Jeremiam*
Hom. Jo.	Chrysostom, *Homiliae in Joannem*
Hom. Josh.	Origen, *Homiliae in Josuam*
Hom. Lev.	Origen, *Homiliae in Leviticum*
Hom. Luc.	Chrysostom, *Homiliae in Lucam*; Cyril, *Homiliae in Lucam*; Origen, *Homiliae in Lucam*
Hom. Matt.	Chrysostom, *Homiliae in Matthaeum*
Hom. Num.	Origen, *Homiliae in Numeros*
Hom. Ps.	Chrysostom, *Homiliae in Psalmos*; Origen, *Homiliae in Psalmos*
Hom. Rom.	Chrysostom, *Homiliae in Romanos*
Hom. Sam.	Origen, *Homiliae in Samuelum*
HTR	*Harvard Theological Review*
In Jo.	Cyril, *In Joannem*
Inv.	Cicero, *De inventione rhetorica*
JECS	*Journal of Early Christian Studies*
JEH	*Journal of Ecclesiastical History*
JTS	*Journal of Theological Studies*
Laud. Paul.	Chrysostom, *De laudibus sancti Pauli apostoli*
Laz.	Chrysostom, *De Lazaro*
LCL	Loeb Classical Library
LNTS	Library of New Testament Studies
LXX	Septuagint
MT	Masoretic Hebrew Text
NPNF	Schaff, Philip, and Henry Wace, eds. *A Select Library of Nicene and Post-Nicene Fathers of the Christian Church*. 28 vols. in 2 series. 1886–1889.
NRSV	New Revised Standard Version

NTS	*New Testament Studies*
OECS	Oxford Early Christian Studies
Or.	Origen, *De oratione* (*Peri proseuchēs*)
Pasc.	Origen, *De pascha*
PG	Patrologia Graeca. Edited by J.-P. Migne. 161 vols. Paris, 1857–1886.
Philoc.	Origen, *Philocalia*
Prax.	Tertullian, *Adversus Praxean*
pref.	preface
Princ.	Origen, *De principiis* (*Peri archon*)
Proph. obscurit.	Chrysostom, *De prophetarum obscuritate*
PTS	Patristische Texte und Studien
QVetChr	Quaderni di Vetera Christianorum
Rect.	Cyril, *De recta fide ad Theodosium Imperatorem*
Resp.	Cyril, *Responsio ad Tiberium*; Plato, *Respublica*
RSR	*Recherches de science religieuse*
SBA	Schweizerische Beiträge zur Altertumswissenschaft
SBLMS	Society of Biblical Literature Monograph Series
SC	Sources chrétiennes
SECT	Sources of Early Christian Thought
SJT	*Scottish Journal of Theology*
SNTSMS	Society for New Testament Studies Monograph Series
ST	Studie Testi
StBi	Studi biblici
StPatr	*Studia Patristica*
SVTQ	*St. Vladimir's Theological Quarterly*
TL	Theologicarum Lovaniensium
TLG	Thesaurus Linguae Graecae
TU	Texte und Untersuchungen
WGRW	Writings of the Greco-Roman World
WUNT	Wissenschaftliche Untersuchungen zum Neuen Testament

Introduction

As is well known, scholars of early Christian exegesis have recently challenged the traditional distinction between the two opposing schools of exegesis, the allegorically inclined Alexandrians and the historical-literal Antiochenes. These scholars have demonstrated that the members of both traditions were trained in the Greco-Roman schools of grammar and rhetoric, and thus, they argue, it is not helpful to speak of two opposing schools of exegesis.[1] In the Greco-Roman schools, all early Christian authors were trained to read texts both literally and nonliterally; depending on the rhe-

---

1. From a young age Origen was trained in scriptural exegesis and was then trained in literature, philology, and philosophy. His education with a *grammatikos* included training in classical literature, mathematics, astronomy, and he was then also trained with a rhetor; see, e.g., Peter W. Martens's discussion of Origen's philosophical and rhetorical education in Martens, *Origen and Scripture: The Contours of the Exegetical Life*, OECS (Oxford: Oxford University Press, 2012), 14–19. Cyril may not have had as much rhetorical and philosophical training as Origen, nor did he have as rigorous a philological education as his contemporary Theodore. However, he had a good knowledge of Aristotelian and Porphyrian logic. For a helpful discussion of Cyril's education, see Norman Russell, *Cyril of Alexandria*, ECF (New York: Routledge, 2000), 4. According to David R. Maxwell, the English translator of Cyril's commentary, Cyril probably also received intensive training in scriptural exegesis under Macarius of the desert; see Maxwell, "Translator's Introduction," in Cyril of Alexandria, *Commentary on the Gospel of John*, ACT, 2 vols. (Downers Grove, IL: InterVarsity Press, 2013), 1:xvi. The Antiochene Chrysostom also studied grammar and rhetoric, under one of Antioch's best rhetors, the sophist Libanius. He received religious education under Meletius, which was supplemented by Diodore, one of the directors of the *asketerion* in Antioch. Theodore joined Chrysostom at a young age in Libanius's grammatical-rhetorical school, where he studied literature and rhetoric; for a discussion of this, see George Kalantzis, "Introduction," in Theodore of Mopsuestia, *Commentary on the Gospel of John*, ECS 7 (Strauthfield: Saint Pauls, 2004), 4. Following this classical education, Theodore too spent about a decade in the *asketerion* in Antioch, where he studied exegesis and theology with Diodore. The Antiochenes did not receive a philosophical education with Libanius, who was not equipped to provide it; see Raffaella Cribiore,

torical needs of the situation at hand, interpreters could either remain at the literal level or they could go beyond the letter to provide a nonliteral reading of the text. In response to this scholarship, I argue that despite much important research to demonstrate the overlap between the two schools of Alexandria and Antioch, the traditional scholarly distinction remains helpful.[2] Of course, the distinction requires more nuance than the simplistic categories of literal and allegorical allow, for, as has been demonstrated, the authors of both traditions, like most early Christian exegetes, were capable of reading both literally and nonliterally.

In order to demonstrate the enduring helpfulness of the traditional distinction, in this study I analyze selections from the exegetical treatments of the Gospel of John by two Alexandrians and two Antiochenes. I examine the commentaries of Origen and Cyril of Alexandria and, on the Antiochene side, the commentary of Theodore of Mopsuestia and the exegetical homilies of John Chrysostom.[3] These authors' treatments of

---

The School of Libanius in Late Antique Antioch (Princeton: Princeton University Press, 2007). I will comment on specific studies arguing against the distinction shortly.

2. While I suspect that we ought to revisit what we mean by *school* as we advance this discussion, such an endeavor is beyond the scope of this study. By school, then, at this stage in my work at least, I mean something similar to a recent definition provided by Peter W. Martens, *Adrian's Introduction to the Divine Scriptures: An Antiochene Handbook for Scriptural Interpretation* (Oxford: Oxford University Press, 2017), 15–16. There he defines the school of Antioch broadly as "an Antiochene exegetical culture" and more specifically as a group of late antique figures who flourished in the diocese of Antioch. I hold that something similar occurred in the diocese of Alexandria. In my view, school means at least a school of thought, which Martens's network suggests; see also Robert C. Hill, *Reading the Old Testament in Antioch*, BAC 5 (Leiden: Brill, 2005), 63. However, we also have literary evidence in both locations of actual classroom settings devoted to the study of Scripture, such as Diodore's *asketerion*, in which Theodore and Chrysostom participated, or Origen's classroom setting, which was probably not affiliated with the episcopally led church; see, e.g., Socrates, *Hist. eccl.* 6.3; and Eusebius, *Hist. eccl.* 6.3.8. The initial founders of both schools are shrouded in mystery, however. For a thorough treatment of the school of Alexandria, see Frances M. Young, "Towards a Christian *paideia*," in *Origins to Constantine*, vol. 1 of *The Cambridge History of Christianity*, ed. Frances M. Young and Margaret M. Mitchell (Cambridge: Cambridge University Press, 2006), 1:484–500; see also Roelof van den Broek, "The Christian 'School' of Alexandria in the Second and Third Centuries," in *Centres of Learning: Learning and Location in Pre-Modern Europe and the Middle East*, ed. Jan Willem Drijvers and A. A. MacDonald, Brill's Studies in Intellectual History 61 (Leiden: Brill, 1995), 39–47.

3. Throughout this study I will be using the following critical editions and English translations, unless otherwise noted. For Origen: *Commentaire sur saint Jean*, ed.

the Gospel of John, a text full of symbolic language and imagery, provide particularly telling evidence of my thesis. That is, if the Antiochenes, traditionally described as historical-literal interpreters, were going to provide nonliteral interpretations of any biblical text, we would expect to find them doing so in their treatments of John, given its symbolic nature. To be sure, the Antiochenes do attend to John's symbolic language in the examples I examine in this study; even so, a demonstrable distinction between the members of the two schools remains. The critical distinction I seek to articulate in this study, however, while related to literal and nonliteral treatments of the text, pertains also to the ways in which these authors found instruction for the spiritual development of their audiences in the biblical text. To demonstrate this, I have focused my analysis on a major exegetical principle shared by all four of these authors: Scripture is inherently beneficial or useful, and it is the exegete's duty to draw out the benefits of the text for the exegete's audience.[4]

Why the Gospel of John?

Before explaining my argument in more detail, a few comments about my choice to study these authors' exegetical works on John are in order. In addi-

---

Cécile Blanc, SC 120, 157, 222, 290, 385 (Paris: Cerf, 1966–1992); *Commentary on the Gospel according to John*, trans. Ronald E. Heine, FC 80, 89 (Washington, DC: Catholic University of America Press, 1989, 1993). For Chrysostom: *Homiliae in Joannem*, PG 59 (Paris, 1862); *Commentary on Saint John the Apostle and Evangelist Homilies 1–88*, trans. Sister Thomas Aquinas Goggin, FC 33, 41 (Washington, DC: Catholic University of America Press, 1957, 1959). For Theodore in Greek: *Essai sur Théodore de Mopsueste*, ed. Robert Devreesse, ST 141 (Vatican City: Biblioteca Apostolica Vaticana, 1949); *Commentary on the Gospel of John*, trans. George Kalantzis, ECS 7 (Strathfield: St. Pauls, 2004); for Theodore in Syriac: *Commentarius in Evangelium Ioannis Apostoli*, ed. Jacques Marie Vosté, CSCO 115 (Leuven: Ex Officina Orientali, 1940); *Commentary on the Gospel of John*, trans. Marco Conti, ACT (Downers Grove: IVP Academic, 2010). For Cyril: *Sancti Patris nostri Cyrilli archiepiscopi Alexandrini in D. Joannem Evangelium*, ed. Philip Edward Pusey, 3 vols. (Oxford: Clarendon, 1864); *Commentary on the Gospel of John*, trans. David R. Maxwell, ACT, 2 vols. (Downers Grove, IL: InterVarsity Press, 2013, 2015). Unless otherwise noted all translations will be by these translators. Translations of other ancient works by these authors will be noted in parenthesis and listed in full in the bibliography. Unless otherwise noted, all scriptural translations are my rendering of the Greek, Latin, or Syriac of the commentaries and homilies themselves.

4. I will explain this in much more detail below.

tion to the fact that these authors' treatments of the Gospel of John provide telling evidence of my thesis concerning the two schools, my choice is justified on two other fronts. First, John's Gospel, "the spiritual gospel," was for the early church of utmost importance due to its unparalleled emphasis on Christ's divinity, a feature that was of no little assistance in the Trinitarian and christological controversies in the third to the fifth centuries.[5] Despite the Fourth Gospel's importance, however, the commentaries and homilies of my study have been relatively unexamined in their own right.[6] When

---

5. Early on in the patristic tradition, the church fathers made a distinction between the three Synoptic Gospels and the Fourth Gospel, which they all believed was written by the apostle John, "the beloved disciple" (John 13:23; 19:26; 20:2; 21:7, 20). The view of Clement of Alexandria (d. 215 CE), that John wrote a "spiritual Gospel" to be distinguished from the "corporeal" Synoptic Gospels, which focused on the historical facts about Jesus's life, became commonplace in the subsequent tradition. Clement's comments on this come from a quotation in Eusebius, *Hist. eccl.* 6.14.7, where Eusebius is drawing from Clement's lost work, the *Hypotyposes*.

6. E.g., in his study of the importance of John's Gospel in the development of the Christology of the early church, T. E. Pollard does not deal with these four authors' exegetical works on John at all; see Pollard, *Johannine Christology and the Early Church*, SNTSMS 13 (Cambridge: Cambridge University Press, 1970). There are, of course, some exceptions to this statement; e.g., Blanc's critical editions of Origen's commentary on John (*Commentaire sur saint Jean*) provide an exception with respect to the excellent introduction and analytical notes. Another is Maurice F. Wiles, *The Spiritual Gospel: The Interpretation of the Fourth Gospel in the Early Church* (Cambridge: Cambridge University Press, 1960). Unlike that which I seek to provide, he conducted his analysis on the basis of modern historical-critical principles and methods, with the result that his contribution, though highly suggestive, was overly evaluative. While his study was comparative, he did not attempt to address the Antioch-Alexandria question directly. Since this publication in 1960, there has been no sustained treatment of these texts for their own sake. A recent work on the reception of John in the early church is Kyle Keefer, *The Branches of the Gospel of John: The Reception of the Gospel of John in the Early Church*, LNTS 332 (New York: T&T Clark, 2006). While his study includes a brief chapter on Origen's commentary, he is more interested in the insight provided by second- and third-century authors for modern biblical scholars' understanding of the text of John, in addition to developing the method of reception history, than in the exegetical practices of these authors themselves. See also C. E. Hill, "The Gospel of John," in *The Oxford Handbook of Early Christian Biblical Interpretation*, ed. Paul M. Blowers and Peter W. Martens (Oxford: Oxford University Press, 2019), 602–13. Another exception is found in Louis M. Farag's work on Cyril's commentary on John in which she studies the structure, grammar, and verse division (Farag, *St. Cyril of Alexandria, A New Testament Exegete: His Commentary on the Gospel of John*, Gorgias Dissertations 29 [Piscataway, NJ: Gorgias, 2007]). It is a helpful resource, but she does

Introduction 5

scholars have drawn on these authors' commentaries and homilies on John, they have tended to focus on their contributions to the doctrinal formulations of the period, with the result that their exegetical literature was studied only for what it might contribute to an understanding of their theology.[7]

---

not work through his application of the exegetical principles of his approach. Finally, a handful of scholars have worked on one passage of John in Origen or on one section of his commentary; see, e.g., Ronald E. Heine, "Stoic Logic as Handmaid to Exegesis and Theology in Origen's Commentary on the Gospel of John," *JTS* 44 (1993): 90-117. Heine deals with Origen's use of Stoic logic in his treatments of John 1:1-2; 8:37-53; 13:31-32. See also Jean-Michel Poffet's work on Origen's and Heracleon's treatments of John 4 in *La Méthode exégétique d' Héracléon et d' Origène commentateurs de Jn 4*, Paradosis 28 (Fribourg: Éditions Universitaires, 1985). In his detailed study, Poffet evaluates these authors' readings of John based on his own contemporary ecclesial concerns and thus does not treat them for their own sake. See also, Jean-Noël Aletti, "D'une écriture à l'autre: Analyse structurale d'un passage d'Origène, commentaire sur Jean, livre II, paragraphe 13-21," *RSR* 61 (1973): 27-47; Henri Crouzel, "Le Contenu spirituel des dénominations du Christ selon le Livre I du *Commentaire sur Jean* d'Origène," in *Origeniana Secunda: Second colloque internationale des etudes, Bari 20-23 septembre 1977*, ed. Henri Crouzel and Antonio Quacquarelli, QVetChr 15 (Rome: dell'Ateneo, 1980), 131-50; Ronald E. Heine, "The Introduction to Origen's *Commentary on John* Compared with the Introductions to the Ancient Philosophical Commentaries on Aristotle," in *Origeniana Sexta: Origène et la Bible; Actes du Colloquium Origenianum Sextum, Chantilly, 30 août-3 septembre 1993*, ed. Gilles Dorival and Alain Le Boulluec, BETL 118 (Leuven: Peeters, 1995), 3-12; John A. McGuckin, "Structural Design and Apologetic Intent in Origen's *Commentary on John*" in Dorival and Le Boulluec, *Origeniana Sexta*, 441-57. McGuckin deals in particular with books 1 and 13 within his discussion of the whole of the commentary. I will return to his treatment of book 13 in ch. 3 as we deal with Origen's treatment of John 4. Chrysostom's *Homilies on John* have received less attention; for a very short study, see Abe Attrep, "The Teacher and His Teachings: Chrysostom's Homiletical Approach as Seen in Commentaries on the Gospel of John," *SVTQ* 38 (1994): 293-301. He deals with Chrysostom's concluding exhortatory comments in his John homilies. The same is true of Theodore's commentary, probably due in part to the fragmentary nature of the Greek text, and the fact that the full translation is in Syriac. To date, the only completed studies of the commentary focus on Theodore's Christology. I will highlight these studies in the following note.

7. See, e.g., T. E. Pollard, "The Exegesis of John 10.30 in the Early Trinitarian Controversies," *NTS* 3 (1956-1957): 334-48; William MaCaulay, "The Nature of Christ in Origen's 'Commentary on John,'" *SJT* 19 (1966): 176-87; J. N. Rowe, "Origen's Subordinationism as Illustrated in His Commentary on St. John's Gospel," *StPatr* 11 (1972): 222-28; E. Früchtel, "Ἀρχή und das erste Buch des Johanneskommentars des Origenes," *StPatr* 14 (1976): 122-44; Lars Koen, *The Saving Passion: Incarnational and Soteriological Thought in Cyril of Alexandria's Commentary on the Gospel according to St. John* (Philadelphia: Coronet, 1991); Koen, "Partitive Exegesis in Cyril of Alexan-

Second, in her *Biblical Exegesis and the Formation of Christian Culture*, Frances Young claims that the traditional account of the two schools was based primarily on these authors' interpretations of the Old Testament, not the New, thus identifying the need for nuanced analyses of their exegesis of New Testament texts, such as that which she initiates in her own work.[8] My study of the fathers' exegetical literature on the Gospel of John goes some way to meeting this need.

THE FOUR EXEGETICAL WORKS OF MY STUDY

Origen wrote his *Commentary on the Gospel of John* over a period of nearly twenty years, probably between 231 and 248 CE, and according to most scholars, he composed the first four or five books in Alexandria and the remaining twenty-seven in Caesarea after his move there.[9] Unfortunately, the commentary is fragmentary, and the nine books left to us of a probable thirty-two cover only parts of John 1–13, though there are no clues as to whether it was ever completed. Even though it is fragmentary, the commentary nonetheless consists of approximately 850 pages of Greek text, and it includes his treatment of portions of John 1, 2, 4, 8, 11, and

---

dria's Commentary on the Gospel according to St. John," *StPatr* 25 (1993): 115–21; Frederick G. McLeod, *The Roles of Christ's Humanity in Salvation: Insights from Theodore of Mopsuestia* (Washington, DC: Catholic University of America Press, 2005); George Kalantzis, "*Duo Filii* and the *Homo Assumptus* in the Christology of Theodore of Mopsuestia: The Greek Fragments of the Commentary on John," *ETL* 78 (2002): 57–78; McLeod, "The Christology in Theodore of Mopsuestia's *Commentary on the Gospel of John*," *JTS* 73 (2012): 115–38. See also a recent study by Michael G. Azar, which is focused on these authors' treatment of another not unrelated concept, namely, the Johannine "Jews": *Exegeting the Jews: The Early Reception of the Johannine "Jews,"* Bible in Ancient Christianity 10 (Leiden: Brill, 2016). Azar examines the exegetical literature on John of three of my four authors, Origen, Chrysostom, and Cyril. He argues that their exegesis of the Fourth Gospel's hostility toward the Jews did not function for them primarily or monolithically as grounds for anti-Judaic sentiments, but rather as a resource for the spiritual formation and delineation of their own Christian communities. While I do not deal with his specific arguments in this study, my work does contribute evidence that generally supports his overall thesis.

8. Frances M. Young, *Biblical Exegesis and the Formation of Christian Culture* (Cambridge: Cambridge University Press, 1997), 201.

9. For a thorough treatment of this timeline, see Anders-Christian Jacobsen, *Christ—The Teacher of Salvation: A Study on Origen's Christology and Soteriology*, Adamantiana 6 (Münster: Aschendorff, 2015).

13. Origen addresses the work to one Ambrose, probably a patron of the work, who was, according to Eusebius, a Valentinian gnostic prior to his conversion to Christianity, and indeed, Origen purportedly refutes the Valentinian exegete, Heracleon, at various points throughout the commentary.[10] That being said, there are long sections of the text in which Heracleon's commentary is not so much as mentioned, and Heracleon and his fellow gnostics are not always in Origen's immediate purview.[11]

Chrysostom delivered eighty-eight homilies in which he commented on the Gospel of John in its entirety, shortly after he had become a priest in Antioch, beginning around 390–391. The record of the full set of homilies consists of about 240 pages of Greek.[12] In each homily, Chrysostom begins with a passage from John and then moves to providing his parishioners with practical moral instruction, often elicited by the passage of focus but not always confined to it. In his comments he defends Nicene orthodoxy, not infrequently refuting the neo-Arian interpreters of his own day.

Theodore originally composed his *Commentary on John* in Greek sometime in the first decade of the fifth century, during what some scholars have characterized as his second period of literary activity (in the years following 383). Only fragments of the original Greek remain, though we have at least a portion of his comments on most of the gospel passages. The fragments amount to about thirty-three pages of Greek. The relatively recent discovery of a full early Syriac translation (conducted ca. 460–65), generally considered reliable by scholars, supplements our knowledge of his treatment of the gospel. The Syriac translation, consisting of about

---

10. See Eusebius, *Hist. eccl.* 6.18.1. Heine has suggested that Ambrose almost certainly knew Heracleon's commentary on John and thus requested that Origen provide a counterpart from the "orthodox" side of the church; see Heine, "Introduction," in *Commentary on the Gospel according to John*, 6. Some scholars, however, suspect that Origen had ulterior motives for refuting Heracleon. As we will discuss in more detail below, John McGuckin has helpfully argued that Heracleon is not really his main concern. Instead, Origen is concerned to defend his own interpretive skills, which some "literalist interpreters" within the church had called into question; see McGuckin "Structural Design," 441–57. See my discussion of this feature of Origen's commentary at 107 n. 23 and 109–10 n. 27.

11. Heine observes that Origen has other aims in composing his commentary, such as providing intelligent interpretations of problems that arise from comparing the Gospel of John with the Synoptic Gospels; see Heine, "Introduction," 7.

12. Goggin, "Introduction," in *Commentary on Saint John*, xvii, observes that many of the homilies are lengthy and would thus take over an hour to be delivered aloud.

360 pages, I use with caution and as a supplement wherever necessary. Like Chrysostom, Theodore presents Nicene theology as he refutes the contemporary Arian thought, though his doctrinal discussions are more developed and complex than those of Chrysostom.

Approximately two centuries after Origen, Cyril wrote his commentary on John's Gospel, between the years 425 and 428, in the early period of his episcopacy. Thus, it was written before the outbreak of the Nestorian controversy, though the commentary contains several instances of his refutations of Antiochene Christology broadly conceived.[13] The work consists of approximately 1600 pages of Greek text. In the commentary, he too takes a firmly Nicene stance, and he frequently refutes neo-Arians, such as Eunomius. As such, he alone of my four authors claims to set out a "doctrinal explanation" (δογματικωτέρας ἐξήγησις) of John, and there are many indications throughout the commentary that Cyril composed the work for the sake of those teaching the central doctrines of the faith to catechumens.[14] Finally, Cyril's commentary is unique in that while it is a verse-by-verse treatment of John, he also took a number of opportunities to devote whole books to central themes that arose for him in John's narrative, such as the Christian treatment of Torah and the sacraments.

Scholarship on Origen and the Two Schools

I will now provide a brief sketch of the developments in scholarship on the two schools in order to situate my study within the discussion.[15] I will first provide an overview of the traditional scholarly description of the two exegetical schools, followed by an excursus on contributions by some of the key studies of Origen's exegesis, which set the stage for the scholarly chal-

---

13. There is no mention in the commentary of the Nestorian controversy's resulting title for Mary, the *Theotokos*.

14. This is the theory of David R. Maxwell in particular, the most recent English translator of Cyril's *Commentary on the Gospel of John*. Based on a great deal of evidence, some of which I will treat in this study, Maxwell argues that Cyril "assumes that his readers are charged with teaching the faith, especially to catechumens"; see Maxwell, "Translator's Introduction," in *Commentary on the Gospel of John*, xviii.

15. There is no need to recount the history of scholarship in too much detail, as this work has already been done by others; see, e.g., J.-N. Guinot, "La frontière entre allégorie et typologie: École alexandrine, école antiochienne," *RSR* 99 (2011): 207–28; Elizabeth Clark, *Reading Renunciation: Asceticism and Scripture in Early Christianity* (Princeton: Princeton University Press, 1999), 70–78.

lenge to the two-schools model. Next, I will present the main arguments of Young, whose work on the two schools changed the shape of the conversation definitively. I will then discuss the work of those who have responded to Young's contribution to the debate.

From the late nineteenth century until the 1980s, scholars of patristic exegesis assumed that the two early Christian centers' schools of interpretation were based on fundamentally different interpretive approaches to the biblical text, as we have already noted.[16] These scholars also argued that in addition to their historical-literal approach, the Antiochenes occasionally employed what they called "typological interpretation," but in a reserved manner; the types they found always maintained a connection between the literal text and the type. Karlfried Froehlich has aptly characterized the traditional account of the dispute in this way: "Alexandrian allegorism, it is claimed, regarded the text of the Bible as a mere springboard for uncontrolled speculation while the Antiochene interpretation took the historical substance seriously and thus was closer to early Christian typology."[17] Froehlich does not count himself among those who hold the traditional position on the question, but his characterization illustrates two correlated points in addition to the obviously major distinction scholars tended to make between the two schools. First, his words highlight the underlying assumption of scholars of the traditional position that allegorical interpretation, as exemplified by the interpretations of Origen and his successors, was arbitrary, for it did not always take the historical account of the text seriously. Second, the nonliteral interpretation of the

---

16. Some notable examples of the traditional approach are as follows: Johannes Quasten, *The Golden Age of Greek Patristic Literature from the Council of Nicaea to the Council of Chalcedon*, vol. 3 of *Patrology* (Westminster, MD: Newman Press, 1960); Robert M. Grant and David Tracy, *A Short History of the Interpretation of the Bible*, 2nd ed. (Philadelphia: Fortress, 1973); D. S. Wallace-Hadrill, *Christian Antioch: A Study of Early Christian Thought in the East* (Cambridge: Cambridge University Press, 1982); Manlio Simonetti, *Biblical Interpretation in the Early Church*, trans. John A. Hughes (Edinburgh: T&T Clark, 1994). These scholars tended to marshal the same group of passages and texts written by the Antiochenes, in which these authors responded to Origen and allegorical interpretation vehemently, e.g., Eustathius, *On the Witch of Endor and against Origen*; Diodore, *On the Difference between Theoria and Allegoria* and *Comm. Ps.* pref.; Theodore of Mopsuestia, *Comm. Mich.* 5:5–6; *Comm. Nah.* 3:8; *Comm. Gal.* 4:24.

17. Froehlich, *Biblical Interpretation in the Early Church*, SECT (Philadelphia: Fortress, 1980), 20.

Antiochenes was acceptable because they attended to a text's historical meaning even when they provided a typological interpretation of the text.[18] Scholars of the traditional position were suspicious of the Alexandrians' exegesis for yet another reason, however. For scholars of the traditional position, whereas the Antiochenes' typological reading of the biblical text, frequently associated in their writings with the interpretive act of θεωρία (insight or contemplation), seemed to be more traditional to early Christianity (i.e., was more akin to the New Testament's interpretation of the Old Testament), the Alexandrians imported allegorical interpretation into their nonliteral reading practice, a method that was based on Platonic philosophical categories.[19] Therefore, the less philosophically inclined school of Antioch was implicitly held in higher regard, as the only apparent trace of philosophy to be found in their interpretive work was an Aristotelian emphasis on observable facts.[20] In this construal, the Antiochene approach was a philological one, unlike that of Origen, based on the model of the Greco-Roman grammatical schools, which many argued accounted for their critical attention to the text itself in its "plain sense."[21]

---

18. For a representative example, see the comments of Wallace-Hadrill, *Christian Antioch*, 33; see also Grant and Tracy, *Short History of the Interpretation of the Bible*, 66.

19. For the importation of allegorical ideas, see, e.g., Simonetti, *Biblical Interpretation*, 34, 37–38; 60. For Platonic categories, see, e.g., J. N. D. Kelly's comments in *Early Christian Doctrines*, 5th ed. (New York: A&C Black, 1977), 74; cf. Karen Jo Torjesen, *Hermeneutical Procedure and Theological Method in Origen's Exegesis*, PTS 28 (Berlin: de Gruyter, 1985), 3. Torjesen argues that Adolf von Harnack's *Lehrbuch der Dogmengeschichte*, which he published in 1883, made this perspective commonplace and that his thesis was the driving force behind much of the scholarship on Origen that followed. An influential example of this is R. P. C. Hanson's *Allegory and Event: A Study of the Sources and Significance of Origen's Interpretation of Scripture* (Richmond: John Knox, 1959).

20. Grant and Tracy, *Short History of the Interpretation of the Bible*, 66.

21. Indeed, while these scholars admitted that Origen had received philological training, he did not put it into practice in his exegesis of Scripture; see, e.g., Wallace-Hadrill, *Christian Antioch*, 29; Simonetti makes a similar statement in *Biblical Interpretation*, 44. Another influence on Antiochene exegesis that most scholars of this position assumed was that of Jewish exegesis; e.g., Grant and Tracy suggest the literalism of the synagogue had a great influence on the Antiochenes (*Short History of the Interpretation of the Bible*, 63). Wallace-Hadrill argues something similar, suggesting that the Antiochenes' recourse to paraphrase in their exegesis was influenced by the Jewish targumim (*Christian Antioch*, 30). For a refutation of this assumption, see Clark, *Reading Renunciation*, 71. Few scholars would claim this as readily today.

Before I describe the challenges to the traditional account of the two schools, it is important to mention the developments in scholarship on Origen's exegesis between the 1960s and the 1980s, for these developments are inextricably linked to developments in scholarship on the two schools.[22] Not only did scholars produce a great number of critical editions of various of Origen's exegetical works during this time, but the third-century exegete's discussion of the principles of biblical interpretation in *Peri archon* and his exegetical works themselves were also reassessed.[23] As a result of this work, Origen's exegesis came to be understood as much more complex than was previously thought; his exegetical treatment of the historical sense of the text and his philological rigor were now much more widely appreciated.[24] Origen also came to be recognized for the influence he had on subsequent patristic biblical interpreters (including the Antiochenes, particularly in regard to his philological methods and rhetorical

---

22. I will not recount all of the details, for this ground has also been covered by others; see, e.g., Joseph W. Trigg, introduction to *Allegory and Event: A Study of the Sources and Significance of Origen's Interpretation of Scripture*, by R. P. C. Hanson (Louisville: John Knox, 2002), i–xxv; cf. Torjesen, *Hermeneutical Procedure*, 1–12.

23. For critical editions, see, e.g., Origen, *Traité des principes (Peri Archon)*, ed. Marguerite Harl, Gilles Dorrival, and Alain Le Boulluec, CEAug.SA 68 (Paris: Études Augustiniennes, 1978); Origen, *La Philocalie 1–20 Sur Les Scriptures*, ed. Marguerite Harl, SC 302 (Paris: Cerf, 1983); *Jeremiahomilien; Klageliederkommentar; Erklärung der Samuel- und Königsbücher*, ed. Erich Klostermann and Pierre Nautin, 2nd ed., GCS 6, Origenes Werke 3 (Berlin: Akademie, 1983); *Mattäuserklärung*, ed. Erich Klostermann, Ernst Benz, and Ursula Treu, 2nd ed., GCS 57, Origenes Werke 11 (Berlin: Akademie, 1976); Origen, *Homélies sur la Genèse*, ed. Henri de Lubac and Louis Doutreleau, 2nd ed., SC 7 (Paris: Cerf, 2003). For the last example, note that the first edition was published in 1976, during this period of reexamination. One of the leading figures of this reassessment was Marguerite Harl. In her articles from the 1970s and 1980s, Harl provided detailed analysis of his exegetical methods, in addition to a reassessment of the form and intention of *Peri archon*; see Harl, *Le déchiffrement du sens: Études sur l'herméneutique chrétienne d'Origène à Grégoire de Nysse* (Paris: Études Augustiniennes, 1993); another notable contributor to this shift is Robert M. Grant, *The Earliest Lives of Jesus* (New York: Harper, 1961), in which he argued that Origen's approach to history was more complex than had previously been thought.

24. This in contrast to previous negative assessments such as those articulated by Hanson, who argued in *Allegory and Event* that Origen sat too loosely to history and thus did not understand the Bible, nor did he attempt to understand the scriptural authors' intentions. Further, for Hanson, through his arbitrary allegorical exegesis, he erased history and misunderstood the doctrinal significance of the incarnation and resurrection.

education).²⁵ Furthermore, his Platonic understanding of reality came to be understood by an increasing number of scholars as the vehicle that lent his allegorical approach to Scripture its coherence.²⁶

Other scholars documented additional aspects of his thought that illustrated the coherence of his exegesis. One particularly notable example is the study by Karen Jo Torjesen, who argued that Origen's exegetical method was coherent by demonstrating that he is consistent in his step-by-step procedure as he treats individual verses and also in the literary form his homilies or commentaries take as a whole. She demonstrated that the organizing principle of his exegesis was that the Christian soul encountered Christ in Scripture. His exegesis assumed the reality of an encounter that led to his readers' or hearers' spiritual transformation. Thus, for Origen, Torjesen argued, exegesis functioned as "a pedagogy of the soul."²⁷

One of the other results of the scholarship in these decades was the growing consensus that the distinction between allegory and typology had been overstated or even falsely constructed.²⁸ In particular, Henri de Lubac insisted in the late 1940s that there was more overlap than had previously

---

25. For Origen's influence on the Antiochenes, see, e.g., the argument of J.-N. Guinot, "L'école exégétique d'Antioche et ses relations avec Origène," in *Origeniana Octava: Origène e la tradizione Alessandrina; Papers of the 8th International Origen Congress 2003, Pisa 27–31 August 2001*, ed. Lorenzo Perrone, BETL 164 (Leuven: Peeters, 2003), 2:1149–66. I will say more below about Origen's rhetorical education, particularly when I outline Young's contribution to this discussion; however, prior to Young, several scholars conducted full-length studies as part of the shift in Origen studies. See, e.g., Manlio Simonetti, *Lettera e/o allegoria: Un contributo alla storia dell'esegesi patristica* (Rome: Institutum Patristicum Augustinianum, 1985), in which he showed how Origen's scientific philological approach to the text used the techniques of Hellenistic grammar, and demonstrated his influence on subsequent patristic exegesis, including the Antiochenes. Pierre Nautin reconstructed the life and works of Origen (*Origène, sa vie, son œuvre*, CAnt 1 [Paris: Beauchesne, 1977]). Apart from his reconstruction of the timeline in which Origen composed his works, it is still heeded today by most. The most extensive work on his philological and grammatical training in the Greco-Roman schools was conducted by Bernhard Neuschäfer, *Origenes als Philologe*, SBA 18, 2 vols. (Basel: Reinhardt, 1987).

26. Young, *Biblical Exegesis*, 25.

27. Torjesen, *Hermeneutical Procedure*, 119; see also Trigg, introduction, xxi.

28. Many were reacting to the thesis of Jean Daniélou, who claimed that typology was legitimate since it was the method used by New Testament authors, whereas (arbitrary) allegory was a later development; see Daniélou, *Origène* (Paris: La Table Ronde, 1948).

been thought between the ways these terms were being used by early Christian exegetes and that θεωρία too was used both by the Antiochenes and the Alexandrians.[29] A growing number of scholars built upon these observations and argued that the ancient authors did not distinguish between typology and allegory the way modern scholars, such as Jean Daniélou, had done.[30] These insights would be taken up again by those who would articulate the challenge to the two schools model, to which we will now turn.

In the 1980s and 1990s, as this shift in the study of Origen's exegesis was taking place, a handful of scholars began to bring together the above-mentioned observations about the areas of overlap between the two exegetical traditions in Antioch and Alexandria in order to question the traditional reconstruction of two distinct exegetical schools. Some, such as Froehlich, combined the observations made within the growing body of scholarly work on Origen and the Antiochenes and argued succinctly that the sharp antithesis of the two schools was nothing more than a scholarly construct, for Origen did not deny the historical referent of most texts, and the Antiochenes often sought a higher sense than that which was indicated by the bare letter, through the procedure of θεωρία.[31] He suggested that the main difference between the schools was that the Alexandrians approached the text from a Platonic philosophical perspective, whereas the Antiochenes did so based on their training in the rhetorical tradition.[32] Their different school training accounted for the Alexandrian subordination of a text's literal sense to its nonliteral sense, and the Antiochene subordination of the nonliteral sense to the literal. Both traditions, however, sought its nonliteral sense because of their common belief in the text's divine authorship. For Froehlich, the

---

29. De Lubac, "Typologie et allegorisme," *RSR* 34 (1947): 180–226; see also Kelly, *Early Christian Doctrine*, 72.

30. Others helped with the erosion of the distinction between allegory and typology; see, e.g., Jean Pepin, *Mythe et allegorie: Les origines grecques et les contestations judéo-chrétiennes*, 2nd ed. (Paris: Aubier, 1976); Erich Auerbach, *Scenes from the Drama of European Literature* (Minneapolis: University of Minnesota Press, 1984); Henri Crouzel, "La Distinction de la 'typologie' et de 'l'allegorie,'" *BLE* 65 (1964): 161–74.

31. Froehlich, *Biblical Interpretation*, 20; see also Bradley Nassif, "'Spiritual Exegesis' in the School of Antioch," in *New Perspectives on Historical Theology: Essays in Memory of John Meyendorff*, ed. Bradley Nassif (Grand Rapids: Eerdmans, 1996), 343–77.

32. This particular observation Young would develop demonstrably.

difference between the two schools lay only in emphasis, for both schools sought both senses of the text.[33]

In her immensely influential 1997 publication, *Biblical Exegesis and the Formation of Christian Culture*, Young developed and sharpened these arguments extensively.[34] For Young, as we saw in Froehlich's comments, the hermeneutical dispute was best understood as a dispute about how meaning is found in texts within the two main Greco-Roman educational programs, namely, the philosophical tradition in Alexandria and grammatical-rhetorical tradition in Antioch.[35] As had already been well documented by Origen scholars, Young made clear that Origen was deeply influenced by Neoplatonic exegesis, which informed his views on the coherence of Scripture.[36] Just as Neoplatonists understood each one of Plato's compositions within the framework of the one and the many, as an "organic unity," Origen saw a unity of intent underlying the various scriptural texts: the one word of God through many words. According to Young, Origen believed that all of the constituent parts of Scripture had a "unitive thrust" (her translation of σκοπός), in the same way the body and soul were unified, and thus that Scripture too consisted of body and soul. The sensible or "bodily" words of Scripture contained intellectual and spiritual realities, and this encouraged the third-century exegete's search for its deeper meanings.[37]

However, as Origen scholars had just previously demonstrated, Young claimed that Origen, and not only the Antiochenes, had an interest in the philological tools of the grammatical-rhetorical schools: τὸ μεθοδικόν (the craft of the examination of the details of the text), which included ἡ διόρθωσις (the restoration of the form of the text), and ἡ ἀνάγνωσις (the act of recognition and correct reading of a text), etymology, linguistics, and in τόν ἱστορίκον, the method of investigation that produced as much information as possible with respect to the background, characters, actions, and elements of the narrative of the text, a procedure in which he asked

---

33. Origen, of course, claimed that a text had three senses, as we will see in the first chapter of this study.

34. Young first made this argument in an earlier article: Young, "The Rhetorical Schools and Their Influence on Patristic Exegesis," in *The Making of Orthodoxy: Essays in Honour of Henry Chadwick*, ed. Rowan Williams (Cambridge: Cambridge University Press, 1989), 182–99.

35. Young, *Biblical Exegesis*, 169.

36. Young, *Biblical Exegesis*, 24.

37. Young, *Biblical Exegesis*, 26.

whether a text was probable or persuasive.³⁸ She rightly argued that Origen was the first to apply these grammatical methods to the Bible in a systematic way.³⁹ However, for Young, the emphasis within Origen's exegesis still lay on the interpretive moves he made once he had dealt with τὸ μεθοδικόν and τὸν ἱστορίκον.

The Antiochenes did not share Origen's philosophical education, according to Young. However, they did share with the Alexandrian an education in the Scriptures, which they received from Diodore of Tarsus (Julian, *CG* frags. 62.253b–254b; 64.262c), and they probably also studied with the great rhetorician, Libanius, and thus they too had a thorough rhetorical education (Socrates, *Hist. eccl.* 6.3.1–7; Theodoret, *Hist. eccl.* 5.27). This training taught them to attend to both τὸ μεθοδικόν and τὸν ἱστορίκον.

One of Young's most important arguments is that the Antiochenes should not be described as literalists in the modern sense, nor should their interest in history be confused with a modern understanding of history; by ἱστορία, these authors were referring primarily to narrative coherence.⁴⁰ Furthermore, the Antiochenes, as a result of their rhetorical education, understood ἱστορία as a genre intended to improve and inform the reader, for they believed that literature was to be morally edificatory. Thus an important aspect of their textual study was that of moral judgment (κρίσις).⁴¹ According to Young, then, it was the Antiochene authors' desire to understand a text's narrative coherence, and not history in the modern sense, that drove their vehement reaction to Alexandrian allegory.⁴² While this concern for narrative coherence could also be found in Origen's exegesis, given his own rhetorical training, he tended to emphasize the "unitive thrust" (σκοπός) of Scripture as a whole and thus the deeper meaning of individual texts. It was, according to Young, Origen's search for a passage's

---

38. For ἀνάγνωσις, see Young, *Biblical Exegesis*, 84; for ἱστορίκον, see Young, *Biblical Exegesis*, 83.

39. Young, *Biblical Exegesis*, 84, 76. Young is here indebted to Averil Cameron, *Christianity and the Rhetoric of Empire: The Development of Christian Discourse*, Sather Classical Lectures 55 (Berkeley: University of California Press, 1991). Cameron articulated that the (pre-Origenian) church established the Bible as the alternative body of classics to those of the Greco-Roman school παιδεία, namely, Homer and Plato, and that it was Origen who transferred the interpretive tools used in the classical context to the Bible.

40. Young, *Biblical Exegesis*, 166.
41. Young, *Biblical Exegesis*, 81.
42. Young, *Biblical Exegesis*, 193.

deeper meaning that the Antiochenes thought led him to destroy the narrative coherence of the passage.

Concerning the traditional scholarly distinction between Antiochene typology and Alexandrian allegory, Young argues, along with the scholars mentioned above, that the ancients did not make such a distinction. In fact, she observed, the notion of typology is a modern scholarly construct, born out of our modern historical consciousness.[43] However, Young insists, there remains a distinction between the two school members' ways of conducting nonliteral interpretation, and it lies in the way each perceived how the text itself related to what it was taken to refer, and here lies another of her major arguments.[44] Young describes the Alexandrian nonliteral reading as "symbolic," in contrast to Antioch's "iconic" nonliteral reading. That is, in Alexandria, the use of allegory involved understanding the words of a given narrative as symbols that referred to other realities, like the application of a code, which bore no necessary relationship to the wording or sequence of the narrative.[45] On the other hand, the Antiochene readers, she claims, desired "to find a genuine connection between what the text said and the spiritual meaning discerned through contemplation [θεωρία] of the text" and found a deeper meaning within the text as

---

43. Young, *Biblical Exegesis*, 152; see also Young, "Typology," in *Crossing the Boundaries: Essays in Biblical Interpretation in Honor of David D. Goulder*, ed. Stanley E. Porter, Paul Joyce, and David E. Orton, BibInt 8 (Leiden: Brill, 1994), 29–48; Torjesen, *Hermeneutical Procedure*, 14.

44. Young, *Biblical Exegesis*, 162.

45. Young, *Biblical Exegesis*, 162. She reiterates this argument in Young, "The Fourth Century Reaction against Allegory," *StPatr* 30 (1997): 120–25. I will argue throughout this study that her iconic versus symbolic distinction breaks down in these authors' treatments of the New Testament Gospel of John passages. In my case studies, the nonliteral interpretation of the Alexandrian authors does not necessarily break the coherence of the narrative, or at least they do not seem to think it does, for they often claim, even if rhetorically, that the nonliteral reading follows naturally from the literal. Furthermore, both Alexandrians provide each passage as a whole with a nonliteral interpretation, rather than treating the words of each narrative as a code to be cracked. By contrast, when Chrysostom provides a nonliteral treatment of 9:6–7, he deals only with this verse in this manner, and thus reads the verses symbolically, a description Young reserves for the Alexandrians. In my view, the distinction is not the most helpful way to articulate the difference between the two schools with respect to their treatment of the Gospel of John, and, I suspect, of the New Testament generally. For a similar critique of Young's distinction, see Karl Shuve, "Entering the Story: Origen's Dramatic Approach to Scripture in the *Homilies on Jeremiah*," *StPatr* 46 (2010): 235–40.

Introduction 17

a coherent whole.⁴⁶ The text was like a mirror, in which the literal narrative reflected the nonliteral meaning. Young provides the example of Origen's and Chrysostom's treatments of the feeding of the multitude in Matt 14 to demonstrate the difference.⁴⁷ For Origen, the loaves and fish symbolize Scripture and the Logos.⁴⁸ For Chrysostom, the text provides proofs of doctrines, such as Christ's unity with the Father, which is expressed by his prayer, and moral lessons, such as Christ's exemplary humility and charity, which his miraculous deed expresses.⁴⁹ The tendency of Alexandrian allegory to destroy the narrative coherence, Young argues, accounts for the Antiochene rejection of allegory as it had been used in Alexandria, but not nonliteral interpretation as such, for, as she observes, they attended to typology and prophecy as they saw fit.⁵⁰ Thus, Young actually remains within the two schools framework even as she critiques the traditional characterization of it. She is still concerned to articulate a distinction between the two schools, which she describes as a difference based on the Neoplatonic philosophical training of the Alexandrians, and the grammatical-rhetorical training of the Antiochenes.⁵¹

---

46. Young, *Biblical Exegesis*, 210; see also Young, "Fourth Century Reaction," 123.

47. Young, *Biblical Exegesis*, 211.

48. Even in this example, if one attempts to understand how Origen might have arrived at this interpretation, it is not difficult to see that he likens the physical nourishment of loaves and fish to the spiritual nourishment of Scripture and the Logos. This is much less arbitrary than Young would have it.

49. Even in this, the only example Young provides as she illustrates her distinction, she admits concerning Chrysostom's treatment of the passage that "this is not exactly typological exegesis as generally understood, but it has similar 'ikonic' features: paraenetic concerns and deductive methods facilitate the discernment of 'theoretic' meanings through the narrative conveyed by the text" (*Biblical Exegesis*, 211). I agree that this is not helpfully understood as typological exegesis. In fact, as will become clear in this study, I understand dogmatic teachings and moral lessons such as the ones identified by Young in this example as a feature of these authors' literal interpretation, for as illustrated in this example, Chrysostom does not indicate that he is providing a nonliteral reading, i.e., he does not use the language of type or *theoria*, which he tends to do when he is moving beyond the letter. In addition, when the Alexandrians find dogmatic teachings and moral lessons like these, they too are operating at the level of the literal text before they indicate a move beyond the letter. I will say more about this in the next section.

50. Young, *Biblical Exegesis*, 173.

51. Young also argued that the Antiochenes were concerned about Origen and his successors' allegorization of specific texts that contributed to the overarching biblical story, such as those that related to creation, the resurrection, and the kingdom of God.

Young's thesis has gained wide acceptance among many of the field's top scholars and their students and is now commonplace in conversations about early Christian exegesis. Development of her thesis has taken two major trajectories: First, there are those who maintain that a distinction between the two schools is helpful in some way but who seek to move beyond the literal versus allegorical description. Second, there are those who wish to do away with the model of the two schools altogether by demonstrating what is, in their estimation, enough overlap between the two schools so as to render the distinction meaningless.

We begin with the scholars of the first (minority) trajectory, who argue that the schools ought to be characterized with more nuance than the simple traditional distinction between allegorical and literal-historical.[52] A recent example is provided by Peter Martens, who, in his 2017 translation and commentary on Adrian's handbook on the literary analysis of Scripture, maintains that there exists a distinctive Antiochene school (and thus by implication an Alexandrian school as well), and he places the fifth-century early Christian author, Adrian, about whom very little is known other than that which the handbook reveals, within the Antiochene school.[53] In his

---

These texts ought not to be allegorized if the Christian story is to provide the Christian life its meaning (Young, *Biblical Exegesis*, 167–68, 296; see also Young, "Fourth Century Reaction," 120–25). For a similar argument, see Guinot, "La frontière," 207–28.

52. We will not examine, e.g., the work of John J. O'Keefe, who argues that the distinction is still important ("Theodoret's Unique Contribution to the Antiochene Exegetical Tradition: Questioning Traditional Scholarly Categories," in *The Harp of Prophecy: Early Christian Interpretation of the Psalms*, ed. Brian E. Daley and Paul R. Kolbet, CJAn 20 [Notre Dame: University of Notre Dame Press, 2015], 191–204). He does not offer any suggestions as to what the difference might be.

53. However, Martens does not address the Alexandrian school directly in this work and brackets the discussion of the differences between the two schools completely, despite his previous work on Origen's exegesis. Similarly, Robert C. Hill avoids discussing the hermeneutical controversy, as well as a comparison of the putative two schools, altogether. In the preface to Hill, *Reading the Old Testament in Antioch*, i, he admits to explicit avoidance of a comparison of the two traditions, for such an endeavor, he claims, has "proven to be unhelpful." Despite what we observed in the previous footnote about O'Keefe's work on the two schools, in O'Keefe and R. R. Reno, *Sanctified Vision: An Introduction to Early Christian Interpretation of the Bible* (Baltimore: Johns Hopkins University Press, 2005), he does not so much as mention the dispute between the two so-called schools, but instead describes patristic exegesis as though it were one monolithic enterprise. It is unclear why they made this decision, though perhaps it is a choice based on the fact that it is an introduction to the exegesis

study of Adrian's handbook, Martens draws our attention to this often overlooked work on scriptural interpretation—indeed the only extant handbook on the subject by one of Antioch's leading exegetes of the fourth and fifth centuries. Martens argues throughout his commentary on the handbook that "it succinctly codifies many of the guiding principles of Antiochene scriptural exegesis," particularly those of Theodore of Mopsuestia, whose corpus has suffered not insignificant damage over the centuries.[54]

Martens describes the Antiochene school of exegesis as an "Antiochene exegetical culture" and as a network of late antique (fourth- to sixth-century) figures who flourished in the diocese of Antioch or were clearly indebted to these figures.[55] According to Martens, this group of authors used the same version of the biblical text, the same technical exegetical terms, the same sequencing of these exegetical procedures, had the same resistance to allegorical exegesis, and announced the same goals for their exegetical activity.[56] Just as figures such as Diodore, Chrysostom, and Theodore had a penchant for rhetorical criticism, so too Adrian begins his handbook by claiming that he will deal with three components of literary style, the text's message, diction, and syntax, all three of which are technical rhetorical terms.[57] Also like his fellow Antiochenes, Adrian instructed his readers that the interpreter ought to first identify a given biblical text's purpose (σκόπος) or subject matter (ὑπόθεσις) before providing a word-by-word or verse-by-verse commentary precisely (ἀκριβέστερον).[58] In

---

of the early church and the scholarly debate about the two schools was deemed unhelpful for such a purpose.

54. Martens, *Adrian's Introduction*, 2. According to Martens, Adrian's exegesis is also similar to that of Eusebius of Emesa. For specific examples concerning both Eusebius and Theodore, see pp. 3, 15–16, 18, 27, 38, 41, 46–50.

55. Martens, *Adrian's Introduction*, 15. However, Martens also argues that the handbook provides evidence of an actual schoolroom setting, given that there is a great deal of overlap between his text and those of the ubiquitous late antique *grammaticus* (52–55).

56. Interestingly, Martens observes that Adrian makes only one mention of the term θεωρία, and that he actually contrasts it with the text's meaning (διάνοια) (*Adrian's Introduction*, 43). In my study as well, we will see that this term, traditionally understood as a distinctive Antiochene term, figures peripherally in Chrysostom's and Theodore's exegesis of John.

57. Martens, *Adrian's Introduction*, 22–24. Martens rightly notes that the use of rhetorical criticism is not unique to the Antiochenes, however.

58. Martens, *Adrian's Introduction*, 43–45. *Precision* is another term commonly associated with the Antiochenes, as Martens highlights; see his discussion of the term

addition, Adrian aimed to clarify the aspects of Scripture that were obscure and peculiar, particularly Scripture's frequent anthropomorphic depictions of God that are erroneous and unworthy of the divine nature if not handled properly, and he frequently did so through his use of the technique of question and answer, and through paraphrase of the biblical words.[59] However, perhaps Martens's most important argument for placing Adrian within the school of Antioch is his extensive documentation of the similarity between Adrian's glosses of specific biblical passages, some of which were verbatim, and those of the other figures associated with Antioch.[60] This is surely a most helpful addition to the discussion about Antiochene exegesis, but it would have been strengthened by a comparison of Adrian's exegetical procedures with those of key Alexandrian figures.

We turn now to the second trajectory: scholars who do not think Young went far enough with her thesis. Since the publication of Young's work, many have observed that there is actually much more overlap than Young acknowledged in regard to the school-members' rhetorical and philosophical training, an argument that, according to these scholars, renders the model of the two schools simply unhelpful. For example, in her work on what she calls ascetic exegesis, *Reading Renunciation: Asceticism and Scripture in Early Christianity*, Elizabeth Clark builds upon Young's dismantling of the neat literal versus allegorical distinction, asserting that these categories are unhelpful since the plain or literal sense of a text is simply what a

---

on pp. 48–49. In my study, however, I will demonstrate that the term is frequently used by the Alexandrians as well, and therefore it ought not to be understood as a distinguishing feature of Antiochene exegesis.

59. See Martens's treatment of the exegetical principle of clarifying obscurity (*Adrian's Introduction*, 26–27, 50–51). For anthropomorphic descriptions, see Martens, *Adrian's Introduction*, 38–39; for question and answer, see pp. 40–42; for paraphrase, see p. 51. Chrysostom and Theodore make extensive use of the technique of paraphrase and Chrysostom in particular uses question and answer. However, so also did Origen.

60. Martens, *Adrian's Introduction*, 15. In the end, however, I wonder how helpful this really is, considering we can find examples in which the Antiochenes repeat rather closely interpretive glosses on particular verses that Origen had already constructed; e.g., we will see that even in this study, the Antiochenes provide readings of passages in John's Gospel that are very close to Origen's treatments of the same passages, such as their interpretations of the harvest parable in John 4:35–38. There are, however, other ways in which the Antiochenes' exegesis differs from Origen's, as we will see throughout this thesis.

given religious community understands it to be.[61] This allows her to say that different schools might disagree on the meaning of the particular nonliteral interpretation but that they all assumed that a text should portend something and that nonliteral reading was necessary to make sense of obscure or problematic texts, no matter which patristic author we are dealing with. It would be more fruitful, Clark argues, if scholars would examine the rhetorical *functions* of nonliteral reading.[62] That is, Clark insists that we examine the different ends to which nonliteral reading is employed by all patristic authors, for these rhetorical purposes are more telling than whether or not an interpreter reads literally or nonliterally as a rule.

Another example of those who follow this second trajectory is Margaret Mitchell, who has made some of the most significant contributions to the discussion through her work on Chrysostom and in her translation of Eustathius's *On the Witch of Endor and Against Origen*.[63] In her 2010 work on the "history of effects" of Paul's Corinthian correspondence, *Paul, the Corinthians and the Birth of Christian Hermeneutics*, Mitchell collates the observations of her previous publications as she demonstrates how Paul's biblical exegesis, particularly in his conflict with the Corinthians, served as an example to all subsequent early Christian interpreters of Scripture.[64] She highlights various aspects of Paul's thought in the Corinthian letters that were taken up by subsequent Christian interpreters, which she argues are more helpful for the analysis of early Christian exegesis than the categories of literal and allegorical interpretation. I will focus on two of them here, as one of them concerns the principle of Scripture's usefulness, which we will discuss below in much more detail, given that it is the major analytical category I will use to examine the four authors' treatments of John's Gospel.

First, Mitchell argues that depending on the needs of his letters' recipients and the situation at hand, Paul would read the biblical text in question either literally or nonliterally, and thus he strategically and

---

61. Clark, *Reading Renunciation*, 71.
62. Clark, *Reading Renunciation*, 77. She, of course, seeks to do so within the context of monastic literature.
63. Mitchell, "John Chrysostom," in *Dictionary of Major Biblical Interpreters*, ed. Donald McKim (Downers Grove, IL: InterVarsity Press, 2007), 571–77; Origen, *The "Belly-Myther" of Endor: Interpretations of 1 Kingdoms 28 in the Early Church*, trans. Rowan Greer and Margaret Mitchell, WGRW 16 (Atlanta: Society of Biblical Literature, 2007).
64. Mitchell, *Paul, the Corinthians and the Birth of Christian Hermeneutics* (Cambridge: Cambridge University Press, 2010).

variably marshaled scriptural texts for his arguments with the Corinthians accordingly.[65] Similarly, argues Mitchell, the authors traditionally placed in the two exegetical schools of Alexandria and Antioch were not taught to be either literalists or allegorists; rather, they were given a set of "commonplaces" that taught them both literal and nonliteral ways of reading, either or both of which could be employed depending on the context.[66] The traditional distinction between the two schools, then, is simply not helpful, in her view. In this study, however, I argue that, despite the school members' shared training in grammar and rhetoric, the frequency with which the members of the respective schools employ nonliteral reading strategies ought also to be considered in our analysis, for the Antiochenes do so much less frequently than the Alexandrians.

Second, Mitchell argues that, in addition to his exemplary hermeneutical adaptability, Paul set the terms for subsequent early Christian interpreters through his apocalyptic sensibilities; for him, the biblical text both hides and reveals glimpses of the divine reality.[67] In the Corinthian correspondence, Paul articulates what Mitchell describes as "a tension between the hidden and the revealed, between clarity and obscurity," which was already present in Paul's discussions of the revelation of the mysterious return of the Lord in 1 Thess 4–5.[68] In his letters to the Corinthians, Paul developed the theme further with the metaphors of the mirror (1 Cor 13:12; 2 Cor 3:18), which emphasized the present partiality of human knowledge, despite God's revelation of his wisdom in Christ, and the veil (2 Cor 3:12–18), which covers the eyes of the mind of the Israelites who do not turn to Christ, and which is removed from the eyes of the one who does turn to him. Further, in the same letter of 1 Corinthians, Paul styles himself in one place as the "purveyor of hidden mystery" (1 Cor 2:1–16), for he has traveled to paradise (2 Cor 12:1–5), and in another place he emphasizes the limited nature of human knowledge, including his own, as he seeks, for example, to manage the tongue-speak-

---

65. Mitchell, *Paul*, x. She refers to this as the "agonistic paradigm" of early Christian interpretation. She notes that Paul operates this way with respect to his own letters, oral statements, and behaviors as well, all of which the Corinthians seemed to misunderstand; see Mitchell, *Paul*, 4, 9–11.

66. Mitchell, *Paul*, 18–27.

67. Mitchell, *Paul*, 11, 49.

68. Mitchell, *Paul*, 58.

ing Corinthians (1 Cor 13:8–12).⁶⁹ Paul thus makes claims about the obscurity or clarity of divine truth depending on the situation and needs of his argument.⁷⁰ Early Christian interpreters, such as Origen, Gregory of Nyssa, Chrysostom, and many others, argues Mitchell, took up Paul's metaphors of occlusion and revelation, in addition to his vocabulary, such as "enigma" (αἴνιγμα) in 1 Cor 13:12, and used them within their discourses about biblical interpretation. Depending on the context and the rhetorical goals of their arguments, early Christian exegetes would claim that the meaning of a text was either clear (φανερός or σαφής) on the one hand, or unclear (ἀσαφής), on the other hand, or that it lay somewhere in between.⁷¹ In this framework, when these authors claimed that the text was clear, they offered a literal interpretation, whereas the obscure passage would require a nonliteral interpretation.⁷² The interpreters from both schools, she argues, operated with these principles, and thus, for Mitchell, analysis of this aspect of their thought is more helpful than analysis that uses the categories of literal versus allegorical.⁷³

By now it will be clear that my own study falls in the first of my two trajectories. That is, I think the distinction between the two exegetical schools remains helpful, but it requires more nuance, as I have said above. I argue that a helpful way of distinguishing between the two traditions is related to

---

69. Mitchell, *Paul*, 59.
70. Mitchell, *Paul*, 59. This Mitchell calls the "veil scale."
71. Mitchell, *Paul*, 76–77. She draws on examples from Origen, *Hom. Jer.* 5.8–9; and Chrysostom, *Proph. obscurit.* 1.6.
72. Mitchell, *Paul*, 77.
73. In fact, she makes this exact point in *Paul*, 147 n. 82. However, I do not think this principle is equally as helpful for all four of these authors. Origen makes the most frequent use of the terminology denoting a text's clarity or obscurity, but there are only a handful of occasions where my other three authors do so, and these occur primarily when they are dealing with Jesus's parabolic speech. I do not deny that these authors were equipped by their rhetorical training to deal with a text either literally or nonliterally, nor do I deny the instances in which they use the language of clarity and obscurity, revealed and hidden, easy and difficult, in their interpretive comments. However, I tend to part ways with Mitchell, who assumes that their similar rhetorical training indicates that their claims to provide, e.g., a literal reading of a given passage ought to be understood as part of a purely rhetorical exercise. I suspect that if early Christian exegetes claim to give a literal reading that is what they thought they were giving, even if to us it does not appear to be literal. For me, then, the categories of literal and nonliteral remain a helpful way to differentiate the exegesis of the members of the schools in Alexandria and Antioch, as long as they are used with the appropriate nuance.

Terminology

Before I proceed to outline the major arguments of this thesis, it is important to comment on the terms *literal* and *nonliteral* in light of the above discussion of previous scholarship on the two schools.[74] First, I assume that the authors indicate explicitly when they are moving beyond the letter of the narrative to provide a nonliteral reading, given the controversies about literal and nonliteral treatments of Scripture during this period. Second, I use the term literal with reference to the various terms and phrases that the authors use as they work at the level of the narrative, such as ῥητός, λέξις, σωματικῶς, πρόχειρος, ἐπιπόλαιος, ἱστορία, and "nonliteral" to describe the interpretation that follows an explicit exegetical move beyond the narrative to provide additional insight or contemplation, signaled by such terms as τύπος, θεωρία, πνευματικῶς, ἀλληγορία, ἀναγογή, σύμβολος. There is no consensus among scholars about whether the various terms used to describe either the literal or the nonliteral sense are synonymous, and I suspect that more detailed studies of the exegesis of individual authors are needed to set us on firmer footing, for it is most probable that each author works with these terms in his own distinctive ways.[75] In any case, it seems clear that, as

---

74. For the sake of simplicity and clarity, and to avoid the confusion that typically accompanies such discussions, I have adopted the umbrella terms *literal* and *nonliteral* from Peter Martens, who uses them in this manner ("Revisiting the Allegory/Typology Distinction: The Case of Origen," *JECS* 16 [2008]: 283–317).

75. The bulk of the scholarly discussion has dealt with the terminology related to nonliteral reading. In particular, scholars have been preoccupied with the question of the degree to which there is a distinction between allegory and typology, a discussion that goes back (at least) as far as the debate begun by Daniélou and de Lubac in the 1940s. Daniélou claimed that typology was native to Christianity, whereas allegory had seeped into the tradition later, and derived from Philo and the Greeks. For Daniélou and the significant number of scholars that followed him in the subsequent decades, the distinction between these nonliteral ways of reading came down to the degree to which the historical biblical narrative was genuinely linked to the spiritual truth to which it pointed. That is, whereas typology maintained the link, allegory did not. De Lubac, however, thought this was too simplistic, and claimed instead that early Christians used allegorical interpretation in order to find the types of Christ in the (Old Testament) biblical narrative. Thus, he suggested that allegory and typology were not actually opposed, but rather they were complimentary. Charles Kannengiesser

Young argues, at the literal level, early Christian authors made either one or some combination of the following five "distinguishable but overlapping" moves: they dealt solely with the wording, examined individual words, attended to the plain sense of words in a sentence, discerned the logic of a narrative or passage, and discerned the implied specific reference.[76] With this in view, I will assume that the terms in question are basically synonymous, but I will note along the way where there seem to be differences in understanding among these four authors.[77]

---

provides a succinct discussion of the development of scholarship on this question in Kannengiesser, "Allegorism," in *Handbook of Patristic Exegesis: The Bible in Ancient Christianity*, BAC 1 (Leiden: Brill, 2004), 248–55. I am inclined to agree with him as he sides with de Lubac and says: "[early Christians] interchanged technical terms with little concern" (Kannengiesser, "Allegorism," 253). Peter Martens provides a thorough and clear account of the state of scholarship on the distinction between allegory and typology in early Christianity in Martens, "Revisiting the Allegory/Typology Distinction," 285 n. 4. He observes that there is still no scholarly consensus on the issue. Further, Martens has demonstrated that Origen uses the terms ἀλληγορία and τύπος interchangeably, and that they frequently occur beside each other within the same context of his exegesis (Martens, "Revisiting the Allegory/Typology Distinction," 301–3). This is the case for Clement of Alexandria as well, which H. Clifton Ward has demonstrated in his recent study, "'Symbolic Interpretation Is Most Useful': Clement of Alexandria's Scriptural Imagination," *JECS* 25 (2017): 531–60, esp. 536–38.

76. See Young's helpful discussion of the literal sense in *Biblical Exegesis*, 187–89. She lays out these five kinds of interpretation through which early Christian interpreters move from the wording of a text and its attendant general associations to the specific referent of the verse in its narrative context.

77. From the outset, we should note that the Antiochenes, particularly Diodore, Chrysostom, and Theodore, tended to reject the use of the term ἀλληγορία in the instances in which they provide a nonliteral interpretation, but they do use τύπος from time to time, most often in the case of Old Testament passages; see Diodore's preface to his *Commentary on the Psalms*. Hill provides a discussion of this in *Reading the Old Testament*, 136–39. In fact, as Reno and O'Keefe observe, by the fourth century, the term ἀλληγορία had become suspect, "in large part because it was associated with Origenist theological speculations that were eventually condemned" (*Sanctified Vision*, 15). The other Alexandrian of my study, Cyril, tends not to use the term ἀλληγορία either, probably for the reasons mentioned by Reno and O'Keefe; see the discussion of Guinot, "La frontière," 207–28, esp. 223. See also Matthew R. Crawford, *Cyril of Alexandria's Trinitarian Theology of Scripture*, OECS (Oxford: Oxford University Press, 2014), 217. Cyril describes his nonliteral interpretation in other ways as well—most frequently as "spiritual interpretation"—which we will see throughout this study. Finally, all four authors provide nonliteral interpretations through the procedure of θεωρία (contemplation or insightful reading), despite some scholars' claims that the term is distinctive

Further explanation of my understanding of the literal sense in particular is required before we proceed. I am aware that early Christian exegetes made additional interpretive moves between their literal interpretations (as outlined in the above paragraph) and their indication of a nonliteral reading. That is, we can observe these authors commenting on issues of doctrine and morality after a careful initial treatment of the letter or wording and before they signal an explicit move to the nonliteral level. I will therefore use the word literal to refer to all of the interpretive moves made by these authors before they signal explicitly a move beyond the level of the narrative to the nonliteral level, including these moral and dogmatic comments. These intermediate comments have been variously described by scholars as separate reified interpretive steps within their exegetical procedures and labeled as moral and doctrinal interpretations, despite the fact that the ancient authors themselves tend not to describe their exegesis with such well-formulated categories.[78] I have chosen not to describe these steps between the literal sense and the nonliteral sense to avoid imposing what are in my view anachronistic categories of exegesis. For, as I will argue below, I understand it to be significant that the authors make observations about doctrine and morality *before* they indicate an explicit move above the letter of the text. Stated negatively, I suspect we miss out on important aspects of their understanding of what is to be dealt with before one moves to the nonliteral plane if we impose our own categorical descriptions on their interpretive procedure, a procedure about which these authors were sufficiently reflective, even in this early period. In my study then, I attend

---

to the Antiochene school of interpretation. One such scholar is Robert Charles Hill; see, e.g., *Reading the Old Testament*, 9. For a very thorough examination of this term and its history of usage, see Andrea Wilson Nightingale, *Spectacles of Truth in Classical Greek Philosophy: Theoria in Its Cultural Context* (Cambridge: Cambridge University Press, 2004). In the passages of my study, however, the Antiochenes use the term very infrequently. In fact, it is the Alexandrians, and particularly Cyril, who make use of the term most often.

78. See, e.g., Young, *Biblical Exegesis*, 212–13. Cyril is an exception, for he indicates in the preface to his *Commentary on the Gospel of John* that he will provide a "doctrinal explanation" of the Fourth Gospel; I will say more about this below. We will see that in practice, however, Cyril works with doctrine in a manner that is very similar indeed to my other three authors, i.e., at the level of the literal narrative's wording. He is simply more reflective than my other three authors, who are earlier in the exegetical tradition, about the kind of reading he provides. I examine his comments about his doctrinal interpretation in ch. 1.

to the specific terminology used by each of these authors as they interpret John's Gospel, and I use the general categories literal and nonliteral for their exegesis with the caveats mentioned above.

Finally, a word of explanation is required concerning how I categorize these authors' treatments of the parables and metaphors they encounter in the text itself within my framework of literal and nonliteral exegesis. In John's Gospel, a great deal of Jesus's speech is symbolic in nature, and several of our passages of focus contain what some scholars have described as "compositional allegory," which is to be distinguished from "interpretive allegory."[79] Whereas compositional allegory refers to metaphors, figures of speech, and parables composed by the biblical authors themselves, interpretive allegory refers to the figurative or nonliteral reading imposed on the text by the reader. This distinction, I contend, these authors made as well, which we will see throughout this study. I therefore consider the authors' treatments of the compositional allegories they encounter in the Johannine narrative to be part of their literal interpretation—a correct understanding of a parabolic passage or verse required a corresponding parabolic interpretation, which is certainly to be distinguished from the nonliteral interpretations the Alexandrians consistently give a whole scriptural narrative.[80] We will see that each of the four authors recognizes John's symbolic language as symbol and operates accordingly, discerning what he understands as the intended meaning of the figure of speech without recourse to the technical exegetical terms used in the context of his provision of an interpretive allegory.[81]

---

79. This applies to my treatment of John 2:19; 4:10–14, 35–38; 10:1–18. This is a distinction used by David Dawson throughout his work (*Allegorical Readers and Cultural Revision in Ancient Alexandria* [Berkley: University of California Press, 1992]); see also Young, *Biblical Exegesis*, 190; Mitchell, *Paul*, 116 n. 4.

80. I make this choice recognizing that in some cases the line between compositional and interpretive allegory is not easily drawn. For one thing, ancient interpreters are not as quick as modern (or even the medieval) readers to label their interpretation of the parable or metaphor they encounter in a given text as literal. In any case, as Young helpfully suggests, "it is one thing for the reader to identify the writer's process of developing a figure of speech in his exegetical analysis and another to suggest a whole text has an 'undersense' and should not be read according to what might be claimed to be its obvious meaning" (Young, *Biblical Exegesis*, 190).

81. Matters are rather more complicated in the case of Origen, who operates slightly differently when he encounters compositional metaphor or allegory. We will see that he often takes the opportunity given by the symbolic language, that if taken literally leads to absurdity or statements unworthy of God, to develop an extended

The Main Arguments of this Study

My argument is twofold. First, I will demonstrate that the Antiochenes provided nonliteral interpretations of the Johannine text much less frequently than the Alexandrians. Despite the Antiochenes' ability to interpret nonliterally, in the case of the Gospel of John at least, they do so infrequently. Second, and most importantly, as mentioned briefly above, I argue that a major distinction between the two exegetical traditions lies in the specific ways the members of the respective schools articulate how the biblical text facilitates the spiritual formation of their Christian audiences.[82] In order to demonstrate this distinction, I examine how these authors worked with the exegetical principle that inspired Scripture is inherently useful (χρήσιμος), beneficial, or profitable (ὠφέλιμος), and that it is therefore the interpreter's duty to draw out its uses or benefits for the Christian.[83] The second argument of this thesis is not unrelated to the first: the exegetical principle of Scripture's usefulness provides an important analytical category for examining these authors' rationale for either remaining at the literal level of the

---

nonliteral interpretation. However, he is not, in my view, ignorant of the genre of metaphor he encounters in Scripture, but on occasion can be seen to feign ignorance for expediency's sake.

82. Young has argued that one important distinction between the two schools lies in the manner in which the respective school members apply the biblical text to their communities; see "Rhetorical Schools," 182–99, esp. 192. In Alexandria, she says, the goal of exegesis was the apprehension of elevated doctrinal concepts, whereas in Antioch, the goal was to find moral lessons that inform and improve the reader. This argument assumes that ancient biblical exegetes thought about biblical interpretation as consisting of two separate stages of interpretation: (1) find the text's meaning, and (2) apply the passage to one's community. I argue that the text's application to their audiences is of immediate interest to these ancient authors as they determine its meaning, and therefore, we cannot so easily distinguish the two separate interpretive stages of discovering meaning and subsequently making an application. In any case, Young's assertion in this respect is inconsistent with her argument that the Antiochenes too in their spiritual interpretation apply the biblical texts to doctrinal matters as well as to moral lessons. I will demonstrate throughout this study why it is rather more complicated than this.

83. Throughout this text I will use the terms *useful*, *beneficial*, and *profitable* interchangeably as they are basically synonyms in Greek. The Latin equivalent to the Greek adjectives is *utilis*. On rare occasions, the authors use other Greek terms for beneficial, such as ἡ ὄνησις, λυσιτελής, or the verb καρπόω. I will say more about this principle shortly.

narrative or moving beyond the letter to provide a nonliteral interpretation of the text. Examining how these authors work with the principle of Scripture's usefulness is one helpful way to move beyond the simplistic categories of literal-historical and allegorical and also to attend to the specific concerns of these authors in their own words. Their use of the principle does not account for the difference between the two exegetical traditions entirely, nor do these authors indicate that they are operating with the principle in every instance I examine, but it certainly governs their overall approach to the biblical text of John, about which I will say more below.[84]

Despite the school members' shared understanding of the inherent usefulness of Scripture, I will demonstrate that the Antiochenes most frequently find the Gospel of John to be beneficial for their audiences at the level of the narrative, without having to make an explicit shift above the letter of the text, except in a small handful of exceptional cases. The Alexandrians, however, spend time at both the literal and the nonliteral levels in order to draw out the usefulness of the text for their readers. I will explain in chapter 1 the various ways in which the school members of my study thought John was beneficial for the church at both levels, in order to demonstrate the important distinction between the two exegetical traditions.

The Usefulness of Scripture

The usefulness of Scripture and the interpreter's duty to render it so were exegetical principles that early Christians adopted from the Greco-Roman rhetorical tradition and were widely agreed upon.[85] To date, however, with the exception of Mitchell, it has been primarily scholars of Origen's exegesis who have observed the importance of the principle of Scripture's usefulness, with respect to his exegesis alone.[86] I will briefly demonstrate

---

84. In ch. 1 I will demonstrate that each of my four authors articulates in his introductory comments that John's Gospel is useful.

85. For classical examples of the principle, see Cicero, *Inv.* 2.41.119; see also Plato, *Resp.* 382d; Ammonius's commentary on Porphyry's *Isagoge*; Alexander's commentary on Aristotle's *Topics* and *Metaphysics*.

86. Mitchell, *Paul*, 1–3, 12, 66. Her argument is based primarily on the exegesis of Gregory of Nyssa in the preface to his *Commentary on the Song of Songs*, and on the Christian roots of the principle in the letters of Paul, primarily the Corinthian correspondence. For Mitchell, the ubiquity of the principle in early Christian exegesis serves as evidence of her thesis that there were not two distinct exegetical schools in Antioch and Alexandria. In this work, as mentioned above, I argue that attending to these

here that the principle was in fact important for all four of these authors as they approached the biblical text.

In Origen's case, I will examine primarily his comments about the usefulness of Scripture in his discussion about the principles of scriptural interpretation in book 4 of *Peri archon*. In the case of the other three authors, however, given that they did not dedicate a specific work to a discussion of scriptural interpretation, we must draw from the comments that are scattered throughout their corpora in order to demonstrate this principle's importance for them. We shall see that, even in these comments, the distinction between the two exegetical schools that I have articulated above emerges. The Alexandrians claim that there are benefits to be found at both the literal and nonliteral levels. However, while Origen has no problem claiming that there are some passages that are not useful at the literal level, Cyril makes clear, at least theoretically, that one must not go beyond the letter to find a text's benefits if one has discovered its usefulness at the literal level.[87] On the other hand, the Antiochenes assume that there is an abundance of benefit to be discovered at the literal level, and both authors articulate explicit suspicion of interpreters who provide, in their view, useless readings at the nonliteral level. I will now turn to examine some examples of their comments.

I will begin with Origen's comments in book 4 of his *Peri archon*. In 4.2.8–9, he claims that it was the Spirit's intention to make "even the outer covering of the spiritual truths, I mean the bodily part of the scriptures, in many respects not unprofitable [οὐκ ἀνωφελές], but capable [δυνάμενον] of improving the multitude in so far as they receive it" (Origen, *Princ.* 6.2.8 [Butterworth, 285]).[88] This quotation demonstrates two major aspects of his understanding of the principle of Scripture's usefulness: (1) the Holy

---

authors' use of the principle actually highlights important distinctions between the two exegetical traditions, for, despite the authors' shared understanding of the inherently useful biblical text, we see different patterns emerging between the two schools in terms of the level of the text at which the members discovered its benefits and therefore the kinds of benefits they drew out of the text. See Ronald E. Heine, *Origen: Scholarship in Service of the Church*, Christian Theology in Context (Oxford: Oxford University Press, 2010), 134–35.

87. In practice, however, Cyril finds benefits at both levels.

88. Here Origen does not mention the third group, the advancing ones, who are capable of understanding "the soul" of Scripture. He discusses the tripartite nature of the biblical text and the corresponding three groups of believers who can access each in *Princ.* 6.2.4–6. For other passages in Origen's corpus where he discusses the useful-

Spirit's authorship results in a useful text; and (2) Scripture is useful both in its "outer covering" or at the literal level for the simple ones, and at its nonliteral level or in the "spiritual truths" it contains for the perfect.[89] The first aspect Origen states explicitly in his twenty-seventh homily on Numbers: "We cannot say of the Holy Spirit's writings that there is anything useless or superfluous in them."[90] For Origen, however, there is another factor involved. When the interpreter encounters a useless or impossible law or statement in an otherwise useful passage, he believes that Scripture's author indicates that the text contains a deeper meaning, in which its usefulness will only then become evident.[91] In Origen's words, "But if the usefulness of the law and the sequence of the narrative were at first sight clearly discernible throughout [Ἀλλ' ἐπείπερ, εἰ δι' ὅλων σαφῶς τὸ τῆς νομοθεσίας χρήσιμον αὐτόθεν ἐφαίνετο καὶ τὸ τῆς ἱστορίας ἀκόλουθον καὶ γλαφυρόν], we would be unaware that there was anything beyond the obvious meaning [παρὰ τὸ πρόχειρον] for us to understand in the Scriptures" (*Princ.* 6.2.9 [Butterworth, 285]). In these cases where Scripture's benefits are not immediately clear, a move beyond the letter of the text is required in order to discern them.

In her study of Origen's exegesis, Torjesen argued that for Origen, different genres of biblical books as a whole have different uses. For example, Pss 36–38 provide moral instruction, Jeremiah provides a call to repentance, the Song of Songs provides revelations of the mysteries of the Logos, Numbers provides instruction in the eschatological mysteries of the age to come, and the gospels instruct the reader in the doctrines of the divine Logos.[92] However, in his treatment of the Gospel of John, Origen draws out each of these benefits for his readers, depending on the level of the narrative at which he is operating and depending on the level of spiritual progress at which his readers find themselves. I will demonstrate that at the literal level, he finds moral instruction, frequently provided by the example set by the narrative's characters, instruction concerning Christ's

---

ness of Scripture, see: *Hom. Sam.* 5.2; *Cels.* 1.18, *Philoc.* 10.2; 12.2; *Hom. Jer.* frag 2.1; *Hom. Josh.* 20.2; *Hom. Ps.* 3.6 on Ps 36; *Hom. Ps.* 77.2.2; *Hom. Num.* 11.1.2.

89. Torjesen, *Hermeneutical Procedure*, 124–25.

90. Origen, *Hom. Num.* 27.1.7 (Scheck, 169) on Num 33:1–49. Heine takes note of this passage in particular in his brief treatment of the principle in Origen's exegesis (*Origen*, 134–35).

91. Martens, *Origen and Scripture*, 60–61.

92. Torjesen, *Hermeneutical Procedure*, 126–30. She made this claim based on Origen's *Hom. Ps.* 36.1.1; *Hom. Jer.* 1.1; *Hom. Cant.* 1.1; *Hom. Num.* 2.1.

fulfillment of Old Testament Scripture, and simultaneous doctrinal teaching and refutation of heresy, primarily concerning the relationship between the Father and the Son and the divinity of Christ.[93] At the nonliteral level, according to Origen, the text is beneficial in its elevated teachings about the place of the church and the individual soul within the drama of salvation history, about the ontological reality resulting from the sacraments of the church, and about the church's present situation.

Chrysostom also articulates his understanding of the principle of Scripture's usefulness. I will examine only two passages from his corpus, though there are many more that I might have included.[94] The first is a passage from his twenty-ninth homily on Genesis. As he turns to interpret the drunkenness of Noah in Gen 9, he says, "what happened to people of former ages proves to be a subject of the greatest instruction for us" and that "every item written in Sacred Scripture has been recorded for no other purpose than our benefit [ἕκαστον τῶν ἐν τῇ Θείᾳ Γραφῇ ἐγγεγραμμένων

---

93. This statement about his discovery of the benefit of doctrinal instruction at the literal level will seem counterintuitive to some readers, but we will provide evidence for this claim in the case studies of each chapter of this study with respect to all four authors. I have not selected John's prologue (1:1–18) as an example of my study, for these authors treat the prologue as a series of doctrinal statements to be interpreted in the face of encroaching heresy, and thus none of them move beyond the letter in their interpretations. J. N. D. Kelly makes a similar argument in his article on Latin interpreters in Kelly, "The Bible and the Latin Fathers," in *The Church's Use of the Bible: Past and Present*, ed. Dennis Eric Nineham (London: SPCK, 1963), 70–82, esp. 54–55, where he says: "It is as a matter of fact noticeable that, when they are discussing strictly theological issues with a view to stating doctrine, Fathers like Hippolytus, Hilary and Augustine tend to adopt much more straightforward, rigorous methods of exegesis than when edification or ascetical instruction is their aim." See also Paul Blowers, "Interpreting Scripture," in *Constantine to c. 600*, vol. 2 of *The Cambridge History of Christianity*, ed. Augustine Casiday and Fredrick W. Norris (Cambridge: Cambridge University Press, 2007), 2:618–36, see esp. 630–33. As we said above, Cyril actually describes his discussion of doctrine in his treatment of various verses throughout his commentary as a doctrinal explanation, which he provides before he makes an explicit shift above the letter of the text. He is the most explicit in describing his doctrinal comments as doctrinal exegesis, probably because doctrine is in his day a more formally studied enterprise than it was in the time of Origen. For him, as for my other authors, doctrinal interpretation is distinctive from nonliteral interpretation. In this line of argumentation, I part ways with Young, who argues that these authors' doctrinal interpretation is a spiritual interpretation (*Biblical Exegesis*, 202, 246).

94. E.g., I have not included his comments in the following homilies: *Hom. Gen.* 58.1; *Hom. Isa.* 2.3; *Proph. obscurit.* 2.1–3; *Laz.* 3.1.

δι' οὐδέν ἕτερον μνήμῃ παρεδόθη, ἀλλ' ἢ διὰ τὴν ὠφέλειαν τὴν ἡμετέραν]."[95] Chrysostom then goes on to argue that his parishioners can learn how not to act from the example of Noah's mistake in becoming drunk, and thus the passage provides moral instruction (*Hom. Gen.* 29.2 [Hill, 198]). Every detail of Scripture, he claims, is beneficial for us. We shall see throughout this study that one of the most common benefits Chrysostom finds in the biblical text is the moral example provided by the characters of Scripture's narratives. Note that Origen too found the literal narrative beneficial in this way.

The second passage is from his thirteenth homily on Genesis in which he interprets Gen 2:8, "the LORD God planted a garden in the East, in Eden; and there he planted the man he had formed."(Chrysostom, *Hom. Gen.* 13.3 [Hill, 175]). Chrysostom claims that the Holy Spirit directed Moses's tongue as he wrote these words and then claims that those who listen to Scripture (and its interpretation) should give attention "for the sake of gaining some profit [τοῖς ὠφελοῦσιν]" (*Hom. Gen.* 13.3 [Hill, 175]). Thus, Chrysostom, like Origen, connects Scripture's usefulness to its inspiration by the Holy Spirit. Unlike Origen, however, Chrysostom, in this example at least, does not think a nonliteral interpretation of the text is necessary to determine the usefulness of the passage.[96] For example, as he deals with Gen 2:8, Chrysostom refutes a group of (unnamed) interpreters whose interpretations are not useful in his estimation, precisely because they provide an interpretation that is "opposed to a literal understanding of the text [μὴ ὡς γέγραπται φρονεῖν]." (By implication, of course, what he claims to provide is a literal reading.) The readings of these nonliteral interpreters might provide the majority of listeners with that which they are eager to hear, namely, that which is "able to bring enjoyment [δυναμένοις προσέχειν σπουδάζουσι]," rather than interpretations that "bring profit [ὠφελοῦσιν]." They understand the garden planted by God in Gen 2:8 to have been planted in heaven and not on earth, Chrysostom claims, which is for him simply out of the question given the wording of the verse (*Hom. Gen.* 13.3 [Hill, 175]). According to Chrysostom, while his interpretive opponents' enjoyable interpretations consist of their own philosophical reasoning and

---

95. Chrysostom, *Hom. Gen.* 29.1 (Hill, 199). See also *Hom. Isa.* 2.1; *Hom. Gen.* 58.1.

96. I am not claiming that Chrysostom himself cannot be found providing nonliteral readings of various biblical texts throughout his corpus, for he does so in these examples: *Comm. Ps.* 8:5; 9:8, 11; 112:4; 113:7. I will address his approach to Scripture more generally in the following chapter.

speculation, a literal interpretation of the verse presents the contents of Scripture itself clearly (cf. *Proph. obscurit.* 1.1). Thus for Chrysostom, at least in this context, useful interpretation is closely connected to a literal interpretation, whereas useless interpretation he associates with certain nonliteral interpretations.[97]

There is no mention on his part of Scripture's benefits for a category of spiritually mature at the nonliteral level as we saw in Origen's comments; for Chrysostom, all Christians, the immature and mature alike, can gain benefit from a literal interpretation.[98] As I have already mentioned, in most instances, Chrysostom finds the biblical text useful because of the moral instruction it provides, often through the examples of the characters of the narrative. However, throughout this study, I will demonstrate that like Origen, at the literal level he too finds in John's Gospel doctrinal teachings, and instruction about Jesus's fulfillment of the Old Testament. In the infrequent instances that he provides a nonliteral interpretation, he finds there instruction for the church about its place within salvation history and, only very rarely, about the present situation of the church in his own day. Thus, in these infrequent instances, the benefits he finds beyond the letter resemble those of Origen's nonliteral treatment.

Like his fellow Antiochene, Theodore worked with the principle of Scripture's usefulness.[99] I will examine two passages from his corpus as well. In the first passage, from his treatment of Galatians in his *Commentary on the Minor Epistles*, it becomes clear that Theodore assumes that Scripture is inherently useful when he expresses concern about how the interpreter is to draw out its use. As he comments on Paul's interpretation of the Gen 16–18 story of Hagar and Sarah in Gal 4:23–24, we get a sense of one aspect of his understanding of a useful interpretation of Scripture. Here Theodore uses a term that for him denotes the exact opposite meaning of the term *useful* to charge his unnamed interpretive opponents with a faulty reading of Paul's words in Gal 4:24, "this is by an allegory"

---

97. He does not claim that all nonliteral readings are useless, but that these particular nonliteral interpretations of Gen 2:8, which resemble their own philosophical speculations more than the content of Scripture, are useless.

98. The closest he comes to this is in his third homily on the rich man and Lazarus in Luke 16:19–31, in which he claims that the passage is beneficial for the rich and the poor alike (*Laz.* 3.1).

99. Some of Theodore's most suggestive comments about the usefulness of Scripture are actually found in his preface to his *Commentary on John*, which I will examine in the first chapter of this thesis; see *Comm. Jo.* preface.

(ἀλληγορούμενα).[100] Theodore describes the opponents' readings not as useful, but rather as "useless" (*superflua*), for they "invert the meaning of everything since they wish the whole narrative of divine Scripture to differ in no way from dreams of the night," an accusation that is similar to Chrysostom's accusations of his opponents that we examined above.[101]

According to Theodore, it seems, readings that are not grounded in the narrative of the text itself are simply fantasies and are therefore not useful for the church.[102] By implication, Paul's reading of the narrative of Hagar and Sarah is useful in Theodore's view, in as much as the apostle makes a comparison (*similitudinem*) between what happened "at that time" and the present dispensation (Theodore, *Comm. Gal.* 4:24 [Greer, 114–15]). Thus it seems that for Theodore, one aspect of providing a useful reading, particularly when dealing with the way the New Testament relates to the Old, is grounding one's interpretation in the similarities between the texts and events themselves. A reading of the Old Testament is not useful if it abandons the parameters set by the scriptural narrative.

In the second passage, Theodore draws out the benefits of Ps 3, a prayer in which the speaker, King David, frequently alternates between expressions of relief and cries for deliverance (Theodore, *Comm. Ps.* 3:8). According to Theodore, both the words of David's psalm and his exemplary attitude are beneficial for the reader. As he treats the words "arise, Lord, make me safe" of Ps 3:8, Theodore describes the "usefulness" (*utilitatem*) of David's words: they provide the reader or hearer with a prophecy of the circumstances to come, whether dire or pleasant. David's words are thus useful in their provision of knowledge of future events. Likewise, David himself, Theodore claims, who "doubtless is filled with the prophetic spirit in saying this," came to realize that although he presently suffered difficulty, he would soon be freed from tribulation, and thus he expressed grief and

---

100. Diodore and Chrysostom deal similarly with the verse; see Diodore, *Comm. Ps.*, pref.; Chrysostom, *Comm. Gal.* 4:24.

101. Theodore, *Comm. Gal.* 4:24 (Greer, 114–15). He most certainly has Origen, and perhaps also Origen's successor Didymus the Blind, in view here, though he does not name them specifically. We should be careful not to understand his statement here as a denial of any benefit beyond the literal level of the biblical text whatsoever, since he is careful to name allegory specifically in his refutation. As we saw in the note above, and as we shall see throughout this study, when Theodore thinks it is warranted by the text itself, he too provides a nonliteral reading.

102. Note that we saw a similar argument in Chrysostom's discussion of his interpretive opponents' reading of Gen 2:8.

thanksgiving throughout the same psalm, "so that his example [*exemplum*] may bring others the benefit of understanding [*utilitatem eruditionis operaretur*]" (*Comm. Ps.* 3:8 [Hill, 38–39]).

Indeed, as I will demonstrate throughout this study, the exemplary nature of Scripture's characters, particularly with respect to morality, is one of the most common benefits Theodore finds in the biblical text. I will also show, however, that like Chrysostom, at the literal level, Theodore too finds simultaneous doctrinal teaching and refutation of heresy, and instruction about Jesus's fulfillment of the Old Testament. There is no mention on Theodore's part either of Scripture's benefits for a category of spiritually mature at the nonliteral level as we saw in Origen's comments. Like Chrysostom, Theodore is suspicious of those who provide nonliteral readings, which he describes, in the first example at least, as useless, in that they have abandoned the parameters set by the biblical text itself. However, also like Chrysostom, when he provides a nonliteral interpretation, the text is beneficial in its instruction about the role of the church within salvation history.

The beneficial nature of Scripture is a major emphasis of Cyril's exegesis as well. We will look at three passages where he comments on Scripture's usefulness.[103] First, as we have seen with our other three authors, for Cyril the biblical text is inherently useful as a result of the Holy Spirit's inspiration. For example, as Cyril comes to John 1:15 in his *Commentary on John*, he claims that John the evangelist and John the Baptist were "Spirit-bearers" (πνευματοφόρων) and, as a result, the Fourth Evangelist "usefully" (χρησίμως) constructs his prologue.[104] In this context he goes on to treat the doctrinal implications of the prologue and to demonstrate its refutation of Trinitarian and christological heresy line by line. I will demonstrate throughout this study that one of the useful features of John's Gospel found by each author is its articulation of doctrine and refutation of heresy.

Second, as mentioned above, like Origen, Cyril believes there are benefits to be found at both the literal and the nonliteral levels of Scripture. However, whereas Origen assumes that there is always benefit to be found at the nonliteral level (unlike the literal), Cyril, as I have already observed, suggests that one ought to move to the nonliteral level only if the useful-

---

103. See also *Comm. Isa.* pref.; 21:3–4; *Comm. Zach.* 3:1; *Comm. Mich.* 7:14–15.

104. Cyril, *In Jo.* 1:15 (Maxwell, 65). Of course, for Cyril, it is not just the prologue that John has written usefully; Cyril finds many other useful teachings in the Fourth Gospel.

ness of the literal level is not evident. For example, in my second passage, after he explains Jesus's words in John 9:4, "We must do the works of him who sent us while it is still day," at the literal level, he chooses not to move to the nonliteral level. He provides his reader with a theoretical comment to explain this decision, seemingly because some have taken to providing a nonliteral interpretation of the word "day" in the verse. Because the words "day" and "night" are rightly interpreted nonliterally in some instances, Cyril argues, there are interpreters who would do likewise in the case of 9:4. In response to this, Cyril says the following:

> But that same meaning when the time is not right—when one should not try to drag by force what ought to be read according to the narrative into a spiritual interpretation [ὅτε μὴ δεῖ περιέλκειν πειρᾶσθαι βιαίως εἰς πνευματικὴν ἑρμηνείαν τὸ ἱστορικῶς ὠφελοῦν]—is nothing other than an unlearned confusion of what would be profitable if understood without elaborate interpretation [οὐδὲν ἕτερόν ἐστιν, ἢ συγχεῖν ἁπλῶς τὸ ἀπεριέργως λυσιτελοῦν]. It is an obfuscation, due to deep ignorance, of what is beneficial from the passage [καὶ τὸ χρήσιμον αὐτόθεν ἐκ πολλῆς σφόδρα τῆς ἀμαθίας καταθολοῦν]. (*In Jo.* 9:4 [Maxwell, 154])

According to Cyril, then, when there is profit enough at the literal level, the interpreter ought not to move beyond the narrative to the nonliteral level, for this only leads to confusion.

However, there are, of course, many instances in which Cyril finds benefit at both levels of the text, for example, in my third passage. As he introduces his interpretation of John 8:31, he tells his readers that they must be eager to "hold onto what is profitable [ἐπωφελέστατον]." He begins with the literal level and says, "As far as the obvious meaning is concerned [ὅσον μὲν οὖν ἧκεν εἰς τὸ νοῆσαι προχείρως], he says 'If they desire to obey his words, they will surely also be called his disciples,'" but, Cyril continues, "As far as the hidden meaning is concerned [ὅσον δὲ εἰς τὸ συνιέναι τι κεκρυμμένον], however, he indicates this: ... he is clearly drawing them away from the teachings of Moses gently ... and removing them from their adherence to the letter."[105] In this example, for Cyril, at the literal level, Jesus's words provide beneficial, practical instruction about how to live as an obedient disciple.[106] At the nonliteral level, Jesus's

---

105. Cyril, *In Jo.* 8:31 (Maxwell, 351–52); see also *Comm. Isa.* 21.3–4; *Comm. Zach* 3.1.

106. All four authors find such benefit in Jesus's words at the literal level.

words provide knowledge of salvation history, for Jesus hints that his own teachings replace the law. I have shown that all three previous authors found similar benefit above the letter. However, Cyril finds many other benefits at the literal and the nonliteral levels. At the literal level, like the other three authors, he finds moral instruction based on the examples of the narrative's characters, doctrinal teachings and refutation of heresy, as mentioned above, and instruction about Jesus's fulfillment of the Old Testament. At the nonliteral level, Cyril finds beneficial teaching about Christ's universal redemptive work within which the gentiles are included in the arch of salvation history, about the nature of the sacraments, and he finds beneficial insight about the situation of the church of his own day. Finally, I should note that for Cyril, unlike Origen, it seems that the benefits at both levels are for all believers, no matter their spiritual progress.[107]

To summarize, all four authors worked with the assumption that Scripture is inherently useful for the church, based on their belief in its inspiration by the Holy Spirit. This assumption informed their interpretation of the text, though they do not always appeal to it or employ the specific language of Scripture's usefulness or benefit in their treatment of a given text. I will note where they do and do not employ it with respect to each example we examine in this study. Origen and Cyril make clear that there are different benefits to be found at the literal and nonliteral levels of the text, whereas the Antiochenes seem to think that most of Scripture's benefits are to be found at the literal level and are actually suspicious of the usefulness of readings provided by those who go beyond the literal level. They do not, as far as I am aware, comment directly on the kinds of benefits one is able to find at the nonliteral level, but they occasionally search for benefit there.[108]

Based on the comments about the usefulness of Scripture just examined and on the comments these authors make about the specific passages of John that I will examine in the following chapters, there are several benefits or uses that I will highlight throughout this study at both the literal and the nonliteral levels. These benefits include not only instruction concerning how to live well as a disciple of Christ but also right belief. That is, these authors seem to conceive of Scripture's benefits in terms of both ethics and

---

107. In some rare instances, however, the characters of the literal narrative are for Cyril examples for specific groups within his contemporary church.

108. I will examine in ch. 1, however, the specific conditions that lead them to offer nonliteral interpretations in which there is benefit to be found.

theology. I will demonstrate that at the literal level, all four authors find examples in the characters of the historical narrative, which they instruct their audiences to follow. The characters in the narrative of Scripture are exemplary disciples of Christ, and they embody virtue and morality. Also, at this level, each author finds the Johannine text to be useful for the church with respect to its doctrinal teachings and its simultaneous refutation of a variety of heresies, particularly with respect to the Son's relation to the Father and the relationship between the Son's human and divine natures. The literal level is also where one can demonstrate that various aspects of Jesus's life and teachings fulfill what had been prophesied in the Old Testament.[109] Whereas the interpretation of the Old Testament frequently required one to operate in a nonliteral way, that is, to demonstrate the true or real meaning of an Old Testament type or prophecy (as pointing forward to events in Christ's ministry or the church's future), when dealing with New Testament passages in which Christ's words and deeds fulfill an Old Testament prophecy or tradition, one provides an aspect of the text's instruction at the literal level.

At the nonliteral level, Scripture is useful in that it teaches about the place of Jesus's ministry and the inclusion of the gentile church within the drama of salvation history.[110] Also at the nonliteral level, the interpreter, of the Alexandrian variety in particular, is able to find direct insight about the present state of the author's contemporary church, and not infrequently, the individual Christian's soul. That is, the various passages of the Gospel of John examined in this thesis provide symbolic representations of the various groups and members of the church, the church's relationship to outsiders, and sometimes the spiritual and psychological state of its individual members. At the nonliteral level, one could also find instruction about the mystical realities related to the sacraments and other church practices.

The distinction I am drawing between the two schools then can be summarized in this way: In Antioch, there is more than enough benefi-

---

109. In the case of Cyril in particular, as will become clear throughout this study, Jesus's life and teachings treated nonliterally can also fulfill Old Testament prophecy. (Perhaps such an exegetical discovery provides further justification for one's nonliteral reading.)

110. I will demonstrate in ch. 3 of this study, however, that Theodore and Chrysostom deal with the place of the gentile church within the drama of salvation history as part of their literal treatment of the passage.

cial instruction to be found at the literal level and it is rarely necessary to move beyond the letter, whereas in Alexandria, both the literal and the nonliteral level alike have much benefit to offer the reader. The Alexandrians find many of the same benefits as the Antiochenes at the literal level, but their belief that the text has inherent benefit at both levels leads them to search beyond the letter in every instance for these benefits. Not only that, but the specific beneficial content the Alexandrians find above the letter, namely, their belief that the biblical text speaks directly to their contemporary church situation, contemporary church practice, and to the individual Christian's mind and soul is only very rarely a feature of Antiochene exegesis.[111]

The Chapters of This Book

In my first chapter, I will examine the four authors' introductory comments to their commentaries and homilies. I examine their descriptions of the circumstances that led to the composition of John's Gospel, in which they each articulate their belief that John's Gospel is superior to the Synoptic Gospels due to John's emphasis on Jesus's divinity. I also examine their statements about the benefits of John. Next, I analyze their descriptions of the ideal interpreter of John's Gospel, in addition to their interpretive principles and assumptions, to the extent that they discuss them in this context. I supplement my analysis in this chapter with material from the rest of the authors' corpora in order to contextualize their statements in their introductory comments on John, particularly as they relate to their interpretive principles. I will show that in their introductory material, all four authors claim that John's Gospel is a beneficial text that is full of great mysteries, and that it is superior due to its doctrinal teachings concerning Christ's divinity. By and large the authors' introductory comments give the impression that their treatment of John will

---

111. In her study of Cyril's and Theodore's commentaries on the Minor Prophets, Hauna T. Ondrey has made a similar distinction between these two exegetes' emphases specifically (*The Minor Prophets as Christian Scripture in the Commentaries of Theodore of Mopsuestia and Cyril of Alexandria*, OECS [Oxford: Oxford University Press, 2018], 227–39). Despite her observation that Theodore's commentary offers "a theological history lesson," whereas Cyril's offers more immediate applications to the church of his day, in the end she suggests that we abandon entirely the distinction between Alexandria and Antioch.

be quite similar, given their shared emphasis on its beneficial provision of instruction about Christ's divinity.[112] However, despite these shared emphases in their introductory comments, the distinction between the two schools nonetheless becomes apparent once we examine their treatment of specific passages from John's Gospel.

Given the great length of these authors' exegetical works on the Gospel of John, I have had to be selective in the passages I will discuss. I have chosen to examine five different kinds of passages as case studies for analysis: the cleansing of the temple in John 2, the woman at the well in John 4, the healing of the man born blind in John 9, the good shepherd in John 10, and the raising of Lazarus in John 11.[113] I will devote a chapter to each passage. I chose the passages I did in part due to the extant material in Origen's commentary, for as I said above, we have his comments only up to John 13. I have chosen the cleansing of the temple in John 2, as it is a passage in which Jesus deals directly with the official Jewish temple cult, and I will examine their treatment of this passage in chapter 2. In chapter 3, I will deal with my author's interpretations of the Samaritan woman at the well in John 4, which provides an example of an extended dialogue between Jesus and the Samaritan woman, as well as an example of a conversion narrative of sorts. The raising of Lazarus in John 11 provides a resurrection story that culminates in one of Jesus's distinctively Johannine "I am" statements (11:25–26), and I will deal with their treatments of this passage in chapter 6.

I have chosen two Johannine passages that Origen's commentary does not cover, however, the healing of the man born blind in John 9 and the good shepherd parable in 10. This I have done due to the richness of my other three authors' treatments of these passages. In John 9, we have a healing miracle combined with a narrative of controversy between Jesus and his Jewish contemporaries, which I deal with in chapter 4, and in John 10, a rare example of a Johannine parable, which I deal with in chapter 5. Both

---

112. There are hints of the distinction between the two schools that we will see throughout this study already in this introductory material; e.g., it is only Origen who claims that the text requires a nonliteral approach in order to discover the mysteries hidden in the Fourth Gospel, but of course Cyril, who does not describe a nonliteral approach to Scripture in his preface, nearly always provides a nonliteral interpretation, which cannot be said for the Antiochenes.

113. I chose these five, but I might have chosen others. The patterns of exegesis that I observe throughout this thesis can be observed in the other passages from John's Gospel that I have not chosen.

of these passages present the opportunity to witness these authors' treatments of different kinds of passages from the other three I have selected. In order to attend to Origen's treatment of these two passages, I have drawn on material from his *Homilies on Isaiah*, in which we have a relatively sustained discussion of John 9, and from his *Commentary on the Song of Songs*, in which he treats the good shepherd parable at some length.

The overall pattern that I demonstrate in this study is that all four authors find beneficial doctrinal and moral instruction about the relationship between the Father and the Son and the two natures of Christ at the literal level. These tend to be the primary benefits the Antiochenes find in each passage. By contrast, the Alexandrians' preference for moving beyond the letter results in their tendency to find in the nonliteral text additional beneficial teachings about salvation history, but also about the sacraments, the present situation of the church in their day, and the individual Christian soul and mind.

1
John, His Gospel, and Its Interpretation in the Schools of Alexandria and Antioch

In this chapter I examine each of the four authors' introductory comments on John's Gospel, in which they each set out the terms for their treatments of the text.[1] In these introductory comments, each of these authors describes John's Gospel as a "beneficial" or "useful" text and each associates its benefits with both its divine inspiration and its distinctive emphasis on the divinity of Christ.[2] In fact, all four authors esteemed the Fourth Gospel above the Synoptic Gospels due to this emphasis.[3] Each author envisioned an ideal reader of the superior gospel text, a reader who could draw out the

---

1. Origen, Cyril, and Theodore make their introductory comments in the prefaces to their commentaries. In the case of Chrysostom, his introduction takes place in the first two homilies on John. There has been some recent discussion as to whether these homilies were ever really delivered or not, but most now think it clear that they were composed with real congregations in view. In more recent discussion, scholars have been concerned with determining *which* congregations Chrysostom was speaking to in a given set of homilies; see the following: Margaret Mitchell, *The Heavenly Trumpet: John Chrysostom and the Art of Pauline Interpretation* (Louisville: Westminster John Knox, 2002), xxii n. 14; Wendy Mayer, "John Chrysostom and His Audiences: Distinguishing Different Congregations at Antioch and Constantinople," *StPatr* 31 (1997): 70–75; Pauline Allen, "John Chrysostom's Homilies on I and II Thessalonians: The Preacher and His Audience," *StPatr* 31 (1997): 3–21.

2. Theodore does not emphasize the inspiration of John's Gospel in his preface, though he mentions vaguely that John received "divine grace." I will discuss this and his somewhat unusual understanding of the inspiration of the biblical authors below.

3. As I noted above, this they inherited from their predecessors. While it is only Origen of my four authors who refers to John's Gospel in Clement's specific terms, i.e., as the "spiritual gospel," my other three authors agreed that it was distinctive in that John was primarily concerned with Jesus's divinity.

benefits it had to offer for his audience.[4] In addition, each author articulated what he saw as the appropriate interpretive approach to John's Gospel.[5]

However, I will examine this material in detail not only because each author returns to many of the interpretive principles he sets out in his pref-

---

4. I have borrowed the term *ideal interpreter* from Martens's work on Origen's ideal reader of Scripture (*Origen and Scripture*, 6, 161–91). According to Martens, for Origen, the ideal interpreter of Scripture was not only a scholar who was trained in Greco-Roman philology, but he was also deeply committed to the Christian tradition and its associated beliefs, practices, and virtues. For Origen, Martens argues, the ideal interpreter was one who had made moral progress on the journey of Christian faith as a participant in the Christian drama of salvation. Of course, none of these authors use the specific language of ideal reader, and each of my four authors has his own emphases as he articulates the characteristics of the interpreter, but each author has a vision of the person who will understand and interpret John's Gospel well.

5. The question of whether my later three authors had access to, or were dependent on, Origen's *Commentary on the Gospel of John* is extremely difficult to answer. For one thing, even if they used his commentary or were otherwise influenced by him, none of the authors admits it, given that, by the time they are writing, Origen represents all dangerous and suspect ideas. Furthermore, the analysis required to demonstrate Origen's influence, beyond the general consensus that all patristic authors were influenced by him to a large degree, requires an extensive knowledge of Origen's (complicated) corpus and sophisticated thought, in addition to painstaking comparative philological work. However, there has been more discussion about whether Cyril had and responded to Origen's *Commentary on the Gospel of John* specifically in his own commentary than is generally the case. While I suspect that he did, it is not our purpose here to prove this definitely. See the following bibliography on the question of whether Cyril had or knew Origen's commentary: Joseph W. Trigg, "Origen and Cyril of Alexandria: Continuities and Discontinuities in Their Approach to the Gospel of John," in Perrone, *Origeniana Octava*, 2:955–65. Trigg does not think that a comparison of the two Alexandrians' commentaries on John provides conclusive evidence that Cyril was responding to Origen in any way. On the other end of the spectrum, see Domenico Pazzini, who argues, based on his analysis of their treatments of John's prologue in 1:1–18, that Origen's work is an ever-present voice in Cyril's mind as he interpreted John (*Il prologo di Giovanni in Cirillo di Alessandria*, StBi 116 [Brescia: Paideia, 1997]). It would be extremely difficult to prove that Cyril knew and responded directly to Origen's commentary specifically, or for that matter, whether the Antiochenes had access to either Origen's or each other's works. It is difficult to claim definitively that Theodore was dependent on or had Chrysostom's *Homilies on the Gospel of John* at his disposal. Again, I suspect that he did, in some form or another, but it is not my aim here to make such an argument. Thus, I will not assume in this study literary dependence in any direction, even if I suspect that it is probable. For a similar suspicion regarding similar and sometimes identical treatments of the same passages by the members of the Antiochene school, see Martens, *Adrian's Introduction*, 15–16.

aces throughout his comments on specific passages of John's Gospel, but also because the juxtaposition of this introductory material with the case studies of each chapter will serve to highlight the important distinction between the traditions. That is, I will demonstrate that despite their agreement about the nature and content of the spiritual gospel, the Alexandrians part ways with the Antiochenes in terms of the manner in which they draw out the gospel's beneficial teachings.

Origen begins his introduction of the Fourth Gospel within the context of a discussion about the nature and context of the term *gospel* and the varying degrees to which the books of the Old and New Testaments can properly be called gospel.[6] For Origen, all of the New Testament is gospel, unlike the Old Testament, which is only gospel insofar as it points forward to Christ, as it is only "a shadow of the good things to come."[7] It is only after Christ took on flesh in the incarnation that the Law and the Prophets can be described as gospel, for it was Christ who revealed their divine nature.[8] For Origen, all of the New Testament is gospel, though "as far as the precise sense of the expression of the gospel [ἐπὶ τῇ ἀκριβείᾳ τῆς τοῦ εὐαγγελίου φωνῆς]," only the four gospels—in Origen's words, "the narration of the deeds, sufferings, and words of Jesus"—deserve the description.[9] Paul's epistles and the Acts of the Apostles, by comparison, provide us only with "the understanding of wise men that have been aided by Christ."[10]

---

6. Origen's preface to his *Commentary on John* can be found in the first twenty-six pages of book 1 (*Comm. Jo.* 1.1–89 [Heine, 31–51]).

7. Origen, *Comm. Jo.* 1.39 (Heine, 35–36, 42). The language of Heb 1:10 assists Origen in this assessment. See 1.14, 17. However, for Origen, even the gospels teach only "a shadow of the mysteries of Christ" (σκιὰν μυστηρίων Χριστοῦ), as he says in 1.39, 60. He will develop the limited nature of Scripture in much greater detail as he treats the woman at the well in John 4, which I examine in ch. 3 of this study.

8. Origen, *Comm. Jo.* 1.14, 33–34, 46–74 (Heine, 35, 40–41, 43–49); see also *Hom. Ezech.* 14.14. 2.3; *Comm. Cant.* 2.8.

9. Origen, *Comm. Jo.* 1.20 (Heine, 36). Note that I have altered Heine's translation slightly. He has "the precise sense of the expression in the gospel."

10. Origen, *Comm. Jo.* 1.15 (Heine, 35). This is corroborated by Origen's comments about Paul in his *Comm. Rom.* 1.4–7. In that context he says that we are able to witness Paul's progress in the stages of perfection. I.e., his letters exhibit Paul's progressive understanding of the divine teachings. This he sees as a contrast to the gospel writers. Not all scholars, however, take Origen's comments about Paul at face value; e.g., Maurice Wiles says that more often than not, Origen attributes perfection to Paul, as is typical in the Eastern tradition; see Wiles, *The Divine Apostle: The Interpretation of St. Paul's Epistles in the Early Church* (Cambridge: Cambridge University Press, 1967), 16;

Therefore, for Origen, the gospels are "the first-fruits" (ἡ ἀπαρχή) of all of Scripture.[11] However, among the gospels, it is John's Gospel that is preeminent for Origen, for in it we find the "greater and more perfect expressions concerning Jesus," because it manifests Jesus's divinity most fully, as evidenced by John's prologue (1:1–18) and Christ's "I am" statements (John 8:12; 10:9, 11; 11:25; 14:6).[12] Not only does Origen claim that among the four gospels it is the fourth that highlights Jesus's divinity most fully, but by designating it "the first-fruits of the Gospels," Origen also suggests that John's Gospel actually *completes* the accounts of the others (*Comm. Jo.* 1.21–22 [Heine, 36–38]). For first-fruits are offered after all the other fruits; whereas the Law and the Prophets were written first, the gospels were written after them, and are therefore the first-fruits of the scriptures.[13] Among the first-fruits then, John's Gospel is preeminent, for he wrote his gospel after the other evangelists had written theirs, in order to write more

---

see also Peter Widdicombe, "Origen," in *The Blackwell Companion to Paul*, ed. Stephen Westerholm, Blackwell Companions to Religion (Malden, MA: Blackwell, 2011), 318.

11. Origen, *Comm. Jo.* 1.12–14, 20 (Heine, 34–36). See also *Princ.* 4.2. 3 where he describes all four gospels as "the mind (or meaning) of Christ" (νοῦς τοῦ Χριστοῦ). See Torjesen's helpful discussion of Origen's understanding of the contents of the gospels (*Hermeneutical Procedure*, 67, 140). She explains that for Origen, unlike the Old Testament, in which the Word is mediated through the experience of the prophet or saint's encounter with the Word, in the gospels, there is no intermediary needed. The interpreter or hearer encounters the Word directly. Origen's introductory comments on Matthew are no longer extant, and he appears not to have written a commentary on the Gospel of Mark, nor to have made reference to the status of Mark's Gospel elsewhere. It is generally the case that most early Christian exegetes did not compose commentaries on Mark's Gospel. For more on the dearth of patristic commentary on Mark, see Thomas C. Oden and Christopher A. Hall, "Introduction to Mark," in *Mark*, ACCS New Testament 2 (Downers Grove, IL: InterVarsity Press, 1998), xxxi. In his *Homilies on Luke*, Origen states briefly that all four gospel writers were filled with the Holy Spirit, a concept that he does not introduce in his introductory comments of his *Commentary on John* (Origen, *Hom. Luc.* 1.1); see also *Princ.* 1.2; 4.2.7–8. In this context, he makes similar comments about all of Scripture; see *Hom. Jer.* 19.11. 2.

12. Origen, *Comm. Jo.* 1.22 (Heine, 37–38). Even though he has such a view of John's Gospel, in 1.24 he will go on to say that it contains a "word, which is stored up in the earthen treasures of paltry language [τὸν ἐν τοῖς ὀστρακίνοις τῆς εὐτελοῦς λέξεως θησαυροῖς ἐναποκείμενον λόγον]" (2 Cor 4:7); see also *Princ.* 4.1.7; 4.2.8–9 where he describes the poor humble style of scripture, which conceals its sublime message.

13. Origen, *Comm. Jo.* 1.13 (Heine, 34–35); see also 1.80. I will say more in due time about Origen's description of John within the framework of the Old Testament sacrificial system, particularly as it relates to the ideal interpreter and to Cyril's preface.

perfect expressions about the divinity of Christ (*Comm. Jo.* 1.13 [Heine, 34–35]). He goes on to describe Matthew's Gospel as the "genesis" of the gospel, Mark's as the beginning (ἡ ἀρχή) of the gospel, and then he names Luke, but at this point there is a lacuna in the text, and we cannot be certain how he described Luke's Gospel in relation to John.[14]

For Origen, the superior Gospel of John is the result of the privileged vantage point given to the Evangelist John, a topic that Origen addresses at some length both in his *Commentary on John* and in a handful of other places in his corpus. According to Origen, the Fourth Gospel is preeminent because the Evangelist John had "leaned on Jesus's breast" (John 13:25).[15] Origen says little more in his preface about how he understands John's leaning on Jesus's breast or why John among the Twelve was chosen to receive this privilege. However, when he comes to the passage of John 13:23–25 in book 32 of the commentary, he claims that John, who was "considered worthy of this privilege because he was judged worthy of remarkable love from the teacher," leans both on the bosom (ὁ κόλπος) (John 13:23) and on the breast (τὸ στῆθος) of Jesus (John 13:25).[16] Origen here reads John's leaning on Jesus's bosom with "symbolism" (συμβολικῶς) to mean that John rested on more "mystical things" (οἱ μυστικώτεροι), that is, on the bosom of the Word, which is "analogous [ἀνάλογον] also to the Word being

---

14. Here Origen plays on the term *beginning* in Mark's Gospel in particular, for Mark begins his gospel by saying that it is the "the beginning of the gospel" (Mark 1:1), whereas John has the final word on the matter as he writes directly of the divine Word who was "in the beginning" (John 1:1). For Luke, see Origen, *Comm. Jo.* 1.22 (Heine, 37–38). A. E. Brooke has reconstructed the text to say: "Luke also having said in the beginning of Acts, 'The former treatise I made of all things which Jesus began to do and teach'"; see Brooke, *The Commentary of Origen on S. John's Gospel*, 2 vols. (Cambridge: Cambridge University Press, 1896, 1939), 17.

15. Origen, *Comm. Jo.* 1.22 (Heine, 37–38); Wiles makes this observation as well (*Spiritual Gospel*, 10). For a thorough and helpful treatment of Origen's comments on John's "leaning on the breast," see Peter Widdicombe, "Knowing God: Origen and the Example of the Beloved Disciple," *StPatr* 31 (1997): 554–58.

16. Origen, *Comm. Jo.* 32.263 (Heine, 391). Note that while Origen claims that John was worthy of Jesus's love, he does not really address why John was more worthy of Jesus's love than the other disciples. I will demonstrate below that both Antiochenes attempt to provide an account of why John is "the one Jesus loved." He does not make this distinction between the bosom and the breast elsewhere, and perhaps the distinction he makes here is to be explained by the fact that it is the text of his immediate focus, whereas in other instances where he comments on the text, it is simply drawn upon to help him explain another scriptural passage or concept.

in the bosom of the Father."[17] Thus the intimacy John had with Jesus as he leaned on his bosom is likened to the intimacy between the Father and the Son. However, Origen thinks John's leaning on the *breast* of Jesus to be superior to his leaning on the *bosom*, for after John moved from Jesus's bosom to his breast, he could then truly be said to be "the disciple whom Jesus loved."[18] Unfortunately, we do not have any further explanation of Origen's distinction between Jesus's breast and his bosom as he discusses it in book 32. In his *Commentary on the Song of Songs*, however, there is a discussion that helps us to better understand how Origen thought about the term *breast* in John 13:23–25, which he draws on in his explanation of the "inner meaning" (*intellectus interior*) of the word *breasts* in Song 1:2, "For thy breasts are better than wine."[19] Whereas breast is to be understood in the same way as "heart" (*corde*) in such contexts as Matt 5:8, "Blessed are the pure in heart," and in Rom 10:10, "with the heart we believe unto justice," in the context of meals (i.e., John 13), the word "bosom" (*sinus*) or "breast" (*pectus*) is used instead (*Comm. Cant.* 1.2.3, 4 [Lawson, 63–64, 65]). Here, Origen argues, the word breast means "the ground of Jesus's heart and … the inward meanings of his teaching [*in principali cordis Iesu atque in internis doctrinae eius sensibus requievisse dicatur*]" (*Comm. Cant.* 1.2.4 [Lawson, 64]). As he reclined at Jesus's breast, John sought "the treasures of wisdom and knowledge" (Col 2:3) that are hidden there.[20] It is this privileged vantage point, then, from which the Evangelist John composes his gospel, according to Origen.

For Origen, then, the Fourth Gospel is preeminent, due in no small part to the Evangelist John's superior vantage point at the breast of Christ,

---

17. See Origen, *Hom. Cant.* 1.3. In this much-abbreviated version of the discussion of this passage, John's leaning on the bosom of Christ allows him to enjoy "full fellowship of thought with Him"; cf. *Hom. Ezech.* 6.4. 3. Origen, *Comm. Jo.* 32.264 (Heine, 391). This is, of course, a reference to 1:18 of John's prologue; cf. Origen, *Hom. Luc.* frag. 223. This fragment provides us with a discussion of John 13:23 that is similar to that which we have in book 32.

18. Origen, *Comm. Jo.* 32.278 (Heine, 394); see also *Comm. Jo.* 32.276.

19. Origen, *Comm. Cant.* 1.2.2 (Lawson, 63).

20. Origen, *Comm. Cant.* 1.2.4 (Lawson, 65). The bride of the Song of Songs receives "more excellent and all-surpassing doctrine [*excellentiorem cunctis eminentioremque doctrinam*]" from the breast of the bridegroom, whom Origen understands as Christ; see *Comm. Cant.* 1.2.20 (Lawson, 68–69). Origen also includes here a related discussion of Lev 10:14–15, which uses the language of "breast of separation." He expands on this in his *Hom. Lev.* 1.4; see also *Pasc.* 1.13.

where he contemplated the mysteries of the divine. This is a kind of articulation of the divine inspiration of John, which is more christocentric than pneumatic.[21] None of my other authors makes an explicit case for the superiority of the Gospel of John based on John's leaning on Jesus's breast in John 13:23–25, although Theodore too makes a probable allusion to this passage, using it to claim that the Evangelist John himself is superior to the synoptic authors, but not in a manner that suggests inspiration.[22] By contrast, Chrysostom and Cyril are willing to grant the superiority of John's Gospel, but not of John's vantage point, skill, or piety, and their articulations of the inspiration of John are much more detailed than Origen's.[23]

I will now turn to examine Origen's comments about the beneficial nature of the Gospel of John. As will become clear, he does not articulate a difference in terms of benefits between John and the other three gospels, despite his comments about the superiority of John's Gospel.[24] For him, each of the four gospels is "a composition of declarations which are beneficial [ὠφελίμων] to the one who believes them and does not misconstrue them, since it produces a benefit [ὠφέλειαν ἐμποιοῦν] in him."[25] He

---

21. As I said above in my discussion of Origen's understanding of Scripture's usefulness in *Princ.* book 4, he believed that Scripture was inspired by the Holy Spirit. He makes similar comments about the Spirit's inspiration of Scripture in *Hom. Num.* 26.3.2; see also *Hom. Ezech.* 2.2.2–3; *Philoc.* 2.4; *Cels.* 1.44; 7.3–4. However, as in this context, Origen also articulates the inspiration of Scripture in relation to the Son; see *Hom. Lev.* 4.1.1; *Hom. Jer.* 9.1.1–2.

22. Perhaps my other authors are aware of the tradition in the gnostic Apocryphon of John in which the apostle John receives "the revelation of the mysteries hidden in silence" and want to avoid potential associations with gnostic circles, which Origen's emphasis on John's leaning on the breast to receive heavenly teachings might have been thought to have resembled too closely; see the translation of John D. Turner and Marvin Meyer, "The Secret Book of John," in *The Nag Hammadi Scriptures* (New York: HarperOne, 2008), 107.

23. I will show below that Chrysostom claims that each member of the Trinity inspires John in the process of the composition of his gospel, whereas for Cyril, it is primarily Christ and the Holy Spirit.

24. Perhaps this is because he has already argued that John's Gospel is superior due to John's emphasis on Jesus's divinity and therefore feels it unnecessary. In any case, it seems that for Origen, even if John articulates Jesus's divinity more clearly than the other three, this doctrine is not altogether absent from the Synoptic Gospels.

25. Origen, *Comm. Jo.* 1.28 (Heine, 39). Origen does go on to explain that the Law and the Prophets are also beneficial, but again, they are only so after the coming of Christ; see 1.32–34. Torjesen claims that for Origen "the usefulness of the gospels is

then goes on to explain in more detail just what kinds of benefits he has in mind. First, the gospels are beneficial in that they teach about "the saving sojourn" of Christ for the sake of humanity, in other words, the doctrine of the incarnation.[26] Second, Origen claims, "it is also clear [σαφές] to everyone who believes that each Gospel is a discourse which teaches about the sojourn of the good Father in his Son with those who are willing to receive him."[27] Again, this is a beneficial doctrinal teaching about the relationship between the Father and the Son. In these two statements also, we have an implicit articulation of the twofold doctrinal nature of the gospels, for each of the four gospels contains beneficial teachings about Christ's humanity (his saving sojourn) and about his divinity (the sojourn of the Father in Christ). So, while John's Gospel provides "more perfect expressions" about the divinity of Christ, as we saw above, such teachings can also be found in the Synoptic Gospels, according to Origen, albeit less clearly than in the Fourth Gospel.

Origen does not articulate here in his preface the level of the text, that is, whether literal or nonliteral, at which one finds such benefits, though as we shall see throughout this study, like my other three authors, he tends to deal with doctrine at the literal level. Origen says more about the level of the text where one ought to search for benefit, however, in book 10 of his *Commentary on John*. In this context, Origen explains the shared "intention" (τὸ βούλημα) of the four evangelists in this way: "[they] wanted to teach us by a type the things they had seen in their mind," and thus, they have "made minor changes in what happened so far as the history is concerned, with a view to the usefulness of the mystical object [πρὸς τὸ χρήσιμον τοῦ τῶν μυστικοῦ σκοποῦ]."[28] That is, according to Origen, the evangelists' main concern was to provide a useful narrative about Jesus in light of their own (noetic) encounter with the Logos, which they present "in a type" for their

---

to be found in the fact that they produce the presence and coming of the Logos in the souls of those who desire to receive him" (*Hermeneutical Procedure*, 129).

26. Origen, *Comm. Jo.* 1.28 (Heine, 39); see also *Comm. Jo.* 10.15, 18–19.

27. Origen, *Comm. Jo.* 1.28 (Heine, 39); see also *Princ.* 4.2.7 where he articulates the doctrines (νοήματα) and teachings (δόγματα) concerning God and his Son, the nature of the Son, the cause of the incarnation, and the nature of Christ's activity, in all of Scripture.

28. Origen, *Comm. Jo.* 10.15, 18–19 (Hiene, 257, 259). This he claims as he introduces his comments on the cleansing of the temple in John 2, where he argues that the nonliteral level provides the true meaning of the passage, since the Synoptic accounts differ not a little from John at the literal level.

cal manner" (μυστικώτερον) (*Comm. Jo.* 1.1 [Heine, 31]). In this mystical reading, the twelve tribes represent the majority of church members, who offer "only a few acts to God," whereas the Levites represent those who "devote themselves to the divine Word and truly exist by the service of God alone" (*Comm. Jo.* 1.10 [Hiene, 33]). Origen identifies himself with the latter group, claiming that "we are eager for those things which are better, all our activity and our entire life being dedicated to God," and then asks (rhetorically) whether there could possibly exist a more excellent activity than "the careful examination of the gospel [τὴν περὶ εὐαγγελίου ἐξέτασιν]."[38] Indeed, his present activity, namely, the careful examination of the Gospel of John, the first-fruits of the gospels, is to be understood as the first-fruits of all activity. Thus, the ideal reader for Origen belongs to the Levitical group, which represents those readers who are entirely devoted to the divine Word.[39] Those who offer only fleeting and infrequent acts of service to God, according to Origen, are not fit for the careful study of John's Gospel.[40] For Origen, then, the ideal interpreter of the Fourth Gospel must have intimacy with Christ (i.e., he must have leaned on Jesus's breast), such as that which John had, he must maintain a posture of prayer, asking for divine aid for the interpretive endeavor, and he must be among those of the (spiritually mature) Levitical order.[41]

Origen also articulates how one ought to approach the task of interpreting John's Gospel in the introductory comments of his preface. Here he claims briefly that his interpretive task is "to translate the gospel perceptible to the senses into the spiritual gospel [τὸ αἰσθητὸν εὐαγγέλιον μεταλαβεῖν εἰς πνευματικόν]," and, further, that it is an attempt "to reach into the depths of the meaning of the gospel and examine the bare truth of the types in it [εἰς τὰ βάθη τοῦ εὐαγγελικοῦ νοῦ φθάσαι καὶ ἐρευνῆσαι τὴν ἐν αὐτῷ γυμνὴν τύπων ἀλήθειαν]."[42] Thus he articulates explicitly his belief

---

38. Origen, *Comm. Jo.* 1.12 (Heine, 34). See also *Princ.* 4.2.7 where he claims that the discovery of the doctrines hidden in scripture requires searching and devotion to deep things; cf. *Comm. Rom.* 7.17.4.

39. Martens, *Origen and Scripture*, 101.

40. Origen describes this type of person in *Hom. Ezech.* 3.1.2; and he warns against the rash thinking about and reading of Scripture in *Ep. Greg.* 3.

41. It is not clear, at least in the context of his *Commentary on John,* whether by the Levitical order he is thinking of either ecclesiastical authorities, such as priests and bishops, or whether he has a specific scribal or scholastic class in mind.

42. The first quotation is from *Comm. Jo.* 1.45 (Heine, 43); see also *Princ.* 1.2; 4.1.7; 4.3.5; *Cels.* 1.18. The second quotation is from *Comm. Jo.* 1.46, 89 (Heine, 43, 51). In

that John contains types that point to the bare truth buried within the letter of the text. He does not explain in this context how exactly he will go about interpreting John's types. However, he does make the (perhaps rhetorical) claim that the exegetical task before him presents "all kinds of difficulties" (πᾶς ἀγών).[43] He does not explain further the difficulties involved in the task in his preface, so perhaps he thinks it self-evident that the careful examination of John is difficult.

However, Origen does describe more specifically the difficulties of the task of translating the literal gospel text into its true nonliteral meaning as he presents his interpretive principles in book 4 of *Peri archon*, to which I will turn briefly. Origen thinks that the gospels (and indeed the rest of Scripture) are filled with passages that "indicate certain mysteries through a semblance of history and not through actual events [διὰ δοκούσης ἱστορίας, καὶ οὐ σωματικῶς γεγενημένης, μηνύειν τινὰ μυστήρια]" and that "the bodily meaning is often proved to be an impossibility [πολλαχοῦ γὰρ ἐλέγχεται ἀδύνατον ὂν τὸ σωματικόν]."[44] Since this is so for Origen, the reader of the gospels must "carefully investigate how far the literal meaning is true and how far it is impossible [ἐπιμελῶς βασανίζειν, πῇ τὸ κατὰ τὴν λέξιν ἀληθές ἐστιν, καὶ πῇ ἀδύνατον]." He provides this rule for the task: where the passage as a whole is "literally impossible [ἀδύνατος μὲν ὁ ὡς πρὸς τὸ ῥητόν]," the reader must seek "the entire meaning" (ὅλον τὸν νοῦν) by connecting the impossible with the parts that are "historically true" (ἀληθέσι κατὰ τὴν ἱστορίαν). Once the interpreter has connected the true and the untrue parts of the narrative, together they are to be "interpreted allegorically [συναλληγορουμένοις]" in order to derive the text's true meaning (*Princ.* 4.3.5 [Butterworth, 297]). In the specific examples of my study,

---

each of these passages, Origen describes Scripture as possessing both an obvious and a hidden meaning. However, in *Princ.* 4.2.4 he claims that Scripture has a threefold meaning, which he describes as the text's body, soul, and spirit. But, as has been noted by most scholars of Origen's exegesis, he rarely finds meaning on all three levels. It is more typical, as is the case in this example in his *Commentary on John*, to find the literal and the nonliteral. See, however, Elizabeth Dively-Lauro's *The Soul and Spirit of Scripture within Origen's Exegesis*, BAC 3 (Leiden: Brill, 2005). She argues that Origen is consistent in finding all three levels of meaning throughout his corpus.

43. Origen, *Comm. Jo.* 1.46 (Heine, 43). See also 1.89. As Crawford notes regarding similar statements made by Cyril, it is a rhetorical convention in antiquity to claim inadequacy for the task at hand; see Crawford, *Cyril*, 184.

44. Origen, *Princ.* 4.3.1, 5 (Butterworth, 288, 297); see also *Princ.* 4.2.5.

1. John, His Gospel, and Its Interpretation 55

I will attend to the ways he went about the difficult task of determining the text's impossibilities, which in turn led him toward its true meaning.

I will turn now to the Antiochene authors and begin with Chrysostom. Here I will examine not only his introductory homilies in his *Homilies on John*, but also the first homily of his *Homilies on Matthew*, where he compares all four gospels. In his introductory homilies, Chrysostom provides a detailed account of the circumstances that led to the composition of John's Gospel, which he crafts from the pages of the gospels themselves. The Evangelist John was of humble origins; he was from the (vilified) village of Nazareth (John 1:46), was the son of a poor fisherman (Matt 4:21–22; Mark 1:19–20), and had no learning whatsoever (Acts 4:13) (*Hom. Jo.* 1.1 [Goggin, 12–13]). However, this same John, the "Son of Thunder" (Mark 3:17), the "beloved disciple" (John 13:23; 21:7, 20), who possessed the keys of heaven (Matt 16:19), who drank the chalice of Christ (Matt 20:20–23), who had been baptized with his baptism (Mark 10:38–39), and who confidently "leaned on the breast of the Lord" (John 13:23–25), "attracted [ἐπεσπάσατο] even Christ himself" with his virtue, which resulted in his receiving the grace of the Holy Spirit.[45] John prepared his soul as a lyre, Chrysostom claims, and "brought it about [ἔδωκε] that the Holy Spirit should send forth a great and sublime sound by its means [δι' αὐτῆς μέγα τι καὶ ὑψηλὸν ἐνηχῆσαι τῷ Πνεύματι]."[46] As a result, not only were John's divinely inspired words sublime, for Chrysostom, but they were also spoken "with accuracy" (μετὰ ἀκριβεία).[47]

---

45. Chrysostom, *Hom. Jo.* 1.1 (Goggin, 5). Note that Chrysostom does not do much at all with the passage in which John leans on Jesus's breast (John 13:23–25). He cites the passage as only one scriptural detail among many.

46. Chrysostom, *Hom. Jo.* 1.1 (Goggin, 5). However, John is not the only scriptural author for whom Chrysostom articulates a process of inspiration in which the human author attracts the divine person with his virtue. See also his introductory comments on the psalmist David in *Comm. Ps.* 45:1. There he says that David speaks inspired words only once he has "purified his soul." Thus, Chrysostom takes seriously the role of the virtuous human author in the process of inspiration, and is careful in his account of the inspiration of John, as he is in the case of his treatment of the inspiration of other biblical authors, not to describe the mysterious process in terms that resemble that of (pagan) seers too closely; see also his comments on the inspiration of David in his *Hom. Ps.* 110; see also *Comm. Ps.* 45:1.

47. Chrysostom, *Hom. Jo.* 1.2 (Goggin, 6). For similar statements about the precision of other biblical authors, see *Comm. Ps.* 47:4; *Hom. Isa.* 2.1; *Hom. Gen.* 4.14; 7.9; 8.10; 12.5–6. I will illustrate how Chrysostom understands this term throughout this study.

56   Interpreting the Gospel of John in Antioch and Alexandria

In these introductory homilies, Chrysostom articulates the "divine power" of inspiration in relation to each member of the Trinity, and in fact, he is my only author to do so.[48] In homily 1, he claims that John "possesses [Christ] speaking within himself and hears from him everything which he hears from the Father" (John 15:15).[49] In the very next paragraph, Chrysostom claims that John also has the Paraclete speaking within him.[50] However, he then says directly that in John's Gospel God, "through his agency, is speaking to humanity [δι'αὐτοῦ πρὸς τὴν τῶν ἀνθρώπων φθέγγεται φύσιν]."[51] Thus, for Chrysostom, the divine words found in John's Gospel are the result of "the divine power moving his soul [τῆς θείας δυνάμεως τῆς κινούσης αὐτοῦ τὴν ψυχήν]."[52] Chrysostom mentions only the inspiring divine power of Christ in his discussion of the composition of John in homily 1 of his *Homilies on Matthew*, to which I shall now turn, for in this context, he provides a discussion of the superiority of John to the Synoptic Gospels.[53]

In his first homily on Matthew, as he discusses the question of why four gospels were needed to tell the same story, Chrysostom argues that despite the overlapping material of the four gospels, none is superfluous, and that each one adds something of its own (*Hom. Matt.* 1.2 [NPNF 1/10:3]). He tells us that Luke wrote in order to provide Theophilus and his subsequent readers with certainty (Luke 1:3-4), Matthew wrote at the request of the Jews who had believed in Christ, and Mark wrote at the request of the

---

48. We might expect Cyril to do the same, but in the preface to his *Commentary on the Gospel of John*, he explains that Christ and the Holy Spirit inspire the Evangelist John, though he does mention the "Spirit of the Father" in this context (Cyril, *In Jo.* 1.pref. [Maxwell, 5]). I will say more about Cyril's discussion of the inspiration of John below.

49. Chrysostom, *Hom. Jo.* 1.2 (Goggin, 6); cf. *Hom. Act.* 1; *Hom. 1 Thess* 8. It should be noted that Chrysostom applies to John specifically Jesus's words to all of his disciples in John 15:15.

50. Chrysostom, *Hom. Jo.* 1.2 (Goggin, 6). This is Chrysostom's most common way of speaking about the inspiration of the biblical authors; see, e.g., *Hom. Matt.* 1.1; 5.2; *Hom. Act.* 3; *Comm. Ps.* 45:1; 49:3-4; *Hom. Ps.* 146.1; *Hom. Isa.* 2.1; *Hom. Gen.* 4.5; 7.7; 22.6.

51. Chrysostom, *Hom. Jo.* 2.1 (Goggin, 12). For similar statements about inspiration, see *Hom. Isa.* 2.1; *Hom. Gen.* 2.5; *Hom. Heb.* 1.3.

52. Chrysostom, *Hom. Jo.* 2.1 (Goggin, 12). See 2.2 where he describes John's words as "God-inspired [θεόπνευστα]"; cf. *Hom. Matt.* 1.3 where he uses the same verb "moved [κινήσαντος]" for Christ's inspiration of John.

53. We do not have any of his comments on Luke's Gospel, should he have made them, and in the case of Mark's Gospel, we have only a handful of fragments of homilies.

disciples who were in Egypt (*Hom. Matt.* 1.3 [*NPNF* 1/10:3]). Concerning John, Chrysostom explains, we can be sure that John did not write his gospel "without purpose" (οὐδὲ ἁπλῶς), for a certain "saying" (λόγος), which has come down to us "from the Fathers" explains that John wrote his gospel after having been "moved by Christ" (τοῦ Χριστοῦ κινήσαντος).[54] In this context, Chrysostom claims that Christ moved John to supplement the Synoptic accounts, for they had dwelt only on "the account of the dispensation" (τῷ τῆς οἰκονομίας λόγῳ), with the result that "the doctrines of the Godhead were near being left in silence [τὰ τῆς θεότητος ἐκιωδύνευεν ἀποσιωπᾶσθαι δόγματα]" (*Hom. Matt.* 1.3 [*NPNF* 1/10:3]). Of course, as Chrysostom says, the other three evangelists were also moved by Christ to provide their accounts.[55] John, however, began his gospel "from above," not "from beneath" as the other three had done, and he composed his entire narrative in this manner, treating "the doctrines of the Godhead" that the others did not, and his gospel is therefore "more lofty" than those of the Synoptic authors.[56]

Chrysostom also made comments in his introductory *Homilies on John* about the beneficial nature of the Gospel of John. He begins by saying that the Fourth Gospel is "teeming with such great mysteries, and productive of so many good things [τοσούτων γέμουσα ἀπορρήτων, καὶ τουαῦτα κομίζουσα ἀγαθά] … that those who receive them … rise superior to

---

54. Chrysostom, *Hom. Matt.* 1.3 (*NPNF* 1/10:3). Purpose is a general principle for Chrysostom: nothing is casual or random in Scripture. See the discussion of Mitchell, "John Chrysostom," 32. This principle relates to his principle of the biblical text's precision, which I will discuss below. In saying "from the fathers," perhaps Chrysostom has something like Irenaeus's account of John's composition of his gospel in view as he makes this comment; see Irenaeus, *Haer.* 3.2.1; cf. Clement of Alexandria as cited in Eusebius, *Hist. eccl.* 6.14.7, where Eusebius is drawing from Clement's lost work, *Hypotyposes*; cf. Jerome, *Comm. Matt.* pref.

55. At the beginning of this homily, he claims that it is the Spirit who inspired Matthew to write his gospel; see Chrysostom, *Hom. Matt.* 1.1 (*NPNF* 1/10:2). He does not seem to think it necessary to articulate a precise account of divine inspiration in terms of the members of the Trinity involved in the process.

56. Chrysostom, *Hom. Matt.* 1.1 (*NPNF* 1/10:3). He describes the contents of the Gospel of John similarly in his *Hom. Jo.* 1.2, 4; 2.1, 3. John's Gospel contains "sublime teachings" (ὑψηλὰ δόγματα), "awesome and ineffable mysteries" (τῶν μυστηρίων τὸ φρικτὸν καὶ πόρρητον), "certain fundamental truths" (τινων νηγκαίων διαλεξόμενος), and the "irresistible power of authentic doctrines" (δογμάτων ὀρθῶν). Of course, Chrysostom discusses Scripture more generally in similar terms; see, e.g., *Proph. obscurit.* 1.1.

everything belonging to this life and change their state to that of angels, so that they dwell on earth as if in heaven."⁵⁷ In other words, John's Gospel is so useful that it is able to spiritually transform the reader or hearer of its teachings. Similarly, according to Chrysostom, the sound of John's voice is "more beneficial" (χρησιμωτέραν) than the sound of any harpist or music, just as his teaching is more beneficial than that of any philosopher, including Plato and Pythagoras, whose works by contrast did not contain "anything useful" (οὐδὲν ὠφέλησε) whatsoever.⁵⁸ Unlike the useless, obscure, perverse, and pompous writings of the philosophers, argues Chrysostom, John's Gospel is "true and useful" (ἀληθῆ ... καὶ χρήσιμα) because he "mingled so much simplicity with his words [τοσαύτην τοῖς ῥήμασιν ἐγκατέμιξεν εὐκολίαν], that all he said was clear [δῆλα] not only to men and scholars, but even to women and children."⁵⁹ Unlike the works of

---

57. Chrysostom, *Hom. Jo.* 1.1 (Goggin, 4). Note that I have changed Goggin's translation of "so many benefits" to "so many good things," given that Chrysostom here uses the term ἀγαθά, not one of our synonyms for "useful" or "beneficial." He probably means something very similar, however; see Chrysostom, *Hom. Jo.* 2.3, where he does use such a term. He claims that John's Gospel teaches "something useful" (τι τῶν χρησίμων), so useful in fact, that its teachings are capable of taking one from earth to heaven. Likewise, in 1.3, he uses a verbal form to express a similar idea about the nature of John's Gospel: it is a text from which one can "derive great profit" (κερδᾶναι τι μέγα) (Goggin, 9).

58. Chrysostom, *Hom. Jo.* 2.2 (Goggin, 17). See Chrysostom's extended discussion of the useless teachings of the philosophers in *Hom. Jo.* 2.2–3. For John's voice, see Chrysostom, *Hom. Jo.* 1.1; cf. *Hom. Jo.* 1.4 (Goggin, 10), where he urges his parishioners to cultivate a desire for "something of advantage" (χρησίμων) in John's Gospel.

59. Chrysostom, *Hom. Jo.* 2.3 (Goggin, 18). For a useful recent study of Chrysostom's treatment of gender, see Wendy Mayer, "John Chrysostom and Women Revisited," in *Men and Women in the Early Christian Centuries*, ed. Wendy Mayer and Ian J. Elmer (Strathfield: St. Paul's, 2014), 211–26. In fact, as will become clear in this study, the "low" or humble nature of John's Gospel is due to the "condescension" (συγκαταβήσις) of God to the weakness of humanity, which is one of the key features of the Bible's usefulness; see *Hom. Gen.* 13.8, 14; *Comm. Ps.* 6:1; *Hom. Ps.* 110.3. For a helpful discussion of Chrysostom's principle of God's condescension in Scripture, see Hill, *Reading the Old Testament*, 36. Hill, however, prefers the word "considerateness" as a translation of συγκαταβήσις, and he observes that Chrysostom views God's considerateness in Scripture as he does the incarnation. I.e., in both the (often anthropomorphic) language of Scripture and the incarnation, God condescends to reach humanity at their own level; see also Bertrand de Margerie, "Saint John Chrysostom, Doctor of Biblical 'Condescension,'" in *The Greek Fathers*, vol. 1 of *An Introduction to the History of Exegesis* (Petersham, MA: Saint Bede's Publications, 1993), 189–212.

these philosophers, Chrysostom argues that the Gospel of John's usefulness is related to the fact that John's words are "God-inspired" (θεόπνευστα), which results in his gospel containing the "irresistible power of authentic doctrines" (δογμάτων ὀρθῶν ἀμήχανον δύναμιν).[60] Chrysostom does not, however, specify in this context that John's Gospel teaches us about both the humanity and the divinity of Christ, as we saw Origen claim above, but instead emphasizes only John's focus on Christ's divinity. For Chrysostom, again unlike Origen, who argued that John's Gospel was difficult even for the most mature interpreter, John's Gospel is beneficial in that it lies open to all due to its simplicity and clarity, and its corrective and transformative benefits are available to all Christians, regardless of spiritual maturity.

Chrysostom has much to say about the ideal hearer of John's Gospel and his comments about the disposition of the ideal hearer resemble Origen's understanding of the ideal interpreter to some degree, which I will note along the way. As he introduces John's Gospel to his parishioners, Chrysostom urges them to attend to his homilies with "attentiveness and eager interest" (σπουδὴν καὶ προθυμίαν). For Chrysostom, as for Origen, the ideal hearer will also receive the words of John "with precision" (μετὰ ἀκριβείας), which is necessary if one wants to understand the precise text, which is full of such great mysteries and benefits.[61] However, as we saw in Origen's comments, for Chrysostom, eagerness and precision are not enough; the ideal hearer will also be one who leads a virtuous life. Therefore, just as Chrysostom highlighted the Evangelist John's virtue, so too does he emphasize the necessity of the hearer's virtuous life for proper understanding of John's Gospel.[62] He urges his parishioners to be of "exemplary conduct," not only while they listen to the gospel, but throughout their lives.[63] Chrysostom goes on to say directly that "the words of John are

---

60. Chrysostom, *Hom. Jo.* 2.2–3 (Goggin, 16, 18); cf. *Hom. Jo.* 1.4.

61. Chrysostom, *Hom. Jo.* 1.1 (Goggin, 4). Note that I have translated μετὰ ἀκριβείας as "with precision" and not "with eagerness" as Goggin has it; cf. 2.3; *Hom. Isa.* 2.1; *Hom. Gen.* 4.13. This is one of Chrysostom's axioms for interpretation, as Mitchell points out ("Chrysostom," 32).

62. Chrysostom highlights the virtue of the other evangelists and biblical authors as well, and frequently exhorts his auditors to emulate such virtuous behavior; see *Hom. Matt.* 1.1, 3; *Hom. Luc.* 1.1; *Hom. Rom.* pref. This is a theme in Chrysostom's homilies on biblical texts; see, e.g., his homilies *Laud. Paul.* 1–7. There he encourages his hearers to emulate Paul in his various virtues.

63. Chrysostom, *Hom. Jo.* 1.2 (Goggin, 6); see also *Hom. Act.* 55. In *Hom. Gen.* 21.1 he claims that the interpreter requires the Spirit's inspiration.

nothing to those who do not wish to be set free from this swinish life," and therefore the ideal hearer is to "transport [herself] to heaven" (*Hom. Jo.* 1.2 [Goggin, 7]). By this he refers to the necessity of his parishioners' work at purifying themselves from the passions. For, he argues, "unless the hearing is purified, it cannot perceive, as it ought, the sublimity of what is said, nor can it grasp, as it must, the awesome and ineffable character of these mysteries, and all the other virtues contained in these divine utterances."[64] In other words, hearers must exemplify in their own lives the virtue that the text teaches. If they do not, they will be unable to recognize the text's virtuous message.[65] For Chrysostom, then, the ideal interpreter of John's Gospel ought to be attentive, eager, precise, and in pursuit of virtue.

Chrysostom says very little in these introductory homilies about how he will go about interpreting John's Gospel, unlike Origen, and, as I will demonstrate below, unlike the other two interpreters, Theodore and Cyril. Elsewhere in his corpus, however, he articulates the interpretive principles that we will see him operating with throughout this study.[66] I will highlight four such principles.[67] First, for Chrysostom (and indeed most early Christian authors), Scripture is united by one goal or mind, with which individual texts must be brought in line. Second, when one encounters a difficult passage of Scripture, there is always an answer to be found either within the passage itself or in other scriptural passages.[68] Chrysostom demonstrates both principles in his thirteenth homily on Genesis concerning Gen 2:7, "he breathed into him the breath of life." He considers the passage difficult given that it could be taken anthropomorphically, thus

---

64. Chrysostom, *Hom. Jo.* 1.2 (Goggin, 8); see also 1.3–4.

65. Such statements lead Mitchell to argue that for Chrysostom exegesis is at the service of catechesis, and is "a tool to inspire changed behavior"; see Mitchell, "Chrysostom," 33; see also Mitchell, *Heavenly Trumpet*, 44.

66. Of my four authors, Origen is the only one who wrote a systematic handbook about how to interpret the Bible (*Princ.* book 4). For the exegetical principles of the other three, we must search throughout their works to find the principles with which they approach Scripture.

67. This is not, by any means, an exhaustive list of Chrysostom's interpretive principles, as that would require its own full-length study. However, I will attempt to discuss those that I consider to be most important and relevant to this study.

68. See, for example, his introductory comments on Ps 45 (Chrysostom, *Comm. Ps.* 45.pref). According to Hill, however, Chrysostom is much less systematic than his teacher Diodore and his contemporary Theodore in his use of the principle of interpreting the whole of a passage, particularly the Psalms, in light of an identified σκοπός or ὑπόθεσις (Hill, *Reading the Old Testament*, 118).

attributing a mouth to God. Therefore he says, "let us follow the direction [σκοπῷ] of sacred Scripture in the interpretation it gives of itself," and "understand the whole narrative in a manner appropriate to God [θεοπρεπῶς ἅπαντα νοοῦντες]" (*Hom. Gen.* 13.2 [Hill, 172–73]). In other words, other aspects of the creation account, such as the words of Gen 1, "Let it be made," which feature God's creative speech rather than actions that attribute to him a body, are to be kept in view in dealing with such interpretive difficulties.

Third, Chrysostom claims that when the text contains symbolic or allegorical language, the text itself also contains the allegory's meaning. For example, in his *Commentary on Isaiah* he says, "Everywhere in Scripture there is this law, that when it allegorizes [ἀλληγορεῖν], it also gives the explanation of the allegory [τῷ τῆς ἀλληγορίας κεχρῆσθαι τρόπῳ]."[69] In both the second and third principles then, Chrysostom makes clear that one need not search too far afield from the text itself as one seeks to interpret either a difficult or symbolic passage.

Fourth, Chrysostom thinks the interpreter is permitted to provide a nonliteral interpretation when the text itself provides an indication that such an interpretation is required, either in the case of words that do not make sense if read literally or if the words are analogous to a verse that one of the New Testament authors has himself read nonliterally.[70] For example, as he turns to deal with the words "The Lord remains forever" of Ps 9:8, Chrysostom claims that in some cases, such as this verse, "it is possible to provide a contemplative reading [θεωρῆσαι]," whereas others, "should be understood only at face value [δεῖ νοεῖν ὡς εἴρηται μόνον]."[71] The first kind

---

69. Chrysostom, *Comm. Isa.* 5.3 (Hill, 1:222–24). Hill discusses this principle in his translator's introduction, 30.

70. He is therefore quite similar to Origen in this regard. See Hill's helpful discussion of this principle in his introduction to Chrysostom's homilies on Isaiah (Hill, "Chrysostom's Six Homilies on Isaiah 6," in *Old Testament Homilies* 2:44). For an example of his recourse to finding types authorized by the New Testament's interpretation of the Old Testament, see *Hom. Isa.* 6.1.2, in which he finds in Achan a type of Christ, given its precedent in Heb 4:8; see also *Hom. Jo.* 27.2; *Hom. Gen.* 36.8.

71. Chrysostom, *Comm. Ps.* 9:8 (Hill, 1:185). For Chrysostom, the words of Ps 9:8 seem to indicate both "Jewish history" if we "take the words as we find them," and a kind of "type of Christ," if we take "the meaning arising from them." He does not explain in any detail the logic of the nonliteral meaning he finds in these words, however, for he goes on to claim that "these considerations ... we should leave to the scholars to work out, and proceed to the next verse" (Hill 1:185–86). Hill translates the

of example, in which the text itself indicates that a move beyond the letter is required, is provided by Prov 5:16–17, "Spend your time with the stag you love, with the filly that has won your favor." Concerning this verse, Chrysostom claims, "if you take this saying as it occurs and do not depart from the surface meaning but stay at that level [ἂν τὸ κείμενον νοήσῃς, καὶ μὴ φύγῃς μὲν τὸ ῥῆμα, διώκῃς δὲ τὸ νόημα]," it teaches something that is problematic because it "reflects little humanity" (*Comm. Ps.* 9:8 [Hill 1:185]). This suggests to Chrysostom that a nonliteral interpretation is needed.

He continues with a comment about the second kind of example, in which there has been a precedent set by a New Testament author who has treated an analogous verse nonliterally. Of such verses Chrysostom says, "while in other places we must take the words as we find them and the meaning arising from them [ἀλλαχοῦ δὲ δεῖ καὶ τὸ κείμενον δέχεσθαι, καὶ τὸ ἐξ αὐτοῦ δηλούμενον]" and then cites the words "as Moses lifted up the serpent" of John 3:14, in which John has Jesus allude to Num 21:9 in application to his own death on a cross. For, he continues, Moses did in fact lift up the serpent, but it is also possible to accept "the meaning that comes from it, namely, a type of Christ [τὸ ἐξ αὐτοῦ, εἰς τύπον τοῦ Χριστοῦ]" (*Comm. Ps.* 9:8 [Hill 1:185]). These words he cites so as to justify his own nonliteral treatment of Ps 9:8, the verse he has set out to comment on. In both of these kinds of case, he claims, one can provide both a literal and a nonliteral interpretation. Chrysostom applies this principle most frequently in the context of his homilies and commentaries on the Old Testament, where in several instances he reads a given passage both literally and nonliterally.[72] For Chrysostom, it seems, one ought not to provide a nonliteral interpretation unless authorized to do so by the biblical text itself, whether the passage at hand or a New Testament author's interpretation of the Old Testament. When the text does provide such an indication, the text itself, or another scriptural passage, also provides an explanation. I will highlight below the instances in which these principles are at work, and I will demonstrate that Theodore operates in a similar way. Finally, it

---

second clause as follows: "in some things you see, it is possible to find a fuller sense," which obscures Chrysostom's use of θεωρέω. Chrysostom cites Gen 1:1 as an example of a text that should not be treated nonliterally and lists Prov 5:16–17, 19 as examples in which one should move beyond the literal level to the nonliteral.

72. See, e.g., *Comm. Ps.* 8:5; 9:8, 11; 112:4; 113:7; *Proph. obscurit.* 2. In such instances, the nonliteral interpretation or the type he finds most often refers to Christ and the church.

should be noted that Chrysostom's comments on his exegetical approach to John specifically are interspersed throughout these homilies on John, and I will highlight them as we encounter them.

The other Antiochene, Theodore, begins his preface with a narration of the situation that led to the composition of John's Gospel in much greater detail than the two previous authors, which, as I will highlight below, is true of Cyril as well.[73] Theodore begins by explaining that John, one of the twelve apostles, settled in Ephesus and traveled throughout Asia teaching the gospel.[74] When the faithful in Asia subsequently encountered the written gospels of the three synoptic writers, they solicited John's interpretation of them, for they considered him to be "the most reliable witness to the gospel," since John had been with the Lord from the beginning and had "enjoyed grace more abundantly because of the Lord's love for him" (John 13:23).[75] Theodore does not elaborate on this verse as we saw Origen do above, but he does allude to it, and as we shall see shortly, Theodore will actually move beyond Origen to claim explicitly not only the superiority of John's Gospel, but also the superiority of John himself. Theodore continues his narrative by claiming that upon reading the three gospels, John saw that what the three had written was true and that they had discussed "the presence of Christ in the flesh," but that they had neglected to write about certain of Jesus's miracles, nearly all of Jesus's instruction, and had most importantly omitted "the statements that concerned his divinity" (τοὺς περὶ θεότητος λόγους) (*Comm. Jo.* pref. [Kalantzis, 42]). Upon the request

---

73. Theodore introduces the Gospel of John in the preface to his commentary, of which we have one two-page fragment in Greek and the full text in about nine pages of Syriac translation. Interestingly, what was for Chrysostom merely a "saying" about the composition of John's Gospel is now for Theodore a more detailed narrative. Cyril also refers to this widely known narrative, which may have been developed based on a felt need to account for the distinctive and superior nature of John's Gospel among the four.

74. This is evidence of Frederick G. McLeod's claim that part of Theodore's interpretation of a text is his introductory provision of background information about the author, date, setting, purpose, themes, and content; see McLeod, *The Image of God in the Antiochene Tradition* (Washington, DC: Catholic University of America Press, 1999), 32; see also Dimitri Zaharopoulos, *Theodore of Mopsuestia on the Bible: A Study of His Old Testament Exegesis* (New York: Paulist, 1989), 122–23.

75. Theodore, *Comm. Jo.* pref. (Kalantzis, 41; Conti, 2). We have only fragments of Theodore's commentaries on each of the Synoptic Gospels, so we do not have access to the comments he made about the other three evangelists when he set to the task of explaining their works.

of the faithful in Asia, claims Theodore, John "elaborated on the teachings that relate to the divinity [περὶ τῶν τῆς θεότητος ἐφιλοσόφησε δογμάτων]," which he judged to be the gospel's "necessary beginning" (ἀναγκαίαν τὴν ἀρχήν), a probable play on John 1:1, in which the evangelist himself begins with the words, "in the beginning" (ἐν ἀρχῇ).[76]

This narrative leads Theodore to join those early Asian believers in their trust of the Evangelist John above the other three, and he goes on to argue that even in the order John presents the events of Jesus's ministry he was "more diligent" than the other evangelists, telling the story in "the proper order" and including what they omitted.[77] Even in those cases where John does recount events that the Synoptic authors included, he does so to add the "necessary teaching" that is associated with a given miracle, such as the feeding of the five thousand in John 6, and its correlated teachings, or "mystical expressions" (τῶν μυστικῶν λόγων), which the other three had not included.[78] Both Antiochenes then heed the tradition that places John's Gospel above the Synoptics, but they are not united in their assessment of the superiority of John the evangelist himself. For Chrysostom, he is an ordinary, unlearned (albeit virtuous) fisherman who was divinely inspired to write his gospel. For Theodore, he is superior to the other gospel writers due to his having received "more grace," and his reliability, diligence, and orderliness in teaching what the Synoptic authors omitted, a claim he does not seem to think problematic vis-à-vis the other three evangelists. In fact, Theodore omits altogether a discussion of the process of the divine inspiration of John.[79] For Theodore, then, the Gospel of John is superior to the

---

76. Theodore, *Comm. Jo.* pref. (Kalantzis, 42). As we saw above, Origen does something similar (*Comm. Jo.* 1.22).

77. Theodore, *Comm. Jo.* pref. (Kalantzis, 42). In the Syriac material, the Evangelist John is described as being "very accurate" (ܚܬܝܬ ܣܓܝ) (Conti, 4); cf. *Comm. Os.* 3:2. The author of the Muratorian fragment claims that John was "a writer of all the wonderful things of the Lord in order." However, he does not, like Theodore, suggest explicitly that the synoptic authors are inferior to John in their ordering of the events of Jesus's life.

78. Theodore, *Comm. Jo.* pref. (Devreesse, 307, Kalantzis, 42). Note that Kalantzis has "eucharistic expressions" for τῶν μυστικῶν λόγων.

79. According to Zaharopoulos, Theodore was more flexible than his contemporaries concerning the doctrine of the inspiration of the biblical authors. While he begins in his earlier years of biblical commentating from the position that God or the Holy Spirit inspired the thought and writing of the biblical authors, he eventually concludes that the human authors have such autonomy in the process of the composition of their writings that he no longer holds the traditional view of inspiration. Theodore's

Synoptic Gospels because it contains the teachings about Christ's divinity that the Synoptics passed over in silence, and he is distinctive among these authors in his claim that John is more reliable and more diligent than the other three evangelists.

According to Theodore, as we mentioned above, the Evangelist John preached the gospel in Asia Minor, which he says brought much "benefit" (τὴν ὠφέλειαν) to the people; he too introduces the gospel text as beneficial (*Comm. Jo.* pref. [Kalantzis, 41]). It seems that for Theodore, John's preaching of the gospel matched the content he included in his written gospel, namely, teachings about Christ's divinity. Accordingly, Theodore claims, at least in the material from the Syriac translation of his preface, that understanding John's thought is more "useful" (ܝܘܬܪܢ) than understanding that of the other evangelists (*Comm. Jo.* pref. [Conti, 1]). He does not say so explicitly, but presumably he makes this statement because of what we discussed above, that is, his belief that John and his gospel are superior, for the fourth evangelist "elaborated on the teachings that relate to the divinity [περὶ τῶν τῆς θεότητος ἐφιλοσόφησε δογμάτων]," about which the other three had remained silent (*Comm. Jo.* pref. [Kalantzis, 42]). Theodore concludes his preface by saying that if it is God's will that his comments on John's Gospel be "useful" (ܢܘܬܪܢ), it will be so (*Comm. Jo.* pref. [Conti, 1]). Theodore claims explicitly, then, as we saw him do in our discussion about the usefulness of Scripture in the introduction, that it is the interpreter's duty to produce a useful interpretation of the useful Gospel of John.

Theodore says very little about the disposition and set of exegetical skills that the ideal interpreter ought to possess. However, he does note briefly two attributes. First, the interpreter must be prayerful, which we saw Origen claim as well. In fact, Theodore claims throughout his preface that divine assistance and strength to interpret John are necessary, both of which will be given as the result of prayer.[80] Second, he claims explicitly that the interpreter must be precise: "The one who inquires with all accuracy (ὅλως ἀκριβῶς τις ζητῶν)" will discover John's diligence in recording the sequence of events of the gospel.[81] By implication, the imprecise or careless reader will not discover the accuracy of John's ordering.

---

treatment of the issue here in his *Commentary on the Gospel of John* seems to fit Zaharopoulos's observations (*Theodore of Mopsuestia*, 82–88).

80. Theodore, *Comm. Jo.* pref. (Conti, 1); see also *Comm. Os.* pref.; *Comm. Jon.* pref. for similar statements about the necessity of prayer in interpretation.

81. Theodore, *Comm. Jo.* pref. (Kalantzis, 42). Note that Kalantzis has taken

Finally, Theodore has much to say about how he will proceed in his exegetical approach to John's Gospel. He claims that as a commentator, he is to explain "the sense" (ܐܠܒܐܘܣ) of the whole book of John, as well as individual texts, whose meanings are determined in light of the whole.[82] As a commentator in particular he claims that he will explain clearly the difficult words (ܡܠܐ ܥܣܩܬܐ) presented by the gospel, and accordingly, he claims that he will not linger on the easy or clear passages, to which the preacher should attend.[83]

Further, it is the job of the commentator to comment "concisely" (ܐܟܣܘܣ), without using superfluous words.[84] However, Theodore claims, a clear explanation sometimes requires many words, particularly in the case of passages that have been "corrupted by the deceit of the heretics"; these texts are to be examined "in detail" (ܐܟܪܘܣ), "accurately" (ܐܟܪܝܒܘܣ), and "with authority" (ܐܘܬܢܛܝܟܘܣ) (*Comm. Jo.* pref. [Conti, 2]). For Theodore, then, interpreting John accurately means, at least in part, interpreting it with an eye to the refutation of heresy. Finally, Theodore also sets up in his preface, even if in passing, a hermeneutical principle that will inform the examples we will examine throughout this study, that of considering the fact that the words of Christ are "varied in their meaning" (ܡܬܚܠܦܬܐ) in the sense that some are about his greatness (i.e., divinity) and others are about his weakness (i.e., humanity).[85] He is the only one of my four authors

---

ὅλως ἀκριβῶς to modify the actions of the evangelist himself, not the interpreter, as I have. While the Greek is ambiguous, I have taken ὅλως ἀκριβῶς to modify the interpreter given the word order of the sentence: ὅλως ἀκριβῶς τις ζητῶν εὑρήσει τοῦτον μνημονεύοντα. His translation reads: "The one who inquires will find that he recounts with all accuracy whatever the sequence of events demanded"; cf. *Comm. Agg.* 2:1–5. Theodore does not claim explicitly that John's Gospel is itself precise in his preface. He does claim that the gospel is in the proper order, and thus perhaps precision is implied, but he does not use the technical term ἀκρίβεια. However, he does describe John's Gospel in this way.

82. Theodore, *Comm. Jo.* pref. (Conti, 1); cf. *Comm. Nah.* 1:1; *Comm. Ps.* 1.pref.

83. Theodore, *Comm. Jo.* pref. (Conti, 2). Theodore does not claim directly that by difficult he refers to those verses that had been misused by heretics, but he tends to spend more interpretive energy on such verses; see McLeod's brief discussion of this principle (*Roles of Christ's Humanity*, 22–23).

84. Theodore, *Comm. Jo.* pref. (Conti, 2). The Syriac reads literally "with a few words"; cf. *Comm. Ps.* 1.pref.

85. Theodore, *Comm. Jo.* pref. (Conti, 5). Theodore is articulating here the interpretive principle that scholars have named partitive or two-nature exegesis; see, e.g., Koen, "Partitive Exegesis," 115–21. Koen claims that "Partitive exegesis implies a sepa-

1. John, His Gospel, and Its Interpretation 67

to make this explicit comment in his preface. However, as I have already noted concerning Origen, and as we will see throughout this study, each of these authors operates with this principle, as from at least the time of Origen it was a commonplace in scriptural interpretation.

Before we turn to Cyril's introductory comments about John's Gospel, it is important to note that we must first note that in his preface, Theodore does not discuss literal and nonliteral interpretation, despite his assertion above that John contains "mystical words." He does, however, provide such discussions elsewhere, and I will examine three correlated principles briefly.[86] First, in a manner that is similar to Chrysostom, Theodore claims that Scripture itself indicates, in a "hyperbolic language" (ὑπερβολικώτερον), when nonliteral interpretation is appropriate.[87] Second, according to Theodore, for one's nonliteral reading to be fitting, there must be similarity (ἅπας) between the narrative and the nonliteral meaning one finds in the narrative.[88] In other instances, which others have noted, Theodore articulates in more detail what is required by the interpreter who finds a type that requires a nonliteral reading.[89] Here is his third principle, then: the exegete ought not to interpret the passage so that each word stands for something else, which Theodore describes as "breaking up" (*incipere*) the narrative.[90] Instead, the interpreter must "maintain a sequence of explanation in faithful

---

ration or partition of the interpretation of certain Scriptural statements vis-à-vis the human and divine natures of Christ" (16). Wiles calls the same phenomenon "two-nature exegesis" (*Spiritual Gospel*, 137–38).

86. For examples of Theodore's comments on literal and nonliteral interpretation, see the following passages: *Comm. Ps.* 1.pref.; *Comm. Gal.* 4:23–24; *Comm. Zach.* 9.9; *Comm. Jon.* pref. It is important to note that such discussions occur within his treatment of Old Testament passages most frequently. This is not an exhaustive treatment of Theodore's interpretive principles; I will mention only those that I have deemed most important for my purposes.

87. Theodore, *Comm. Zach.* 9.9 (Hill, 367).

88. Theodore, *Comm. Mic.* 4:1–3 (Hill, 220); see also *Comm. Jon.* pref. Rowan A. Greer observes that Theodore rarely uses the interpretive approach that scholars have named "typology," but that when he does, he points to the New Testament as providing an authorization (Greer, *Theodore of Mopsuestia: Exegete and Theologian* [Westminster: Faith Press, 1961], 109).

89. E.g., Greer, *Theodore of Mopsuestia*, 108–9; McLeod, *Image of God*, 19–22; Zaharopoulos, *Theodore of Mopsuestia*, 116. This they describe as typological interpretation.

90. Theodore, *Comm. Gal.* 4:24 (Greer, 114–15). Presumably he would have expanded on these comments in his now lost treatise, *On Allegory and History*; see Young's helpful discussion of this passage (*Biblical Exegesis*, 180–82).

accord with the narrative [*secundum historiae fidem tenorem expossitionis aptemus et concinnenter*]."[91] Theodore makes this statement in the context of an accusation against some unnamed allegorizing opponents, whom he accuses of breaking up the narrative into separate words that refer to something else, without regard for the coherence of the narrative (*Comm. Gal.* 4:23–24 [Greer, 114–15]). Thus while he agrees with Chrysostom that the interpreter must have a textual indicator to authorize nonliteral interpretation, he articulates a more developed principle about the content of the nonliteral interpretation: it must reflect the narrative itself. I will examine how these principles operate for him throughout the course of this study.

Like Theodore, Cyril introduces John's Gospel with a narrative account of the circumstances that led to the composition of John's Gospel, although as we will see, there are some striking differences in their presentations of the story.[92] According to Cyril's understanding of the story, immediately following Christ's ascension, false teachers began to spread their ignorant and impious teachings about God the Word, teachings that challenged the doctrine of the Son's eternal generation from the Father. In response, even though John was aware that his thought and speech were not worthy of "the dignity that befits God," he wrote his gospel at the request of some wise representatives of the faithful.[93] Thus for Cyril, the believers in John's own day were dealing with the same heresies that would later come to plague the church in Cyril's lifetime, and this is what led John to write his gospel. John did not write in response to his reading of the Synoptic Gospels, which he deemed incomplete, as we saw Theodore articulate above. In fact, Cyril is the only author of the four that does not claim in his introductory comments that John wrote his gospel so as to complete what is lacking

---

91. Theodore, *Comm. Ps.* 1.pref. (Hill, 6–7); see also *Comm. Zach.* 9.9. Note that I have translated *historiae* as "narrative," where Hill has "history," for I agree with Young that *historia* for these authors tends not to refer to history as we understand it.

92. Unlike Theodore, Cyril indicates that he has inherited the narrative account from others, who "study these matters most intensely," and justifies his doing so with an interpretive maxim: "those who are engaged with the Holy Scriptures need to approach all writings that might be good, noble, and free from harm … gathering what many people have observed from various points of view about the same thing, and by bringing them all to bear on one point, they will climb to a good measure of knowledge" (Cyril, *In Jo.* 1.pref. [Maxwell, 5]). He is probably referring to the tradition mentioned by Irenaeus, Clement, and Eusebius.

93. Cyril, *In Jo.* 1.pref. (Maxwell, 5–6). Note that for Cyril, "the faithful" are not limited to believers in Asia Minor.

1. John, His Gospel, and Its Interpretation   69

in the Synoptic Gospels. Instead, for Cyril, the timing of the four gospels' composition is left undefined as he claims that John "left to the other evangelists the task of explaining the human matters more fully," as he himself sought to address the dangerous teachings of the false teachers with his distinctive focus on the divinity of Christ (*In Jo.* 1.pref. [Maxwell, 6]). Thus the doctrines about Christ's divinity and the refutation of the heresy of the Son's subordination to the Father are an integral part of the very composition of John's beneficial Gospel for Cyril.

Cyril also understood John's Gospel to be superior to those of the other evangelists. He claims that "One might with good reason say that the composition of the book of John far surpasses even wonder itself when one looks at the excellence of his thoughts, the sharpness of his reasoning, and the unceasing introduction of one idea after another." Unlike the other three gospel authors, Cyril claims, John directs his thoughts "to reach for subjects that are beyond human comprehension," and he "dares to narrate the ineffable and unutterable birth of God the word" (*In Jo* 1.pref. [Maxwell, 5]). In a similar manner to our other three authors, Cyril maintains that John's Gospel is superior to the Synoptics due to John's focus on Jesus's divinity. Cyril does not, however, make a claim such as that of Origen that John's intimate act of leaning on the breast of Jesus provided him with the privileged vantage point of direct contemplation of the divine teachings, nor does he claim like Theodore that John himself is superior to the Synoptic authors in any way.[94]

In any case, Cyril also articulated his understanding of the beneficial nature of John's Gospel. Like Origen, he discusses the benefits of John alongside those of the Synoptic Gospels. Before discussing John, he highlights three attributes that all four gospel writers share.[95] The first attribute is that the four gospels share the same goal (σκοπός), namely, the "interpretation

---

94. In fact, Cyril does nothing with the leaning on the breast passage in John 13:23–25 in his preface, unlike Origen. Even the Antiochenes make use of the verses, though they differ from each other as to the weight they give them. Whereas Chrysostom mentions them in a long list of other scriptural verses about John, Theodore alludes to the description of John as "the beloved disciple," as mentioned above, in order to claim that John is superior to the synoptic authors. In Cyril's actual comments on the passage, he is forced to deal with the words "the one Jesus loved," and explains Jesus's love for John as the result of "the glory of [John's] purity." However, he quickly clarifies that John is not boasting in his use of the epithet; instead claims Cyril, he "buries his name in silence" (*In Jo.* 9 on 13:23–26 [Maxwell, 128]).

95. Unfortunately, we do not have much more than fragments of his commentaries

of divine teachings [περὶ τὴν τῶν θείων δογμάτων ἐξήγησιν]," despite exhibiting different characters.[96] Cyril provides two analogies to illustrate this for his reader. In the first analogy, the evangelists are like a team of horses who race toward the same goal from the same starting gate. In the second, they are like people who have been instructed to meet in a city, though they need not travel by the same route. The second attribute the evangelists share is that the thought of all four is "instructed by God" (θεοδίδακτος), and all four have "the Spirit of the Father" speaking in them.[97] As a result, each author is concerned to present something of "benefit" (χρήσιμον) to his hearers, and their thought is "precise" (ἀκρίβεια).[98] However, whereas the Synoptic authors are precise (ἀκριβείας) in their account of "our Savior's genealogy according to the flesh," in Cyril's view, John addresses "the chief of all divine doctrines," as expressed in his prologue (John 1:1–2), and he is thus precise in his treatment of Christ's divinity.[99] Unlike Origen, then, Cyril does not suggest that both John and the Synoptics address the

on Matthew and Luke, and, like Origen and others, he seems not to have written a commentary on Mark. We do, however, have a Syriac translation of his *Homilies on Luke*.

96. Cyril, *In Jo.* 1.pref. (Maxwell, 5). For a helpful discussion of Cyril's use and understanding of σκοπός, see Marie-Odile Boulnois, *Le paradoxe trinitaire chez Cyrille d'Alexandrie: Herméneutique, analyses philosophiques et argumentation théologique*, CEAug.SA143 (Paris, Études Augustiniennes, 1994), 77–80. Boulnois claims that for Cyril, identifying a given biblical passage's σκοπός, which he understands as the intention or sense, is key to its interpretation. A passage is to be understood in light of the context of the aim or sense of the whole book.

97. Cyril, *In Jo.* 1.pref. (Maxwell, 4–5). It is such statements as these that lead Crawford to argue that for Cyril, the process of the inspiration of the apostles is to be understood as "spiritual mystagogy" rather than the visions given to the prophets; see his helpful discussion of inspiration in Cyril's thought in *Cyril*, 72–114. For Cyril it is often the Holy Spirit who inspires the scriptural authors; see, e.g., *Comm. Isa.* 26:17–18; 29:11–12; *Comm. Joel.* 2:28–29; *In Jo.* 1:1; 7:39; 16:23–24; 20:1–9. However, at times he claims that it is Christ by the Holy Spirit who inspires, and in some instances, he describes the Holy Spirit as the mind of Christ, or as Christ indwelling the authors by the Holy Spirit; see *Comm. Heb.* 1:1; *Comm. Isa.* 43:9; *In Jo.* 7:39; 14:21; 16:12–13; 17:24.

98. For the benefit, see Cyril, *In Jo.* 1.pref. (Maxwell, 4); cf. *Comm. Isa.* 26.17–18. Note that unlike Theodore, Cyril thinks each of the gospel writers is as precise and beneficial as the others. For precision, see Cyril, *In Jo.* 1.pref. (Maxwell, 5). See Cyril's similar comments about the precision of Isaiah's prophetic text in *Comm. Isa.* pref.

99. Cyril, *In Jo.* 1.pref. (Maxwell, 5); cf. *Comm. Luc.* 1.1, in which he comments on Luke 1:2.

1. John, His Gospel, and Its Interpretation   71

humanity and the divinity of Christ.[100] The specific benefits that John's Gospel offers are directly related to the doctrines of Christ's divinity, and it is for this reason that Cyril thinks John to be the superior gospel.

Like Origen, Cyril introduces the ideal interpreter of John in an elaborate fashion; he too places the proclamation of the gospel, of which the interpretation of John's Gospel is a part, within the framework of a spiritualized sacrificial system.[101] For Cyril, those who were called to the Levitical priesthood to administer the law for the people of Israel represent the church leaders of Cyril's own day.[102] Despite the dangers involved in speaking about the divine mysteries of the transcendent essence, claims Cyril, silence was not an option for the Levitical priests as they gave the people the law of Moses, nor is it an option for the present leaders of the church, who have been "enlightened by grace from above" and "called to the divine priesthood," particularly in the face of the false teachings of the heretics.[103] Clearly Cyril understands himself as a member of this group, and thus he offers the commentary as his priestly offering.[104] It seems then that he makes an implicit claim here that it is the priest, or leader of the church—in his case, the bishop—who has been given divine enlightenment and authority to interpret John's Gospel.[105]

However, there are other attributes that the ideal readers of John's Gospel must possess. Such interpreters, who will have the assistance of the Spirit, according to Cyril, are "those who thirst for the true exposition of divine teachings and who search with good intentions," who have "simple minds" and are "without guile," and who "avoid superfluous sophistry."[106] Thus for

---

100. However, as Cyril deals with specific examples throughout his commentary, he also finds instruction about the doctrine of Jesus's humanity.

101. See Crawford's helpful discussion of the prologue (*Cyril*, 184–85).

102. Cyril, *In Jo.* 1.pref. (Maxwell, 1–3). We might have here an indication that by Cyril's time the ecclesiastical interpreters in Alexandria have managed to gain authority over the quasi-independent schoolroom academics that probably flourished during the lifetimes of Clement and Origen.

103. Cyril, *In Jo.* 1.pref. (Maxwell, 1). Cyril claims elsewhere, including later on in his *Commentary on John*, that the interpreter of Scripture requires the Spirit's enlightenment; see, e.g., *Hom. Luc.* 78.2; *In Jo.* on 5:37–38; 14:20.

104. As I noted in the introduction, Maxwell has argued convincingly that Cyril composed his commentary for those charged with teaching the faith. See my discussion on above.

105. Crawford makes this observation as well (*Cyril*, 216).

106. Cyril, *In Jo.* 1.pref. (Maxwell, 5). Note the Holy Spirit's role in revealing the meaning of Scripture in the interpretive process; see also *Hom. Luc.* 38.1; 48.1.

Cyril, ideal interpreters must have good intentions as they approach the text, and they will have a desire for that which the text has to offer. Furthermore, for Cyril, ideal, precise (ἀκριβεστάτης) interpreters must also search the scriptural text "with painstaking attention and a sharp mind [τοῦ νοῦ προσβολῆς τε καὶ ὀξύτητος]" in order to understand the sharp mind of the evangelist.[107] As I noted above, Origen and Chrysostom emphasized this kind of eager attentiveness as well.

Finally, according to Cyril, the ideal (church-leading) interpreter must have undergone the proper doctrinal training and must therefore be poised for battle against heretics (*In Jo.* 1.pref. [Maxwell, 2–3]). We do not see such a claim in any of my other three authors' comments, though Theodore too is concerned to refute those who have misused the Gospel of John. Like Theodore, Cyril thinks John is a difficult book to interpret since it has been interpreted by those of "false opinion" and thus he claims that it requires an appropriate counterinterpretation.[108] This is possible only if one has faith in God, who will provide the wisdom necessary for him to overcome his weakness and to accomplish the task.[109] The ideal interpreter as the doctrinal defender of the church is an aspect that is not at all present in either Origen's or Chrysostom's comments, and it is much stronger in Cyril's comments than in Theodore's.[110] Thus

---

107. Cyril, *In Jo.* 1.pref. (Maxwell, 1). Note Cyril's use of the term ἀκριβεστάτης here. The interpreter, like the scriptural author, is to be precise, as discussed concerning our other three authors' introductory comments. Cyril makes similar comments about the painstaking attention and thorough investigation of the interpreter in the following examples: *Hom. Luc.* 38.1; 48.1; *Comm. Isa.* pref.; *In Jo.* on 1:1, 9; 5:37–38; 14:20; 15:9–10.

108. Cyril, *In Jo.* 1.pref. (Maxwell, 3). Like Theodore, Cyril vows not to "extend the length" of his comments on John despite its difficulty. However, this claim is not as formalized an interpretive rule for Cyril as it is for Theodore, who claimed that the commentator is to be concise. In any case, Cyril was not as successful as Theodore at maintaining brevity in his comments on the passages that he understood to have been interpreted falsely by heretics.

109. As I noted with respect to Origen, this claim of inadequacy for the task was a common rhetorical move, as pointed out by Crawford (*Cyril*, 184). Cyril's comments in his preface about his humble offering ought to be understood in this light as well (*In Jo.* 1.pref. [Maxwell, 3]).

110. Origen clearly has heresy in view, however. He responds to Heracleon explicitly throughout the commentary, as we mentioned above. There has been considerable scholarly debate about the role that Origen's apologetic against Heracleon played in his overall purpose in writing the commentary. For some, these polemics against

1. John, His Gospel, and Its Interpretation   73

for Cyril, the ideal interpreter, who has been called and enlightened by the Spirit to lead the church, must match the Evangelist John in possessing a sharp, precise and attentive mind, noble intentions, faith in God, and doctrinal knowledge.[111]

Given the discussion above about the ideal interpreter's doctrinal training, it is no surprise that Cyril's articulation of the appropriate exegetical approach to the Fourth Gospel reflects a doctrinal emphasis as well. For, according to Cyril, the Evangelist John opposed heretical doctrines in the very *composition* of his gospel, and thus its interpretation requires a corresponding doctrinal approach. In fact, interpretation of John for Cyril, in this context at least, means that one "contends for the holy doctrine of the church" (*In Jo.* 1.pref. [Maxwell, 2]). One ought to "turn the words around to the right argument of the faith [εἰς τὸν ὀρθὸν τῆς πίστεως περιτρέποντες λογισμόν]" so as to avoid being found unprepared in the face of opposing heretical teachings, he argues, and proceeds to promise his readers a "doctrinal explanation" (δογματικωτέρας ἐξήγησιν) of John's Gospel.[112] Throughout this study I will trace both Cyril's assumption that John intentionally refutes heresy and his claim to provide what he calls a doctrinal explanation against the heretical opponents of his own day.

Finally, I must note here that despite the fact that Cyril assumes that in the text there are to be found "divine and mystical thoughts" (τὰ θεῖά τε καὶ μυστικὰ θεωρήματα), which require a search of painstaking attention, like the other three authors, he does not articulate an explicitly nonliteral approach to John's Gospel in his preface.[113] In fact, Origen is the only one

---

Heracleon loomed large, particularly because of book 13, which we will examine in our next chapter. Others, however, note that Origen does not consistently refute the Valentinian throughout his treatment of John. For a helpful discussion of the issues involved in this debate, see McGuckin, "Structural Design," 441–57. I am inclined to agree with McGuckin and others who remind us that in his commentary, Origen is "resurrecting the text of Heracleon from an obscure past" and that in his use of Heracleon's "antiquated" commentary, Origen has other purposes, such as likening Heracleon's hermeneutical errors to Origen's opponents within his contemporary church setting; see McGuckin's "Structural Design," 44 in particular. Interestingly, in his preface, Origen does not make mention of Heracleon. Both he and Chrysostom deal with what they view as heretical interpretations of John throughout their commentaries, however.

111. For a similar, much more detailed treatment of Cyril's understanding of what is required of the reader to interpret scripture rightly, see Crawford, *Cyril*, 182–232.

112. Cyril, *In Jo.* 1.pref. (Maxwell, 2–3). On the doctrinal nature of his exegesis, see Boulnois, *Le paradoxe trinitaire*, 57–58.

113. Cyril, *In Jo.* 1.pref. (Maxwell, 1). As I have already observed, he does, how-

to do so. Cyril does, however, articulate such an approach throughout the rest of his corpus, and as we shall see, it is an interpretive principle that he brings to his interpretation of John's Gospel as well. For example, in his *Commentary on Isaiah* he articulates clearly the principle that the text contains both a literal and a nonliteral meaning to be discovered.[114] After commenting on the literal words of Isa 11:12–13, for instance, he claims that the prophet "turns what happened in actual fact into an image of a spiritual reality [Δέχεται γὰρ τὸ ἱστορικῶς γεγονὸς εἰς εἰκόνα πράγματος νοητοῦ]."[115] Because the text itself possesses both a literal and a nonliteral meaning, Cyril claims that the interpreter must "move [πεπραήσεις], as it were, from what occurred in actual fact [ἀπό γε τῶν ἱστορικῶς] to a spiritual interpretation [εἰς θεωρίαν ἐρχόμενος τὴν πνευματικήν]."[116] Thus Cyril assumes that it is appropriate to interpret passages on both the literal and nonliteral level, for the biblical text inherently contains both.

In conclusion, I have observed that each of the authors thought John was self-evidently distinctive among the four gospels, for above all, the Fourth Gospel emphasized Jesus's divinity. For all four authors, John's emphasis on Jesus's divinity led them to maintain the position of John's superiority to the Synoptic Gospels, and each of them claimed that John's Gospel is beneficial because of the doctrinal instruction it provides concerning Jesus's divinity.[117] For all except Cyril, John's Gospel completes the accounts of the Synoptic Gospels, and only Theodore articulates the position that the Evangelist John is more orderly, diligent, and reliable than the Synoptic authors. Given the Evangelist John's emphasis on Christ's divinity, all but Chrysostom agreed that John's Gospel is difficult to interpret, and for Cyril and Theodore in particular, the interpretation

---

ever, provide a nonliteral interpretation of the Levitical priesthood and the wood and ax of Eccl 10:9–10, both of which frame his preface.

114. For similar comments, see *Comm. Isa.* pref.; *Comm. Zach.* 3:1; *Comm. Am.* 8:9; *In Jo.* on 8:31.

115. Cyril, *Comm. Isa.* 11:12–13 (Hill, 267).

116. Cyril, *Comm. Isa.* 11:12–13 (Hill, 269); cf. *Comm. Isa.* pref.; *Comm. Am.* 8:9; 9:13–15; *Comm. Mich.* 7:11–15; *In Jo.* on 6:12–13.

117. Of course, as I noted above, Origen thinks that the Synoptic Gospels also contain teachings about Christ's divinity, though it is not, for him, their main emphasis. There are other benefits to be found in John's Gospel in addition to teachings about Christ's divinity for all four authors, and I have already begun to outline these additional benefits in the introduction.

of John is particularly difficult due to its misuse by unnamed heretical groups.[118]

Each of the authors articulates his understanding of the ideal reader of John's Gospel in his preface. Both Alexandrians associate themselves with the Levitical priestly class of Israel, which symbolizes the ideal reader of John's Gospel. For Origen, the Levite is the one who has devoted his life to the word of God, offering the first-fruits of all one's activity to painstaking study of Scripture, probably as an academic, who may or may not have a leadership role in the church, whereas for Cyril, the Levite priest is the church leader, who has been enlightened by the Spirit. Theodore, on the other hand, seems to make a distinction between the interpretive roles of the commentator and the preacher, and he of course identifies with the former. Chrysostom does not comment on the ideal interpreter as explicitly as he does the ideal hearer of John's Gospel, which for him is simple and clear. However, as a leader of the church himself, he clearly understands his role to include extensive exegetical, homiletic treatment of John's Gospel. In any case, all four authors agree that divine aid is required if one is going to provide a worthy interpretation of John.[119] They also agree that both precision and eager attention are required of the interpreter of the precise Evangelist John.[120] Finally, all but Theodore are explicit that the life and character of the ideal interpreter must match that of the Fourth Evangelist.

All four of these authors thought John's Gospel contained divine doctrines, but it is the two latest authors, Theodore and Cyril, who seem to have a more formal or studied concern with heresy than the other two. This is perhaps simply because by their time doctrine itself was more formally studied. In any case, both introduce the interpretation of John in the context of the refutation of heresy.[121] Only Cyril, however, explicitly articulates the view that John composed his gospel with the refutation of such heresy in view, and he alone articulates the necessity for the astute

---

118. Chrysostom claims (perhaps rhetorically) that John's content is sublime, yet simple. Throughout Cyril's and Theodore's commentaries, they frequently name their opponents, who are typically Arian. Chrysostom and Origen also name their opponents from time to time.

119. Chrysostom does not make this claim explicitly in his introductory homilies to John. However, he makes such comments elsewhere; see, e.g., *Hom. Gen.* 37.1.

120. As we noted above, Origen and Theodore do not mention explicitly that John's Gospel is precise, but we will see them do so throughout their commentaries.

121. Wiles makes a similar observation (*Spiritual Gospel*, 5).

interpreter to provide a "doctrinal explanation" of John's Gospel. Theodore gestures in this direction by asserting that he will devote more attention to explaining those verses that have been misinterpreted by heretics.

Finally, it is important to note here that while all four authors claim that John is "full of great mysteries," it is only Origen who articulates a corresponding mystical or nonliteral method of interpretation in his introductory comments. I will demonstrate in each subsequent chapter that Cyril provides a nonliteral interpretation for each passage of John that we will examine, but he does not explain his procedure for movement beyond the letter of the text in his preface. The Antiochenes did not articulate a nonliteral interpretation of John in their introductory comments either, and I argue that very rarely do they go beyond the letter to provide a nonliteral interpretation, despite their claims that John is full of great mysteries. They do so only when they believe that the text itself provides indication that they should, a principle that we saw both of them articulate above.

2
The Cleansing of the Temple of John 2

The first passage of my study is the cleansing of the temple in John 2:14–22. In this passage, Jesus enters the temple in Jerusalem just before Passover and finds that those present had been using the temple precincts to buy and sell the animals required for sacrificial offerings. Jesus then accuses these vendors of turning his "Father's house" into "a marketplace" and expels them (2:14–16). As they approach the passage, the four authors each deal with the potential problem of the ways in which John's narrative differs from the Synoptic accounts of the cleansing of the temple; they also find it necessary to address the doctrinal implications of Jesus's apparent anger in the temple. For each of them, the passage is instructive concerning Jesus's relationship to God the Father, giver of the law. The authors reproach the Jews present in the temple because of their demand of a sign from Jesus that he has the authority to perform such an act (2:18), for, they contend, a sign has already been provided through his actions in the temple. Jesus's symbolic statement in response to the Jews, "Destroy this temple, and I will raise it up in three days" (2:19) and the evangelist's explanation of his saying (2:21–22) provides these authors with the occasion to discuss the nature of Jesus's death and resurrection.

In terms of the authors' approach to the passage, we will see that Origen moves from the literal to the nonliteral in search of its usefulness and indeed claims that the passage is beneficial only at the nonliteral level. For Origen, the nonliteral narrative not only provides instruction about the place of the church within salvation history, but it also speaks directly to the present situation of the church, and to the individual souls of those within the church. My other three authors, however, find much that is beneficial at the literal level: the cleansing of the temple narrative offers beneficial doctrinal teaching, instruction about Christ's resurrection, and in Theodore's case, instruction about the place of the church in salvation history.¹ In addition, both Cyril and Theodore find instruction for their readers concerning the way in which Jesus's actions in the temple relate to Old Testament prophecies. Cyril, however, goes beyond the Antiochenes when he, like Origen, discerns benefits in the passage above the letter as well. For Cyril too, the passage provides instruction about the place of the gentile church within salvation history; the gentiles who have faith in Christ are included and the disobedient Jews' sacrificial cult is rejected. In this chapter, then, we can see a clear distinction between the two schools in that the Antiochenes do not move beyond the letter to discern the passage's benefits, whereas the Alexandrians find much instruction for the church at the nonliteral level.

I will begin by examining Origen's lengthy treatment of the passage, to which most of book 10 of his commentary is dedicated.² This amounts to approximately seventy-three pages of Greek text. Origen provides an introduction to the passage, and to gospel interpretation in general, in which he discusses the exegetical principle of Scripture's usefulness in order to prepare his readers for his treatment of the passage. While he provides a verse-by-verse treatment of the narrative, he also finds occasion for lengthy discussions about the nature of the resurrection, the heavenly Passover feast, and the heavenly temple. Throughout his comments, he provides quotations of Heracleon's comments on the passage for the purpose of refuting the Valentinian and moves from the nonliteral plane to the literal to do so.³ As I said above, however, Origen's primary focus is on the

---

1. I will not deal in any detail with Cyril's treatment of 2:19, for he comments very briefly on Jesus's symbolic words, saying that Jesus "gives a subtle hint [ὑπαινίττεται] at what is about to happen," presumably in reference to Christ's death and resurrection; see Cyril, *In Jo.* 2:19–20 (Maxwell, 94). What Origen discerns within his nonliteral treatment of the passage, Theodore seems to understand as part of the literal text's meaning. I will say more about this below.

2. See the full section of his treatment of the cleansing of the temple narrative: Origen, *Comm. Jo.* 10.119–323 (Heine, 281–327). I will focus on select passages from this extensive book. I have chosen not to deal with Origen's treatment of 2:12–13, in which he provides lengthy discussions of Christ's descent to Jerusalem and the Passover; John's account of Jesus's cleansing of the temple proper begins in 2:14.

3. Despite Origen's claims that the passage is not useful at the literal level, claims that I will examine below, throughout his treatment of the passage Origen returns to the literal level to refute the Valentinian interpreter, Heracleon. He does not always announce his move back to the literal level, but he does tend to work with the literal wording of the text in these instances. See, e.g., Origen's refutation of Heracleon's treatment of Jesus's words in 2:16, "Take these things out of here! Stop making my Father's

2. The Cleansing of the Temple of John 2

passage's meaning at the nonliteral level, which he describes variously as the passage's "hidden things," its "type," "anagogy," and "symbol."

I will first examine his introductory comments about gospel composition, in which he discusses the interpretive principle that the exegete must render a given scriptural passage useful. From there I will examine his comments about the literal narrative of the cleansing of the temple, where he, as we mentioned above, finds countless problems, which lead him to move beyond the letter. Next, I will examine this shift to the nonliteral level, followed by an examination of the benefits he discerns in the passage once he has moved beyond the letter.

In his introduction to book 10, Origen provides a discussion of gospel composition, a discussion that resembles his comments in *Princ.* 4.[4] Here he says that the evangelists composed their gospels "with a view to the usefulness of the mystical object [πρὸς τὸ χρήσιμον τοῦ τῶν μυστικοῦ σκοποῦ]," which explains for him the "minor changes" that have been made to their narratives "so far as narrative is concerned [ὡς κατὰ τὴν ἱστορίαν]" and thus the discrepancies between them.[5] Therefore, he argues, "The spiritual truth is often preserved in the material falsehood, as it were [σῳζομένου πολλάκις τοῦ ἀληθοῦς πνευματικοῦ ἐν τῷ σωματικῷ ὡς ἂν εἴποι τις, ψευδεῖ]," and as a result, the interpreter ought to be looking beyond the letter in such cases (*Comm. Jo.* 10.20 [Heine, 259]).

The cleansing of the temple narrative provides one such case for Origen. He compares John's account of the narrative with those of the Synoptic authors and claims that it has been necessary to quote the Synoptics at length "to show the disagreement according to the literal meaning [ὑπὲρ

---

house a marketplace!" in *Comm. Jo.* 10.214, 216. Despite Heracleon's apparent silence about Jesus's relation to the Father, as Origen presents his opponent's interpretation to his reader, he says "if Jesus says that the temple in Jerusalem is the house of his own Father, and this temple was constructed for the glory of him who created the heaven and the earth, are we not taught openly [ἄντικρυς] to consider the Son of God to be a Son of none other than the creator of heaven and earth?" In other words, the creator, the God of the Old Testament, is the same God and Father of the Son, Jesus Christ, which Jesus's words in 2:16 indicate; cf. *Princ.* 4.4.1. John 2:16 had already been used by Tertullian in *Adversus Praxean* as evidence for a distinction within the unity of the Father-Son relationship in the Godhead in order to refute the monarchians; see Pollard, *Johannine Christology and the Early Church*, 66.

4. Origen, *Comm. Jo.* 10.19–20. I discussed this passage in ch. 1.

5. Origen, *Comm. Jo.* 10.19 (Heine, 259). I have used the term *narrative* where Heine has *history*.

τοῦ καταστῆσαι τὴν κατὰ τὸ ῥητὸν διαφωνίαν]" (*Comm. Jo.* 10.129 [Heine, 285]). Consideration of these disagreements, Origen argues, is indicative of "he who is concerned about a more accurate insight [ᾦ μέλει τῆς ἀκριβεστέρας ἐξετάσεως]" (*Comm. Jo.* 10.145 [Heine, 289]). The first issue is that John records two trips to Jerusalem, which are "separated by many acts revealed between them, and by visits of the Lord to different places," whereas the Synoptic authors record the same event to have taken place in one visit to Jerusalem (*Comm. Jo.* 10.129 [Heine, 285]). Furthermore, this was for the Synoptic authors not just any visit; Jesus's cleansing of the temple took place just prior to his triumphal entry. Another issue is that of Jesus's action in the temple itself. Origen suspects that given Jesus's position in life, namely, the fact that he was a carpenter's son, the account of his driving the merchants and such a great number of animals out of the temple was simply implausible, for the money-changers would more probably have accused Jesus of "an outrage." Another issue, which is of doctrinal import, is Jesus's anger in the temple. Concerning Jesus's anger, Origen says, "let us consider if [the fact that] the Son of God takes cords and weaves a whip for himself and drives them out of the temple does not point to one who is self-willed, and rather rash, and undisciplined in nature" (*Comm. Jo.* 10.145 [Heine, 289]). Before moving to the nonliteral level, Origen acknowledges that the person who wishes "to preserve the historical sense [τὴν ἱστορίαν σῶσαι]" has one argument in his favor, namely, the divine power of Jesus "to prevail over tens of thousands with divine grace," as the words of Ps 32:10–11 indicate: "For the Lord will bring to naught the counsels of nations, and he rejects the arguments of peoples." Thus he reservedly concedes, "the historical meaning in our passage [τὴν κατὰ τὸν τόπον ἱτορίαν], if indeed it even occurred, indicates that a miracle was executed no less than any which he performed most incredibly" (*Comm. Jo.* 10.148 [Heine, 289]). Clearly, however, Origen is not convinced by this argument, for he spends most of his interpretive energy on his nonliteral reading.

Given the problems with the literal narrative that he has demonstrated, Origen believes that he is justified, and in fact required, to go beyond the letter to find the usefulness of John's cleansing of the temple narrative. Before he provides his nonliteral interpretations of John 2, however, Origen acknowledges the difficulties involved in the endeavor, in addition to his own inadequacy, and therefore his need for God's assistance, again exemplifying (however rhetorically) one of the exegetical virtues of the ideal reader of the Gospel of John he has outlined. He says: "we have asked him who gives to everyone who asks and struggles intensely to seek, and we are knocking, in order that the hidden things of scripture may be opened to us by the keys of knowledge [ὑπὲρ τοῦ ἀνοιχθῆναι ἡμῖν ταῖς τῆς γνώσεως κλεισὶν τὰ κεκρυμμένα τῆς γραφῆς]."⁶ Having provided the rationale for his move to the nonliteral level and having thus prayed, Origen begins his nonliteral interpretation of the passage, to which we will now turn. He provides three distinct but related nonliteral interpretations of the passage, each of which provides benefit for his contemporary readers, and I will examine them in turn. The first nonliteral reading concerns the whole contemporary church, the second concerns the individual Christian soul, and the third presents instruction about the place of the gentile church within salvation history.

I will begin with Origen's first nonliteral interpretation, which establishes his overarching nonliteral treatment of the passage. As he interprets 2:13–14, in which Jesus goes up to Jerusalem and enters the temple, it becomes clear that the temple represents the church in Origen's own day. Origen describes this interpretation as that which is "beyond the historical meaning" (πέρα τῆς ἱστορίας) and claims that Jesus "found in the temple, which is also said to be the house of the Savior's Father, that is, in the church, or in the proclamation of the sound message of the church," some who made the Father's house into a house of merchandise (*Comm. Jo.* 10.130, 133 [Heine, 286]). He goes on to say that there are always those in the temple qua church who "prefer the mammon of iniquity," who "despise what is honest and pure and devoid of all bitterness and gall," and who "abandon the care of those who are figuratively called doves."⁷ When Jesus overturns the tables, according to Origen, then, he overturns the tables in the souls of those in the church who are fond of money. Thus, the first benefit to be found at this level relates to the situation of the church, in which there will always be those who are present for impious reasons of personal gain, and Jesus clears such ones out.

Origen develops this line of interpretation as he deals with Jesus's symbolic words in 2:19, "Destroy this temple and in three days I will raise it up." He claims that with these words Jesus is "joining as one [συνάπτων ... ὡς

---

6. Origen, *Comm. Jo.* 10.131 (Heine, 285); see also *Comm. Jo.* 10.266. This criterion of the ideal reader we saw Origen mention in his preface: 1.46, 89; cf. *Princ.* 4.2.3. See my discussion of the necessity that the interpreter asks for God's assistance in ch. 1.

7. Origen, *Comm. Jo.* 10.134–36 (Heine, 286–87). As Wiles describes this nonliteral reading, the cleansing of the temple refers to "the ever-necessary work of Christ in purging his church" (*Spiritual Gospel*, 44).

ἕνα] the saying about his own body with that about the temple" and then proceeds to find a type (τύπος) of the temple qua church in Jesus's own body (*Comm. Jo.* 10.226, 228 [Heine, 305]). Two New Testament texts help him in this interpretation. Regarding the temple as the body of Christ, that is, the church, Origen notes that Eph 2:21 says, "In him the whole building is joined together and rises to become a holy temple in the Lord," and in 1 Cor 12:27, Paul tells the Corinthian church, "Now you are the body of Christ."[8] With the aid of such verses, Origen argues that, just as the "perceptible body of Jesus [τὸ αἰσθητὸν τοῦ Ἰησοῦ σῶμα]" has been crucified, buried, and raised, so too "the whole body of the saints of Christ have been crucified with Christ and now no longer live" (Gal 2:20). Origen introduces another Pauline text into his argument in order to address the Christian's resurrection with Christ: "we were buried with Christ" (Rom 6:4), and "we were raised with him" (Rom 6:5). For, Origen argues, the apostle says this as though he had attained a pledge of resurrection, since the Christian "has not yet arisen so far as concerns that anticipated blessed and perfect resurrection." He concludes his nonliteral treatment of these verses by claiming that, "The mystery of the resurrection, however, is great, and difficult for many of us to understand" (*Comm. Jo.* 10.230, 231–232 [Heine, 306]). Within another pastiche of scriptural references to the resurrection, Origen returns to the Johannine verse of focus, 2:19, "Destroy this temple and in three days I will raise it up," and associates it with the words, "Zeal of your house will devour me" of 2:17. Both verses apply to the individual Christian: "Each person likewise, when Jesus cleanses him, by putting aside those things which are irrational [τὰ ἄλογα] and which engage in business, will be destroyed because of the zeal for the word which is in him," Origen argues (*Comm. Jo.* 10.239, 242 [Heine, 308]). Thus in Jesus's words in 2:19, it is not only Christ's resurrection that Jesus predicts (as John tells us in 2:21); Jesus's resurrection is also a type for the death and resurrection of his body, the church, and the individual members of it. Having established this meaning at the nonliteral level, Origen proceeds to take great pains to "refer each of the things recorded about the temple anagogically [ἕκαστον τῶν ἀναγεγραμμένων περὶ τοῦ ναοῦ φιλοτιμνητέον ἀνάγειν] to the saying about the body of Jesus, whether it be the body which he received from the virgin, or the church, which is said to be his body."[9] Notice here Origen's use of the terms *type* and *anagogical* in the same interpretive context;

---

8. He also uses 1 Pet 2:5 here (Origen, *Comm. Jo.* 10.228–229 [Heine, 305–6]).
9. Origen, *Comm. Jo.* 10.263 (Heine, 313). This he develops at length in 10.263–287.

clearly he does not think it a problem to do so and does not seem to view them as indicating distinct exegetical procedures.

In the previous reading, Origen found the text useful at the nonliteral level because of its ability to address the situation of the collective church primarily, although individual members are also implicitly in view. However, in this, his second nonliteral reading, he also finds another more explicit use for the text that is focused on the needs of the individual soul, to which we will now turn. Origen claims that it is possible that the human soul is a temple by nature "because of the intelligence which is united with it [διὰ τὸν συμπεφυκότα λόγον]," to which Jesus ascends from Capernaum. In this reading, senseless, harmful, earthly emotions are driven out by the discipline of Jesus's word of "reproving doctrines," so that the soul, his Father's house, might receive the worship of God that is performed according to heavenly and spiritual laws.[10]

I will now examine Origen's third nonliteral interpretation, in which he explains for his readers what the narrative signifies or symbolizes, and which he indicates by saying the following:

> In addition, that he has also performed a more profound sign [σημεῖον βαθύτερον] through what has been said [in 2:16], so that we recognize that these events have occurred as a symbol [σύμβολον] of the fact that no longer will the ministry related to that temple still be able to be performed by the priests so far as the sacrifices perceptible to the senses [κατὰ τὰς αἰσθητὰς θυσίας] are concerned, nor will the law still be able to be observed even as the corporeal Jews would wish. (*Comm. Jo.* 10.138 [Heine, 287])

Accordingly, in this nonliteral reading of the passage, Origen finds another benefit, namely, its instruction about the church's place within salvation history.[11] This cleansing of the temple Jesus performed once and for all, Origen continues, and as a result the law was nullified and its office given to the gen-

---

10. Origen, *Comm. Jo.* 10.141–42 (Heine, 288). Each animal that is referred to in the cleansing of the temple narrative corresponds to a different kind of thought or emotion, which needs to be driven out; see 10.142; cf. *Hom. Ps.* 77.8.5. See Torjesen's treatment of the cleansing of the temple passage (*Hermeneutical Procedure*, 135–36). It provides one of her examples of the encounter of the mature, careful reader of Scripture with the Logos.

11. Origen, *Comm. Jo.* 10.138 (Heine, 287). Note that the term "sign" (σημεῖον) is present in the passage itself (2:18). Perhaps Origen is playing on John's use of the term

tile members of the church, "who believe in God through Christ."[12] Not only the office of the Mosaic legislation, but the very kingdom of God was taken from "the corporeal Jews" and given to the gentile believers in Christ, argues Origen. We will see that this is the use at the nonliteral level Cyril finds, and that Theodore too finds in his literal treatment. Indeed, it is the most frequent of the nonliteral readings given to the passage in the subsequent tradition.[13]

This concludes my analysis of the benefits that Origen finds at the nonliteral level. I have shown that for him, the text is useful in its instruction concerning salvation history, in which the Jewish temple cult is abolished and the gentile church now observes the spiritual law, and in its ability to speak directly to the present situation of the corporate church and to the individual Christian soul. I will show below that Cyril and Theodore also find instruction concerning the place of the gentile church within their nonliteral interpretations of the narrative, but not of the present situation of the church and the individual soul.

Chrysostom provides his brief treatment of the passage in the majority of one homily, which amounts to approximately three columns of Greek text (*Hom. Jo.* 23.2–3 [Goggin, 225–31]). He claims explicitly that the passage is beneficial and proceeds to provide a verse-by-verse explanation of the passage for his hearers, explaining potential problems and questions, and providing historical detail, all the while remaining at the literal level of the narrative. (I should note, however, that Chrysostom does not claim explicitly that he is providing a literal reading. This is my own assessment, based on his tendency to indicate his shift to the nonliteral plane in other instances, and the absence of such a claim here.) Having explained the passage, again as his custom, Chrysostom turns to provide his parishioners with moral exhortation in the final section of his homily. In this case, his exhortation is uncharacteristically brief, and he urges them toward lives of virtue in imitation of Jesus's disciples, who enjoy the Spirit's grace. I will examine first his general comments about the usefulness of the passage, and then turn to examine the particular benefits he finds in the literal narrative.

Chrysostom's claim that the scriptural passage of the cleansing of the temple is useful is much less explicit than Origen's, for he likens the "use-

---

in this context, but he is not as explicit about it as we should like. I will argue below that Theodore seems to do so more explicitly in his treatment of the verse.

12. Origen, *Comm. Jo.* 10.140 (Heine, 288). Here Origen uses Matt 21:43.

13. Wiles, *Spiritual Gospel*, 44–45. As evidence for this claim, Wiles lists the interpretations of Isidore, Cyril, and Theodore.

fulness" (χρείαν) of his homily on the passage to that of Scripture, which is itself many-sided in its remedy for the various ills suffered by humankind (*Hom. Jo.* 23.1 [Goggin, 223]). Thus it seems that Chrysostom understands his preaching on the scriptural passage of the cleansing of the temple narrative in John 2 to be by extension of comparable benefit for his audience to that of the scriptural passage itself. For him, the passage is useful primarily for its doctrinal teaching about the Son's relationship to the Father, and in its instruction about Christ's resurrection.

Chrysostom spends most of his interpretive energy in his treatment of the narrative's doctrinal implications, and I will therefore begin here. For Chrysostom, the passage provides an occasion to discuss Christ's relationship to the Father. Like Origen, Chrysostom acknowledges the potential doctrinal issue of Jesus's apparent anger in the temple (2:15–16), and despite the verses' implications for our understanding of Jesus's divinity, finds the verses doctrinally beneficial. For Chrysostom, however, these verses are not historically problematic, as they were for Origen, and thus he remains at the immediate level of the narrative, asking with his audience rhetorically, "'And why,' you will ask, 'did Christ do this very thing and show indignation against these men such as He did not seem to show anywhere else?'" Chrysostom answers his audience's hypothetical question: "Because he was going to heal on the Sabbath ... which would seem to them to be transgressing the Law." With these zealous actions for the house of the Lord, claims Chrysostom, Jesus demonstrated that he "would not withstand the Lord of the house who was worshiped in it" and that he was not "doing these things like some enemy of God, who has come out of opposition to the Father." To the contrary, argues Chrysostom—in cleansing the temple, he showed his "harmony" with the Father. Jesus's words display his agreement with the Father as well: "for he did not say 'the holy house,' but 'the house of my Father'" (*Hom. Jo.* 23.2 [Goggin, 225–27]). For Chrysostom, then, Jesus's zealous words and actions in the temple in John 2 simply demonstrate that he is in agreement with the Father.[14]

Chrysostom's treatment of Jesus's symbolic words in 2:19, "Destroy this temple and in three days I will raise it up," provides an example in which he operates according to one of the exegetical principles examined in the previous chapter. The verse provides for him instruction about Christ's

---

14. This is a doctrinal theme Chrysostom returns to throughout his *Homilies on John*; see, e.g., his treatment of 10:1 in *Hom. Jo.* 59.2; and his treatment of Matt 27:45–48 in *Hom. Matt.* 78.1.

resurrection. Chrysostom claims that in this verse Jesus "speaks enigmatically" (ἠνίξατο), and then he moves to clarify his words.[15] Chrysostom finds the explanation of the obscure words within the narrative context of John 2 itself, and he claims, the Evangelist John's subsequent words "interpret what Christ said [ἑρμηνεύει τὸ εἰρημένον]" and thus provide an explanation of his symbolic words in 2:21–22: "But he was speaking of the temple of his body," and "After he was raised from the dead, his disciples remembered that he had said this" (*Hom. Jo.* 23.3 [Goggin, 228]). According to Chrysostom, along with the Evangelist John, Jesus refers symbolically to his resurrection, as we saw in Origen's treatment as well. For Chrysostom, however, unlike Origen, the resurrection of the whole church at the end of the age is not also in view.

For Chrysostom, then, as we have seen, the text was beneficial at the literal level alone, where it provided doctrinal instruction about the Son's agreement with the Father, in addition to teaching about Christ's resurrection as he dealt with Jesus's symbolic words in 2:19.

Theodore's treatment of the passage is also rather brief. In this case we have only two small Greek fragments on 2:19 and 2:23 (two small paragraphs of Greek), so I must rely on the full Syriac translation, which is itself only three and a half pages of Syriac text (Greek: Kalantzis, 54; Syriac: Conti, 28–30). Theodore too provides a verse-by-verse treatment of John 2, and like Chrysostom, he remains at the literal narrative, which he does not claim explicitly.[16] Many of his comments are brief paraphrases of the biblical text, with the exception of his doctrinal comments on 2:19–21.

In his literal treatment, Theodore, too, finds several benefits for his readers. For him, the passage provides beneficial doctrinal teaching, particularly concerning Christology, as he seeks to refute a group of unnamed heretics. In addition, the passage provides an occasion to instruct his readers about the relationship between Old Testament Scripture and Christ's actions in the temple, which we will also see in Cyril's treatment below. Like Origen, and as we will see, like Cyril, Theodore also finds beneficial instruction concerning the place of the church within salvation history, however, for him, this interpretation is part of the passage's literal meaning.

---

15. Chrysostom, *Hom. Jo.* 23.3 (Goggin, 229); see my discussion of the authors' treatment of parable and metaphor in the introduction.

16. Again, I assume, based on examples where he is explicit about his shift to the nonliteral plane, that had he understood his reading as nonliteral, he would have acknowledged it. I discuss this in the introduction.

Finally, Theodore too finds in the passage useful instruction about Christ's resurrection, as we have seen in our previous two authors' treatments, and his treatment of 2:19 is very similar to Chrysostom's. I will begin with Theodore's discussion of why John included the story of the cleansing of the temple in his narrative, followed by an examination of the benefits he finds in the literal narrative.

While Theodore does not evoke the language of usefulness explicitly in his comments on this passage, he does provide a discussion about why John included the narrative of the cleansing of the temple, given that the synoptic authors had already dealt with it. The Evangelist John provided his own account of Jesus's actions in the temple "because of the power of the doctrine [ܪܟܘܠ ܪܬܘܠܩܘܚ] that was connected with the miraculous event," and John also supplied the exchange between Jesus and the Jews in 2:18–19.[17] He explains that the Jews asked Jesus for a "sign" in 2:18, about which he says, "if a sign [ܪܬܐ] was required, it had already been given" (in Jesus's actions in the temple), and then he moves to provide a fitting explanation of the sign. Theodore claims that in the temple, Jesus was *acting* in parables (ܒܡܬܠܐ ܗܘܐ ܥܒܕ ܡܪܢ), and that "he did not do anything openly [ܐܠܐ ܗܘܐ ܓܠܝܬܐ ܥܒܕ ܡܪܢ]."[18] For Theodore, on the surface Jesus simply expelled those buying and selling in the temple, but "in truth" (ܒܫܪܪܐ), he symbolically abolished the ritual sacrifice of animals altogether through this act, saying through his actions that, "those ancient and obsolete rites will be replaced with a new rite, a new order, and a new age that will be proclaimed after my resurrection" [*Comm. Jo.* 2:19 [Conti, 29]). Like Origen then, Theodore finds beneficial instruction concerning salvation history, in which the Jewish temple cult is abolished, and a new order inaugurated by the resurrection of Christ is ushered in. For him, however, this is part of the passage's literal meaning.

Theodore too finds instruction for his readers concerning Jesus's resurrection as he deals with Jesus's words in 2:19, in addition to doctri-

---

17. Theodore, *Comm. Jo.* 2:21 (Conti, 30). In his preface Theodore claims that John included only that which the other evangelists did not mention, and when he did include narratives that the Synoptics included, he did so for the sake of attaching what he saw as important accompanying doctrinal teachings and mystical expressions; see Theodore, *Comm. Jo.* pref. (Kalantzis, 42). See my discussion of this aspect of his teaching in chapter 1.

18. Theodore, *Comm. Jo.* 2:19 (Conti, 29). Conti has translated the first of these phrases rather liberally as "he had a symbolic purpose in mind that only foreshadowed his intention with allusions."

nal instruction concerning Christology. Of Jesus's words, "Destroy this temple and in three days I will raise it up," Theodore says: "our Lord said these things in an obscure and mysterious way [ܬܐܘܪܝܐ]."[19] However, he continues, because the Evangelist John "believed it was appropriate to explain the meaning of these more obscure words of Christ," he did so in 2:21: "But he was speaking of the temple of his body."[20] For Theodore too, then, with these words, Jesus "not only alluded (ܪܡܙ) to the event of his resurrection, but also to the time when it would happen, hinting that there was thought to be a great difference between the one who suffered the passion and the one through whom he was raised."[21] So like Chrysostom, Theodore finds the explanation of the obscure words in the passage itself. Unlike Chrysostom, however, for Theodore, Jesus not only hints about the fact of his resurrection, but also about the relationship between the operations of his human and divine natures at the time of his resurrection.

Once Theodore has clarified the meaning of Jesus's symbolic words in 2:19, he can explain in great detail the christological statement quoted in the previous paragraph. As he explains his statement, he does so with the aim of refuting an unnamed group of heretics, probably Arians, whom he charges with misunderstanding Jesus's words, "I will raise it up" in 2:19. Theodore seems to shift gears as he charges his opponents with not dealing carefully with the words of the verse, in a way that is similar to Origen's refutation of Heracleon in his commentary; that is, he deals carefully with the wording of the verse. Theodore claims that these heretics miss the words "I will raise it up," and therefore mistakenly assume that Christ does not have the power to raise the dead.[22] He then proceeds to provide a representative articulation of his distinctive christological thought, for which he was later condemned: his understanding of two sharply separated natures of Christ,

---

19. Theodore, *Comm. Jo.* 2:19–21 (Conti, 29). See my discussion of the authors' treatment of parable and metaphor in the introduction.

20. Theodore, *Comm. Jo.* 2:19–21 (Conti, 29). He too finds the meaning of the obscure words in the text itself.

21. Theodore, *Comm. Jo.* 2:19–21 (Conti, 30). I will say more about this statement shortly.

22. Theodore, *Comm. Jo.* 2:19 (Conti, 29); we also have part of his treatment of the verse in the Greek fragments (Kalantzis, 54). Theodore probably has such verses in mind when he promises to provide an explanation of "difficult verses" in his preface. See my discussion in ch. 1.

divine and human.²³ He argues that by these words Christ makes clear that "he does not refer the destruction to himself [ܫܘܒܩܢܐ ܐܝܬ ܡܪܝ ܠܗܘ], but to the temple [of his body] [ܐܠܐ ܠܗܘ ܗܝܟܠܐ ܢܣܬܬܪ] that was going to be destroyed." He did not need anyone or anything else to raise the temple of his body, claims Theodore, but he could raise it himself. He goes on in his refutation of his heretical opponents to argue that even though it is said (elsewhere) that the Father raises Christ, the meaning he provides of the verses at hand is undoubtedly correct, for "the agreement" between the Father and Son in their operations indicates that "with equal right" they are attributed to both persons (*Comm. Jo.* 2:19–21 [Conti, 29]). Curiously, Theodore is the only one of these authors to articulate in any detail a christological position concerning 2:19. Cyril, the other author from whom we might expect such a discussion, does not take the opportunity, despite his use of the verse for such purposes in later works, which we will highlight below.²⁴

Finally, the literal narrative provides the opportunity for Theodore to draw out one final piece of beneficial instruction. As he deals with 2:17, Theodore finds occasion to instruct his readers about the way in which Jesus's actions in the temple relate to the Old Testament.²⁵ According to Theodore, in 2:17 John tells us that once Jesus had risen from the dead, Jesus's disciples remembered the words, "Zeal for your house will consume me," from Ps 68:10 (*Comm. Jo.* 2:17 [Conti, 28]; LXX 68:10/MT 69:9). Theodore makes clear for his readers that this prophecy was not originally about Christ, but that Jesus simply acted in a manner that was appropriately zeal-

---

23. Cf. *Comm. Jo.* 10:18; 11:42. He uses 2:19 as he interprets both verses. See also his rather ambiguous comments on 2:19 in his *Comm. Phil.* 2:8 concerning Paul's words, "made obedient up to death, even the death of the cross."

24. Cyril uses 2:19 in christological discussions elsewhere; see *Ep.* 6.6, which is dated sometime between the years 428–431 and thus written after his *Commentary on the Gospel of John*; he cites 2:19 as evidence of the two distinct natures and their conjunction into one person as part of a larger argument about the hypostatic union. Similarly, in his *A Defense of the Twelve Anathemas against Theodoret*, he maintains this position, whereas Theodoret argues that the verse implies that there are two inseparable natures. (The verse is cited in Theodoret's critiques of the second and twelfth anathemas and Cyril's responses to the fifth anathema.) See Cyril's *A Defense of the Twelve Anathemas against Bishops of the Diocese of Oriens* in his response to the seventh anathema.

25. In his treatment of this verse, Chrysostom briefly compares the disciples' memory of the psalm verse's prediction with the Jews' request for a sign (2:18), claiming that the disciples rightly understood Jesus's zealous actions in the temple; see Chysostom, *Hom. Jo.* 23.2.

ous for the temple, which his disciples later recognized.[26] It will become clear below that for Cyril, the disciples aptly understand Jesus's actions in the temple as the fulfillment of the prophetic psalm. This instruction concerning Jesus's actions in the temple in relation to the Old Testament psalm, and that concerning Jesus's anger that we observed above, is the extent of Theodore's literal treatment of the passage.

Cyril's treatment of the narrative is, like the Antiochenes', relatively brief, amounting to eight and a half pages of Greek text (*In Jo.* 2:14–22 [Maxwell, 92–95]). He too provides a verse-by-verse treatment of the literal narrative, in which he clarifies the problems he encounters in the text, doctrinal and otherwise, and explains Jesus's symbolic speech. However, it only becomes clear that Cyril has been working at the literal level when he shifts to the nonliteral plane—and here he parts ways with the Antiochenes.[27] Jesus's actions in the temple, as described in John 2:14–15 in particular, lead Cyril to suggest that the passage requires further "contemplation" concerning its communication of "higher matters" which are woven throughout the narrative in a type.[28]

I will demonstrate that at the literal level Cyril finds doctrinal instruction for his readers, in addition to instruction about discipleship, and about Jesus's fulfillment of Old Testament Scripture. Above the letter, Cyril finds additional beneficial instruction concerning the place of the church within salvation history, just as I observed in one of Origen's nonliteral treatments of the passage (and in Theodore's literal treatment).

---

26. Theodore makes similar comments about this particular verse of Ps 68 in his *Commentary on the Psalms* in which he generally looks for the fulfillment of Old Testament prophecies only in the Old Testament itself. See his comments on Ps 68:10, in which he finds the psalm's fulfillment in 1 Macc 2:24–25 in contrast to both John 2:17 and Rom 15:3. This is characteristic of Theodore's interpretation of the prophets more generally; e.g., there are instances within his *Commentary on the Twelve Prophets* where he is content to disagree with the New Testament authors' use of the Psalms in their writings when they find their fulfillment in Christ, rather than in a more immediate Old Testament historical event. See Robert Hill's discussion of Theodore's approach to the Psalms in particular in Hill, "Introduction," in *Commentary on Psalms 1–81*, trans. Robert C. Hill, WGRW 5 (Atlanta: Society of Biblical Literature, 2006), xxx, and the list of examples included in Hill, "Introduction," in *Commentary on the Twelve Prophets*, 24–27.

27. I discuss my choice to deal with the four authors' comments in this way in the introduction.

28. I shall comment on the specific terminology Cyril uses in more detail below.

Given Cyril's emphasis on his provision of a doctrinal explanation of the Gospel of John in his preface, we will begin our examination of his treatment of the literal narrative with the doctrinal instruction he draws from the text. As he treats 2:15–16, Cyril too must deal with Jesus's anger in the temple, lest any reader is led to question Jesus's divinity. Unlike Origen and Chrysostom, Cyril simply claims that Jesus is "angry for good reason," for he observes, the temple was to be a "house of prayer" (Matt 21:13).[29] Jesus is justified in his actions in the temple, thinks Cyril, not because his divinity is already evident from previous miracles, as we saw Theodore argue above, but because, as Paul said in his first letter to the Corinthians, "If anyone destroys the temple of God, God will destroy them" (1 Cor 3:17) (*In Jo.* 2:16 [Maxwell, 92]). That is, claims Cyril, the divine Son of God destroys those he finds destroying the temple of his Father with whom he acts in accordance. Not only do his actions in the temple demonstrate his agreement with the Father, as Chrysostom argued, but for Cyril, these actions actually demonstrate Christ's own divinity.

Cyril finds additional doctrinal instruction, of a Trinitarian nature, as he deals with Jesus's words in John 2:16, "Get these things out of here. Stop making my Father's house a house of merchandise!" For Cyril, as for Origen and Chrysostom, these words provide evidence of the unique relationship between God the Father and Jesus the Son. According to Cyril, Jesus does not say "our Father's house," for he is not a son by "adoption, that is, and only by the will of the Father" but he is the Son of the Father "by nature" and is "truly begotten," which he makes clear when he says "my Father's house." Here Cyril uses classical Nicene Trinitarian language to describe the relationship between the Father and the Son: "the Word knows that he is from the substance of God the Father and not included among those who are sons by grace" (*In Jo.* 2:16 [Maxwell, 92–93]). It may be that Cyril has Arius and his followers more squarely in view than did my other three authors; however, he does not say so explicitly in this instance.

---

29. Cyril, *In Jo.* 2:16 (Maxwell, 92). In *Comm. Am.* 2:8, Cyril cites John's account of Jesus's actions in the temple, prompted by the words, "binding their garments with ropes, they laid hangings near the altar, and drank the wine of calumnies in the house of their God." The prophet Amos indicts the Israelites' illicit treatment of the temple in this context, and Cyril likens it to the situation Jesus finds in John 2, and goes on to apply both passages to the churches of his day, saying "we shall become better from sins committed by others if we avoid theirs."

When Cyril turns to treat the words, "But he was speaking about the temple of his body" in 2:21, he finds another beneficial doctrinal teaching, this time concerning the relationship between the two natures of Christ. Cyril reflects briefly on Christ's divine nature as he deals with these words, arguing that they provide clear evidence that the only begotten Word, dwelling in a body called a temple, is "God by nature," for one who is not God cannot dwell in a temple. After this brief statement, Cyril moves on to argue that it is Christ alone whose body Scripture describes as a temple in its own right.[30] Likewise, when Scripture describes Christ's body as a corpse (Matt 24:28), that is, in a way decidedly unfitting for divinity, it does so "in a parable-like way" (ἐν τρόπῳ παραβολῆς), and as "an image" (εἰς εἰκόνα), in order to describe the future gathering of the saints to Christ, and this does not "damage the force of the truth" (*In Jo.* 2:21–22 [Maxwell, 95]). Thus it is clear, argues Cyril, that only Christ's body can be described as a temple, which for him provides clear evidence of his divinity.[31]

Cyril, however, provides more than a doctrinal explanation in his treatment of the literal Johannine narrative. He also thinks it necessary to instruct his readers concerning the relationship between Jesus's ministry and the Old Testament, which we saw Theodore treat as well. For Cyril, the situation in the temple and its worship in John 2 fulfill the prophecy of Jer 12:10–12:[32] "Many shepherds have utterly destroyed my vineyard. They have defiled my portion and made my desired portion a trackless desert. It has become a great ruin." The Lord's vineyard, says Cyril, "was truly destroyed since the vineyard was being taught to trample the divine worship itself ... being turned into a desert of complete ignorance by the sordid greed of its leaders" (*In Jo.* 2:14 [Maxwell, 92]).

In his treatment of the remainder of the Johannine passage, Cyril continues to highlight the passages from the prophets that the cleansing of the temple fulfills. For example, when he arrives at 2:20 where the Jews

---

30. Cyril, *In Jo.* 2:21–22 (Maxwell, 95). For, he argues, Christians are described as "temples of God" in Scripture (e.g., 1 Cor 6:19), not as temples of themselves.

31. As I mentioned above, Cyril does not discuss Christology as he interprets 2:19.

32. All throughout his commentary on John, Cyril seems to understand himself as a guide for his readers in comparing what occurred at the time of Christ's coming with the Old Testament passages about him. This he discusses in *Comm. Habac.* 3:2, prompted by the words "in the approach of the years you will be acknowledged; when the time arrives, you will be brought to light." In this instance he cites John 2:15–17 as an example of prophecy and fulfillment. Perhaps this is related to his understanding of his position as bishop as well, which I discussed in ch. 1.

respond to Jesus's symbolic words, "Destroy this temple and I will raise it in three days," he finds that their failure to understand "the depth of the mystery" is a fulfillment of Ps 68:24: "Let their eyes be darkened that they may not see, and bend their backs forever" (*In Jo.* 2:19–20 [Maxwell, 94]).

Cyril finds a different kind of instruction at the literal level, which is provided by the disciples' positive behavior as he treats 2:17. In the verse, Jesus's disciples witness his actions in the temple and then the Evangelist John tells us that at a later time, they remembered a Scripture about it: "Zeal for your house will consume me" (John's quotation of Ps 68:10). For Cyril, this verse demonstrates the disciples' progress in their knowledge of the Scriptures, for in a short time they developed skills in "comparing what is written with its fulfillment in deeds" [ταῖς τῶν πραγμάτων ἐκβάσεσι τὰ γεγραμμένα συμβάλλοντες]" (*In Jo.* 2:17 [Maxwell, 93]). Thus in one sentence, Cyril gives us an indirect statement about one of the ways his readers are to emulate the disciples, namely, in their careful study of the Scriptures so as to find Christ in the Old Testament in particular.[33]

Cyril returns to the instruction provided by the behavior of the disciples as he treats 2:22, "When he was raised from the dead, his disciples remembered that he had said this, and they believed the Scripture and the word that Jesus had spoken." He argues in this instance that, "since the disciples have a good disposition, they become wise," and not only that, but they also "ruminate [ἀναμασῶνται] on the words of Holy Scripture, nourishing themselves to gain more exact [ἀκριβεστέραν] knowledge and from there come firmly to faith" (*In Jo.* 2:22 [Maxwell, 95]). Thus he highlights the disciples' reflection on Scripture, which results in their precise knowledge of the faith. As I observed above in the first benefit Cyril finds in the literal narrative, namely, the passage's fulfillment of Old Testament Scripture, Cyril himself provides a similar model for his readers of how to ruminate on Scripture, and therefore also of how to relate the events of Jesus's life to the Old Testament. As bishop, he sees himself as an inheritor of the apostolic tradition of dwelling on and interpreting Scripture.

In addition to the benefits offered by the literal narrative described above, Cyril also moves to the nonliteral plane, where he provides an interpretation of the passage that resembles those of Origen and Theodore. Cyril indicates explicitly that he is moving to the nonliteral plane once he has dealt

---

33. Or, as Maxwell would argue, this is a clue about how Cyril would have his readers teach their catechumens. See my discussion of Maxwell's theory about the audience of Cyril's *In Joannem* above.

with 2:14–16 at the level of the narrative. He claims that giving adequate attention to these verses also requires the interpreter to "spiritually apply it to higher matters [λογικώτερον ἐφαρμόσαι τοῖς ἀνωτέρω καὶ ταῦτα]" and to "contemplate the passage differently [θεωρητέον ἑτέρως τὸ ἀνάγνωσμα]."[34] In this instance, the "higher matters" to which the passage applies relate to the place of the church within the arch of salvation history. He instructs his readers to "look again at the entire shape of God's plan, as far as it concerns us. It is woven throughout with two realities [Θέα δὴ πάλιν ὅλον τῆς καθ᾽ ἡμᾶς οἰκονομίας τὸ σχῆμα διὰ δύο πραγμάτων ἐξυφασμένον]."[35] Note that Origen also used the language of spiritual matters being woven throughout the narrative in his introductory comments to the cleansing of the temple narrative. Cyril, unlike Origen, however, is not led to the nonliteral level of the text because he finds problems with the literal level as did Origen.

These two realities, wherein lies the substance of Cyril's nonliteral treatment of the passage, require further examination. The first Cyril describes as the reality that Christ feasts with those who have invited him, namely, the inhabitants of Galilee, who have faith in him, as he performs signs for them. Concerning this reality, Cyril claims that Christ teaches through "a type" (τύπου) that he will accept the gentiles because of their faith. Cyril goes on: these ones God will lead to the heavenly bridal chamber to take part in the heavenly feast with the saints (Matt 8:11). The second, corresponding reality of God's plan is that the disobedient Jews will be punished; they will be driven out from the holy places, and God will no longer receive their sacrifices. Therefore, by devising the whip of cords in 2:15 in particular, Cyril argues, "[Jesus] signifies this most excellently in a type [ἄριστα διὰ τύπου σημαίνει]" that he will subject them to the punishing whip, as they are "bound by the cords of their own sins."[36] The Lord's prophesy through Isaiah in Isa 1:11–14, "I have had enough of your burnt offerings of rams. I do not want the fat of lambs and the blood of bulls and goats … my soul hates your fasting and rest and feasts. I have had enough of you. I will

---

34. Cyril, *In Jo.* 2:14 (Maxwell, 93). Note that it is Cyril who uses the term θεωρία in his treatment of the passage and not the Antiochenes, with whom scholars tend to associate the exegetical term.

35. Cyril, *In Jo.* 2:14 (Maxwell, 93). I have altered Maxwell's translation by using the word "realities," for he translates πραγμάτων as "facts." This is purely a stylistic choice.

36. Cyril, *In Jo.* 2:14 (Maxwell, 93). Here too we probably have a kind of play on words through Cyril's use of the verb "signify" (σημαίνω), the cognate verb of "sign" (σημεῖον) in 2:18.

no longer pardon your sins," which Cyril quotes immediately following his nonliteral reading, surely bolsters this interpretation (*In Jo.* 2:14 [Maxwell, 93]). Thus in this instance, the type Cyril finds in the narrative fulfills the prophecy of Isaiah about the corruption of Israel's worship. Clearly for him, the events presented in this New Testament passage, whether at the literal or the nonliteral level, fulfill the Old Testament Scriptures.

In conclusion to Cyril's nonliteral reading, I should say that it resembles closely Origen's second spiritual interpretation: Jesus's temple action symbolized the cessation of the sacrificial system's efficacy. His nonliteral interpretation is much less thorough than Origen's, and it is not the result of his rejection of the text's meaning according to the letter. His understanding of the whip in particular we did not see in Origen's nonliteral treatment of the passage. In any case, the narrative should be "applied spiritually to higher matters," Cyril claims, by which he means, in this case, that it should be applied to salvation history, in which the gentiles are brought into the people of God and the disobedient Jews are put out of the holy places, a higher matter to which he frequently applies the Johannine narrative throughout his commentary.[37] Origen of course provides several other nonliteral interpretations at the individual and corporate levels, but both interpreters think the passage teaches about God's plan in salvation history, just as did Theodore.

In conclusion to his treatment of the passage as a whole, I argued that Cyril found a great deal of instruction to assist the spiritual development of his readers in the passage at both the literal and the nonliteral levels, despite the brevity of his treatment. The literal level provided doctrinal instruction concerning the divinity of the Son and concerning the relationship between the Father and the Son. Cyril found occasion as well to demonstrate for his readers how Jesus's actions in the temple fulfilled Old Testament Scripture at the level of the narrative, and the disciples provided for his readers examples to be followed in terms of their own rumination on the relationship between the Old Testament and Christ. We witnessed Cyril's shift above the letter to the nonliteral level, and the nonliteral interpretation he gave, which provided his readers with instruction about God's rejection of the Jewish temple cult and the place of the gentile church within salvation history.

---

37. Maxwell observed this in his introduction to his English translation; see Maxwell, "Translator's Introduction," in *Commentary on the Gospel of John*, xxiii.

CONCLUSION

In this chapter I argued that Cyril and the Antiochenes found instruction for the spiritual development of their audiences at both the literal and the nonliteral level of the passage. Within their literal treatments, each author found doctrinal instruction for their audiences, but Cyril and Theodore drew out other teachings from the literal text, such as Cyril's exhortations to his audience to emulate the example set by Jesus's disciples, and Theodore's and Cyril's discussions of Jesus's relationship to Old Testament Scripture.

The Alexandrians alone made explicit shifts to the nonliteral plane before drawing out the beneficial instruction offered by the nonliteral sense of the passage. Origen claimed explicitly that the nonliteral level contained the passage's useful teachings, given the problems he found at the literal level, whereas Cyril simply claimed that a careful consideration of the passage required additional contemplation, and thus provided a nonliteral reading.[38] The Alexandrians discovered instruction about salvation history in the nonliteral passage, in which Jesus ends the sacrificial system of the Jews once and for all, making way for a new era, which is ushered in by Christ, a reading Theodore found at the literal level. For Origen, there are additional benefits to be found on the nonliteral plane; the passage provides direct insight about how Christ interacts with the church in its present state, and how he interacts with the individual Christian's soul.

This example of these four authors' exegesis has demonstrated discernable differences between the two schools, despite the overlap that we have observed along the way. The Antiochenes draw out instruction for the spiritual development of their audiences primarily from the literal text. Conversely, the Alexandrians found as much instruction for their readers at the nonliteral level as at the literal, and they do not require the text itself to authorize this kind of interpretive maneuver.

---

38. Origen's claim about the (useless) literal level is also a kind of textual indicator that a move beyond the letter is required. However, this is not the same kind of interpretive move as to recognize the text's use of symbolic words.

3
The Samaritan Woman at the Well of John 4

In this chapter I will examine the four authors' treatments of the Samaritan woman at the well in John 4:4–42. In this passage, John tells us that Jesus had to go through Samaria on his way to Galilee, and because he was tired from his journey, he stopped at Jacob's well near the Samaritan city of Sychar (4:3–6). The Samaritan woman meets Jesus there "at midday" (4:6), where he requests from her a drink of water (4:7). The evangelist informs us that Jews and Samaritans do not "share things in common" and thus the woman's skeptical response to his request is justified (4:9). Jesus, however, uses the occasion to offer her "living water" (4:10–15) and to reveal himself to her (4:16–26). For these authors, this is a story that demonstrates Jesus's love for all humanity and his provision of the Spirit's indwelling. The passage also instructs their audiences about attentiveness to doctrinal teaching or spiritual things, over and above material things, through the example of the Samaritan woman. For, once Jesus demonstrates his knowledge of her past, she suspects that he is the messiah (4:28–29) and returns to her city to share with those she meets about her encounter with Jesus, inviting them to come and see him for themselves (4:28–30). The story's conclusion, in which many of the Samaritans believe in Jesus (4:39–42) provides occasion for the authors to discuss God's inclusion of non-Jews in the people of God.

In their treatments of John 4, once again the Antiochenes find beneficial instruction for the spiritual development of their audiences at the literal level, whereas the Alexandrians find it both at the literal and the nonliteral levels. As for the literal narrative's benefits, all four authors find the text to be spiritually helpful in its provision of examples to be followed in the characters of the narrative. The Samaritan woman and Christ are to be emulated in various ways by their audiences. At the literal level, all four also find doctrinal instruction concerning Jesus's words, "God is

Spirit."[1] Despite the potential doctrinal issue concerning Jesus's claim to worship the Father in 4:22, all three post-Nicene authors find beneficial doctrinal teaching in the verse concerning Christ's humanity, and Origen discusses its implications for the relationship between the God of the Old and New Testaments. Similarly, Cyril finds beneficial christological teaching as he discusses Jesus's weariness by the well in 4:6. For Chrysostom, Jesus's departure from Judea to Galilee, the journey that takes him through Samaria in 4:4–5, provides the occasion to instruct his audience concerning the role of the gentiles within salvation history. Chrysostom and the Alexandrians find occasion to discuss for their readers the relationship between Christ and the Old Testament as they deal with the literal level. Finally, as Cyril and the Antiochenes deal with Jesus's symbolic words about Jesus's living water and the harvest, they find instruction about the work of the Holy Spirit in the life of the believer and about the arch of salvation history from Moses and the prophets to the apostles and their successors.[2]

The Alexandrians find much that is useful at the nonliteral level. For Origen, the passage teaches his readers about the relationship of the heterodox to the orthodox church, and it also provides instruction concerning the journey of the individual Christian's soul in relation to Scripture and to Jesus's teachings. Jesus's harvest parable in 4:35–38 is to be dealt with at the nonliteral level according to Origen, due to problems he finds in the words taken literally, though he provides a reading that features the arch of salvation history, which my three subsequent readers adopt. For Cyril, at this level the passage provides teaching about Jews and non-Jews

---

1. Origen is an exception, for after he struggles with the literal text he eventually turns to deal with it at the nonliteral level to solve the difficulties he finds with the words at the level of the narrative.

2. Jesus's symbolic words about his food in 4:32 provide another example in which all four authors work on the nonliteral plane to interpret them. I have chosen not to include their treatments for this verse, however, because Jesus himself decodes his obscure words in the passage itself (4:34), and so as to avoid unnecessary repetition, for all four of these authors deal similarly with his explanation. This is another instance in which the passage both introduces an allegory and provides its explanation. For all four authors, Jesus's food is to do the will of his Father. For Cyril and the Antiochenes, the immediate narrative context also indicates to them that the Father's will in this instance is for the Samaritans to come to saving faith in Christ; see Origen, *Comm. Jo.* 13.203-249 (Heine, 111–19); Chrysostom, *Hom. Jo.* 34 (Goggin, 333–34); Theodore, *Comm. Jo.* 4:32–34 (Conti, 43); Cyril, *In Jo.* 4:32–34 (Maxwell, 130–32).

within the overarching narrative of salvation history, and Jacob's well in 4:6 presents a type for the present church's practice of venerating the saints. In this chapter I will demonstrate that not only do both Alexandrians provide nonliteral interpretations, but in addition to the passage's instruction about salvation history, both find beneficial instruction above the letter that relates directly to their own church setting, which is absent from the Antiochenes' treatments.

As in the previous chapter, I will begin with Origen's extensive treatment of the passage. We do not have his comments on 4:1–12, which he claims to have treated in the now lost book 12 of his commentary, but his extant treatment of the rest of the narrative gives us approximately one hundred pages of Greek text to work with from book 13 (*Comm. Jo.* 13.1–363 [Heine, 69–143]). Just as we saw in his treatment of the cleansing of the temple narrative, in his comments on the Samaritan woman at the well Origen frequently quotes and refutes Heracleon's readings of John 4. In his verse-by-verse treatment of the passage, he moves frequently between the literal narrative and his nonliteral treatment of it, though he spends a great deal more time at the nonliteral level, which he describes with several apparently interchangeable terms, such as the text's "anagogical sense," "allegorical sense," and its "spiritual meaning." Furthermore, within his nonliteral treatment of the passage, he provides a discussion of the benefits (as well as the limits) of Scripture.

I will first examine the benefits he finds at the literal level. Once I have demonstrated what he does with the text at this level, I will examine the shifts he makes at various points to the nonliteral level, followed by the benefits he draws from the text at the nonliteral level. Origen finds three main uses for the passage before he moves above the letter to the nonliteral level. First, the passage is full of doctrinal instruction, which refutes heretical teachings, particularly Heracleon. Second, the characters of the story provide examples for his readers to follow. Third, at this level, he draws out teaching about Jesus's fulfillment of Old Testament passages.

I will begin with Origen's treatment of the doctrinal aspects of the literal narrative, for this is where he places the greatest emphasis. I will examine the verses on which he makes comments that concern doctrine in the order of the biblical narrative. As he deals with Jesus's words in 4:22, "You worship what you do not know, but we worship what we know because salvation is from the Jews," Origen claims to have the gnostic Heracleon in view (*Comm. Jo.* 13.101–118 [Heine, 89–92]). Before dealing with the reading of his opponent, Origen sets out his own understanding of the referent of the verse's "you," which he says, "taken literally [ἐπὶ τῇ λέξει] means the Samaritans," and of the "we," "the Jews according to the letter [ἐπὶ τῷ ῥητῷ]."[3] Note that he is explicit here that he is operating at the literal level. Having given his own reading, Origen then charges Heracleon with misunderstanding what is for him an important aspect of the literal level. According to Origen, Heracleon took the word "you" in a way that is "peculiar and contrary to the natural sequence of the words [ἰδίως καὶ παρὰ τὴν ἀκολουθίαν τῶν ῥητῶν]," by which he means "the 'plain sense' of words in combination" (the unit of the sentence in this verse).[4] One must not attend to the individual words of the literal text alone, but also to the meaning of the words in combination with one another. According to Origen, Heracleon's failure to do so leads to his misunderstanding of the natural referent of "you" and to identify it with either the Jews or the gentiles, but not the Samaritans. Thus, the distinction Jesus makes between Jews and Samaritans is obscured. Misunderstanding of this aspect of the literal level of the verse has, according to Origen, disastrous results. For in 4:22, Jesus says, "in a straightforward manner" (ἄντικρυς φάσκοντος) that "salvation is from the Jews," which confirms for Origen that the God of Abraham, Isaac, and Jacob is "the fathers of the Jews," a teaching that the heterodox deny to their peril. He adds further evidence to corroborate his understanding of the literal level of the passage: the Savior fulfills the Law and the Prophets. Therefore, Jews and gentiles, he says, have the same God; the law is not abolished but established through faith, and thus, he asks his rhetorical opponent, "is it not clear [σαφές] how 'salvation' comes 'from the Jews'?" (*Comm. Jo.* 13.106–107 [Heine, 90]). According to Origen then, it is important not to misunderstand ἡ ἀκολουθία of literal words of this verse, which he describes here as "the natural sequence of the words," for in this case it leads to misunderstanding God and the role of the Old Testament within the arch of salvation history.

Origen comments extensively as well on the doctrinal implications of Jesus's words, "God is Spirit" in 4:24. In this case, while he ends up giving

---

3. Origen, *Comm. Jo.* 13.101 (Heine, 89). In this passage Origen also summarizes his nonliteral interpretation of the verses as well, in which the Jews are taken as the church, which he describes here and in *Princ.* 4.3.6, 9 as "spiritual Jews" and the Samaritans are the heterodox, such as Heracleon. I will explore this in much more detail below. Cf. *Comm. Rom.* 6.12.6.

4. Origen, *Comm. Jo.* 13.102 (Heine, 89). See Young's discussion of the grammatical notion of sequence in *Biblical Exegesis*, 172, 189.

4:24 a nonliteral interpretation, he begins at the literal level where he goes to great lengths to deal with the verse, trying to find doctrinal meaning.[5] However, in this instance he not only cannot, but he also believes the verse to have been doctrinally misused, and thus he must of necessity move to the nonliteral level, where he solves the problem by providing a reading that is not directly doctrinal at all, or at least it is not about the doctrine of God.

According to Origen, a failure to understand these words results in a failure to understand the divine essence. He begins by claiming that, "In this passage it is stated as if his essence were spirit." For Origen, the problem with taking the words "literally, making no inquiry above the letter [ἁπλούστερον, μηδὲν πέρα τῆς λέξεως]," is that they suggest that God has a body (*Comm. Jo.* 13.124–125 [Heine, 93]). Such a claim leads to absurd conclusions, such as those of the Stoics, for whom there is no incorporeal reality, and thus a "spirit" is the purest form of corporeal existence, or those of Christian interpreters under Stoic influence, for whom spirit and fire are bodies. According to Origen, however, if God has a body, then he is mutable and corruptible, and therefore the interpretive options are clear: he can either accept the blasphemous things that the "preserving of the literal meanings [τηροῦντας τὰς λέξεις]" requires, or he can "examine and inquire what can be meant when it is said that God is spirit, fire, or light."[6] In other words, to his mind, the words "God is spirit" are like other cases of scriptural anthropomorphisms, where one must "change what is written into an allegory [μεταλαμβάνομεν εἰς ἀλληγορίαν τὰ γεγραμμένα]," and thus, he claims rhetorically, it is "clear indeed" (καὶ δῆλόν γε) that the words must be treated "consistently" (τὸ ἀκόλουθον) with our practice in such cases.[7] Origen concludes that at the nonliteral level, the words "God is spirit" refer to God's power to make a person spiritually alive; the divine power "entrusts itself to the abode in the soul" of the person deemed worthy (*Comm. Jo.* 13.143 [Heine, 98]).

---

5. In fact, he devotes approximately ten pages of Greek text to the verse, in sharp contrast to the other three authors, who devote only a few sentences to it (Origen, *Comm. Jo.* 13.123–153 [Heine, 93–100]); cf. *Princ.* pref. 9; 1.1.1–2. This example complicates my argument that these authors tended to deal with doctrine at the literal level.

6. Origen, *Comm. Jo.* 13.130 (Heine, 95); cf. *Cels.* 6.70.

7. Origen, *Comm. Jo.* 13.131 (Heine, 95). I will not discuss in detail here the fact that in his extensive wrestling with the literal words, Origen compares what could be meant by "God is Spirit" with what could be meant by the literal words "God is a fire" and "God is light." The claims that God is fire or light also indicate that God has a body. For these comments see *Comm. Jo.* 13.132–139; cf. *Comm. Jo.* 13.136, 140–146.

We are given further indication that Origen feels the need to account for going beyond the letter of the text to deal with these words, for he goes on to claim, perhaps rhetorically, that "we need more training ... that we may be able more attentively and in a way more worthy of God to understand how God is light and fire and spirit, so far as this is humanly possible."[8] In defense of his reading, he asks, "But who could more properly speak to us about who God is than the Son?" for it is the Son who alone knows the Father (Matt 11:27), and it is the Son's words in 4:24 that have caused such interpretive difficulty (*Comm. Jo.* 13.146 [Heine, 99]). Thus Origen concedes here that it just might have to be sufficient that the Son himself has called the Father "spirit," and he exhorts his readers to trust Jesus's words about the Father.

Origen draws another benefit concerning doctrine from the literal level, namely, its capacity to refute what he considers a heretical reading of Heracleon. Having provided his own explanation of the words "God is spirit," Origen returns to the literal level, which becomes clear only after he has dealt (at the literal level) with the next verse, 4:25, at which point he claims, "but this is enough on the literal sense [ταῦτα μὲν ὡς πρὸς τὴν λέξιν]" (*Comm. Jo.* 13.162 [Heine, 102]). Origen begins by telling his reader that for Heracleon the words "God is spirit" mean that "his divine nature is undefiled, pure, and invisible [ἀόρατος]."[9] Origen is suspicious that his opponent could come to such a conclusion, however, given that he understands the verse's following words "those who worship must worship in spirit and in truth" to indicate that those who worship God spiritually are "of the same nature with the Father [τῆς αὐτῆς φύσεως ὄντες τῷ πατρί] and are themselves also spirit." For Origen, the implications of such a literal interpretation are impious, for if the worshipers' nature is the same as the one who is worshiped, the interpreter implies that, for example, God is capable of committing fornication.[10] Origen does not provide his own understanding of the words "those who worship must worship in spirit

---

8. Origen, *Comm. Jo.* 13.144 (Heine, 98). For similar (even if rhetorical) confessions of his inability to deal with particularly difficult passages, see *Hom. Exod.* 4.2; *Hom. Num.* 1.3.5; *Hom. Ezech.* 13.3.1.

9. Origen, *Comm. Jo.* 13.147 (Heine, 99). This is the same kind of literal interpretation that each of my later three authors provide the words.

10. Origen, *Comm. Jo.* 13.148, 150 (Heine, 99–100). Origen goes on to argue that not even the Son and the Spirit are "comparable with the Father in any way," therefore humans are certainly not of the same nature as God; see *Comm. Jo.* 13.151–153.

and in truth" in response to Heracleon in this context, but instead proceeds to articulate what is for him an orthodox understanding of the relationship between the members of the Trinity, so as to demonstrate just how disastrous is Heracleon's suggestion that the worshipers of God share his nature.[11] Unlike Heracleon, Origen argues, "we are obedient to the Savior who says, 'the Father who sent me is greater than I' (John 14:28)" (*Comm. Jo.* 13.151–153 [Heine, 100]). He provides his famous apparently subordinationist Trinitarian statement: "This is why we say the Savior and the Holy Spirit transcend all created beings, not by comparison, but by their exceeding preeminence. The Father exceeds the Savior as much (or even more) as the Savior himself and the Holy Spirit exceed the rest" (*Comm. Jo.* 13.151 [Heine, 100]). In other words, he argues, if the Son and the Spirit do not share the same essence as the Father, as in his view Scripture itself demonstrates, how could the faithful interpreter suggest that created beings could do so?

As I said above, for Origen the literal narrative is not only beneficial in its provision of doctrinal instruction and simultaneous refutation of heresy; it also provides other benefits, such as examples set by the narrative's main characters, Jesus and the Samaritan woman. In both instances, Origen is explicit that it is the literal level of the text that offers this kind of instruction. For Origen, Jesus's conversation with the Samaritan woman concerning "great matters" in 4:26–27 shows him to be exemplary in that he is meek and lowly of heart. To introduce this teaching, Origen says, "But let us learn from him on the basis of the literal meaning [ἐπὶ τῷ ῥητῷ]." Unlike Jesus, Origen tells his reader, "we" are proud and arrogant, forgetting that each person has been made in the image and likeness of God, of which Jesus's conversation with the Samaritan woman reminds us (*Comm. Jo.* 13.166–167 [Heine, 103–4]).

For Origen, the Samaritan woman herself is also an exemplary (and "apostolic") figure from whom we can learn, for once she learns that Jesus is the Messiah, she leaves her water jar and goes to her city to tell its inhabitants immediately (4:28–29) (*Comm. Jo.* 13.169 [Heine, 104]). In fact,

---

11. He deals elsewhere with these words of 4:24; see Origen, *Comm. Jo.* 13.109–110, 146 (Heine, 90–91, 99). For Origen, "true worshipers," however, worship the Father not in the "types" of the law, but in reality, having partaken of "the spirit that makes alive," and following the "spiritual meanings of the law" (Rom 3:27–31). True worshipers, then, have been inspired by the Holy Spirit and can thus interpret the law aright.

Origen claims, the Evangelist John includes the detail about the water jar "not to no purpose" (οὐ μάτην), for at its "literal level" (κατὰ τὴν λέξιν), the detail demonstrates her eagerness to benefit the many rather than complete her humble task of drawing water, which is "related to material things."[12] At the literal level, then, Origen claims, the Evangelist John challenges the reader through her example to "forget things that are more material in nature and leave them behind, and be eager to impart to others that benefit of which we have been partakers" (*Comm. Jo.* 13.174 [Heine, 105]). I will demonstrate below that Chrysostom spends a great deal more time on this beneficial aspect of the text than does Origen.

Finally, Origen's treatment of 4:25 demonstrates a third use that Origen finds in this passage at the literal level, namely, instruction about the relationship between Jesus's ministry and the Old Testament. As he deals with the Samaritan woman's words "I know that the Messiah is coming, who is called the Christ," he discusses for his readers the Samaritan canon, which consists of the Torah only, and lists a string of passages from the Torah that he suspects have led the Samaritans to expect a messiah.[13] Origen then cites Jesus's words in John 5:49, "If you believed Moses, you would believe me, for he wrote about me" in order to affirm this Samaritan interpretive tradition before claiming himself that "one can find, therefore, that most of the things recorded in the law refer typically and enigmatically to the Christ [τυπικῶς μὲν οὖν καὶ αἰνιγματώδως ἀναφερόμενα εἰς τὸν Χριστον τῶν ἀναγεγραμμένων ἐν τῷ νόμῳ πλεῖστα ὅσα ἔστιν εὑρεῖν]." Having presented for his reader these examples, which he argues are "plainer and clearer" (γυμνότερα δὲ καὶ σαφέστερα) than any others, he states, as we have mentioned above: "But this is enough on the literal sense [ταῦτα μὲν ὡς πρὸς τὴν λέξιν]" (*Comm. Jo.* 13.161–162 [Heine, 102–3]). Here then we have a very clear example indeed of one of our authors providing instruction for his audience concerning Jesus's fulfillment of the Old Testament, which he claims is part of the passage's literal level. This Chrysostom and Cyril do as well.

Having drawn adequate benefit from the literal narrative, Origen moves above the letter, where he spends most of his interpretive energy, and I will now examine Origen's treatment of the passage at the nonliteral

---

12. Origen, *Comm. Jo.* 13.173 (Heine, 105). Origen describes her as "an apostle, as it were [Οἱονεί δὲ καὶ ἀπόστολος]" here.

13. Origen, *Comm. Jo.* 13.154–163 (Heine, 101–3); he lists Gen 49:8, 10; Num 24:7–9, 17–19; Deut 33:7.

level. I will note Origen's explicit shift from the literal to the nonliteral level along the way. At the nonliteral level Origen draws out three main kinds of instruction, two of which relate directly to the present situation of the church in his day, and one concerning salvation history as he deals with the harvest parable in 4:35–38. The first such teaching has bearing on the relationship of the church to the heterodox other, particularly with respect to their competing approaches to scriptural interpretation.[14] The second relates to the role of Scripture within the soul's journey to the Father, and it is in this context that Origen discusses the usefulness of Scripture.

For Origen, the overarching nonliteral meaning of the passage is its instruction about the church's relation to the heterodox. His treatment of 4:22, "You worship what you do not know, but we worship what we know, because salvation is from the Jews," presents this clearly. Origen tells his reader that, "The 'you' taken literally, means the Samaritans," but then he moves explicitly to suggest that, "in the anagogical sense it means [ὅσον δὲ ἐπὶ τῇ ἀναγωγῇ] those who are heterodox concerning the Scriptures."[15] Likewise, Origen continues, "the 'we' according to the letter means the Jews" but "taken allegorically means [ὅσον δὲ ἐπὶ τῇ ἀλληγορίᾳ] I the Word, and those formed in accordance with me, who have salvation from the Jewish words."[16] In other words, for Origen, at the nonliteral level, the Jews of the passage represent those who understand the (Old Testament) Scriptures as being fulfilled by Christ, namely, the members of the orthodox church. Such a reading Origen provides explicitly as he deals with 4:20, "you say in Jerusalem is the place to worship": "And what else would the city of the great king, the true Jerusalem, be than the Church that is built of living stones?"[17]

Within this nonliteral treatment of the passage, as he interprets 4:13–14, he indicates that he understands Jacob's well to represent Scripture itself and proceeds to compare the two waters, that of the well and that of the living water offered by Christ, claiming that the Samaritan woman at the well is "a representation" (εἰκών) of the heterodox, who "busy themselves

---

14. Origen deals with the meaning of Jesus's living water of 4:13–14 within this overarching interpretation of the passage.

15. Origen, *Comm. Jo.* 13.101 (Heine, 89); cf. *Comm. Jo.* 13.6.

16. Origen, *Comm. Jo.* 13.101 (Heine, 89); cf. Origen, *Comm. Jo.* 13.81.

17. Origen, *Comm. Jo.* 13.84 (Heine, 85). He might also mean that "we" represents all those within the church who understand Old Testament Scripture aright.

concerning the divine Scriptures."[18] According to Origen, even though the Samaritan woman drank from the well, she still had thirst and therefore asked for Jesus's water, which for Origen represents Jesus's teachings.[19] Thus, within his nonliteral reading, Origen holds the well of (Old Testament) Scripture and the living water of Jesus's teachings in contrast.

Given that Origen separates the teachings of Scripture from those of Christ, he must explain Scripture's purpose in the life of the Christian, which he does here in terms of its usefulness.[20] Scripture is useful (χρήσιμον) in that it stirs up the thirst for righteousness that only Jesus's teachings can fill, and therefore, it is good to drink first from the fountain of Jacob. According to Origen, this Jesus himself indicated when he sat at the well and asked the woman for a drink (John 4:7), which he would not have done if Scripture were not useful for the initial stages of spiritual development (*Comm. Jo.* 13.23–24 [Heine, 73]). Even so, he continues, Scripture is where one begins, and thus it is the more simple and innocent "so-called sheep of Christ" that begin with the "elementary rudiments of and very brief introductions to all knowledge [στοιχεῖά τινα ἐλάχιστα καὶ βραχυτάτας εἰσαγωγάς ... τῆς ὅλης γνώσεως]" contained in the Scriptures.[21] However, there are teachings that surpass it, and this narrative reveals the difference between the benefits of Jesus's teachings and the benefit that is derived from the Scriptures, even if "accurately understood" (νοηθῶσιν ἀκριβῶς) (*Comm. Jo.* 13.26 [Heine, 74]). For, Origen argues, some of "the more lordly and more divine aspects of the mysteries of God [τὰ κυριώτερα καὶ θειότερα τῶν μυστηρίων τοῦ θεοῦ]" are not contained in Scripture, as is evidenced by the examples of the Evangelist John and the apostle Paul, who

---

18. It seems that for Origen wells often stand for Scripture; see Origen's *Hom. Gen.* 7.5–6; 10.3; 11.3; *Hom. Num.* 12.2.5. In *Comm. Cant.* pref., he calls this Old Testament book itself a well, for it "holds the living water." Quotation from Origen, *Comm. Jo.* 13.6 (Heine, 70).

19. Origen, *Comm. Jo.* 13.6–7 (Heine, 70). For my other three authors, it represents the Holy Spirit.

20. He does so at length; see *Comm. Jo.* 13.23–42. See Mitchell's brief treatment of this passage (*Paul*, 35–37). She examines Origen's use of various Pauline verses within the section of book 13, an aspect of his discussion that I have not dealt with here.

21. Origen, *Comm. Jo.* 13.39 (Heine, 76); cf. 1.30, 60–61, 68. In this context, Origen also mentions those who are wise in their scriptural interpretation, such as Jacob and his sons, and those who interpret incorrectly, namely, gnostic interpreters; cf. *Princ.* 4.2.1–6 and my discussion of the tripartite division of believers depending on spiritual maturity in the introduction.

were forbidden from recording the unspeakable things they had heard.[22] Both figures can say, "we have the mind of Christ" (1 Cor 2:16), and thus the things beyond Scripture are revealed to them.[23] Therefore, whereas the well water of Scripture leaves one in want, the living water of Jesus's teachings, which is beyond Scripture, provides understanding that wells up to eternal life, and, he continues, perhaps it allows one to go even beyond eternal life, to the Father himself.[24]

The Samaritan woman herself provides an illustration of the person on this journey to the Father. When she asked Jesus for the water he offered her, she received it and could now, apart from Jacob's fountain, "contemplate the truth in a manner that is angelic and beyond man [θεωρῆσαι τὴν ἀλήθειαν ἀγγελικῶς καὶ ὑπὲρ ἄνθρωπον δυνηθῇ]."[25] Before she could go up from the Scriptures to the water Jesus offered, the Samaritan woman had

---

22. Origen, *Comm. Jo.* 13.27–29, 32–35 (Heine, 74–75). He alludes here to Rev 10:4; 2 Cor 12:4; and 1 Cor 6:12.

23. Origen, *Comm. Jo.* 13.35 (Heine, 75). Given that Origen frequently claims throughout his exegetical endeavors that he has been given "the mind of Christ," thus likening himself to these apostolic figures, it is probable that he is providing here an implicit defense of his own nonliteral interpretation of Scripture, as we noted that McGuckin has argued. See McGuckin, "Structural Design," 452–57.

24. Origen, *Comm. Jo.* 13.16, 19 (Heine, 72); cf. *Comm. Jo.* 13.31, 37; *Hom. Isa.* 7.3. However, in *Comm. Jo.* frag. 36, Origen defines Jesus's living water as the Holy Spirit, which is the most common interpretation of these words in the early church. As Wiles has demonstrated, there were two main ways of understanding Jesus's living water in the early church, and both can already be found in Origen (*Spiritual Gospel*, 45). Eusebius followed Origen in identifying the living water as Jesus's teachings in *Dem. ev.* 6.18.48–49. Irenaeus identified the Holy Spirit as the referent of the living water in *Haer.* 3.17.2. We will see below that Chrysostom, Theodore, and Cyril do likewise. One outlier of the tradition is Cyprian, who thought the living water was a reference to baptism; see Cyprian, *Ep.* 63.8. However, Origen provides additional interpretations for Jesus's living water elsewhere; see *Or.* 15.3. Here Origen discusses the line, "deliver us not into temptation" of the Lord's prayer and says that the one who has living water in his soul, has the divine thoughts formed in the soul of him who studies to become spiritual, by his contemplation of the truth; cf. *Comm. Rom.* 8.5.6; cf. also *Hom. Ezech.* 13.4.2, *Hom. Gen.* 12.5, and *Hom. Num.* 12.1.3–5, 7 where Christ himself, and not simply his teachings, seems to be the living water.

25. Origen, *Comm. Jo.* 13.42 (Heine, 77). Angels have no need of Scripture, for each has in themself a fountain of water leaping to eternal life, revealed by the Word himself and by Wisdom herself. See my forthcoming article on Origen's presentation of angels in relation to Scripture and his own exegesis: "Angels, Scripture, and the Exegesis of Origen," *Patristica Nordica Annuaria* 34 (2020): 27–50.

"engaged very diligently" with the fountain of Jacob, in order to gain an accurate understanding of Scripture (*Comm. Jo.* 13.30, 37 [Heine, 74, 76]). Therefore, at the nonliteral level, the Samaritan woman provides an illustration of the person who has made such progress vis-à-vis Scripture and Jesus's teachings.

Origen draws from this passage at the nonliteral level a related benefit, namely, its refutation of the heterodox, and specifically gnostic scriptural interpretation. As I observed above, before she believes in Christ, the Samaritan woman is for Origen an image of the heterodox, who do not have the superior teachings of Christ, and thus while they read Scripture intensively, they continue to thirst (*Comm. Jo.* 13.15–16, 19 [Heine, 72]). Origen's interpretation of the Samaritan woman's husband (4:16–18) demonstrates well this aspect of his nonliteral reading. Her husband represents for Origen "the law that rules the soul, to which each has subjected itself" (*Comm. Jo.* 13.43 [Heine, 77]). He explains how this is worked out within his understanding of the narrative in the following quotation:

> If, then, the husband is to be identified as the law, and the Samaritan woman has a husband because she has subordinated herself to some law on the basis of a misunderstanding of the sound teachings, a law by which each of the heterodox wishes to live, herein the divine Word wishes the heterodox soul to be exposed when she introduces the law that rules her, that ... she might seek another husband. He wants her to belong to another, to the Word who will be raised from the dead, who is not overthrown, nor will he perish, but he remains forever and rules and subordinates all his enemies. (*Comm. Jo.* 13.48 [Heine, 79])

In this reading, then, the Samaritan woman's husband represents her misunderstanding of sound teachings, to which her soul is subjected, and which the Word wishes to expose so that she might seek another husband, namely, Jesus, the Word of God.

Origen goes on in this vein to warn his readers that the Samaritan woman could also represent every soul who comes to the Scriptures. For he says, "I think that every soul who is introduced to the Christian religion through the Scriptures and begins with sense-perceptible things called bodily things [ἀπὸ τῶν αἰσθητῶν σωματικῶν λεγομένων ἀρχομένην] has five husbands"; each husband is related to one of the senses. After the soul associates with "the matters perceived by the senses," she wishes to rise to "the things perceived by the spirit," at which point, she may encounter false teachings based on "allegorical and spiritual meanings [ἀλληγορίας καὶ πνευματικῶν]," such as those provided by the heterodox (*Comm. Jo.* 13.51 [Heine, 80]). Thus the Samaritan woman's separation from her previous five husbands, and her subsequent association with her current partner provide for Origen a map of sorts for the soul's movement toward the Word, in which the soul begins with Scripture, understood in its literal or "bodily" sense, and then soon desires to move beyond the bodily sense to things "perceived by the spirit." This is the critical moment for Origen, for the soul's desire to move beyond the bodily sense of Scripture is the time in which she is most susceptible to the unsound teachings that are based on (heterodox) allegorical interpretations of Scripture. These unsound teachings are represented by the sixth husband of the Samaritan woman, against which every soul ought to be on guard.[26] Here then Origen indicates that not only are his readers to find in the passage a description of the heterodox gnostics, that is, the "other" outside the church, but they are also to turn inward so as to ascertain whether or not they themselves have been held captive by unsound teachings.

This Origen develops on a more corporate level as he turns to interpret 4:21. Within his nonliteral reading, Jesus's words "neither on this mountain" refer to "the heterodox in their fantasy of gnostic and supposedly lofty doctrines." However, with Jesus's words "nor will you worship the Father in Jerusalem" he speaks of the limits of "the Church's rule of faith [τὸν δὲ κανόνα <τὸν> κατὰ τοὺς πολλοὺς τῆς ἐκκλησίας]," which will also be surpassed by the worship of the Father undertaken by "the perfect one," who will worship in a way that is "more contemplative, clearer, and more divine [θεωρητικώτερον καὶ σαφέστερον καὶ θειότερον]" (*Comm. Jo.* 13.98 [Heine, 88]). In other words, for Origen true worship goes beyond grasping the doctrines derived through the application of the interpretive rubrics of both the heterodox and the church, and it is only achieved by a group of perfect individuals.[27]

---

26. Such unsound teachings, which are based on allegorical and spiritual interpretations of Scripture, are represented by Heracleon's exegesis of John, which Origen includes so as to refute them throughout his own *Commentary on John*, as we have seen.

27. Origen undoubtedly considers himself to be part of this group, and here again we see evidence of McGuckin's thesis that in book 13 Origen refutes both the heterodox and literalist interpreters within the church. He argues that the heterodox teacher Heracleon, whom Origen refutes in great detail here, is not really his main concern. Instead, Origen is concerned to defend his own interpretive skills, which some within the church have called into question. McGuckin proceeds to reconstruct the situation that led Origen to compose book 13, in which news has begun to spread about his

Origen concludes his overarching nonliteral interpretation of the passage as he turns to deal with 4:28, in which the Samaritan woman leaves behind her water jar to tell the inhabitants of the city of Sychar about Christ (4:28). This action signals for Origen that in its "anagogical sense" (ἀναγωγὴν σκοπητέον), she leaves behind her previously held opinions and the teachings of the heterodox, having received some of the living water promised by Jesus. By leaving her jar and going to her fellow Samaritans with her message, she "obtained benefit" for those who dwelt also in the city of "unsound doctrines" (*Comm. Jo.* 13.175, 181 [Heine, 105, 107]). In fact, it is "not difficult" (οὐ χαλεπόν), Origen claims rhetorically, "to see how those who have been frustrated with false teachings leave the city of opinions, when they happen upon sound teaching."[28] Thus on the nonliteral plane, the passage provides proof of the superiority of Jesus's (and by extension the church's) teachings over those of the heterodox, for once the Samaritan woman and her fellow Samaritans of Sychar encounter Christ, they leave their previously held teachings behind.

Finally, Origen deals at length with Jesus's symbolic teaching about the harvest in 4:35–38. As we saw in the previous chapter, here Origen finds problems with the words as understood at the literal level, which lead him to provide a nonliteral interpretation (as we would expect given his comments in book 4 of *Princ.*), which provides beneficial teaching concerning both the drama of salvation history, and the work of the Word in the individual soul.[29] Origen begins by claiming that Jesus's words, "Do you not say that there are yet four months and the harvest comes? Lift up your eyes and see the fields, for they are already white for harvest," are "spiritual"

---

recent trip to Athens, where he encountered one Candidus, a contemporary gnostic thinker who challenged an unprepared Alexandrian. This leads to Origen's comparison of the literalists within the church to Heracleon, the unfaithful gnostic interpreter; see McGuckin, "Structural Design," 452–57. While I am not comfortable following the details of McGuckin's reconstruction of this situation, we do see hints throughout his treatment of John 4 that Origen uses his refutation of Heracleon to charge the literalists, or "the simple ones" in the church, with infidelity to the text.

28. Origen, *Comm. Jo.* 13.340 (Heine, 141); cf. 13.343 where he continues on the nonliteral plane and claims concerning 4:40–41 that "to enter a city of the Samaritans is to be engaged in some knowledge falsely so-called (1Tim 6:20) of those who claim to devote themselves to the words of the Law or the Prophets or the Gospels or the apostles."

29. Origen, *Comm. Jo.* 13.250–326. This amounts to approximately twenty-four pages of Greek text.

(νοητά) and "lacking meanings that are literal and factual [γυμνὰ αἰσθητῶν καὶ σωματικῶν]" (*Comm. Jo.* 13.250 [Heine, 120]). Such an assessment of the literal words is based on his calculations of John's chronological "sequence of the account" (τὸ ἀκόλουθον τῆς ἱστορίας) of harvest time, which Origen claims is "cramped," given the number of Passovers John recorded in this time frame.[30] It could not possibly have been harvest time when Jesus spoke these words; in fact, Origen argues, "it is obvious [δῆλον] that it was winter" when he spoke them (*Comm. Jo.* 13.251 [Heine, 120]). Therefore, he claims, these words of Jesus require "a clearly allegorical explanation [ἀλληγορῆσαι σαφῶς]," and I will examine it here.[31]

I will begin with the referents he finds for "the fields, white for harvest" of 4:35. "These fields are already white for harvest," he says, "when the Word of God is present clarifying and illuminating [σαφηνίζων καὶ φωτίζων] all the fields of the Scripture that are being fulfilled by his sojourn." In addition to the first referent of the "white fields" concerning Jesus's present fulfillment and clarification of the Scriptures, however, Origen supplies another: perhaps the fields also represent "all the beings that are perceptible to the senses, including heaven itself and the beings in it." Thus, with these words, Origen says, Jesus urges the disciples to lift up their eyes both to the fields of Scripture and to the fields of "the purpose in each of the things that exist," for the light of truth is omnipresent. The work of harvesting, then, is for Origen, the work of the Word, who by his coming "clarifies the interpretation of the Scriptures [περὶ τῆς σαφηνείας τῶν γραφῶν τρανής]" or his work in the human person, so that it refers to "the way in which everything that God made can be said to be very good" (*Comm. Jo.* 13.279, 280, 284, 297 [Heine, 126, 127, 130]).

He assigns referents to the reaper and the sower of 4:36–37 as well.[32] The sowers are Moses and the prophets, "who wrote for our admonition" (1 Cor 10:11), by proclaiming the coming of Christ. Those who reap are the apostles, who saw Christ's glory, a glory that "agreed with the intel-

---

30. Origen, *Comm. Jo.* 13.259 (Heine, 122); cf. 13.269.
31. Origen, *Comm. Jo.* 13.270 (Heine, 124). I suspect that Origen is well aware of the fact that this John's Jesus here uses a figure of speech, but he feigns ignorance for the sake of his desire to move above the letter. My three subsequent authors provide the same interpretation as that given by Origen, though none of them does so because of the supposed difficulties of the literal words. Instead they each observe that Jesus's words are figurative and act accordingly.
32. He also explains the rewards of each in 13.298.

lectual seeds of the prophets" concerning him. These seeds were reaped by the apostles' understanding and explanation of "the mystery that has been hidden from the ages, but manifested in the last times" (Eph 3:9).[33] Now concerning Jesus's statement that the sower and reaper will "rejoice together" in 4:36, Origen thinks it obvious that this will occur in the age to come, as the Evangelist Matthew makes clear when he says, "many will come from east and west and recline with Abraham and Isaac and Jacob in the kingdom of heaven" (Matt 8:11); but perhaps, he claims, such an occasion has already taken place at the transfiguration (Matt 17:1–13).[34]

Origen concludes his treatment of these symbolic words by inviting his readers, that is, those who are "genuine disciples" of Jesus, to find their place within the drama of the parable, for he exhorts them, "let us also lift up our eyes and see the fields sown by Moses and the prophets … to see their whiteness and how it is possible already to reap their fruit and gather fruit to eternal life" (*Comm. Jo.* 13.308 [Heine, 132–33]). His readers are to search the Scriptures that have been sown by Moses and the prophets and illumined by the Word, in order to join the apostles in reaping and gathering the spiritual meanings to be found there, with the assistance of the Word's illumination. As I mentioned above, my other authors take up this same interpretation in their treatments of the passage.

In Origen's extensive discussion of John 4, he draws out various and sundry benefits. At the literal level both Jesus and the Samaritan woman provide examples for his readers to follow, and he dealt with the passage's doctrinal instruction and Jesus's fulfillment of Old Testament Scripture. At the nonliteral level, the Samaritan woman and her fellow Samaritans represent the heterodox, whereas the Jews represent the church. The nonliteral level, within this framework, provides instruction about the role of Scripture within the individual soul's journey to Christ. Again, the Samaritan woman provides a helpful illustration of the person who is on such a journey, for she herself moved from a rigorous engagement with Scripture to the living water of Jesus's teachings. For Origen, the harvest parable instructs the reader concerning the place of the church within salvation

---

33. Origen, *Comm. Jo.* 13.305 (Heine, 132); cf. 13.320–321. Origen also provides a discussion of whether or not the prophets understood the obscure teachings the Spirit spoke through them. He introduces this with the device of the hypothetical interpretive opponent, but does not resolve the issue; see *Comm. Jo.* 13.314–319.

34. Origen, *Comm. Jo.* 13.309–310 (Heine, 133). For at the transfiguration, the reapers Peter, James, and John were present alongside the sowers, Moses and Elijah.

3. The Samaritan Woman at the Well of John 4

history beginning with Moses and the prophets to the time of the apostles, in addition to its instruction about the work of the Word within each field of the receptive individual soul.

Chrysostom provides his treatment of the passage in four lengthy homilies, which amount to approximately twenty-two columns of Greek text (*Hom. Jo.* 31–34 [Goggin, 296–341]). As I mentioned above, once again in his treatment he remains at the level of the literal narrative, though again he is not explicit about this. However, it is telling that he draws out the same benefits in his treatment of John 4 as did Origen within his literal treatment of the passage, and as we saw above, Origen did in fact claim explicitly that he was operating at the literal level as he provided these readings. Like Origen, Chrysostom provides an explicit discussion of Scripture's benefits in the context of his treatment of this passage. He moves verse-by-verse through the text, as is typical, commenting on textual and doctrinal issues, providing background details such as the historical relationship between Jews and Samaritans, and clarifying Jesus's symbolic speech. Again, in each homily devoted to the passage, he dedicates the last section to exhorting his hearers toward virtuous lives. In this case, his exhortation relates directly to the passage at hand, for he instructs his readers to embody the virtues displayed by the Samaritan woman and the disciples, concerning which I will say more below.

For Chrysostom, John 4 provides various benefits at the level of the narrative. In fact, this he claims explicitly as he rebukes his parishioners for their neglect of that which would provide them with "help and profit" (ὠφελείας καὶ κέρδους), that is, the contents of the books of Scripture.[35] The Scriptures, he argues in this context, are beneficial in their provision of remedies for the passions of the soul, and in their provision of advantageous exemplary figures, whose just lives are to be imitated (*Hom. Jo.* 32.3 [Goggin, 320]).

There are five distinct kinds of benefit that Chrysostom draws out of the literal narrative. First, he draws out the benefit of the examples provided by the characters of the narrative, Christ and the Samaritan woman, as we saw Origen do above. Second, he deals with the passage's doctrinal teachings, such as the christological implications of Jesus's claim to worship the Father in 4:22 and the nature of God the Father as he comments on 4:24. Third, Chrysostom finds in the passage instruction about how

---

35. Chrysostom, *Hom. Jo.* 32.3 (Goggin, 319); cf. 57.1.

Jesus's ministry fulfills Old Testament Scripture. Fourth, for Chrysostom the passage provides beneficial instruction for his readers concerning the place of the gentiles within salvation history. Fifth, Jesus's words about his living water provide instruction about the role of the Holy Spirit in the life of the believer.

I will begin with Chrysostom's comments on the exemplary nature of Christ and the Samaritan woman, the latter of which he deals with at great length. In fact, he places the most emphasis on this aspect of his treatment of the text. We will begin with the example set by Jesus, who, according to Chrysostom, displayed his scorn for "a soft and easy life" by traveling by foot through Samaria, through which he "taught us to work with our hands, to be simple, and not to want many possessions." Similarly, as he treats the words, "Jesus, tired by his journey, was sitting by the well" in 4:6, and the words, "His disciples had gone to the city to buy food" (4:8), Chrysostom claims that "we learn both his endurance with regard to journeys and his disregard of food, and also how casually he treated the matter of food." Unlike Jesus, Chrysostom claims, "We take care of earthly needs before spiritual ones," so that "everything is upside down [ἄνω καὶ κάτω]" (*Hom. Jo.* 31.3 [Goggin, 304–5]). Like Jesus, he urges his parishioners, we ought to deal first with spiritual matters before providing for our material needs. Finally, as Origen said concerning Jesus's act of conversing with the Samaritan woman at the well, we learn from Jesus's "exceeding humility," for despite his exalted dignity, Christ spoke with a poverty-stricken Samaritan woman (*Hom. Jo.* 33.3 [Goggin, 328]).

I will now examine Chrysostom's comments on the Samaritan woman's example for his parishioners. In these comments he consistently compares the Samaritan woman's exemplary response to Jesus with the inexcusable response of the Jews, as presented throughout John's Gospel. For example, the Samaritan woman paid attention and listened to Jesus as soon as she learned who he was, "something which could not be said of the Jews," who did not desire to learn from him upon discovering his identity, but instead insulted him and drove him away. Similarly, her question in 4:12, "Are you greater than our ancestor Jacob, who gave us the well?" demonstrates a degree of understanding of the "lofty idea" Jesus communicates, unlike the Jews, to whom Jesus spoke about the same lofty ideas, from which they "derived no profit" (οὐδὲν ἐκέρδαναν) (*Hom. Jo.* 31.4 [Goggin, 308, 309]). When Jesus reveals his power by "acting as a seer" and tells her "Go, call your husband and come here" (4:16), says Chrysostom, she receives this proof of his power with "great wisdom," with "docility," and with astonishment, for she was hearing his words and seeing his power for the first time. The Jews, to the contrary, acted with neither docility nor wonder but with insults and threats to put him to death, despite having seen so many of his miracles.[36] Thus at almost every turn, Chrysostom praises the Samaritan woman, while denigrating the narrative's Jewish figures as examples not to be heeded.[37]

Chrysostom also provides his parishioners with specific ways in which they might embody the Samaritan woman's character traits. For example, just as the Samaritan woman "made such an effort to learn something beneficial [τι χρήσιμον] and stayed at Christ's side, though she did not know him," so also we, he says to his audience, "who know him, and are not beside a well, nor in a desert at midday," ought to "persevere in listening to anything that is said."[38] Chrysostom goes on: "Let us, then, imitate the Samaritan woman: let us converse with Christ. For even now he has taken up his stand in the midst of us, speaking to us through the Prophets and the disciples" (*Hom. Jo.* 31.5 [Goggin, 310]). So like the Samaritan woman, he asks his parishioners to listen and converse with Christ, presumably through the liturgy, the readings from Scripture, and his own homily that explains Scripture. Chrysostom finds another direct way in which his parishioners ought to imitate the Samaritan woman, this time based on her response to learning that Christ is a prophet. That this Samaritan woman, who had had five husbands no less, demonstrated "such deep interest in doctrine [τοσαύτην περὶ δογμάτων σπουδήν]," should make us blush, he says. The woman is therefore exemplary in her undivided focus on Jesus's teaching, unlike us, he says, who not only do not inquire about doctrine but are "indifferent and casual about everything" (*Hom. Jo.* 32.3 [Goggin, 318–19]).

Finally, just as we saw in Origen's treatment of the text, Chrysostom highlights the Samaritan woman's fervor and zeal, as she "left her water jar and went away into the town," in order to tell the people about Jesus (4:28–

---

36. Chrysostom, *Hom. Jo.* 32.2 (Goggin, 316–17). Chrysostom lists many more examples in 32.2–3 that I have not included here.

37. See *Hom. Gen.* 44.1–2 for a succinct presentation of his understanding of the Samaritan woman's exemplary virtue.

38. Chrysostom, *Hom. Jo.* 31.5 (Goggin, 310). Note that Goggin has "something worthwhile" where I have translated the text as "beneficial," given the emphasis of my argument. For Chrysostom, Jesus's words to the Samaritan woman and, by extension, to the reader in Chrysostom's day are beneficial.

29). For Chrysostom, she is a "fervent disciple," who was "on fire with zeal and prepared to risk any danger." Such zeal, he claims, is necessary to attain eternal life. Furthermore, in her encounter with Jesus the woman "attained to the fountain of truth," and thus scorned the fountain, which is "perceptible only to bodily senses" (Chrysostom, *Hom. Jo.* 34.1 [Goggin, 332]). This, Chrysostom claims, in a manner reminiscent of Origen, "was intended to teach us" that when listening to spiritual things, we ought to put aside material things.[39] In this the Samaritan woman demonstrated that she was even more willing than the apostles, for she left her water jar and worked as an evangelist without being called.

According to Chrysostom, another benefit to be found in the literal narrative is its doctrinal instruction, to which he devotes substantial attention as well. Chrysostom has different doctrinal difficulties than Origen to deal with, given the developments in Trinitarian theology since the time in which Origen was writing. Concerning Jesus's words to the Samaritan woman in John 4:22, "You worship what you do not know; we worship what we know, for salvation is from the Jews," Chrysostom thinks it necessary to deal with the christological issue posed by Jesus's self-identification with those who worship, for, he claims, "it is evident to all universally [παντί που δῆλον] that he is to be worshiped," and, he continues, worship "is the part of the creature." He solves the potential issue, however, by claiming that in this instance, Jesus speaks as a human Jewish man.[40] Chrysostom will go on, however, to explain for his parishioners that although Jesus has seemingly praised the tradition of his human ancestors, his praise is qualified by his subsequent (prophetic) statement, which Chrysostom understands as a declaration concerning the end of the Jewish holy rites. Even so, Chrysostom goes on to claim, like Origen, that with these words Jesus was "commending the Old Testament," and demonstrating that his ministry was not contrary to the law.[41] He does not name interpretive opponents such as Marcion or gnostics explicitly in his treatment of the verse, as we

---

39. Chrysostom, *Hom. Jo.* 34.1 (Goggin, 332). For Chrysostom too, she is to be compared with the apostles, as he says: "she herself did as the Apostles had done; nay, with even more alacrity than they.... She of her own accord, with no summons, left her water-jar and did the work of an evangelist."

40. Chrysostom, *Hom. Jo.* 33.1 (Goggin, 323); cf. *Hom. Matt* 63.1 where he cites 4:22 as words similar to Jesus's words "no one is good" in Matt 19.16. Here then Chrysostom solves the potential issue with recourse to partitive exegesis. Theodore deals with the verse in a similar manner, as I will demonstrate below.

41. Chrysostom, *Hom. Jo.* 33.1 (Goggin, 324–25). Chrysostom made the same

saw Origen do above, though he probably has such figures in view. In any case, despite the potential doctrinal issue posed by Jesus's claim to offer worship alongside his fellow Jews, Chrysostom draws from this verse beneficial instruction concerning the Son's agreement with the Father about the Old Testament law.

Like Origen, Chrysostom deals with the words "God is spirit" in 4:24, but he devotes only two sentences to the verse. For Chrysostom, the words mean "nothing else than that he is incorporeal [τὸ ἀσώματον]." Since God is "a spiritual being," he says, that which is spiritual in us, namely, the mind, must offer him worship (*Hom. Jo.* 33.2 [Goggin, 326]). According to Chrysostom, both the Jews and the Samaritans disregarded the soul and took too much care for the body, and so Jesus declared that it is by the mind that God is to be worshiped.[42]

Chrysostom finds a third kind of beneficial instruction at the literal level, which concerns the ways in which Jesus's actions in this passage fulfill Old Testament Scripture. This we saw in Origen's reading above as well. As he treats 4:6, "Jesus, wearied by his journey, was sitting by the well," Chrysostom claims that David foretold the simple way of life that Jesus modeled in this verse when he said, "From the brook by the wayside he will drink" (Ps 109:7) (*Hom. Jo.* 31.3 [Goggin, 304]). Similarly, as Chrysostom deals with 4:25, in which the Samaritan woman says, "I know that the messiah is coming," like Origen, he instructs his readers about the passages that declared Christ from the writings of Moses, the source of the Samaritans' messianic expectations. He lists Gen 1:26, "Let us make man in our image," and Gen 49:10, "the scepter shall not depart from Judah" for his hearers.[43] Therefore, it seems that for Chrysostom, instruction about Christ's fulfillment of Old Testament Scripture takes place primarily at the literal level.[44] We will see below that Cyril finds such beneficial teachings for his readers as he works with both the literal and the nonliteral levels.

---

argument as he treated John 2, and I will demonstrate below that he returns to it again as he deals with John 10.

42. He fills out what this means in his *Hom. Heb.* 11.5 where he cites John 4:24 in a discussion about spiritual worship: moderation, temperance, mercifulness, enduring suffering, and humbleness of mind; cf. *Adv. Jud.* 5.10; *Hom. Rom.* 2.1. Here he interprets the words, "for God, whom I serve with my spirit by announcing the gospel of his son" of Rom 1:9.

43. Chrysostom, *Hom. Jo.* 33.2 (Goggin, 326–27). He also lists Deut 18:15; Num 21:8; Gen 22; Exod 12.

44. I will highlight an exception to this in ch. 5, however.

Chrysostom discerns in the literal narrative another related kind of beneficial instruction for his hearers concerning the place of the gentile church within the arch of salvation history.[45] As he comments on 4:3–4, in which the evangelist tells us that Jesus withdrew from Judea to Galilee, a journey that caused him to pass through Samaria, Chrysostom finds occasion to discuss the place of the gentiles within salvation history. According to Chrysostom, Jesus went "to perform a significant mission among the Samaritans," and his withdrawal to Galilee was not "without purpose" (οὐ ... ἁπλῶς). Because the Jews had driven him away (4:1), Chrysostom claims, Jesus "took the gentiles in hand," and in fact, he continues, the Jews themselves "opened the door for the gentiles."[46] Chrysostom returns to this theme as he comes to 4:21–24, in which Jesus teaches the Samaritan woman about true worship. According to Chrysostom, Jesus's words "the hour is coming when you will worship the Father neither on this mountain nor in Jerusalem" (4:21) indicate that Jesus "declared their holy rites at an end," and furthermore, when Jesus says, "the hour is coming, and is now here, when the true worshipers will worship the Father in spirit and truth" he is "speaking of the Church, because it itself is the true worship, worship befitting God." He continues, claiming that God merely tolerated the worship of both the Jews and the Samaritans until he might guide them through Christ to the true worship. Paul helps him with this reading, for he quotes Rom 1:9, "whom I serve in my spirit in the gospel of his Son" and Rom 12:1, "present your bodies as a sacrifice, living and pleasing to God, your spiritual service."[47] For Chrysostom, this teaching about the cessation of Jewish (and Samaritan) worship and the culminating place of the church's worship within the arch of salvation history is part of the text's literal offerings. Cyril finds this teaching as he treats 4:4–5 as well, but according to him one must move to the nonliteral level to discern it.

According to Chrysostom, Jesus's symbolic words about the harvest in 4:35–38 provide further instruction about the arch of salvation histo-

---

45. I demonstrate below that the Alexandrians find this teaching above the letter.
46. Chrysostom, *Hom. Jo.* 31.2 (Goggin, 300); cf. 31.3 (Goggin, 306).
47. Chrysostom, *Hom. Jo.* 33.1, 2 (Goggin, 324, 325). We would expect both Theodore and Cyril to provide a similar reading. However, both have other concerns in their treatments of these verses, and both merely claim that both Jewish and Samaritan worship will end; see Theodore, *Comm. Jo.* 4:21 (Conti, 42); Cyril, *In Jo.* 4:23 (Maxwell, 127).

ry.⁴⁸ Chrysostom's treatment resembles Origen's, though it is less detailed and complex. Chrysostom does not claim to find the same problems with these words at the literal level as we saw in Origen's treatment; for Chrysostom they are uncomplicatedly "figures of speech" (αἱ τροποί), "an image" (εἰκόνος), and "a parable" (τῆς παραβολῆς), which had been given by the grace of the Spirit, "not by chance" (οὐ ἁπλῶς). He simply proceeds to clarify these words' meaning. For Chrysostom, "the field and the harvest signify [δηλοί] ... the multitude of souls ready to receive their preaching," for Jesus saw the Samaritans on their way to him and the "receptiveness of their dispositions." Thus, while we saw that for Origen, the fields could represent individual souls, he did not seem to have the Samaritans of the immediate narrative context as specifically in view as does Chrysostom here, and he placed more emphasis on the other referent he found for the fields, namely, the Scriptures. Chrysostom proceeds to identify the sowers as the prophets, and the reapers as the apostles, as we saw in Origen's treatment, and then he argues that Jesus showed that he himself gave the prophets their sowing mission and that therefore the Old and New Testaments are in agreement.⁴⁹ The Samaritans once again provide for Chrysostom the referent of the fruit of the parable, for they "assembled in a dense throng," which is why Jesus said "lift up your eyes and behold the fields are already white for the harvest" (4:35).⁵⁰ In Chrysostom's treatment we have a good example of Chrysostom finding the meaning of the figure of speech from the context of the narrative itself.⁵¹

As Chrysostom concludes his treatment of the harvest parable, he indicates in passing that he sees himself, and perhaps Christians in general, to possess a role similar to the apostles in the parable, for he says that the prophets are not "deprived of the pleasure accruing from their toils ... but they join with our pleasure and joy, even if they do not reap with us"

---

48. See my discussion of the authors' treatment of parable and metaphor in the introduction.

49. Chrysostom, *Hom. Jo.* 34.2 (Goggin, 334–35). Chrysostom also claims that in the parable, Jesus wishes "to intimate" (κατασκευάσαι) that it is the prophets' desire that people come to Jesus, and this is foreshadowed in the law too. Chrysostom (and Theodore) provides a similar interpretation of the good shepherd parable, which I examine in ch. 5 below.

50. Chrysostom, *Hom. Jo.* 34.2 (Goggin, 337); cf. *Hom. Matt.* 37.1, where he interprets the harvest parable in Matt 13:37–43. He deals with the problem of comparing the harvest in John's Gospel and that which is yet to come in the Matthean parable.

51. We saw Chrysostom articulate this interpretive principle in ch. 1.

(*Hom. Jo.* 34.2 [Goggin, 335–36]). This is a move similar to that which we saw Origen make above, though it is much less developed and seems not to be related to scriptural interpretation. However, both authors assume that their audiences are part of the salvation history drama presented by the parable.

The fifth and final benefit that Chrysostom draws from the literal narrative of the Samaritan woman at the well occurs in his treatment of another exchange in which Jesus speaks symbolically, this time with the Samaritan woman concerning the living water he has to offer (4:10–14).[52] Chrysostom finds here instruction about the work of the Holy Spirit in the life of the Christian. He tells his audience that "Scripture at one time calls the grace of the Spirit fire, at another, water, to show that these appellations are applicable [ταῦτα παραστατικὰ τὰ ὀνόματα] not to his substance [οὐσίας], but to his work [ἐνεργείας]."[53] The Spirit is not a literal fire, nor literal water, Chrysostom continues, and he is not "made up of different substances [ἐκ διαφόρων συνέστηκεν οὐσιῶν]," but he is "invisible and simple" (ἀόρατόν τε καὶ μονοειδὲς ὄν) (*Hom. Jo.* 32.1 [Goggin, 312]). These names that Scripture gives to the person of the Holy Spirit connote his actions, just as many of Scripture's anthropomorphic statements about God the Father connote his character and actions. Chrysostom's straightforward identification of the living water with the Holy Spirit suggests that it was a widely assumed tradition.[54] However, using Scripture to interpret Scripture, he does summon the assistance of John's explanatory gloss of Jesus's words about living water in John 7:38–39 as he deals with these words in John 4, "He said this, however, of the Spirit whom they were to receive."[55] Chrysostom claims that Jesus called the Spirit "water," to illustrate the purification and refreshment for the souls who receive it. The Spirit waters and "beautifies the well-disposed soul," causing it to bear fruit, preventing the feeling of despondency, and protecting it from "the wiles of Satan" (*Hom. Jo.* 32.1 [Goggin, 312]). We will see below that both Theodore and Cyril deal similarly with these

---

52. As I mentioned above concerning the harvest parable, see my discussion of the authors' treatment of parable and metaphor in the introduction.

53. We saw above in his treatment of the harvest parable that Chrysostom claimed in passing that Jesus speaks about the water in the same way he does the harvest, which he claims explicitly is "a parable" (*Hom. Jo.* 34.2 [Goggin, 312]).

54. See above for the early church's interpretation of Jesus's living water. Most interpreters associated the living water with the Holy Spirit.

55. Chrysostom, *Hom. Jo.* 32.1 (Goggin, 312); see a similar discussion in *Hom. Jo.* 50.1 on John 7:38–39.

verses, whereas for Origen they were subsumed within his overarching nonliteral treatment of the passage.

In conclusion to Chrysostom's treatment of the Samaritan woman at the well, we have seen that he found various benefits for his parishioners as he dealt with the literal narrative. The characters of the story, Christ and the Samaritan woman, provided examples to emulate, and despite the potential christological issue posed by Jesus's claim to worship in 4:22, the passage was doctrinally beneficial in that it provided instruction concerning Christ's divinity and God's incorporeal nature. The literal narrative also provided Chrysostom with the occasion to discuss how Jesus's ministry fulfilled the Old Testament, and the place of the church's worship within the context of salvation history, and about the regenerative work of the Holy Spirit.[56] Although we saw some overlap between Origen's and Chrysostom's treatments of the passage, we also saw that Origen spent most of his interpretive energy dealing with the passage above the letter, whereas Chrysostom worked with the passage at the level of the narrative.

Theodore's treatment of the passage is very similar to Chrysostom's, and considerably longer than his treatment of the cleansing of the temple narrative, though again, briefer than Chrysostom's. Except for one small fragment consisting of one sentence concerning 4:9, we have none of the original Greek of Theodore's treatment of John 4, and thus we must rely solely on the Syriac translation, of which we have about fifteen pages of Syriac text (*Comm. Jo.* 4:1–42 [Greek: Kalantzis, 57; Syriac: Conti, 39–44]). Like his fellow Antiochene, Theodore too provides a line-by-line literal treatment of the passage, in which he paraphrases the biblical text, solves potential problems, both textual and doctrinal, and clarifies Jesus's symbolic speech.

Like Chrysostom, Theodore draws several kinds of beneficial instruction for his readers from the literal narrative. First, he too finds the virtue of the Samaritan woman to be instructive.[57] Second, the passage has doctrinal instruction to offer as well. Third, Jesus's symbolic words about the harvest provide instruction concerning the arch of salvation history. Fourth, the other symbolic words of Jesus in the passage, which concern his living

---

56. This is as close as Chrysostom will come to discussing the nature of the sacraments in his treatment of John.

57. Unlike my other three authors, Theodore only addresses the exemplary nature of the Samaritan woman.

water, provide the opportunity for Theodore to discuss the role of the Holy Spirit in the life of the believer.[58]

As I examine Theodore's treatment of the narrative of John 4, I will begin, as he does, with his words about the virtue of the Samaritan woman. He is less explicit than my other three authors that she is to be emulated by his readers, but he does, nonetheless, draw his readers' attention to her positive behavior. For Theodore, "It is evident [ܝܕܝܥ] that the blessed John wanted to reveal the virtue of the woman through this story." He goes on to demonstrate, throughout his treatment of the passage, her integrity, her high esteem of Jesus, her wisdom, and her knowledge of torah and the messianic promises it contains. As he treats her words in 4:9, "How is it that you, a Jew, ask a drink from me, a woman of Samaria?" Theodore claims that they demonstrate her "great integrity" (*Comm. Jo.* 4:9 [Conti, 40]). For, he explains, it was not that the woman did not want to give water to a stranger out of meanness, but she wanted to warn him not to transgress the law (*Comm. Jo.* 4:10 [Kalantzis, 57; Conti, 41]). According to Theodore then, by her question the woman displays not only her integrity, but also her knowledge of Jewish torah. Similarly, concerning 4:11–14, Theodore claims that once the Samaritan woman has understood that Jesus did not ask for water so as to quench his thirst, but that he offered living water, she admirably "treated his words with the appropriate dignity" and asked for the living water he offered (*Comm. Jo.* 4:11–14 [Conti, 41]). Furthermore, once she understood that Jesus was teaching her "a new doctrine higher than the traditional one and superior to Jewish weakness" by his words about true worship (4:21–24), she responds appropriately, demonstrating her knowledge of messianic expectation (4:25) (*Comm. Jo.* 4:21–25 [Conti, 42]). Finally, according to Theodore, she displays her wisdom in the way she responds to Jesus's confirmation that he is the Messiah in 4:26, for she leaves her water jar and goes to the city to invite others to see Jesus. Once she arrives in Sychar, her cautious speech to the Samaritans also demonstrates her wisdom, for it indicates that she thinks her fellow countrymen should make their own judgment about Jesus (*Comm. Jo.* 4:26–29 [Conti, 43]). Thus for Theodore, as we saw in Origen's and Chrysostom's treatments of the passage, the behavior of the Samaritan woman is to be celebrated.

Theodore too drew doctrinal instruction from the literal narrative, and in his treatment of 4:21–24, he too saw fit to deal with some of the challenges

---

58. See my discussion of the authors' treatments of parable and metaphor in the introduction.

3. The Samaritan Woman at the Well of John 4   123

posed by Jesus's exchange with the Samaritan woman concerning worship and the nature of God. The words "salvation comes from the Jews" of 4:22 give him pause, as they did Origen and Chrysostom. Theodore makes clear for his reader that Jesus did not say, "in the Jews" but "from" them. For salvation, which he defines as "Christ-in-the-flesh," came from them, he explains (*Comm. Jo.* 4:22 [Conti, 42]). Like Chrysostom, then, Theodore makes clear that Jesus speaks in his humanity and not in his divinity in this instance.[59]

Concerning the words, "God is spirit, and those who worship him must worship in spirit and truth," Theodore argues that the time when God is worshiped in a way "appropriate to his nature" is here, for God is "incorporeal in nature [ܠܘܬ ܕܠܐ ܓܫܘܡ] and cannot be circumscribed into any place."[60] Thus, just as we saw in Chrysostom's treatment of the words, "God is spirit" in 4:24, for Theodore it is not a problem to understand them as referring to the incorporeality of God. Therefore, for Theodore, the "true worshiper" is the one who "honors him with the right intention" and believes "with a pure conscience that he can speak with the Infinite one anywhere."[61] Again, Theodore's comments on these verses are remarkably shorter than Origen's, just like his fellow Antiochene, Chrysostom's. Like Chrysostom, who focused on the aspect of humanity that allows for worship "in spirit" (i.e., the mind), Theodore claims that the right intentions (and a pure conscience, i.e., a virtuous life), and not the right place—"neither this mountain nor in Jerusalem"—are what counts in the worship of the incorporeal God, who cannot be circumscribed.

According to Theodore, as we saw in Origen's and in Chrysostom's treatment of the passage, Jesus's symbolic words in 4:35–38 provide instruction about the arch of salvation history, from the time of Moses to that of the apostles, though Theodore's treatment is characteristically brief. He is less explicit than Origen and Chrysostom about the parabolic nature of these words, but he does begin by claiming that with them Jesus is "alluding [ܪܡܙ]" not to a literal harvest but to the "better and more immediate

---

59. Here, then, we have an example of the two-nature exegesis he promised his readers in his preface, namely, his attention to the verses that relate to either Christ's humanity or divinity; see my discussion of this interpretive principle in ch. 1.
60. Theodore, *Comm. Jo.* 4:24 (Conti, 42); see also his comment on and use of 4:23–24 in *Comm. Phil.* 3:3, as he comments on the words "we who serve God in spirit and boast in Christ Jesus and have no confidence in the flesh."
61. Theodore, *Comm. Jo.* 4:24 (Conti, 42); cf. *Comm. Mich.* 4:1–3. There he cites John 4:24 to claim that Jewish worship has been replaced, and that good and bad worshipers are no longer defined by place but manner of worship; cf. *Comm. Mal.* 3:2–4.

harvest" of the conversion of the Samaritans, and thus like Chrysostom, he too has the immediate narrative context in view as he interprets the parable.[62] Theodore's interpretation of the harvest parable deals with the story of salvation history, as we saw in Origen's and Chrysostom's treatments; however, for Theodore, because of his earthly ministry, Jesus himself is the sower, rather than the prophets (*Comm. Jo.* 4:36 [Conti, 44]). For Theodore, the prophets are the "other laborers" of 4:38.[63] For even though Jesus called himself the sower, the teaching concerning the worship of God had clearly begun before his incarnation, and this through the prophets and the righteous ones who came after them, Theodore claims. In any case, he continues, the distinction matters not, for he initiated the prophets' labor, as well as that of the reapers of 4:36, who represent the apostles in his interpretation, for they too have received from Christ the preexistent Word, who, from the beginning, "portioned out the different phases of cultivation" (*Comm. Jo.* 4:38 [Conti, 44]). Theodore is thus much more explicit about Jesus's role in the sowing and reaping than Chrysostom and Origen, but like these earlier interpreters, the parable presents a picture of God's revelation of himself through his Son in salvation history. For Theodore, however, in contrast to Origen and Chrysostom, there is no indication that the parable is to draw his readers into the story; it simply instructs them about salvation history from the pages of Scripture itself.

Finally, like Chrysostom, Theodore finds useful instruction in the passage about the role of the Holy Spirit in the life of the believer, as he deals with Jesus's symbolic words in 4:10–14. Unlike the Samaritan woman, who "understood these words in a bodily sense [ܐܢܫܘܬܐ]," for Theodore, the words are properly understood, not in "a bodily sense," but in "a spiritual sense" (*Comm. Jo.* 4:10–14 [Conti, 41]). Like Chrysostom he identifies the living water with the Holy Spirit.[64] This water, he says, offers "perpetual refreshment" and "perpetual help," for it always preserves and prevents the one it indwells from perishing, so that the one who receives it will never

---

62. Theodore, *Comm. Jo.* 4:35–38 (Conti, 44). The words "not to a literal harvest" do not appear in the text, but they are implied.

63. I should note, however, that in the parable itself, the "other laborers" of 4:38 are indeed the sowers of 4:35.

64. According to Wiles, for Theodore, the living water is more clearly the activities of the Holy Spirit. This we saw in Chrysostom's statements explicitly. However, in the case of Theodore, at least in this Syriac translation, it is not so easily parsed out in my view (Wiles, *Spiritual Gospel*, 48); cf. *Hom. cat.* 10.9.

die. While Chrysostom dealt more with the action of the Spirit within the heart of the believer, Theodore focuses on the outward fruit of the Spirit's indwelling, saying that the one who has this living water, has "virtues superior to human nature." Furthermore, for Theodore, the Spirit's indwelling is the source of the hope of a future resurrection and perfect grace through participation in him.[65]

In conclusion to Theodore's treatment of the passage, we saw that he drew several kinds of beneficial instruction for his readers from the literal narrative: The Samaritan woman's virtue was instructive for his readers, as was Jesus's doctrinally laden conversation with her. As we saw in Chrysostom's treatment, Jesus's symbolic words concerning the harvest and living water provide instruction about salvation history and the Holy Spirit's work in the Christian's life, respectively.

Cyril's treatment of the narrative is lengthy; he deals with the passage in about thirty-eight pages of Greek text (*In Jo.* 4:1–42 [Maxwell, 116–34]). In his treatment as well Cyril provides both a literal and (several) nonliteral interpretations, which he describes as "types," though in 4:6, where Jesus sits at the well, he finds what he describes as both a "type" and "an enigma." Cyril spends significantly more time dealing with the literal narrative, which he explicitly claims is beneficial, particularly in its provision of the characters' exemplary behavior. In his verse-by-verse treatment, he too comments on potentially difficult verses—in particular, doctrinally difficult verses—and spends a great deal of interpretive energy treating Jesus's weariness at the well in 4:6 and Jesus's self-identification with the Jews and his words, "salvation is from the Jews" in 4:22.[66]

As mentioned above, Cyril draws out of the passage instruction for the spiritual development of his readers at both the literal and the nonliteral levels. As we have done in the case of our other three authors, we will first examine the benefits he finds at the literal level, before carefully examining his explicit shift to the nonliteral level and the benefits he finds there. Like the other three authors, at the literal level, Cyril draws out the passage's doctrinal teachings, and he also finds the narrative's characters to be exemplary in different ways. Along with the Antiochenes, he finds in Jesus's symbolic words about the harvest in 4:35–38 instruction about the arch of salvation history, and in 4:13–14, instruction for his readers con-

---

65. Theodore, *Comm. Jo.* 4:10–14 (Conti, 41); cf. *Comm. Jo.* 6:27 where he compares Jesus's words concerning food for eternal life with John 4:13–14.
66. I will deal with this in more detail below.

cerning the work of the Holy Spirit in the life of the believer.[67] Once Cyril has shifted to the nonliteral plane, he draws out further beneficial instruction concerning salvation history, this time with an emphasis on the role of the gentiles, as well as instruction about his present church's practice of venerating the Old Testament patriarchs.

As I did in the previous chapter, I will begin in Cyril's case with the passage's doctrinal instruction, for this is where he spends most of his interpretive energy. Indeed, Cyril spends a great deal more time than my other three authors on the passage's doctrinal teachings and simultaneous refutation of heresy.

My first example is a discussion Cyril has immediately following that of our previous paragraph, and it too is concerned with the words, "Jesus was wearied by his journey" of 4:6, "as it is written," an indication that Cyril here deals with the literal verse. Unlike the other three authors, Cyril comments on this verse at length. According to him, the verse refutes the Arians. Whereas the Jews are at fault for crucifying Jesus "in the flesh," he says, the Arians "slander the Word's ineffable nature itself."[68] In response to the Arian's use of the verse to claim that Jesus is subordinate to the Father, Cyril claims that Jesus's weariness "is proper to the human nature, not to the Word," and thus he resolves the potential issue with recourse to the partitive exegesis we have seen the Antiochenes use above.[69] However, lest anyone should think that this understanding of 4:6 "divide[s] the one Christ into a pair of sons [διέλῃς εἰς υἱῶν δυάδα τὸν ἕνα Χριστόν]," Cyril makes clear that Jesus "makes the experience of human nature his own [τὰ τῆς ἀνθρωπότητος εἰς ἑαυτὸν οἰκειοῦται πάθη]," whilst simultaneously remaining impassible. He concludes his classically Alexandrian treatment of the verse by saying, "In no other way could we know clearly that, while being God and Word, he became human, unless the impassible is recorded as suffering something and the highest as saying something humble" (*In Jo.* 4:6 [Maxwell, 118–19]). Cyril has dealt with the Arians, but also anyone who would charge him with an Antiochene treatment of the verse, such as

---

67. I will demonstrate below that the nonliteral passage as a whole provides such instruction as well.

68. Cyril, *In Jo.* 4:6 (Maxwell, 118); cf. Irenaeus, *Haer.* 3.22.2; 4.22.2. Irenaeus used this verse in his refutation of the docetists, in order to demonstrate that Jesus had a real fleshly experience.

69. Cyril, *In Jo.* 4:6 (Maxwell, 118). For his much briefer comments on other such verses in the passage, see Cyril, *In Jo.* 4:7–9, 17–19 (Maxwell, 119, 122).

that which would have been found in the writings of Diodore and Theodore, in which the two natures of Christ are discussed as such different entities that they appear to their opponents as "two sons."

Similarly, as Cyril treats 4:22, "You worship what you do not know. We worship what we know, for salvation is from the Jews," here too he says that Jesus is "speaking as a Jew and a human being," as is required in the situation at hand.[70] This interpretation the Antiochenes gave as well. Cyril too, however, must deal with Jesus's words "we worship," by which Jesus appears to count himself among the worshipers. Here again, Cyril solves the christological issue of the Son's worship of the Father, raised by a rhetorical (Arian) opponent, by claiming that Jesus worships as a man "since he became human" and in any case, "he is always worshiped with the Father since he was, is, and will be true God by nature." Here again, Cyril solves the christological issue of the Son's worship of the Father, raised by a rhetorical (Arian) opponent, by claiming that Jesus worships as a man "since he became human" and in any case, "he is always worshiped with the Father since he was, is and will be true God by nature." The Son, Cyril concludes, "does not worship as Word and God," but since he became human, he accepts the experience of worshiping God "in a way that befits a human being, because of the *oikonomia* with the flesh."[71] He concludes this discussion by asking rhetorically, "Is it not clear [καταφανές] to everyone from this statement that, since he uses the plural number and numbers himself among those who worship from necessity and servitude, he says these things on the grounds that he came to be in human nature, which is a slave?" (*In Jo.* 4:22 [Maxwell, 127]).

Concerning the words, "God is spirit" in 4:24, like Theodore and Chrysostom, Cyril does not regard them as problematic but treats them in one sentence, saying simply that Jesus speaks these words "in contrast to embodied nature [ὡς πρὸς ἐνσώματον ... φύσιν]."[72] Thus God receives the spiritual worshiper, who worships through achievements of virtue and "by the correctness of divine doctrine," and not the one who worships in

---

70. Cyril, *In Jo.* 4:22 (Maxwell, 123); cf. *Comm. Habac.* 3:2; *Rect.* 32.
71. Cyril, *In Jo.* 4:22 (Maxwell, 124, 126). Cyril deals with this verse and its misuse by heretics at length in ten pages of Greek text.
72. Cyril, *In Jo.* 4:24 (Maxwell, 127). He expounds 4:24 in a great many other places, however; see, e.g., *Resp.* 2, 10; *Ep. Calos.* 2–3; *Doctrinal Questions and Answers* 1–2; *Ep. Val.* 50.3.

a Jewish way, that is, "in form and types" (ἐν μορφώσει καὶ τύποις).⁷³ Note that it is Cyril alone of my four authors who explains that true worship is related to both correct doctrinal understanding and to virtue, though a virtuous life is implied in Theodore's comments.⁷⁴ Cyril's distinctive emphasis on worship as right doctrinal understanding is not surprising given his discussion of the doctrinal nature of John's Gospel and his promise to provide a fitting "doctrinal explanation" of the text. In any case, Cyril too, in his emphasis on understanding doctrine aright, instructs his readers that the arena for true worship is now located in the mind.

Lastly, as Cyril deals with Jesus's symbolic words in 4:34, "My food is to do the will of him who sent me and to complete his work," he claims to provide a "doctrinal explanation," which he had promised his readers in his preface.⁷⁵ In this instance, after he has dealt with the type and pattern provided by the verse, Cyril indicates that he is shifting to a different kind of interpretation by saying, "But if we must add something more doctrinal [δογματικώτερον προσβάλλοντας] to what we have already said," and then proceeds to discuss the words "him who sent me."⁷⁶ Clearly for him, as I have argued throughout this study, doctrine is to be dealt with separately from the passage's nonliteral meaning. Cyril begins his treatment of the words "him who sent me" by providing some options for the meaning of the Son's claim to be "sent." It could, he claims, "refer to the incarnation," or, "it could refer to the fact that, as Word, he proceeds in a way from the mind who begat him." In any case, for Cyril, the fact that Jesus was sent to fulfill the will of the Father does not imply Christ's subordination to the Father, for the Son himself *is* the Father's will, a fact that is "perfectly clear [καταφανές] to everyone." In response to yet another rhetorical opponent

---

73. Cyril, *In Jo.* 4:24 (Maxwell, 127). As I demonstrated above, Origen also described the Jewish manner of worship as that of "forms and types." Cf. *In Jo.* 7:8, where Cyril cites 4:24, claiming that Christ would naturally take pleasure in spiritual honors and offerings, since the others were a type of those who now worship in spirit; cf. *In Jo.* 8:46; 9:38; 15:3. He also uses John 4:21–24 extensively in his *Commentary on Zechariah*; see *Comm. Zach.* 8:3, 8; 9:9; 11:3; cf. *Comm. Mal.* 1:11.

74. In his treatments of 4:22 and 4:24, Cyril does not claim anything about the level of the text that he is working with, or the kind of reading he is giving, but I will argue that for him this has been the level of the narrative, for he does not indicate any kind of shift concerning the level until he arrives at 4:32.

75. Cyril, *In Jo.* 1.pref. (Maxwell, 3). See my comments on this aspect of his interpretation of John in ch. 1 above.

76. Cyril, *In Jo.* 4:34 (Maxwell, 131).

who says, "If the Son himself is the will of the Father, what 'will' was he sent to fulfill?," Cyril concedes, by saying that "The assigning of names does indeed demand a difference in the things signified." Rather than attempt to solve this conundrum of the seeming two wills, Cyril simply argues that "When it comes to God … a discussion of the highest nature is exempt from accuracy [τὸ ἀκριβές] in these matters." Thus Cyril provides a concession to the limits of human language in speaking of the divine nature and concludes by indicating that in the case of 4:34 the "will" of God refers to the divine intention to save the lost, "without differentiating" between the Father and the Son (*In Jo.* 4:34 [Maxwell, 131–32]).

Within his literal treatment, Cyril also spent significant interpretive energy explaining how the narrative's characters, Jesus and the Samaritan woman, are examples to be followed by his readers. This kind of instruction we have seen our previous three authors draw out of the narrative as well, and we will see below that Cyril describes this kind of instruction explicitly as "beneficial." For Cyril, however, the Samaritan woman's exchange with Jesus provides a "catechetical discourse" (τοῦ τῆς κατηχήσεως … λόγου), and thus her keen response to Jesus's teaching is to be followed by initiates into the faith specifically.[77] The Samaritan woman is exemplary in her hunger for knowledge, in her disregard for material needs, and in her desire to initiate others into her newfound faith. Concerning Jesus's words in 4:26, "I am [the Messiah], the one who is speaking to you," Cyril claims that Christ reveals himself to all those souls who want to learn and hasten toward the knowledge of the perfect, as exemplified by the Samaritan woman, who, despite her unrefined ideas about God, still had the desire to know something, receiving his accusations against her "as medicine for salvation." Jesus, therefore, rewarded her desire to learn, by revealing himself as the Messiah (4:26) (*In Jo.* 4:26 [Maxwell, 128]). In addition, the exemplary woman leaves her water jar and goes back into her Samaritan city as a result of her conversation with Jesus (4:28), for she now disregards the "necessities of the flesh" and embraces a new disposition marked by virtu-

---

77. Cyril, *In Jo.* 4:26 (Maxwell, 128). For a few scattered comments about her quick intelligence and the development of a vigorous mind leading up to Cyril's explicit statement that she is an example "for us," see *In Jo.* 4:12–13, 17–19 (Maxwell, 120–22). Perhaps this passage too provides evidence of Maxwell's theory, which we discussed above, particularly Cyril's treatment of Jesus's example for church leaders, which I will discuss below.

ous love for others.[78] While Cyril does not use the term *apostle* with respect to the Samaritan woman, as we saw Origen and Chrysostom do above, his comments are similar: she is "already a worker skilled in speaking who initiates others into the mysteries," as she skillfully speaks with the Samaritans (*In Jo.* 4:29 [Maxwell, 129]).

As I mentioned above, for Cyril, as we saw in Origen's and Chrysostom's treatments, Christ is an example to be followed.[79] This he says explicitly of Christ's humility as he comments on 4:22: "Do you see how the Son became an example [ὑπόδειγμα] of humility for us when, though he was equal to and in the form of the Father (Phil 2:5–8) … he came down for our sakes into willing obedience and humility?"[80] Unlike Origen and Chrysostom, however, Cyril's understanding of the passage as a "catechetical discourse" dictates that Christ is primarily an example for teachers of the church, just as the Samaritan woman was a model for catechumens. As he treats Jesus's revelation of himself to the Samaritan woman in 4:26, Cyril says to his readers,

> Therefore, let those who have the teaching task in the church entrust to the newcomers the message of catechesis for rumination, and thus let them finally show the newcomers Jesus as they lead them up from a little instruction to a more perfect knowledge of the faith. (*In Jo.* 4:26 [Maxwell, 128])

Just as Jesus led the Samaritan woman to greater and greater knowledge before finally revealing himself to her, so too must teachers of the church instruct catechumens, Cyril exhorts.[81] Cyril gives the leaders of the church another piece of instruction based on the example of Jesus's speech with

---

78. Cyril, *In Jo.* 4:28 (Maxwell, 129). Cyril describes the Samaritan woman's actions in this verse as a "type and sketch" (ἐν τύπῳ καὶ γραφῇ), but in this instance, Cyril uses "type" so as to indicate that she is an example. For a discussion of the different ways the word "type" is used by patristic authors, of which "example" is one, see Young, *Biblical Exegesis*, 201; see also Ward, "Symbolic Interpretation," 531–60. Ward discusses Clement's use of type as example on p. 535.

79. Cyril claims in passing that the disciples too ought to be "marveled at" in 4:28, for they demonstrate wisdom, understanding, and knowledge, when they refrain from asking Jesus why he is speaking with the woman (Cyril, *In Jo.* 4:28 [Maxwell, 128]).

80. Cyril, *In Jo.* 4:22 (Maxwell, 123); cf. *In Jo.* 4:10–11, 14–15.

81. The theme of church leadership will surface again in my treatment of the good shepherd parable in John 10.

the woman as he treats 4:27. Jesus is gentle and meek with this woman, and unlike others, who choose not to speak to women, Christ "extends his loving kindness to all," regardless of their sex. Accordingly, Cyril exhorts his reader, "Let the one who teaches in the church profit [ὠφελεῖν] from this as a model [πρὸς ὑπογραμμόν], and let him not refuse to help women" (*In Jo.* 4:27 [Maxwell, 128]). For Cyril, Jesus provides the church leaders with yet another useful example as he describes his "food" in 4:31–32. As he deals with these verses, Cyril makes the general comment that the Evangelist John "leaves out nothing which he believes will be at all useful [λυσιτελῆ] to the readers." In fact, he goes on to say that nothing has been placed in Scripture "in vain" (μάτην), but even a person's thoughts are sometimes "found to be pregnant with a profit [ὠδῖνον ἔσθ' ὅτε τὴν ὠφέλειαν εὑρίσκεται] that is not to be despised." Clearly the exchange of 4:31–32 is useful in Cyril's view, for here again, Jesus is "an example of the most remarkable behavior [ἀξιολογωτάτου πράγματος γεγονότα πάλιν ὑπογραμμόν]." His character is exemplary here, says Cyril, because Jesus is focused solely on the salvation of those who are called. This he does, according to Cyril, "so that he might thereby help the teachers in the churches and persuade them to disregard all weariness and to consider zeal for those who are being saved to be more important than care for the body."[82] Thus in his treatment of John 4, Cyril specifies just who within the church is to follow whom, and he explicitly names this kind of interpretation a benefit of the passage.[83] He does not claim explicitly that his interpretive work of drawing out the beneficial instruction from the examples set by the narrative's characters has been part of his literal interpretation, but I will demonstrate below that he makes an explicit shift to the nonliteral plane once he has drawn out the literal narrative's benefits. Finally, I should also note that for Cyril, the body of the

---

82. Cyril, *In Jo.* 4:31–32 (Maxwell, 130); cf. Cyril, *In Jo.* 4:34 (Maxwell, 131). Concerning Jesus's "dark saying" (σκοτεινὸν λόγον) about his spiritual food, Cyril claims that Jesus "introduces himself as a type [τύπον] for future teachers of the world" in that he thinks care for the body is secondary to "the task of the apostolic ministry." As I demonstrated in the case of his treatment of the Samaritan woman's neglect of things corporeal in 4:28, in which he used the term "type" to mean example, in this instance he does likewise.

83. Note that this is similar to Origen's belief that different aspects of the text are useful for different people. For him, however, the literal level of the text is useful for the spiritually immature, and the mature find benefit in the nonliteral level. For Cyril, the benefits he finds here, for the initiates and the teachers respectively, are at the literal level.

text, that is, its literal level, is useful in different ways for different groups within the church, unlike Origen, for whom the literal text is useful for the spiritually immature alone. I will show throughout this study that the Antiochenes make no such differentiation concerning the ways in which the text is useful for different kinds of members of the church.

Cyril finds another kind of beneficial instruction in the literal narrative concerning the arch of salvation history, as he deals with Jesus's symbolic words about the harvest in 4:35–38, as we saw in the Antiochenes' treatments as well.[84] He deals with the parabolic speech at some length. Cyril indicates that he understands these words figuratively by announcing that they are an example in which Jesus "takes the occasion for his discourse from what is going on at the moment" by which he "fashions an explanation of spiritual ideas [πνευματικῶν θεωρημάτων ἀναπλάττει διήγησιν]" (*In Jo.* 4:35 [Maxwell, 132]). Like the Antiochenes, he straightforwardly recognizes a parable that requires a fitting interpretation, whereas Origen claimed the words problematic at the literal level so as to move beyond the letter.

Before Cyril offers his treatment of the parable, he claims that his reader "will see the meaning [θεωρήσεις τὸ δηλούμενον]" because of "the likeness to the events in the narrative [ἀπὸ δὲ τῆς ὁμοιότητος τῶν ἐν ἱστορίᾳ πραγμάτων]." In other words, Cyril indicates that he is operating with the principle typically associated with the Antiochenes, that when a passage contains an allegory or parable, the text itself provides the interpretation of the parable. Having made this aside, Cyril proceeds with his interpretation of the parable. The symbolic words of Jesus in 4:35, "lift up your eyes, and see how the fields are already ripe for harvest," Cyril paraphrases to mean the following: "lift up the eye of your understanding a little from earthly affairs and behold that the spiritual [τὸν πνευματικὸν] sowing has whitened … and calls the reaper's sickle to itself." Like Origen and Chrysostom, he claims that the spiritual sowers are "the voice of the prophets," who tilled beforehand "the multitude of the spiritual ears" (*In Jo.* 4:35 [Maxwell, 132]). Cyril is not explicit here that he has the Samaritans in view as were the Antiochenes, but it is certainly implied given this identification of the fields with those who have spiritual ears.

Cyril continues with a great deal more attention to the details of the image: the sickle of the reaper is the "sharp word of the apostles, which cuts

---

84. Again, I discussed the authors' treatment of parable and metaphor in the introduction.

3. The Samaritan Woman at the Well of John 4   133

off its hearers from the worship prescribed by the law and transfers them to the threshing floor, that is the church of God." When the Logos comes, Cyril claims, he shows those who heard the Law and the Prophets that they are now fulfilled at his coming, and now in the words of the apostles, a reading that resembles that of Origen. For Cyril, with his words in 4:38, Jesus "reveals the whole mystery [τὸ σύμπαν ... ἀποκαλύπτει μυστήριον]" to the disciples, for Jesus "removes the cloak of enigma from his words [τὴν αἰνιγματώδη τῶν λόγων ἀποστήσας περιβολήν]," by claiming that both prophets and apostles receive credit for their mutual effort and thus, Jesus exhorts the apostles to honor the prophets who preceded them "in both labor and time" (*In Jo.* 4:35, 36–37, 38 [Maxwell, 132–33]). As we have seen in the previous three authors' treatments of the parable, for Cyril as well, these words instruct the reader about salvation history, from the time of the prophets to that of the incarnation and the apostolic ministry. He does not extend the referent of the reapers to include the church leaders of his own day, as we might expect, however.

Finally, let us now turn to Cyril's treatment of Jesus's words about his living water in 4:10–14, which for him, as for the Antiochenes, provide instruction about the work of the Holy Spirit in the life of the Christian. Cyril indicates his belief that these words are symbolic by commenting on the fact that the Samaritan woman thinks he speaks of the water that flows from the well, indicating that he knows better. The "living water" refers to "the life-giving gift of the Spirit," through which human nature can "run back up to the original beauty of its nature."[85] That is, claims Cyril, through the gift of the Spirit, human nature receives grace, and "blooms with all kinds of good things." Thus Cyril describes the Spirit's life-giving action within the life of the Christian in horticultural terms, in keeping with Jesus's symbolic description of the Holy Spirit as water, a common scriptural idiom.[86] Concerning Jesus's words of 4:14, "The water that I will give them will become in them a spring of water gushing up to eternal life," Cyril claims that anyone who partakes of the living water will have their own supply of divine knowledge springing up inside of them, "so that they no longer need admonition from others." Lest his readers thinks his words apply to just anyone, however, Cyril makes clear that the recipients of such living water were "the saints, prophets and apostles during their lives while

---

85. Cyril, *In Jo.* 4:10–11 (Maxwell, 120); cf. *In Jo.* 7:38–39; *Epistles to Anastasius, Alexander, Martinian, John, Paregorius, Maxiums, and Others*; *On the Creed* 40.

86. Cyril, *In Jo.* 4:10–11 (Maxwell, 120); e.g., he lists Isa 43:20–21; Jer 38:12.

they were still living on earth, and the heirs of their service," by which he probably means those given the task of church leadership, such as himself and possibly also his readers.[87] In fact, Cyril claims, the prophet Isaiah spoke about these saints and their heirs when he said, "draw water with joy from the springs of salvation" (Isa 12:3) (*In Jo.* 4:14–15 [Maxwell, 121]).

For Cyril, as for Origen, the passage has additional benefits to offer if one moves beyond the letter of the narrative; I now turn to examine them here. I will show that he provides 4:4–5 and 4:6 in particular with nonliteral interpretations. The types he finds in these verses provide beneficial instruction concerning the role of the gentiles within salvation history, and in 4:6 in particular, he also finds teaching that relates directly to the present church's practice of venerating the Old Testament saints, which he describes as both a type and an enigma, perhaps indicating that for him these terms are interchangeable. I will observe the explicit shifts that Cyril makes from the literal to the nonliteral level and vice versa as we proceed.

I will begin with the nonliteral treatment that Cyril provides the passage's introductory verses in which Jesus withdraws from Judea and goes through Samaria (4:1–5), for this is his overarching nonliteral reading. Once Cyril has dealt with the wording of 4:4–5, he shifts to the nonliteral level, claiming briefly that through Jesus's hastening "to the land of a different race," he "depicted typologically by the nature of his action [ἐν τύπῳ ζωγραφουμένη τῇ τοῦ πράγματος φύσει]" that the Jews will imminently lose God's grace completely and send Christ to others (*In Jo.* 4:1–5 [Maxwell, 118]). This passage, then, at the nonliteral level, is for Cyril primarily about the Jews' rejection of Christ and the subsequent inclusion of non-Jews within salvation history. This interpretation we saw Chrysostom provide as well, though for the Antiochene, it was part of his literal treatment of the narrative.

Cyril's only other move above the letter this time relates to the practices of his contemporary church setting. As he treats 4:6, "Jacob's well was there, and Jesus, wearied by his journey, was sitting by the well," Cyril begins with the nonliteral level and claims that Jesus shows us "in another type and enigma [ἐν τύπῳ καὶ δι' αἰνίγματος], that even though the gospel proclamation departs from Jerusalem, and the divine word goes out to the gentiles, love for the fathers will not be cast out along with Israel." That is,

---

87. Cyril, *In Jo.* 4:14–15 (Maxwell, 121). Perhaps he means bishops such as himself. See my discussion of this in ch. 1. He may also be referring to those given the task of instructing catechumens, as per Maxwell's theory.

by sitting at the well Jesus teaches in an enigma that the patriarchs such as Jacob are saints, and that they are not to be lumped together with those that Cyril perceives as the sinful generation of Israel. In fact, by sitting at the well, Jesus is "preserving to them the unfading grace they had in the beginning." Not only does Jesus's dwelling at the well provide this instruction about "the fathers" for Cyril, but it also shows him to be "a type for us [τύπον ἡμῖν]," and thus Jesus becomes the first to honor the fathers (*In Jo.* 4:6 [Maxwell, 118]). That is, Jesus's seat at the well provides a type for the present church's practice of the veneration of the saints, and particularly the patriarchs. In this passage, Cyril's use of the term "type" is not unambiguous; in the first assertion, Jesus's seat at the well teaches something about the role of the patriarchs within the story of salvation history that Cyril began to tell in his treatment of the preceding verses, and in the second, he provides for Cyril's readers a picture of the church's present practice of the veneration of the saints.[88] Once he has explained the type of the verse, Cyril returns to the literal level, to deal with the verse, "as it is written," which we examined above.

This concludes my treatment of Cyril's interpretation of the Samaritan woman at the well. We have seen that he found beneficial instruction for his readers at both levels of the narrative. Just as we saw in my previous three authors' treatments, at the literal level the passage provided exemplary characters to be followed by his readers in Jesus and the Samaritan woman. As we saw in Origen's and Chrysostom's literal readings, Cyril too draws out instruction concerning how Jesus's ministry fulfills the Old Testament. Again, as with my other authors, Cyril finds much doctrinal instruction in his literal treatment of the passage, in this case concerning the humanity of Christ in 4:6 and 22, christological teaching about how the two natures of Christ interact in 4:6, about the incorporeal nature of God in 4:24, and about Christ's divinity in 4:34. Again, as for the Antiochenes, for Cyril, the passage, particularly Jesus's harvest parable, provided instruction concerning salvation history and concerning the Holy Spirit's redemptive work (4:10–14).

---

88. I showed above that Cyril used the word "type" to connote "example" as I dealt with his literal treatment of the text. Cyril may also be using "type" here to indicate that Jesus provides an example for the practice of saint veneration. In this passage that is not as clear as it is in those I dealt with above or in some of the passages I will deal with in the next chapters below.

However, as in Origen's treatment of the passage, for Cyril too there was additional benefit to be found beyond the letter of the narrative; he provided nonliteral readings of 4:4–5 and 4:6 that instructed his readers concerning salvation history and present church practice. However, I should note that in this case his nonliteral interpretation was not as thoroughgoing as Origen's and he spent significantly more time at the level of the narrative than his third-century predecessor, possibly because the literal narrative provided a great deal of benefit in its own right.

CONCLUSION

In conclusion to this chapter as a whole, again all four authors found instruction for the spiritual development of their audiences at the literal level. Within their literal treatments, for example, despite the potential issue of Christ's claim to worship the Father in 4:22, each author found doctrinal instruction for their audiences. We also saw that all four authors found the Samaritan woman to be an example for their readers to follow, and for all except Theodore, Christ too was found to be exemplary at the literal level. Both Alexandrians and Chrysostom found instruction concerning Jesus's fulfillment of Old Testament Scripture. Chrysostom drew out additional instruction from the literal narrative concerning the place of the gentile church within the arch of salvation history as he dealt with 4:4–5.[89] Cyril and the Antiochenes found for their readers instruction about the arch of salvation history in Jesus's harvest parable and in Jesus's words concerning his living water. These three exegetes found similar beneficial instruction concerning the redemptive work of the Holy Spirit.

Again, however, the Alexandrians found additional benefit for their readers beyond the letter of the literal narrative. Origen and Cyril found the nonliteral text to be useful for their readers in its provision of further instruction concerning the place of the church within salvation history, but also in its capacity to speak directly to their own church settings. For Origen,

---

89. While it is worth noting that Chrysostom finds the passage's instruction concerning salvation history to be a feature of the literal narrative, whereas for Cyril, this reading is described as a nonliteral meaning, it is unclear why this is the case. Perhaps it is simply a commonplace reading of the narrative, and it is the immediate or "ready-to-hand" meaning that comes to his mind. We saw this kind of reading surface in Theodore's literal treatment of John 2, and I will demonstrate another example of this in the following chapter.

the nonliteral text teaches about the individual soul's journey to the Father vis-à-vis Scripture, in addition to its instruction concerning how the church is to relate to the heterodox. In Cyril's case, the nonliteral text instructs his readers about the church practice of Old Testament saint veneration.

As in the previous chapter, despite this overlap, the four authors' treatments of John 4 also demonstrate discernable differences between the two schools. First, the Antiochenes draw out instruction for the spiritual development of their audiences from the literal text alone. In this instance, they devoted the most attention to the exemplary nature of the Samaritan woman. Second, aside from Chrysostom's brief injunction to his parishioners to join the apostles in their reaping of the figurative ripe fields, we do not see the Antiochenes drawing from the text instruction that relates directly to their immediate church settings, as we saw in the Alexandrians' treatments. This distinction will become clear in my subsequent chapters as well, and indeed it is one of the most important distinctions between the schools that I will demonstrate in this study.

4
The Healing of the Man Born Blind of John 9

In this chapter I will examine the four authors' treatments of the story of the healing of the man born blind, which follows a dispute between Jesus and the Jews in John 8 concerning Jesus's claim to be the "the light of the world" (8:12). This statement Jesus confirms through his healing of the man born blind, in which he provides him with both spiritual and physical sight. Once again, this passage concerns, for these authors, God's rejection of the Jews and the inclusion of non-Jews within his people. The healing leads to the blind man's own dispute with the Jews, the Pharisees in particular. Jesus encounters the blind man as he exits the temple (9:1), and spits on dirt to make mud, which he then rubs on his eyes (9:6), an image that causes these authors to reflect on the divinity of Christ, the preexistent creator. The blind man is healed, however, only after Jesus orders him to go and wash in the pool called Siloam (9:7). This healing took place on the day of the Sabbath (9:14), a fact that caused much controversy among those present, not least, the Pharisees (9:8–34). The healed man's interactions with these Jewish leaders demonstrate, according to these authors, his exemplary faith and courage.

I will demonstrate that, as they deal with the literal narrative, the later three authors draw out beneficial instruction for their audiences concerning exemplary discipleship, based on the character of the man born blind and Jesus's disciples. Jesus himself also provides a virtuous example to be followed.[1] These three authors also find the passage doctrinally beneficial. For the Antiochenes, Jesus demonstrates his divinity by using clay to heal the blind man (9:6-7). For Chrysostom, Jesus's words in 9:4, "I must do the

---

1. In a couple of instances within the material on the passage from his *Homilies on Isaiah*, Origen provides interpretations that are quite similar to the literal treatment we saw him provide in the previous chapter. In this context, however, he does not claim to give a literal treatment of the passage, so I will be careful not to label it too hastily.

work of him who sent me" provide beneficial teaching concerning Jesus's unity with the Father. In the case of Cyril, the literal text is doctrinally beneficial in that it provides him occasion to discuss the relationship between Jesus's two natures as Jesus reveals himself to the blind man in 9:37. Finally, for Cyril, the passage is also useful in its instruction about Jesus's fulfillment of Old Testament prophecy.

While Chrysostom gestures toward a nonliteral interpretation of 9:6–7 with an ambiguous and passing comment, it is only the Alexandrians who draw out the narrative's usefulness at the nonliteral level. As I mentioned in the introduction, for Origen we have limited material on this passage, but we do have his nonliteral treatment of it. Once both Origen and Cyril have made explicit shifts to the nonliteral level, both find the passage to be instructive of the role of the gentile church within salvation history. However, both find additional benefits at the nonliteral level that relate directly to their readers. For Origen, the blind man also teaches about Christ's visitation and healing of the individual Christian soul. For Cyril, however, the passage also teaches about the church's sacrament of baptism.[2]

In this example, then, the main distinction between the two schools' treatments of the passage is that in Antioch the text is primarily useful at the level of the narrative, and neither Antiochene indicates that an explicit shift above the letter is warranted.[3] In the material with which we have to work from the Alexandrian side, both authors draw out instruction from the nonliteral level. This is all that we have definitively in Origen's case, and as for Cyril, the passage is useful at both levels. Both authors find nonliteral instruction concerning salvation history and, as I demonstrated in the previous chapter, instruction that addresses their immediate church settings directly.

I will again begin with Origen, whose comments on John 9 are not extant in his *Commentary on the Gospel of John*, and thus I will be working with his discussion of the passage from his *Homilies on Isaiah*, which provides us with about four pages of Jerome's Latin translation of the homilies.[4] While it is probable that Origen found much that was useful in the literal narrative of John 9 in his now lost commentary on the passage, we

---

2. See Wiles's description of Cyril and Origen's treatment (*Spiritual Gospel*, 35).

3. Of course, as I mentioned above, Chrysostom makes an unclear comment to this effect as he treats 9:6–7, but it is remarkably brief.

4. Origen, *Hom. Isa.* 6.3, 7 (Scheck, 910–13). Origen's treatment of John 9 would have been included in the now lost books 21–27 of his *Commentary on John*.

may have only hints of this in our material of focus. I am on surer footing with respect to his nonliteral treatment, concerning which it is probable that the reading he gives in the Isaianic homily would not be demonstrably different, even if abbreviated, from that which he would have provided in his original treatment in his John commentary.[5] I will begin with his introductory comments on the passage from Isaiah, in which he introduces our passage of focus, followed by an examination of that which I suspect might constitute his literal treatment of the story of the man born blind. I will demonstrate Origen's explicit nonliteral reading and the instruction it provides his readers, which in this context relates to the place of the gentiles within salvation history, and Jesus's healing of the individual Christian soul's blindness.

Origen introduces the narrative of John 9 within his treatment of Isaiah's prophecy in 6:9-10:

> You shall hear with hearing, and you shall not understand; and seeing you shall perceive, and you shall not see. For the heart of this people has become fat, and they have not heard with their ears with heaviness, and they have closed their eyes; lest they should see with their eyes, and hear with their ears, and understand with their heart, and be converted; I would heal them.

For Origen, these words prophesy about the events that took place at Christ's coming, about the witnesses of Jesus's miracles, and about the auditors of his teachings, for there were many who did not comprehend what they had seen and heard. As he explains the meaning of the prophecy, Origen states that the prophet Isaiah knew that there would be "two ways to hear his words" and that there would be a twofold issue, "one physical, the other spiritual" (*hoc est aliud eorum corporale, aliud spirituale*). It is here that he summons my passage of interest, for in the story of the man born blind, he claims, Isaiah's prophecy is fulfilled; when Jesus healed the man, "not everyone ... could in 'seeing,' immediately 'understand' why [the healing] was done."[6]

---

5. Furthermore, as I shall show below, Cyril's nonliteral treatment is quite similar to that offered by Origen in his homily on Isaiah, and this might also suggest that we are getting an abbreviated version of a similar interpretation in his original treatment in his now-lost section of the John commentary.

6. Origen, *Hom. Isa.* 6.3 (Scheck, 910-11). Prophetic "seeing" prompts his use of the man born blind in John 9 in a number of other instances as well, e.g., *Hom. Jer.*

The connection he has made between Isaiah's prophecy and Christ's ministry leads Origen to discuss the gospel literature itself, and he exhorts his reader to seek vision of the events of the gospels as well "in a twofold way" (*dupliciter*), both physical and spiritual. He proceeds to articulate his twofold approach to the gospels with these words: "each thing that was done in his body was the image and type of things to come [*similitude ... et typus futurorum*]" (*Hom. Isa.* 6.3 [Scheck, 912–13]). For Origen then, not only is Isaiah's prophecy twofold, but so also are the events of Jesus's ministry recorded in the gospels.[7]

Having established the twofold nature of the gospels, Origen turns to deal directly with the story of the man born blind. He begins by claiming that since he does not know "what man 'blind from birth' recovered his sight," the narrative presents "the image and type of things to come," and the people of the gentiles, who were "truly blind from birth [*caecus iste a nativitate*]" (*Hom. Isa.* 6.3 [Scheck, 913]). It seems that Origen is unsure whether there was truly a man born blind; in any case, he is sure about the referent of the type presented by the blind man.[8] Whereas Christ was said to have restored the sight of the blind man, in the case of the gentiles, Christ was also "anointing their eyes with his saliva," that is, the Spirit. Furthermore, just as Jesus sent the blind man to Siloam (which John tells us means "sent" [9:7]), likewise he "sent" the gentiles to the apostles and teachers (*Hom. Isa.* 6.3 [Scheck, 913]). Thus Origen's overarching nonliteral interpretation of the passage concerns the inclusion of the gentiles within salvation history, at least as he presents it in this homily on Isaiah.

As we mentioned above, for Origen, the story of the man born blind also provides additional instruction at the nonliteral level for the individual Christian soul, and by implication, for the relationship of the individual soul to the church. We too are "sent to Siloam," he says to his readers, "whenever we begin to be visited by Jesus to receive the sight of the soul."

13.12–17; 15.10. Origen's comments in these instances are much briefer. It is not clear in this context whether he sees the story of the man born blind's fulfillment of the prophetic passage in Isaiah as part of its literal meaning, though we saw in the previous chapter that he dealt with Jesus's fulfillment of Old Testament Scripture as he worked at the level of the narrative.

7. He makes such claims elsewhere; see *Princ.* 4.2.4–6; *Cels.* 2.69; *Comm. Jo.* 20.26; 10.35–36; *Hom. Luc.* 7.

8. Origen comes close to saying that the narrative of the healing of the man born blind is not plausible at the level of the narrative, as in his treatment of the cleansing of the temple narrative in John 2. However, there is not enough material here to be sure.

4. The Healing of the Man Born Blind of John 9

Jesus's healing of the blind takes place then at the individual level as well. However, Origen continues by adding to this nonliteral interpretation by instructing his readers that when "we are sent to Siloam," we are sent to the apostles and teachers of the church (*Hom. Isa.* 6.3 [Scheck, 913]). Therefore when Jesus comes to bring sight to the individual soul, the result will be their desire to heed the authoritative voices of the church, the apostles in Scripture, and their own church leaders.

Let us examine one final example. In this case, Origen does not use any of the technical terms he usually does to indicate nonliteral reading, and the interpretation he provides here resembles those we have seen him make at the level of the narrative in our previous chapter, though he does not label it thus. As Origen turns to interpret the words of Isa 6:10, "and they have closed their eyes, lest at some time they should see with their eyes, and hear with their ears, and understand with their heart," he returns once more to John 9 and draws on Jesus's statement to the Pharisees in verse 41: "If you were blind, you would have no sin; but now that you say, 'we see,' your sin remains" (*Hom. Isa.* 6.7 [Scheck, 917]). Concerning 9:41, Origen claims that it is much worse for those who have physical sight but have closed their eyes of their own accord than it is for those who were blind naturally and yet receive spiritual sight.[9] This claim has direct implications for his audience: In the reading of Scripture, he says, if a gifted and able soul does not meditate on the utterances of God, this soul is in darkness because it closes its own eyes (*Hom. Isa.* 6.7 [Scheck, 917]). In other words, in their reading of Scripture, his readers are not to emulate the Jews of John 9, who have become blinded to the Scriptures and thus fail to recognize Christ. His readers are to learn from the Jews' mistakes so that when they have the opportunity to encounter Christ in the reading of the Scriptures, they do not darken their own eyes.

For Origen, then, at least in the context of the sixth homily on Isaiah, the narrative of the healing of the man born blind, dealt with at the nonliteral level, provides instruction concerning the role of the gentiles within

---

9. A similar discussion can be found in his *Hom. Ezech.* 2.3.4 on Ezek 13:1–19. There he explains that one needs inner eyes to see Jesus, and that sinners see nothing. More generally, from the rest of Origen's corpus, we have a few other instances from which we are able to piece together aspects of his understanding of the story of the man born blind; e.g., as he discusses the title "the light of the world" (9:4–5) in his *Comm. Jo.* 1.162–168, 180, he states that Jesus has this title because he is the one who enlightens the intellects of men and spiritual beings.

salvation history, and instruction for the individual soul that receives Christ's visitation. He also considered the passage to fulfill Isaiah's prophecy in Isa 6:9–10, and he found in the narrative a negative example in the Pharisees, who claimed that they are not blind, despite the fact that their spiritual blindness is implied in the Johannine passage.

Chrysostom's exegesis of the narrative is relatively lengthy, consisting of four homilies and approximately nineteen columns of Greek text (*Hom. Jo.* 56–59 [Goggin, 85–123]). In this case Chrysostom provides the passage with a literal treatment, but he reads 9:6–7 in particular both literally and nonliterally; these verses he claims "conceal a great deal of meaning in their depths," and he summons the exegetical principle of Scripture's usefulness as part of his justification for this nonliteral reading. Again, he comments on the passage verse-by-verse, dealing with problems of meaning and doctrine, and in some cases simply paraphrasing the interactions between the man born blind and the Jewish leaders. As is his practice, Chrysostom concludes each of these four homilies on John 9 with a section of exhortation on topics not directly related to the passage at hand, such as the proper use of wealth, upright living, attentiveness in prayer, and the reading of the Scriptures.

At the literal level, the Antiochene finds the passage beneficial in two major ways. As expected, for Chrysostom, the narrative provides his audience with one primary model of exemplary behavior, that of the man born blind. The literal narrative also provides his audience with beneficial doctrinal teaching concerning Christ's divinity as evidenced by the healing in 9:6–7 and despite his claim to have been sent in 9:4. I will also demonstrate that he makes an explicit claim to move above the letter, which he justifies with recourse to the principle of Scripture's benefits, thus reflecting explicitly on his method of exegesis. His explicit move above the letter demonstrates that the beneficial instruction he drew from the text prior to (and again after) this juncture he considers to be a result of his literal treatment of the narrative. Once he is above the letter, he provides a brief nonliteral reading of 9:6–7 in relation to Christ's healing power through the water at Siloam.

I will begin with his literal treatment of the passage and deal first with the benefit provided by the exemplary behavior of the blind man, who demonstrates exemplary faith and discipleship.[10] According to this Antiochene,

---

10. Chrysostom also mentions briefly that Christ is exemplary in the narrative in that after he heals the blind man, he made himself scarce, demonstrating a "lack of vanity" (*Hom. Jo.* 57.2 [Goggin, 100]).

the exemplary faith of the blind man was indeed one of the primary reasons the evangelist John included the story in his narrative, and he draws this teaching out in all four of his homilies on the passage. For example, as he deals with 9:6–7, in which Jesus healed him by spreading the mud he made on the blind man's eyes and telling him to wash in the pool of Siloam, Chrysostom notes the blind man's trust in Christ. Strange as Christ's actions were, he says, the man did not hesitate or question him (*Hom. Jo.* 56.2 [Goggin, 93]). Again, the blind man submitted completely to Jesus despite the judgment of his contemporaries, and he obeyed Jesus's command to go to Siloam to wash. In fact, Chrysostom claims, Jesus commands him to go and wash his eyes "so that you might learn the faith of the blind man." Not only that, but after the healing also the blind man continued to stand firm in the face of peril, and "he neither denied nor contradicted his previous statements" (*Hom. Jo.* 57.1, 2 [Goggin, 97, 100–101]). He was therefore both steadfast and honest. In his final dispute with the people (9:24–33), the blind man serves yet again as an example, this time of the courage he demonstrated. According to Chrysostom, "this was certainly the act of a soul courageous in speech, lofty of ideals, and disdainful of their anger." In this exchange with his adversaries, then, the blind man demonstrated that following Christ is a dignity, and that what his adversaries took as insult, to him was an honor (*Hom. Jo.* 58.3 [Goggin, 112]).

Finally, in his treatment of 9:34, Chrysostom is most emphatic in his view of the exemplary blind man: he asks his parishioners, "Are you taking note of the messenger of truth?" Regardless of his lack of learning, says Chrysostom, this wise man endured great sufferings as he "bore witness to Christ by word and deed." Chrysostom then proceeds to claim explicitly that "these things have been recorded in order that we also may imitate [μιμώμεθα] him" (*Hom. Jo.* 58.3, 4 [Goggin, 115]). In other words, for Chrysostom, John included the narrative of the healing of the man born blind so that the church might receive the benefit of learning from this exemplary disciple, who was found to have spiritual sight, as opposed to the Pharisees of the passage, who were found to be spiritually blind (9:38–41) (*Hom. Jo.* 59.1 [Goggin, 122–23]). For, even though the blind man had never seen Christ, he was very courageous, and chose to be turned out of the synagogue rather than to betray the truth, claims Chrysostom.[11] We, on the other hand, he says to his parishioners, have

---

11. Chrysostom, *Hom. Jo.* 58.4 (Goggin); cf. *Hom. Jo.* 59.1.

seen miracles and "ineffable mysteries," and thus ought to show even greater courage than the blind man in the face of those who indict Christ and malign Christians so as to silence them. He concludes by suggesting that his parishioners might begin in the footsteps of the blind man by being brave and by paying greater attention to Scripture.[12]

I will now turn to examine the other kind of benefit that Chrysostom draws out of the passage, that of doctrinal instruction. For Chrysostom, the passage teaches primarily about the divinity of Christ. For example, as he treats Jesus's words in 9:3, "he was born blind so that God's works might be revealed in him," Chrysostom claims that Jesus is speaking of himself not the Father, for the glory of the Father had already been made manifest. That is, it was the Son's glory that was in focus, not the Father's. However, for Chrysostom it is 9:6–7 that indicate most clearly Christ's divinity, for in Jesus's act of spreading the mud he made with his spittle on the blind man's eyes, he evokes the creation account in Genesis in which man was formed from clay. Concerning this act, Chrysostom states that Jesus used clay for the healing "to teach that he himself was the Creator in the beginning of the world" (*Hom. Jo.* 56.2 [Goggin, 89, 91]). Again, Chrysostom argues, Jesus's hearers already knew that God created man from the dust of the earth (Gen 2:7), and so for this reason, Jesus made clay by mixing the earth with his saliva to heal the man born blind so as to reveal that he too created in the beginning.

Chrysostom also deals with the doctrinal implications of Jesus's words in 9:4, "I must do the works of him who sent me," which he paraphrases to mean the following: "I must manifest myself and do things that have the power to prove that I do the same works as the Father—not 'similar' works, but 'the same' ones, a proof of closer identity, and a fact predicated of those who differ from one another not even in a small way."[13] For Chrysostom, then, Jesus speaks here of his unity with the Father, and thus we are to learn from this passage not only Jesus's divinity, but also his unity with the Father in action and will. These words do not provide evidence of the problematic position of those who believe Jesus to be subordinate to the Father, according to this Antiochene.

---

12. Chrysostom, *Hom. Jo.* 58.4 (Goggin, 115). Perhaps also, by extension, he argues that they ought to pay greater attention to his own homilies on Scripture.

13. Chrysostom, *Hom. Jo.* 56.2 (Goggin, 91). Chrysostom highlights this teaching again as he deals with Jesus's words in 9:35, "do you believe in the Son of God?"; see *Hom. Jo.* 48.2.

4. The Healing of the Man Born Blind of John 9

As he interprets this passage, Chrysostom makes an explicit shift to the nonliteral level of the narrative, at which point it becomes clear that the rest of his treatment he considers to be part of his literal interpretation of the narrative. With his shift above the letter he summons the principle of Scripture's benefit. In his second homily on John 9, Chrysostom addresses 9:6–7 for a second time. He says:

> Those who are to gain any profit [καρποῦσθαι] from what they read must not skim over even the smallest part of the words ... because it seems that many texts, though their literal meaning is easy to comprehend [αὐτόθεν ὄντα εὔκολα], actually have a great deal of meaning concealed in their depths [πολλὴν ἐν τῷ βάθει διάνοιαν ἔχειν ἀποκεκρυμμένην].[14] Notice, in fact, how true this is in the present instance, also.[15]

Clearly for Chrysostom Jesus's actions and words in 9:6–7 indicate that in addition to the literal treatment we saw him give these verses above, a nonliteral treatment is warranted, and he uses the concept of the text's profit to justify his move beyond the literal text, as we have seen Origen do in our second chapter, and will see Cyril do below. I should note that despite his comment that "many texts" have "a great deal of meaning concealed in their depths," a comment that he (and indeed all four authors) made concerning John's Gospel specifically in his introductory homilies, in the material I have examined in this study, it is very rare indeed that he searches for this concealed meaning.

---

14. Here Chrysostom claims that the literal reading (that he provided in his previous homily) is easy to understand, but that there is also a deeper meaning, that requires more difficult and further searching with a nonliteral interpretation. Note, however, that he does not use the term θεωρία here. For another example of Chrysostom's nonliteral treatment of a New Testament passage, see his treatment of Matt 21:1–11 in *Hom. Matt.* 28; see Peter Widdicombe's discussion of Chrysostom's treatment of the passage in "The Patristic Reception of the Gospel of Matthew: The Commentary of Jerome and the Sermons of John Chrysostom," in *Mark and Matthew II: Reception and Cultural Hermeneutics: Reading Mark and Matthew from the First to the Twenty-First Century*, ed. Eve-Marie Becker and Anders Runesson, WUNT 304 (Tübingen: Mohr Siebeck, 2013), 105–19.

15. Chrysostom, *Hom. Jo.* 57.1 (Goggin, 96). Note Chrysostom's claim that careful reading of John is needed. Only the person who does not skim over the words will profit from the text. For a similar comment about the avoidance of "casual" (ἁπλῶς) reading, see *Hom. Jo.* 58.1. See also my discussion of such an exegetical virtue in ch. 1.

Perhaps the concealed meaning of the verses is self-evident to his audience, for Chrysostom does not explain this point in any detail, but repeats much of his previous treatment of the verses. That is, he argues that the healing demonstrates Jesus's divinity and agreement with the Father, the God of the Old Testament, in addition to its illustration of the blind man's faith (cf. *Hom. Jo.* 46.2). In this context, however, he adds an additional explanation of the verses, using Paul's identification of Christ with the rock Moses struck in the desert (1 Cor 10:4) as a second justification for his interpretation of the pool at Siloam. Like the "spiritual rock," says the Antiochene, "so also He was a spiritual Siloe," and that "it was the power of Christ which accomplished everything."[16] Thus we have an example in which Chrysostom feels he is justified in providing a nonliteral interpretation because of the analogous example of Paul's interpretation of the rock in the desert, the content of which happened also to involve Christ's miraculous use of water. Chrysostom concludes his nonliteral treatment of these verses by saying: "it seems to me that the suddenness with which he mentioned the water hints to us of an ineffable mystery [αἰνίττεσθαι μυστήριον ἡμῖν ἀπόρρητον]," which he explains briefly as "the unexpectedness of the manifestation of his power" (*Hom. Jo.* 57.1 [Goggin, 98]). He does not elaborate on this statement, and perhaps even more curiously, he does not make an association with the sacrament of baptism, but he simply moves to the next verse. One should not miss the fact that Chrysostom's treatment of 9:6–7 is the only instance in which either Antiochene author provides a nonliteral interpretation of any aspect of John 9.

Theodore's treatment of the passage is again fragmentary in the Greek, though we have more material to deal with than we had of his treatment of the previous two examples. We have fragments of his interpretation of John 9:1–9, 12, 15–22, 24–33, 35–41, which amounts to about twelve pages of Greek text, and I have therefore been able to work mostly with the Greek for his treatment of the passage (*Comm. Jo.* 9:1–9, 12, 15–22, 24–33, 35–41 [Kalantzis, 66–76]). In Syriac translation, the passage is fifteen pages, and I will draw on it where necessary (*Comm. Jo.* 9:1–41 [Conti, 83–89]). Theodore alone of my four authors deals with the passage at the literal level only, and he claims explicitly that the story of the healing of the man born blind is one that provides benefit for the reader. Much of his verse-by-verse treatment of the passage is, as in Chrysostom's treatment, paraphrase of

---

16. Chrysostom, *Hom. Jo.* 57. 1 (Goggin, 98). See my discussion of this interpretive principle in ch. 1.

the Jewish leaders' conversation with the man born blind, and he too deals with the passage's potential doctrinal and textual issues. I will first examine his comments concerning the beneficial nature of the passage before dealing with the benefits he draws from the literal narrative.

As he comments on 9:1–3, he claims that it is "quite clear" that the healing was "of great benefit" (χρήσιμος) to the blind man himself, for through it he received understanding of the only-begotten, and also that many others "were taught to prefer faith in Him above everything else."[17] Thus for Theodore, as for Chrysostom, the story teaches about appropriate faith in Christ through the example of the blind man, and about the divinity of Christ. I will show that he highlights these and other benefits throughout his treatment of the passage, and that his literal treatment is remarkably similar to Chrysostom's. Of my four authors, he is the only one who does not move beyond the literal level of the narrative.[18]

I will begin with his description of the behavior of the narrative's characters. Theodore draws his readers' attention to the behavior of both the man born blind and of the disciples. Let us begin with his brief comments about the disciples, who according to Theodore, "were moved by their pious thoughts, as well as by human nature," to ask Jesus, "who sinned, this man or his parents, that he was born blind?" (9:2).[19] For, he claims, it is through such questions that one learns "those things that lead to piety," and therefore Jesus indicates that such questions are appropriate (*Comm. Jo.* 9:1–2 [Kalantzis, 66]). In other words, for Theodore, the disciples rightly supposed that because God in his providence is in charge of human affairs, the circumstance of the man born blind could not be accidental. It was their human weakness, however, which led them to think about his sin as the only possible explanation for his blindness, and thus the disciples

---

17. Theodore, *Comm. Jo.* 9:1–3 (Kalantzis, 67). Devreesse's edition of the Greek fragments includes two parallel fragments containing Theodore's comments on 9:1–3. In the other fragment not quoted within the body text, Theodore uses the term λυσιτελής instead of χρήσιμος. I am drawing on both fragments in this paragraph.

18. He does not describe his treatment as literal using the terms available to him, but he does not indicate an explicit shift above the letter either, as we saw Chrysostom do above.

19. Theodore, *Comm. Jo.* 9:1–2 (Kalantzis, 66). I did not comment on Chrysostom's assessment of the disciples' question in 9:2–3 above, for he says only in passing that "this question was a blundering one," and goes on to refute the theology implied by their question with a series of scriptural verses; see Chrysostom, *Hom. Jo.* 59.1.

remain for him steadfast examples of virtue in their quest for piety, limited only by their human perspective.

Theodore too draws attention to the exemplary faith and wisdom of the blind man, though unlike Chrysostom, he does not dwell on this particular benefit to the same extent. When he comes to the blind man's final dispute with the Jews in 9:26–32, Theodore briefly tells his readers that "we must also admire his wisdom and his ability to garner arguments against [the Pharisees] on many different fronts" (*Comm. Jo.* 9:32 [Conti, 88]). Similarly, according to Theodore, in the course of his disputes with the Jews, the blind man demonstrated to Christ through his noteworthy faith that he was "worthy" to receive the knowledge of his divinity.[20] In addition, the blind man's worship of Jesus upon learning that he is the Son of God in 9:37–38, suggests to Theodore that his behavior is to be celebrated, for in this act of confession and worship the man was "showing through his deed the faith of his soul." Indeed, claims Theodore, the blind man "received his sight on both accounts, being enlightened both in faith and deed, while those who thought they were able to see … were shown to be blind—neither accepting the truth nor believing the very thing they saw with their own eyes" (*Comm. Jo.* 9:39 [Kalantzis, 75]). Thus Theodore highlights the exemplary faith of the blind man and, like Origen, demonstrates that the Pharisees of the passage are not to be emulated.

Like Chrysostom, Theodore also finds at the literal level beneficial doctrinal instruction, though again his comments are much briefer. In fact, only 9:6 elicits such a discussion. As he deals with 9:6, Theodore claims that Jesus needed the mud not only because he aimed to use "that through which all human nature was constituted from the beginning," but also, he claims, again like Chrysostom, "to reveal through it that he was the creator of humankind" (*Comm. Jo.* 9:6 [Kalantzis, 70]). It seems this is the major doctrinal lesson of the passage for the Antiochenes.[21]

Cyril's extensive treatment of the passage consists of seventy-three pages of Greek text (*In Jo.* 9:1–41 [Maxwell, 21–55]). He deals with the difficulties presented by such verses as 9:3, which he felt had been misused by heretics. In his treatment as well, like Chrysostom, Cyril finds occasion to discuss the exegetical principle of Scripture's benefits as he deals with Jesus's symbolic words in 9:4–5, a passage I examined in the introduction. Unlike Chrysostom, however, Cyril evokes the principle so as to remain at

---

20. Theodore, *Comm. Jo.* 9:35–36 (Kalantzis, 74–75); cf. *Comm. Jo.* 9:34 (Conti, 89).
21. I will show below that for Cyril, this teaching is to be found beyond the letter.

4. The Healing of the Man Born Blind of John 9   151

the literal level of the narrative, though he does claim that the type he finds in the narrative is beneficial as well. In any case, as I have demonstrated in previous chapters, Cyril deals significantly with the nonliteral level of the narrative as well, and he describes the textual indications that he must go beyond the letter as the narrative's "sign," "type," and "mystical meaning."[22]

At the literal level, like the Antiochenes, he too finds the text beneficial in its provision of both exemplary figures, doctrinal teachings, and Jesus's fulfillment of Old Testament Scripture. For him, Christ himself is the primary model to be followed by his readers, but he also draws attention to the positive behavior of Jesus's disciples, as well as to the blind man. He corrects the doctrinal error of those who believe that God punishes subsequent generations for their ancestors' sins as he treats 9:2–3. He provides a christological discussion concerning Jesus's self-revelation to the blind man in 9:37. I will demonstrate that Cyril makes an explicit move to the nonliteral plane, where he discovers additional benefits. At the nonliteral level, the text provides beneficial instruction about the place of the gentile church within the drama of salvation history, just as Origen argued in his brief treatment of the passage, though Cyril provides much more detail. As already mentioned, Cyril also finds beneficial instruction about the sacrament of baptism. Like Origen, then, within his nonliteral interpretation he finds instruction that applies directly to his contemporary church, though his reading is for the whole church, not the individual soul in this case.

I will begin by examining Cyril's take on the beneficial instruction provided by the model behavior of the narrative's characters, which in this example is where he spends most of his interpretive energy at the literal level. For Cyril, Christ, his disciples, and the blind man provide examples to be followed, and I will briefly examine his comments on all three figures, beginning with Christ. Like Chrysostom, Cyril does not spend much time at all on Christ's exemplary behavior, but nonetheless we will look at the one passage in which he does, for in it, Cyril not only draws out Christ's model behavior, but he also makes a clear statement about the fact that he does so at the literal level, due to the benefits he finds there. He thus provides us with a statement concerning his rationale for either remaining at the literal level or moving beyond it to the nonliteral level.[23]

---

22. Thus, his treatment of John 9 provides evidence that he thought it appropriate to use these terms interchangeably.

23. We saw Chrysostom evoke the concept of the benefit of the nonliteral level in order to justify his move beyond the letter to provide a nonliteral interpretation of 9:6–7.

I dealt with this passage of Cyril's commentary in the introduction, but I will examine it again here in more detail.[24] Cyril provides a brief treatment of Jesus's symbolic words in 9:4, "We must do the works of him who sent us while it is still day; night is coming, when no one can work," and claims that by these words Jesus warns his disciples that now is not the time to search out matters that are beyond them, such as they had done in 9:2–3, and that the word "day" simply refers to the time we have on earth, while "night" refers to death (*In Jo.* 9:4 [Maxwell, 30]). Cyril then acknowledges that in other instances, Scripture refers to figurative days and nights, but for him, Jesus's words in 9:4 are not such an instance, and he explains why this is the case in what follows:[25]

> But that same meaning when the time is not right—when one should not try to drag by force what ought to be read according to the narrative into a spiritual interpretation [ὅτε μὴ δεῖ περιέλκειν πειρᾶσθαι βιαίως εἰς πνευματικὴν ἑρμηνείαν τὸ ἱστορικῶς ὠφελοῦν]—is nothing other than an unlearned confusion of what would be profitable if understood without elaborate interpretation [οὐδὲν ἕτερόν ἐστιν, ἢ συγχεῖν ἁπλῶς τὸ ἀπεριέργως λυσιτελοῦν]. It is an obfuscation, due to deep ignorance, of what is beneficial from the passage [καὶ τὸ χρήσιμον αὐτόθεν ἐκ πολλῆς σφόδρα τῆς ἀμαθίας καταθολοῦν]. (*In Jo.* 9:4 [Maxwell, 30])

According to Cyril, then, in a statement not unlike that which we would find in the writings of the Antiochenes, when there is profit enough at the literal level, or more specifically here, within the narrative itself, the interpreter ought not to move beyond the narrative to the nonliteral level. By implication of course, his comments here imply that there are times when the passage's benefit is to be sought above the letter, but the interpreter is to use his discretion.

Having defended his choice to remain at the level of the narrative, Cyril turns to interpret Jesus's words in 9:4–5. He claims that Jesus's words, "We must do the works of him who sent us while it is still day; night is coming, when no one can work" mean the following: "it would be better to devote themselves to doing what pleases God and to give up the search for anything beyond that." Cyril goes on to claim that after he has said these

---

24. See the introduction.
25. This is an interesting example as Cyril seems to want to avoid even acknowledging that these words of Jesus are figurative, which he does elsewhere, though he provides an interpretation that decodes them.

things, Jesus "holds himself up as an example [εἰς εἰκόνα] of this," and he paraphrases Jesus's words to mean, "See, I too ... do the work that is appropriate for me," that is, healing the man born blind. Thus Cyril claims that he would like to treat Jesus's words in these verses literally, and he thinks the narrative itself provides their meaning. This he says explicitly: "Therefore, we will take the statement in a simple sense as it reads in the narrative ['Εκληψόμεθα τοιγαροῦν ἱστορικώτερον, καὶ ὡς ἐν ἁπλῷ λόγῳ τὸ εἰρημένον" (*In Jo.* 9:4–5 [Maxwell, 31]). Cyril clearly feels the need to defend his interpretive choice to provide a literal meaning of Jesus's symbolic words in this instance.[26] It is not clear exactly why, but perhaps he has specific interpretations of the words in view that he wishes to distance himself from, interpretations that in his estimation go beyond what is indicated by the narrative itself. In any case, he seems to think it appropriate to treat the words literally, or according to their simple sense within the narrative, and in so doing, he understands Jesus to provide a model for the called person, who performs tasks that are appropriate for him.

Before I turn to examine another benefit that Cyril draws from the literal narrative, I should note that even though Cyril chooses to deal with Jesus's words in 9:4–5 literally, he allows room for a nonliteral interpretation of the verse as well, though he clearly does not think the nonliteral meaning is to be the main emphasis. He says of the verse, "there is no doubt that the Only Begotten is also spiritual light [φῶς νοητόν], with the knowledge and power to illuminate not only what is in the world but also all the rest of the creation beyond this world." This interpretive move he describes as follows: "if we join the sense of the words to the contemplative meaning" (πρὸς δὲ τὴν τῶν ἐν χερσὶ θεωρίαν τὴν ἐκ τῶν λαλουμένων διάνοιαν συναρμόζοντες).[27]

I will now turn to examine Cyril's comments on the behavior of the man born blind. Just as we saw in the Antiochenes' treatments, for Cyril, the blind man is to be celebrated due to his steadfast faith in the face of

---

26. Therefore, I agree with Maxwell, who claims that "Cyril seems concerned that the reader might object to him taking the passage literally"; see Cyril, *Commentary on the Gospel of John*, 31 n. 123. However, this example of Cyril's exegesis is one in which the line between compositional and interpretive allegory is blurred. I discussed this in the introduction.

27. Cyril, *In Jo.* 9:5 (Maxwell, 31). Note that Maxwell has translated θεωρίαν as "spiritual meaning." I have chosen to avoid this, as it is not the most precise translation of this technical exegetical term.

tribulation. For example, as Cyril deals with the blind man's words, "he put mud on my eyes," in 9:15, he draws his readers' attention to the blind man's bold confession of the truth concerning the healing, which he made in front of the malicious audience of the Pharisees. Cyril paraphrases the blind man's statement in 9:15 extensively, in order to explain the significance of his words for his readers, attributing to him such words as, "I will honor my physician by confessing him" and "he did not inflict an elaborate medical procedure on me … but he exercised his power and strange devices." Cyril even encourages his readers to admire the man born blind for his intelligence and his argumentative abilities in his report of the events, for by the words "now I see," the man "says these things with integrity to uphold the genuine power of the healer as best he can" (*In Jo.* 9:15 [Maxwell, 36]). In fact, for Cyril, the blind man's exchange with the Pharisees in 9:28–31 is itself "profitable and fitting" (τὴν τοῦ χρησίμου καὶ τοῦ πρέποντος), for he argues with sound reasoning, drawing on concepts that the Jews agreed upon.[28] The blind man's exchange with the Pharisees in 9:28, in which they revile him for being a disciple of Christ rather than Moses, Cyril claims, teaches that "enduring reproach for the sake of Christ is an enjoyable and fully glorious experience," and in receiving their rebuke, he proves himself wise.[29] Finally, for Cyril, the conduct and the words of the blind man in 9:36, "Who is he, Lord? Tell me, so I may believe in him," provide proof that "The soul that is equipped with sound reasoning and that searches for the truth with clear eyes of understanding reaches it without impediment" (*In Jo.* 9:36 [Maxwell, 51]). Therefore, after the blind man witnessed Christ's power in amazement, he was ready to believe, and Christ honored him by revealing himself to him. Accordingly, the blind man "regained his sight not only physically but mentally as well," whereas the Pharisees "suffered the opposite" (*In Jo.* 9:39 [Maxwell, 54]). It is he that Cyril's readers ought to emulate.

As we saw in Theodore's treatment, Cyril too finds the disciples' behavior in the narrative worthy of comment. In particular, Cyril highlights the fact that the disciples seek to learn from Jesus in 9:2–3, as evidenced by their question concerning who sinned. Cyril, however, goes beyond Theodore in his treatment of these verses, in that for him they provide not only the benefit of the disciples' exemplary and wise behavior, but also important doctrinal instruction and the simultaneous refutation of heresy. In

---

28. Cyril, *In Jo.* 9:31 (Maxwell, 47); cf. *In Jo.* 9:27.
29. Cyril, *In Jo.* 9:34 (Maxwell, 50); quotation from Cyril, *In Jo.* 9:28 (Maxwell, 45).

fact, it is for the sake of the latter that the disciples (are urged by God to) ask the question. Thus, concerning the disciples' question, Cyril says:

> Their curiosity is profitable [χρησίμως] not so much for themselves as for us. We receive immeasurable benefit [ὠφελούμεθα γὰρ οὐ μετρίως] by hearing from the omniscient one what the true glory is in this situation and also by being warned away from the abomination of fleeting doctrines. (*In Jo.* 9:2–3 [Maxwell, 22])

Clearly Cyril thinks it necessary to correct such fleeting doctrines immediately. For, he claims, in addition to the erroneous thinking of the Jews who complained that their suffering was the result of the sin of their parents' generation, there are those at present who hold such opinions as the Jews, those, he claims, "who are insufferably conceited about their knowledge of the inspired Scripture and seem to pass for Christians."[30] These interpreters he charges with willingness to "mix Greek error with the doctrines of the church," for they insist that human souls existed before their bodies and that their souls sinned, resulting in the punishment of birth in the flesh.[31] Cyril goes on to deal with both errors extensively.

The "Jewish error" he corrects through a long discussion of their misunderstanding of the Scriptures, particularly Exod 34:5–7:

> The Lord God, compassionate and merciful, longsuffering and abundant in mercy and true, preserving righteousness and showing mercy to thousands, taking away iniquities, unrighteousness, and sins. He will not clear the guilty but will visit the sins of the fathers on the children and the children's children to the third and fourth generation.

For Cyril, the qualities to emphasize are God's kindness and love for humanity, not his wrath, which is said to extend to the third and fourth generation, as the Jews claim. Thus, argues Cyril, the Jews err in supposing, based on this passage alone, that the sins of parents are actually visited upon their children in the third and fourth generations. They ought to

---

30. He lists as proof of this charge of the Jews, Ezek 18:2 and Exod 34:5–7 (Cyril, *In Jo.* 9:2–3 [Maxwell, 22]).

31. Cyril, *In Jo.* 9:2–3 (Maxwell, 22). I should note that Origen was, of course, famous for this view, as were subsequent "Origenists," in addition to certain gnostic groups. Cyril does not name anyone specifically here, so one can only speculate about whom he has in view.

understand the verse as highlighting God's love for humankind, and his generous and patient delay of punishment until the fourth generation of their descendants, who, if they are punished, are punished justly.[32]

Cyril's doctrinal comments continue with his treatment of 9:3, "Neither this man nor his parents sinned," words that the Alexandrian takes to refute the erroneous teaching of those who mix "Greek error" with church doctrine, namely, the teaching that embodiment is the result of the sins of the soul before birth. In fact, despite the verse's "excessive difficulty" (τὸ σφόδρα δυσέφικτον), he says, "it seems profitable (χρησίμως) ... to say a few words about this in order to defend against the damage from this error," and this due to the verse's potential to indicate that "human bodies are called to suffer so that God's work might be revealed in them." According to Cyril, by saying that the man's blindness was not the result of his sin, Jesus showed this particular doctrine to be very foolish indeed, for his words refute such teaching directly. Thus all those who hold this erroneous view need to do is read Jesus' words in 9:3 in order to be corrected. Cyril goes on to claim that it is the divine nature alone who can understand the mysterious reason that the man in John 9 was born blind, and for this reason Jesus moves the discussion to the topic of God's glory, which will be revealed by the man's healing (*In Jo.* 9:2–3 [Maxwell, 27–28]).

According to Cyril, Jesus's response to the blind man in 9:37, "You have seen him and the one speaking with you is he," also provides the church with beneficial doctrinal instruction and the refutation of contemporary erroneous christological teachings. With these words, Cyril claims that Jesus "is giving thorough forethought to our benefit [ὠφελείας τῆς ἡμετέρας πανταχῇ προνοῶν]." Cyril goes on to warn his readers that there are some even now who "do not understand accurately [ἀκριβῶς] the point of the *oikonomia* with the flesh," for they "dare to separate from the Word of God that temple that was assumed for us from the woman, and they divide the one true Son into two sons just because he became a human being."[33] The

---

32. Cyril, *In Jo.* 9:2–3 (Maxwell, 23–28). Cyril deals with a number of biblical texts here to demonstrate his point: Num 14; Ezek 18; Jer 6:11; Gen 15:16; 3 Kgdms 21.

33. Cyril, *In Jo.* 9:37 (Maxwell, 51). Most agree that Cyril wrote his *Commentary on John* in 428, before the christological controversy broke out in 429, and thus, his treatment of the issues pertaining to Christology are here less precise than the much fuller statements he eventually made in response to Nestorius. He does, however, seem to have the Antiochene articulation of the two natures of Christ, as represented by, e.g., Theodore of Mopsuestia in view already in this context.

benefit of Jesus's statement, according to Cyril, is that it presents clearly the inseparable unity of Christ's two natures, the divine and the human, in direct refutation of those who maintain too great a distance between the divine and human natures. Cyril continues by arguing that the words "You have seen [the Son of God]" refer to his divine nature, whereas the words "the one speaking to you is he" show the Word dwelling in the flesh, that is, to the human nature of Christ. In placing these statements together, says Cyril, he makes no distinction, but emphasizes the great unity. Those in Cyril's day who are in christological error are "excluding the temple assumed from the woman from true sonship" and end up saying that the Word begotten of the Father's substance is one, and that the son of the woman is another (*In Jo.* 9:37 [Maxwell, 52]). It is for this very reason then that the Lord said these words in 9:37 in his foresight, argues Cyril. Thus, as Cyril works here at the level of the narrative, he finds Jesus's words beneficial in that they speak directly to the doctrinal issues of Christology in his own day.

Cyril finds one final benefit at the literal level, namely, instruction about Jesus's fulfillment of the Old Testament. According to Cyril, Jesus's healing of the blind man fulfilled "the word of the Spirit," which was spoken in Isa 35:5–6, "Then the eyes of the blind will be opened, and the ears of the deaf will hear" (*In Jo.* 9:24 [Maxwell, 42]). Like his Alexandrian predecessor, then, Cyril thinks the narrative of the healing of the man born blind fulfills an Isaianic prophecy.[34] The context of Cyril's comments on this is a polemic against the Jews in his treatment of their claim that Jesus is a sinner, while urging the blind man to "give glory to God" for the healing (9:24). Although the Jews claim in this verse that "they know" Jesus is a sinner based on their knowledge of God through the law, Cyril argues, for their failure to recognize Jesus, they will pay a great penalty since "it was possible for them to know the mystery of Christ, who was typified and proclaimed [ἐκτυπούμενόν τε καὶ βοώμενον] in many ways in the Law and the Prophets."[35] For Cyril, then, Jesus's healing of the man born blind clearly literally fulfills that which was spoken by the prophet Isaiah, who typologically proclaimed the event in advance.

---

34. I demonstrated above that for Origen, Jesus's healing of the man born blind fulfills Isa 6:9–10, though it was not clear in that context that he thought of such comments as part of his literal treatment of the passage.

35. Cyril, *In Jo.* 9:24 (Maxwell, 41); cf. *In Jo.* 9:29.

I will now examine Cyril's nonliteral treatment of the passage. As I proceed, I will take note of his articulation of his explicit shift to this level. I will demonstrate that Cyril provides a nonliteral interpretation of the passage as a whole, but, as in previous chapters, isolated verses also contain benefits to be discovered at the nonliteral level. For Cyril, the nonliteral meaning of the passage as a whole is that the blind man represents the place of the gentiles within salvation history, as we saw in Origen's interpretation.

Cyril makes his clearest statement about the overall nonliteral meaning of the passage as he introduces his comments on 9:6–7, the verses that record the actual healing. In fact, these verses receive only a nonliteral treatment. Cyril says immediately: "We will take [παραδεξάμενοι] the healing of this blind man as a type [εἰς τύπον] for the calling of the gentiles, and we will explain the meaning of the mystery, summing it up in a few words [ἐροῦμεν ὡς ἐν βραχέσιν ἀνακεφαλαιούμενοι τοῦ μυστηρίου τὸν λόγον]." Cyril goes on to explain that because Jesus decided to heal the man without being asked, "we will profitably take [χρησίμως ἐποίσομεν] the healing as a kind of sign [σημεῖον] that when there was no request from the multitude of the Gentiles ... God, who is good by nature, invited himself, so to speak, to come and have mercy on them."[36] In this instance, then, Cyril again invokes the principle of the usefulness of the nonliteral level as an implicit justification of this move beyond the letter, as we saw Chrysostom do above.

Having presented the overarching nonliteral meaning of the passage, Cyril develops it throughout his treatment of the passage, as particular verses provide supplementary details for this instruction in salvation history. For example, as he encounters 9:10, in which the witnesses of the healing ask the blind man, "Then how were your eyes opened?," Cyril claims that the reader may "take as a beautiful image [ὅπερ εἰς εἰκόνα λήψῃ καλήν] of the gentile converts becoming teachers of the Israelites, after escaping from their ancient blindness and obtaining illumination from Christ our Savior through the Spirit" (*In Jo.* 9:10 [Maxwell, 33]). At the nonliteral level, the blind man is no longer a mere example of steadfast and courageous faith, as he was at the literal level, but now he is a representation of the whole gentile people, who through God's mercy and Christ's illumination in the Spirit, have come to instruct God's chosen people, the Israelites. Cyril develops this line of argumentation concerning the Israel-

---

36. Cyril, *In Jo.* 9:6–7 (Maxwell, 31); cf. *In Jo.* 9:1, 28.

ites even further in his treatment of 9:34, in which the Pharisees cast the man born blind out of the synagogue. Again, once he has dealt with the verse at the literal level of the narrative, Cyril instructs his readers that they should "take this act as a type of the true event [δέχου πάλιν εἰς τύπον πράγματος ἀληθοῦς τὸ τετελεσμένον], namely, that the Israelites, because of their unfair prejudice, were going to detest the gentiles as being raised in sin." Not only does he suggest to his readers that this reading is permissible, but he also claims rhetorically that "Anyone can see this from what the Pharisees said to him" (*In Jo.* 9:34 [Maxwell, 50]).

Finally, as Cyril deals with the narrative's last scene, in which the blind man worships Jesus as God (9:38), Cyril adds to this overarching nonliteral interpretation, and he describes (all too briefly) his exegetical procedure. As he turns to deal with the blind man's worship of Christ, he says, "Since we transferred his entire experience and applied it to the gentiles [ἐπειδὴ δὲ ὅλην ἐπ᾽ αὐτῷ πραγματείαν εἰς τὸ τῶν ἐθνῶν μετηγάγομεν πρόσωπον], come, let us discuss this next."[37] After this brief comment, Cyril claims that by his worship of Christ, the blind man "brings to fulfillment [πληροῦντα] the type of spiritual service [ἐν πνεύματι λατρείας τὸν τύπον] to which the Gentiles were led by faith." That is, the blind man's act of worshiping Christ, which is placed right next to his confession of Christ, fulfills the type of the gentiles' spiritual worship, which is to be distinguished from the Jews' bodily worship of sacrificing oxen and incense according to the law.[38]

Cyril finds another interpretation at the nonliteral level, namely, one that provides instruction about the sacraments. After he has dealt with the overall nonliteral meaning of 9:6–7 we examined above, he suggests that "the power of the action contains a mystical meaning [λόγον μυστικόν] as well."[39] The healing of the blind man is then, according to Cyril, also an "anticipatory type" (πρόωρον ... τὸν τύπον) and an "image" (εἰκόνα) of holy baptism, in which Jesus's saliva, and the waters of Siloam, are a kind of

---

37. Cyril, *In Jo.* 9:38 (Maxwell, 52). He uses this vocabulary in his treatment of 9:28 as well (*In Jo.* 9:28).

38. Cyril, *In Jo.* 9:38 (Maxwell, 52–53). Cyril goes on to list various scriptural passages to bolster his nonliteral interpretation: Pss 50:13–14; 66:4; John 4:21, 23–24.

39. Cyril, *In Jo.* 9:6–7 (Maxwell, 32); see Crawford, *Cyril*, 192–98. He compares Cyril's treatment of the passage to that of Didymus the Blind within his discussion of Cyril's innovation of the interpretative tradition on this passage vis-à-vis the redemptive illumination and participation in Christ one receives through baptism.

anointing that provides participation in Christ, and by extension, knowledge of the "holy and consubstantial Trinity."[40] Cyril continues his mystical interpretation by playing on the word "sent," the meaning John provides for the name Siloam; he claims that since Jesus is "the sent one," he was sent by God the Father. Jesus, therefore, "swims invisibly in the waters of the holy pool," Cyril claims, and he washes away "the defilement and impurity of the eyes of the mind" in order that those with faith might "gaze purely at the divine beauty" (*In Jo.* 9:6–7 [Maxwell, 32]). For Cyril, then, the additional nonliteral benefit of the narrative of the healing of the man born blind, which he describes here as its "mystical meaning," relates to the reception of Christ and the resulting knowledge of the Trinity in the waters of baptism.

Cyril provides yet another nonliteral interpretation related to the sacrament of baptism as he deals with 9:35, but in this instance he does not describe it as a mystical interpretation, but as a "type."[41] In this verse, Jesus finds the healed man born blind after he is cast out of the synagogue, and asks him, "Do you believe in the Son of God?" Once Cyril has dealt with the literal verse, which we observed above, he explains that Jesus's question to the blind man is to be understood as Jesus's initiation of the blind man into "the mysteries," that is, baptism, for Jesus asks him for an assent of faith. Cyril continues: "The type [τύπος] of this practice is first found in this passage, and we have learned from our Savior Christ himself how this profession of faith should be made" (*In Jo.* 9:35 [Maxwell, 51]). Again the practice of Cyril's present church is represented "typically" in Jesus's actions.[42]

In one final instance Cyril shifts to the nonliteral level in his treatment of the passage. Just as we saw Chrysostom provide 9:6–7 with a nonliteral reading, we see Cyril do something similar with these verses. As I showed above, the verses provide Cyril with the opportunity to articulate his understanding of the nonliteral meaning of the passage as a whole.

---

40. Cyril, *In Jo.* 9:6–7 (Maxwell, 32). This tradition is not distinctive to him, but goes back at least to Irenaeus, *Haer.* 5.15.3; see also Tertullian, *Bapt.* 1.

41. This might indicate that Cyril, like Origen before him, uses such terms for nonliteral interpretation interchangeably. However, this might also provide another example of Cyril's ambiguous use of the term "type" synonymously with "example."

42. This might be yet another piece of evidence for Maxwell's theory that Cyril's ideal readers are those who teach catechism and are thus leaders in the church. See my discussion of his theory above.

However, he also provides another nonliteral reading, which is not directly related to the overarching nonliteral interpretation examined above. Cyril suggests that—again using different terminology to denote a nonliteral meaning to be discovered—"there is a deep meaning buried [βαθύς τις τοῖς εἰρημένοις ἐγκέχωσται λόγος]" in John's description of the manner in which Jesus healed the blind man, that is, by making mud out of dirt and his saliva and spreading it on his eyes: "he shows that he is the one who formed us in the beginning, the creator and fashioner of all" (*In Jo.* 9:6–7 [Maxwell, 32]). Unlike the Antiochenes, then, who gave this interpretation at the literal level, Cyril claims he has uncovered a nonliteral meaning, that was hidden in the depths of these words, and thus not part of the text's immediate literal meaning. Notice that he does not suggest that this is a doctrinal meaning, but also that it does not conform to my argument that these authors tend to deal with doctrine at the literal level.[43] In any case, Cyril does not dwell on this reading as he does other verses that are of doctrinal import, nor does he discuss the implications for the church's understanding of Christ's divinity as we might expect, but he clearly thinks his reading is an additional beneficial teaching of the nonliteral variety.

In conclusion to Cyril's treatment of this passage then, we have seen that he found the text beneficial at both levels of the text. We saw that Christ, the disciples, and the blind man provided models for his readers to follow and that the literal text provided the occasion for extensive doctrinal instruction. Also, at the literal level he instructed his readers concerning Jesus's fulfillment of Old Testament prophecy. We also saw Cyril shift to the nonliteral level on several occasions, to draw out additional benefits for his readers, such as the passage's teaching about the place of the gentiles within salvation history and about the sacrament of baptism.

Conclusion

In this chapter we saw again that both the Antiochenes and Cyril found much that was beneficial in the literal narrative of the healing of the man born blind. As mentioned above, we saw suggestive hints that Origen may have done so as well, but I cannot claim this definitively. We also saw that except for Chrysostom's brief nonliteral discussion about Jesus's ineffable power in the waters of Siloam in 9:6–7, the Antiochenes remained at the

---

43. In fact, this is one of two instances that complicate my argument that doctrine is dealt with at the literal level. The other one is Origen's treatment of John 4:24.

level of the narrative to articulate the passage's benefits. For Cyril as well, the passage has a great deal of benefit to offer at the literal level, and it teaches primarily about appropriate discipleship, as represented by the blind man, and about Christ's divinity. Of course, we have only Origen's nonliteral treatment, but in Cyril's case, we saw that he made a number of explicit shifts to the nonliteral level to draw out additional benefit. For both authors, above the level of the narrative, the man born blind is primarily a type for God's visitation of the gentiles within salvation history. Both, however, find additional benefit at this level, which relates directly to their contemporary church settings. In Origen's case the passage contains instruction for the individual Christian soul's healing encounter with Christ. In Cyril's case, it offers instruction concerning the sacrament of baptism, and he describes this nonliteral reading as the mystical interpretation. As we saw in the previous chapter, these nonliteral readings, in which the text provides direct instruction about the life and practice of the contemporary church and the individual Christian soul, are typically not present in the Antiochenes' treatments of the passage. Here again lies one of the key distinctions between the two schools that this study demonstrates.

5
The Good Shepherd Parable of John 10

In this chapter I examine the four authors' treatments of one of Jesus's few sustained parable-like discourses in John's Gospel, that of the good shepherd (10:1–19), which is addressed to the Pharisees and which the Fourth Evangelist calls a "figure of speech" (ἡ παροιμία) in 10:6. Within the parable, Jesus uses a combination of two metaphors, the good shepherd, and the gate for the sheep, which are introduced with the distinctively Johannine "I am" (ἐγώ εἰμι) statements. That is, Jesus claims that he is the good shepherd and the gate for the sheep. Through the parable, Jesus distinguishes his ministry, which is marked by self-sacrificial provision, care, and guidance, from that of the Pharisees, whose leadership is marked by transience and negligence of the flocks of the Jewish people.

All four authors attend to the parabolic genre of the passage, and accordingly, they each provide it with a fitting interpretation in which they identify the referents of the parable's images and characters.[1] Within their readings of the parable, all four authors find the text useful for its ability to instruct their audiences concerning salvation history, from the time of Moses to that of Jesus's ministry, in which Jesus's Jewish contemporaries are found wanting in their leadership, and are thus rejected and replaced by Christ and his apostles. In addition, Cyril and Chrysostom argue that Jesus as a metaphoric shepherd of the sheep of Israel fulfills the prophecy of the prophet Ezekiel (Ezek 34). Finally, Cyril and the Antiochenes find much beneficial doctrinal teaching in Jesus's final words of the parable, in which he describes his relationship with his followers and with the Father (10:14–18). Though these words are technically within Jesus's parabolic speech, once all three post-Nicene authors have clarified the passage's

---

1. See my discussion of the authors' treatment of parable and metaphor in the introduction.

obscurities, they shift gears as it were and treat them as doctrinal propositions that provide instruction about the relationship between the Father and the Son.[2]

Despite the similarities mentioned above, there are still discernible differences between the two schools' treatments of the passage. First, the Antiochenes deal primarily with the context of the immediate passage and with other New Testament passages as they identify the veiled references of the parable.[3] While Cyril provides a similar line of interpretation, he does not stop there; he also provides a complex interpretation of Christ the Shepherd's eschatological salvation of all humanity. Furthermore, Cyril (and Origen as well, in the limited material we have of his treatment of the passage) not only draws from the pages of the New Testament to interpret the parable but also claims explicitly that the parable has direct bearing on his contemporary church setting.[4]

For Origen, the passage explains the role of Christ in the individual believer's life, whereas for Cyril, the benefits for his contemporary church setting are primarily corporate. We will see that the Antiochenes too make some brief comments about the passage's implications for their contemporary church settings, but they are much less developed than those of the Alexandrians.

I will again begin with Origen. As I mentioned in the introduction, Origen's treatment of the passage in his *Commentary on the Gospel of John* is now lost, but he does deal with it in a sustained passage of approximately ten pages of Rufinus's Latin translation of his *Commentary on the Song of Songs*, in which he uses the good shepherd passage to explain the role of Christ in the individual Christian's spiritual journey toward the Father.[5] I will use this passage primarily, but I will also supplement it with a few other texts from his corpus in which he draws on John 10.

---

2. This we saw was also true of Theodore's treatment of Jesus's symbolic words in 2:19; see ch. 2 above.

3. This kind of interpretation at the nonliteral level they provided in their treatments of John 2 and John 4 in chs. 2 and 3 respectively, albeit on a smaller scale.

4. As I mentioned in the introduction, we no longer have Origen's treatment of the parable extant in his *Commentary on the Gospel of John*. I have thus had to draw from the rest of his corpus, his *Commentary on the Song of Songs* in particular, in order to comment on his treatment of the passage.

5. He also uses the image of the gate and the good shepherd from John 10 in his *Letter to Gregory*, in *Contra Celsum*, and in *Peri archon*, but these discussions are very brief and not helpful for my purposes.

In Origen's *Commentary on the Song of Songs*, John 10 provides him with assistance in both his literal or "historical" (*historicus*) and his nonliteral or "mystical" (*mysticam*) interpretation of Song 1:7, "Tell me, O you whom my soul has loved, where you feed, where you have your couch in the midday, lest perchance I be made as one that is veiled above the flocks of your companions." As he turns to deal with this verse, it is the word "flocks" (*greges*) that provokes his discussion of the good shepherd image. When the bride asks the bridegroom where he feeds at midday and where he keeps his flocks, explains Origen, "It is plain" (*ostenditur*) that this bridegroom is also a shepherd who feeds his sheep (*Comm. Cant.* 2.4.1, 3, 4 [Lawson, 118–19]). From this observation at the historical or literal level of the Song of Songs verse, Origen moves to the nonliteral level, which, as I mentioned above, he describes as the mystical, in which he discusses the role of Christ as shepherd in the life of the Christian, and the good shepherd of John 10 is one of the major sources for his comments.[6] At the nonliteral level, the bridegroom-shepherd's flocks are the very flocks of which Christ says in the gospel, "My sheep hear my voice" (John 10:27), and he says explicitly, "it seems fitting to support what we say out of the Gospels also," for, "There too have I encountered this good shepherd talking about the pastures of the sheep."[7]

As he continues his treatment of Song 1:7 at the nonliteral level, Origen claims that within the church there are "different classes of believers in Christ, associated with him in different relationships."[8] In this context the different classes of believers are represented by the queens, who are at the highest level, followed by the less noble concubines, then the maidens, and last, the souls of those who are sheep, that is, the flocks of this verse (*Comm.*

---

6. The other major source is Ps 23 (22 LXX). Origen is surprisingly the only one of my four authors to draw on Ps 23 in relation to the good shepherd of John 10. We will see him do so again below.

7. Origen, *Comm. Cant.* 2.4.13, 24 (Lawson, 122, 124). He goes on to quote John 10:9 explicitly.

8. Origen, *Comm. Cant.* 2.4.5 (Lawson, 119). This is an example of Origen's well-known articulation of Christ's various "aspects" or "functions" (ἡ ἐπίνοια), which one encounters depending upon his or her need. As the soul of the believer progresses toward perfection, Origen suggests that he or she relates to different aspects of Christ at each stage. In such a schema, Christ as the good shepherd is the aspect of Christ that the believer encounters initially as one of the sheep. This idea he develops throughout his corpus, but also in his *Commentary on John* in particular; see, e.g., *Comm. Jo.* 1.118; 6; 10.21–23; 13.39.

Cant. 2.4.4 [Lawson, 119]). According to Origen, as a sheep, the Christian needs Christ the good shepherd in particular because "he feeds or refreshes his sheep," that is, he takes care of the Christian's material needs.[9] As the believer is perfected, she encounters Christ in his other aspects, as Word or as Wisdom, aspects that "have to do with progress and perfection" (*Comm. Cant.* 2.4. 23 [Lawson, 124]). Clearly Origen thinks the bride of Song of Songs has not yet encountered Christ as Word or Wisdom, for in 1:7, as she asks the bridegroom-shepherd to tell her where he feeds his flocks and where he has his couch in the midday, she is just now relating to him as the shepherd.[10] For Origen then, at least in this context, the good shepherd passage provides instruction concerning the individual Christian soul's encounter with Christ, and specifically the individual who is in the primary stages of discipleship within Origen's tripartite schema.

I will now turn to the manner in which Origen uses the parable of the good shepherd throughout the extant materials of his *Commentary on John* and throughout the rest of his corpus. In this section I will provide something of a reconstruction of Origen's treatment of the good shepherd parable based on this material. For each of the various figures and images of the parable—we have extant comments on the bandits and flocks in particular—Origen assigned two kinds of referent, the first from the pages of Scripture, and the second from his own contemporary church setting.

I will begin with the referents that Origen draws from the pages of the New Testament. Concerning the parable's bandits and thieves of 10:1, 8, and 10, in the context of his *Homilies on the Gospel of Luke*, the thieves are identified with those of the good Samaritan parable in Luke 10:29–37, and in his *Commentary on the Gospel of Matthew*, they are associated with those who might break through and steal that which Christ's followers have stored in heaven (Matt 6:19).[11] The flock of the parable's shepherd

---

9. Origen, *Comm. Cant.* 2.4.11 (Lawson, 121); cf. *Hom. Ps.* 77 9.6.

10. Origen will go on in his treatment of Song 1:7 to interpret the bride's request of the shepherd, "tell me ... where you feed, and where you have your couch in the midday" to interpret the word "midday" nonliterally, suggesting that with her request she seeks more perfect and higher knowledge of Christ, but he does not suggest a clear referent for the pastures of the shepherd; see Origen, *Comm. Cant.* 2.4.24–26.

11. Luke: Origen, *Hom. Luc.* 34.4 (Lienhard, 138). In this context, Origen quotes John 10:8 and says that "the robbers are none other than they of whom the Savior says, 'All who came before me are thieves and robbers.'" He does not elaborate any further than this, however, and he does not name the Pharisees of John 10 explicitly. Matthew: Origen, *Comm. Matt.* 10.14.

Origen also identifies with groups of people from the pages of the New Testament. For example, the shepherd and his sheep provide him the image with which to make a distinction between Christ and the church on the one hand and Moses and the old covenant people of Israel on the other, and this he argues in his *Homilies on Numbers*, as he deals with the leprosy of Miriam in Num 12:10 (Origen, *Hom. Num.* 6.4.2 [Scheck, 24]). However, he proceeds to argue that both groups will become "one flock" with "one shepherd" (10:16) at the end of the age (*Hom. Num.* 6.4.2 [Scheck, 24]). Origen deals similarly with the "other sheep" (10:16) in his *Commentary on Romans*. As he treats Rom 11, he claims that Jesus's other sheep represent Israel within Paul's discussion of the place of Israel within God's people (*Comm. Rom.* 8.7.3 [Hammond Bammel, 673–80]). In this context, the other sheep are not the gentiles, as most modern biblical interpreters (and the three subsequent ancient interpreters of this study) suggest, but to the contrary, they are the Israelites whom Jesus must bring back into his fold at the end of the age.[12] Here again Origen finds the referent in the pages of Scripture, though he has his eye on the relationship between the church and the Jews in the drama of salvation history.[13]

Concerning Origen's second kind of referent, that is, the kind in which he draws from the situation of the church in his day, the parable's bandits are heretics representing figures such as Marcion, Valentinus, and Basilides. For example, he makes this claim briefly in his *Homilies on Jeremiah* as he treats Jer 17:11, "The partridge cried out; she gathered but did not lay."[14] Origen charges the heretics of his day with deceiving and leading astray Christ's sheep, just as the partridge of Jer 17 gathers the creatures of another.[15] Origen also identifies groups of believers from his own contemporary setting with the parable's flock. In his interpretation of John 4,

---

12. See, e.g., the rather standard comments of the following modern biblical scholars on the gentiles as the "other sheep" of 10:16: Adele Reinhartz, *The Word in the World: The Cosmological Tale in the Fourth Gospel*, SBLMS 45 (Atlanta: Society of Biblical Literature, 1992), 46; Raymond Brown, *The Community of the Beloved Disciple* (New York: Paulist, 1979), 55–58.

13. I suspect that this is one of the nonliteral treatments Origen would have given this passage, for he articulates similar readings in his nonliteral treatment of the parable in John 4:35–38.

14. Origen, *Hom. Jer.* 17.2.1 (Smith, 181). Heretics are also represented by those in the parable who are not the sheep of Christ (10:26), according to Origen; see his brief comments in 20.54–55.

15. Origen, *Hom. Jer.* 17.2.1 (Smith, 181); cf. *Hom. Ps.* 77.2.4.

which I treated above, Origen says that the flock is an identifiable group within the church in his own day, that his, his well-known category of "the so-called 'sheep of Christ'" (οἱ λεγόμενοι πρόβατα Χριστοῦ), who are in the initial stages of the spiritual journey and whom we saw represented by the bride of the Song of Songs above.[16]

Finally, in a very brief section of one of Origen's recently discovered *Homilies on the Psalms*, Origen provides us with a discussion in which he has both the pages of Scripture and the members of his own community in view. This happens as he discusses the referent of the passage's "pasture." In his first homily on Ps 73, as Origen interprets the words "why has your wrath been stirred against the sheep of your pasture?" of Ps 73:1, the word "sheep" elicits his quotation of John 10:9, "I am the gate; if anyone enter through me he will be saved and come in and out and find pasture." After he quotes the Johannine verse, he explains the pasture: "the pasture is the holy Scriptures; the law is pasture, the prophets are pasture, the gospels, the apostles." Following this brief explanation, Origen turns to his audience and says, "let us enter into this pasture, and it is the Lord's task to shepherd us, so that we can say, 'the Lord shepherds me and nothing is lacking for me, in a place of new growth, there he encamps me' (Ps 22:1–2)" (*Hom. Ps.* 73.1.3). The very pages of Scripture themselves provide the context in which Christ the Shepherd might nurture and care for his flock, the members of Origen's congregation.[17] We will see below that the Antiochenes' too think Scripture an integral part of the shepherd's care for his flock.

To conclude my analysis of Origen's treatment of the passage, we saw that he used the good shepherd passage within his nonliteral treatments of various biblical passages. Within his treatment of Song 1:7, we saw that the passage instructed his readers concerning the individual (immature) Christian soul's encounter with Christ. Wherever we find him assigning referents to the parable's images, we saw that some are more historical or derived from the Johannine and New Testament narrative, whereas at other times the referents are drawn from his own church setting. I suspect that we would find such or similar readings in his *Commentary on the Gospel of John* had his treatment of John 10 not been lost.

---

16. Origen, *Comm. Jo.* 13.39 (Heine, 76); cf. *Hom. Ps.* 77.7.6.

17. Therefore, this section of Origen's first homily on Ps 73 provides a helpful clue about the audience of the new homilies, a question concerning which there is little agreement to date. Certainly, some of Origen's hearers were initiates, an observation that aligns with Origen's mention of catechumens in several instances.

Turning now to the Antiochenes' treatment of the good shepherd parable of John 10, we will begin with Chrysostom, who treats the parable in the majority of two homilies, which consist of approximately thirteen columns of Greek text (*Hom. Jo.* 59–60 [Goggin, 124–51]). I will demonstrate that within his interpretation of the parable, he too seeks to provide a referent for each of the parable's characters and images within the pages of the New Testament, as we saw in my reconstruction of Origen's treatment of the passage. The referents he finds in the New Testament contribute to his understanding of the parable's instruction about the drama of salvation history, which is his primary emphasis in his treatment of the passage. Chrysostom too finds his present church and its opponents in the parable, though this interpretation he provides only in passing. Finally, once he has clarified Jesus's parabolic speech, he deals with the doctrinal instruction provided by 10:14–18.

Chrysostom makes clear that he is dealing with symbolic speech by claiming that Jesus speaks the words of the passage and keeps to "the metaphor" (τῇ μεταφορᾷ) and by explaining to his readers that "if you wish to interpret the parable word by word (κατὰ λέξιν ἐθέλοις τὴν παραβολὴν ἐξετάζειν), nothing prevents you from considering Moses as the gatekeeper, since he has been entrusted with the words of God."[18] Thus he indicates that because the passage is written in the genre of parable, the interpreter is free to interpret each word of the parable in like manner. This comment sets the tone for his treatment of the rest of the parable, and he goes on to identify the referents of its other words.

Chrysostom claims that the shepherd, Christ, is "in complete agreement with the Father," for he "brought the Scriptures to the fore in support of what he said," unlike the thieves and bandits of the parable. Indeed, just as Christ instructed the Jews to "search the Scriptures" in John 5:39–47, through this parable he "expresses the same idea metaphorically [ἐνταῦθα δὲ τὸ αὐτὸ μεταφορικῶς]" (*Hom. Jo.* 59.2 [Goggin, 125]). Chrysostom makes clear that within the drama of salvation history, which is brought

---

18. Chrysostom, *Hom. Jo.* 59.2 (Goggin, 125–26). As I noted above, the Evangelist John describes Jesus's words here as a "figure of speech" (τὴ παροιμία), and this seems to indicate to Chrysostom that it requires a fitting interpretation. Origen provides a similar interpretation to that of Chrysostom here in his *Ep. Greg.* 3. Here he refers to the (unnamed) gatekeeper of the Scriptures as he encourages Gregory to apply himself to the study of Scripture. For the person devoted to the study of Scripture will the gatekeeper open the gate.

into sharp focus through the parable, Christ enters through the gate, that is, he interprets and fulfills the law and indeed all (Old Testament Scripture) correctly, for he is the fulfillment of the law, unlike his contemporary Jewish opponents.

Chrysostom develops a sharp contrast between Christ and the various villainous characters of the parable, which he identifies with characters either from the Gospel of John itself, or from elsewhere in the pages of the New Testament, as we saw Origen do as well. For example, concerning the parable's "robbers" (10:1), by "making a veiled reference" (αἰνίττεται), Jesus refers to both the false Jewish teachers, the Pharisees, of the immediate narrative context and to those who would follow them: the insurrectionists Judas and Theudas of Acts 5:34–36.[19] These figures are robbers, Chrysostom claims, because they do not enter through the gate, that is, they are "not in accordance with Scripture."[20] It is not clear from the context exactly what Chrysostom means by this, though it might refer to the robbers' conduct that does not accord with the requirements of Scripture, specifically torah, which the gatekeeper, Moses, oversees. Unlike Christ, they do not interpret and thus fulfill Scripture aright. Similarly, for Chrysostom, when Jesus indicates that there are those who "climb in another way" (10:1), he "was referring indirectly to the Scribes," for they taught the teachings of men, and transgressed the Law (Matt 15:9) (*Hom. Jo.* 59. 2 [Goggin, 125]). Here again, it is New Testament characters that Chrysostom has immediately in view as he interprets the parable, and they are summoned because of their inability to interpret torah. Finally, Chrysostom again has the Pharisees and scribes of the present narrative of John in view when he identifies the hired hand of 10:12–13, for instead of tending to the sheep in their care, they run away when the wolf comes (10:12), choosing to care for themselves instead of the flock.[21] None of these villainous figures is a match for the parable's good shepherd, Christ.

---

19. Chrysostom, *Hom. Jo.* 59.2 (Goggin, 124). He has the insurrectionists of Acts 5 in view as he interprets the "stranger" of 10:5 and again, the "thieves and bandits" of 10:8; see *Hom. Jo.* 59.3.

20. Chrysostom, *Hom. Jo.* 59.2 (Goggin, 124). I will demonstrate below that the polemics against the Jewish teachers of Jesus's day, while present in Chrysostom's treatment of the passage, are heightened considerably in Cyril's comments.

21. Chrysostom, *Hom. Jo.* 60.1 (Goggin, 134). Even the wolf has a referent that comes from the pages of the New Testament. Chrysostom suspects that the wolf might be "a spiritual wolf" (νοητὸν λύκον), for Christ did not actually allow him to seize the sheep. He thinks himself justified in this interpretation, for he claims that Scripture

In fact, once Chrysostom has set up this contrast between Christ the shepherd and the thieves qua contemporary Jewish teachers, he provides his audience with instruction about how the events surrounding Jesus's ministry fulfill the Old Testament prophecy of Ezekiel. He claims that "Ezekiel of old also reproached the notorious figures Theudas and Judas by saying: 'Woe to the shepherds of Israel! Surely shepherds do not feed themselves? Do not the shepherds feed their flock?'" (Ezek 34:2) (*Hom. Jo.* 60.1 [Goggin, 134]). In other words, according to Chrysostom, the prophet Ezekiel had these contemporaries of Christ in view as he spoke these words. These leaders did not act as true shepherds, but instead paid no heed to their flock, Chrysostom continues, which Ezekiel also claimed in advance. I will show below that Cyril provides a more detailed interpretation of the passage's fulfillment of Ezekiel's prophecy.

I will now examine Chrysostom's understanding of the parable's sheep. He begins by saying generally that Christ's sheep are all people who follow him but then goes on to find a more specific referent within the (nearby) pages of the New Testament, and claims: "he seems to be referring indirectly also to the blind man" (9:1–42). Chrysostom finds another referent for the shepherd's sheep as he treats 10:9, "if anyone enter by me, he shall go in and out, and find pasture," this time in the gospels more generally. As he explains 10:9, he claims that the person who follows Christ will receive safety and security and that the word "pasture" specifically refers to Christ's care, nourishment, supervision, and guardianship. He continues by providing an example in which Christ's care and supervision actually happened, namely, in the case of the apostles, who came in and went out of his pasture freely, "as if they had become masters of the whole world" (*Hom. Jo.* 59.2–3 [Goggin, 124–128]). Thus for Chrysostom we can think of both the blind man and the apostles as sheep. I should note here how unlike Origen's treatment of the parable's sheep Chrysostom's is; for this Antiochene, all followers of Christ, including the exemplary apostles and the man born blind, are sheep, whereas for Origen, with his various categories of spiritual need, only those of the most rudimentary faith ought to be called sheep.

The sheep of 10:1–15, however, are not the parable's only sheep, for Jesus also mentions "other sheep, which are not of this fold, them also

---

is full of representations of the devil as animals; e.g., the apostle Peter himself refers to the devil as a lion in 1 Pet 5:8. Therefore, he argues, the devil is in view when one encounters a wolf, a lion, a serpent, or a dragon in the pages of Scripture; see *Hom. Jo.* 60.3. Again, for Chrysostom, Scripture interprets Scripture.

must I bring" (10:16). Concerning these "other sheep," Chrysostom argues, Jesus "introduces a reference to the Gentiles." With these words, Chrysostom argues, Jesus himself predicted that his one flock would consist of both Jews and Gentiles, just as Paul says: "circumcision does not matter and uncircumcision does not matter" (Gal 5:6) (*Hom. Jo.* 60.2 [Goggin, 136]). Thus here again the parable provides instruction for his audience concerning the place of the gentile church within the people of God in salvation history.

Chrysostom, then, tended to look for the referents of the parable's figures and images in the pages of the New Testament, either within the narrative of John's Gospel or throughout the rest of the New Testament. However, as we saw in Origen's treatment above, there are several instances where we see Chrysostom also providing an interpretation of the parable with reference to the situation of the church in his own day. I will examine them briefly here.

First, as he discusses the gate of 10:1–3, which refers, in his view, to Scripture, Chrysostom instructs his readers that the Scriptures bring the community of faith to the knowledge of God.[22] In fact, he continues, it is Scripture that "makes us his sheep," for "it guards us" and "does not permit the wolves to enter." It becomes clear who the wolves are in this reading, as Chrysostom goes on to claim that, "just as a gate provides security, so Scripture prevents the entrance of heretics." If the gate of Scripture remains in place, Chrysostom argues, the church will be able to distinguish the true shepherds from the false, heretical enemies. Here then the parable's gate has direct bearing on his own community; the gate of Scripture protects Christ's flock, the church, by providing them with the measurement against which to judge the teachings of heretics. However, for Chrysostom, the gate of Scripture also protects the members of the church from themselves; he claims that it "places us in safety with regard to all our desires, and does not permit us to go astray" (*Hom. Jo.* 59.2 [Goggin, 124]).

Second, as he concludes his first homily on the parable, Chrysostom exhorts his parishioners to "remain in the care of the Shepherd," which he tells them, they shall do if they obey him, following not a stranger but hearing his voice. He assures them that they indeed know Jesus's voice, for his are the words, "Blessed are the poor in spirit, blessed are the pure

---

22. Chrysostom, *Hom. Jo.* 59.2 (Goggin, 124). As we saw above, Origen too thinks Scripture is part of the equation of the shepherd's care for his flock. For Chrysostom, however, the gate of the parable refers to Scripture, not the pasture.

in heart, and blessed are the merciful" (Matt 5:3, 8, 7), which, if practiced, result in the Christian's remaining in the shepherd's care (*Hom. Jo.* 59.4 [Goggin, 130]).

Third, as he treats Christ's words in 10:11, "I am the good shepherd," and 10:15, "I lay down my life for my sheep," Chrysostom claims briefly that "a great thing is the role of leader in the church" and that the role requires wisdom and courage, "sufficient to lay down one's life for the sheep" (*Hom. Jo.* 60.1 [Goggin, 133]). He clearly speaks about his own role within the church, in addition to all other leaders of the church of his day. I will demonstrate below that Cyril develops this line of interpretation significantly in his treatment of the parable.

Like the other two post-Nicene authors, Chrysostom treats 10:14–15, and 10:17–18, verses that are technically part of Christ's parabolic speech, as straight doctrinal sentences. I begin with Chrysostom's treatment of Jesus's words in 10:14–15, "I know my own and my own know me, just as the Father knows me and I know the Father." Once Chrysostom has explained for his audience who are the shepherd and the sheep, he thinks it necessary to explain also the nature of the knowledge shared between them, given that Jesus here compares it to the knowledge shared between the Father and the Son. According to this Antiochene, the knowledge shared between Father and Son "is not the same" as that which is shared between the Son and his followers, for theirs is "a certain unique kind of knowledge, and such as no one else can possess." He does not explain why exactly Christ would compare the knowledge shared between Jesus and his human followers with that between him and his Father, but he simply says that Christ "frequently placed himself within the ranks for ordinary men" (*Hom. Jo.* 60.1 [Goggin, 136]). He thus hints at a solution to the issue with recourse to the partitive exegesis we have seen our authors use throughout this study in those cases in which Jesus speaks or acts in a manner unworthy of his divinity. Theodore and Cyril provide more by way of explanation of Christ's words in these verses, which I will show below.

Chrysostom provides a lengthy treatment of the doctrinal teachings offered by Jesus's words in 10:17–18, which read:

> For this reason, the Father loves me, because I lay down my life in order to take it up again. No one takes it from me, but I lay it down of my own accord. I have power to lay it down, and I have power to take it up again. I have received this command from my Father.

Concerning the words, "For this reason does my Father love me" of 10:17, Chrysostom anticipates interpreters who would argue that Jesus had to earn his Father's love, by arguing that these humble words demonstrate that Christ "condescended to our lowliness [κέχρηται τῇ συγκαταβάσει]," a common interpretive move for the Antiochene, for it provides the rationale for Christ's speech as a human. According to Chrysostom, Christ speaks this way in order to demonstrate his agreement and unity with his Father and theirs because the Jewish teachers had called him a deceiver, who was alien from the Father. He expands his explanation by paraphrasing Christ in this way: "If nothing else, at least this would impel me to love you; namely that you are loved by my Father as I am, and I am loved by him for this reason—because I am to die in your behalf." Chrysostom concludes his treatment of this verse by saying that Jesus wishes to prove that he willingly lays down his life and that his willingness was "in conformity with His Father's will," which is the true cause for his love. For Chrysostom, it is Christ's love of his own people that leads him to condescend with these words, which demonstrate his unity with God the Father, whom they know. It is therefore not marvelous, then, Chrysostom assures his parishioners, if he speaks "as a man" in this verse. Jesus's words in 10:18, "I have power to lay it down, and I have power to take it up again," by contrast indicate to Chrysostom that Jesus also speaks as God. Christ's power over death is a power that does not belong to any other man, he argues, for we have no such power to lay our lives down in any other way than killing ourselves. However, the following sentence, "I have received this commandment from my Father," requires a great deal of explanation, for he must hold these statements together somehow. Chrysostom decides first to specify what Jesus is being commanded by the Father to do: "to die in behalf of the world." He then proceeds to claim that just as Jesus's words "For this reason does the Father love me" (10:17) indicated that his death would be in conformity with the Father's will, so also here when he claims that he received a command from the Father, he really means, "I do what he wills." For Chrysostom, the commandment means nothing other than the Son's unanimity with the Father, and if he speaks in "so humbly and in human fashion," it is because of his hearers' infirmity (*Hom. Jo.* 60.2–3 [Goggin, 136–40]). Again, for the Antiochene, Christ's humble words are explained with recourse to his concept of condescension. Cyril in particular makes a similar interpretive move in his treatment of the passage, though his comments are more extensive, while Theodore takes his interpretation in another direction.

In conclusion to Chrysostom's treatment of the good shepherd parable, we saw that he proceeded to identify word by word the referents of each of the parable's figures and images. We saw that he searched for the meaning of the parable within the immediate narrative context of John and from elsewhere in the New Testament. Thus, for him the parable primarily provided instruction about salvation history, in which the gatekeeper Moses approved of Jesus's scriptural interpretation over that of Jesus's Jewish contemporaries, the Pharisees, and later, the insurrectionists, Theudas and Judas of the Acts narrative. The New Testament itself proved Jesus the shepherd's care for the blind man and the apostles. We also saw that Chrysostom turned to his own church setting briefly to discern how the parable related to his own ministry as a church leader, to Christ's and his own flock of his parishioners, and to the role of Scripture in differentiating true and false shepherds, which for him are an unidentified group of heretics. Finally, he dealt with the parable's final verses similarly to the way we have seen him and our other authors treat verses of doctrinal import: he changed modes and dealt with these verses as straightforward doctrinal statements.

We have a substantial amount of Theodore's treatment of the parable in his Greek fragments— about seven pages of Greek text—and the whole of the twelve-page Syriac translation with which to work (*Comm. Jo.* 10:1-18 [Greek: Kalantzis, 76–83; Syriac: Conti, 90–97]). We shall see that his comments largely resemble those of Origen and Chrysostom, in that the referents he finds for the parable's images and figures also come either from John's Gospel or from elsewhere in the New Testament. Unlike Origen and Chrysostom, however, Theodore does not find referents for the passage's images and figures within his contemporary church setting, except for one passing comment in which it is merely implied that his readers are sheep. For Theodore, like Chrysostom, the parable also provides instruction about salvation history, from Moses to the time of Christ's ministry. As I mentioned above, Theodore also shifts modes to deal with the doctrinally significant verses of 10:14–15 and 10:17–18 as straightforward doctrinal statements. I will examine Theodore's introductory comments on the passage first, in which he indicates explicitly that Jesus's words are symbolic, and then we will examine the details of his treatment of the passage.

Theodore begins his treatment of the parable by indicating immediately that the passage at hand ought to be dealt with in a fitting manner, for he claims that with these words Jesus speaks "figuratively" (ܐܘܟܝܬ) in reply to the Pharisees' question "Surely we are not blind, are we?"

(9:40), in order to announce his authority over them as teacher.[23] Having set out the context within the narrative of the Fourth Gospel, and the overarching meaning of these words, he again reminds his readers that in this chapter, the Lord spoke to them "by way of a parable" [ܐܬܠܐܒܡ ܒܐ], and thus, he explains, the interpreter ought to treat these words differently than what has preceded them. In fact, it is necessary to give the entire parable "a full explanation" (ܡܦܫܩܘ).[24] Furthermore, says Theodore, in order that Jesus's words not be as "obscure" (ܚܫܝܢ) to us as they were to the Pharisees in the passage, it is necessary to prepare with God's help "to explain the meaning of this parable (ܐܬܠܐܒ ܡܚܘܝܢܘܬܐ)" for all who encounter it in John's Gospel (*Comm. Jo.* 10:1–6 [Conti, 90]). Thus Theodore models for his readers one of the characteristics of the ideal reader he presents in his preface; according to him, the ideal reader maintains a posture of prayer as he interprets Scripture, asking for God's help, particularly as he deals with the difficulties presented by a passage such as a parable.[25]

Similar to what we saw in Chrysostom's treatment, for Theodore, the gatekeeper is Moses, but unlike Chrysostom, it is not the parable's gate that represents the teachings of the law, but the sheepfold, and therefore in his reading, the sheep are those who subject themselves to the law, and "who are exact and attentive to the truth [οἱ ἀκριβεῖς καὶ τῆς ἀληθείας ἐπιμελόμενοι]," in the face of false teachers. Within this framework, for Theodore, when Christ the good shepherd claims to use the lawful entrance, he claims that he has conducted himself according to the precision (ἀκριβείας) of the law, and was therefore given the authority by Moses to teach the law. Christ the good shepherd leads the sheep out to the pastures, which means for Theodore that he will provide the sheep instruction in terms of "how they ought to understand Scripture [πῶς δεῖ

---

23. Theodore, *Comm. Jo.* 10 (Conti, 90). For these introductory comments, we must rely on the Syriac translation as we do not have them in the Greek. The first Greek fragment on the passage begins with Theodore's treatment of the word "sheepfold" in 10:1.

24. Theodore, *Comm. Jo.* 10 (Conti, 90). I have translated the Syriac ܐܬܠܐܒ as "parable" instead of "allegory" as Conti has it, as we do not have access to the original Greek, and it is not certain that Theodore would have used the term *allegory*.

25. As I noted above, Theodore claims that he will deal with difficult passages in his preface; see *Comm. Jo.* pref. (Conti, 2). See also my discussion of this trait of the ideal interpreter in ch. 1.

νοεῖν τὰς γραφάς]."[26] More specifically, the Good Shepherd will give them "instruction in parts," that is, "of what they ought to partake first and of what second" (*Comm. Jo.* 10:1–6 [Kalantzis, 77]). The shepherd thus guides the sheep from the more rudimentary commandments of the law toward the loftier. Not only that, but the shepherd also trains the sheep to avoid the interpretations they should flee, such as those of "thieves and bandits" (10:8) (*Comm. Jo.* 10:7–8 [Conti, 92]).

For Theodore, as for Chrysostom, the parable's "thieves and bandits," who are "scaling the entrance and the office" of teacher of the flock, are Theudas and Judas of Galilee from Acts 5:36–37, the two insurrectionists who asserted that they taught something new and useful, thus causing their followers many calamities (*Comm. Jo.* 10:1–6 [Kalantzis, 77]). Likewise, concerning the hired hand in 10:12–13, Theodore too has the Pharisees and scribes of the present narrative in view, for these teachers thought they had been entrusted with the leadership of the people, says Theodore, but they did not actually take care of the flock, and were in any case only hired temporarily until the approach of the true shepherd, Jesus (*Comm. Jo.* 10:12–13 [Kalantzis, 80–81]).

Theodore explains in more detail than Chrysostom how Jesus is the "gate for the sheep" (10:7). With these words, he argues, Jesus means that "he has become for everyone the basis of entering into virtue and the true knowledge of God—that is, the teaching of the gospel, that which is considered to be different from the one outlined roughly in the law." In fact, Theodore argues, "he has given complete control of the entrance into the Truth"; that is, Moses, who let Christ through the gate, has now handed his role of gatekeeper over to Christ, whose sheep will "enjoy true salvation and will be sated and will enjoy abundantly the pasture of the divine teachings" (*Comm. Jo.* 10:7–9 [Kalantzis, 79]). Within the drama of salvation history, then, Moses himself makes way for the teachings of Christ in the gospel, for he demonstrated himself to be the accurate interpreter and indeed the embodiment of the law.

Having explained the gate in this way, Theodore comes as close as he will to finding the church of his own day within the drama of the parable, for he turns to address his reader as the parable's sheep and says:

---

26. Theodore, *Comm. Jo.* 10:1–9 (Kalantzis, 76–77, 79). As I observed above, Theodore, like both Origen and Chrysostom before him, thinks one aspects of the shepherd's care for the sheep is instruction in the law and Scripture more broadly.

Therefore, we have abandoned the works of the law and have applied ourselves to obeying Christ's commandments instead. We have devoted our lives to the principles of the gospel and diligently seek to fulfill his laws.... We can then delight in the blessings we possess through him, thanks to his access to the Father. (*Comm. Jo.* 10:7 [Conti, 91–92])

In other words, Theodore assures his reader, "we are the sheep." He does not belabor the implication that the church has now replaced the people of the Jews as the sheep, but he does provide a similar interpretation to Chrysostom when he comes to 10:16, "I have other sheep that do not belong to this fold." Theodore too thinks Jesus foretells God's inclusion of the gentiles in his people with these words, and that these "other sheep" refer to the faithful of the nations, who will join those faithful from Israel (*Comm. Jo.* 10:16 [Kalantzis, 81]). Here again, the parable instructs his reader concerning the shape of the drama of salvation history, in which the gentiles are brought into God's people under the shepherding of Christ. We have seen that for Theodore, like Chrysostom, the parable provides instruction about the place of Jesus's ministry within the arch of salvation history, and it is primarily the pages of the New Testament that supply the referents of the parable's figures and images, though I also noted some suggestive hints about how he thinks it applies to the church of his day.

Theodore too draws doctrinal instruction from 10:14–15 and 10:17–18. Like Chrysostom, once Theodore has made clear Jesus's parabolic words, he sets to work treating these verses as he has done the other doctrinally significant verses in previous chapters. While he deals with the same issues, his doctrinal treatment is in many ways more complex than that of Chrysostom, as I have shown in previous chapters.

Concerning Jesus's comparison of the sheep's knowledge of Christ with that shared between the Father and the Son in 10:14–15, Theodore explains that there are two different kinds of knowing represented in these verses.[27] Christ and his sheep know each other, for he has made them his own possession, thus "providing for them the virtue that comes from free choice"; in this case knowledge amounts to their recognition of Christ as

---

27. Theodore, *Comm. Jo.* 10:14–15 (Kalantzis, 81). We do not have Theodore's transition to his treatment of these verses in the Greek fragments, but even in the full Syriac translation, he does not provide much of a transition or indication that he is shifting to deal with verses that have been mistreated by heretics. However, it becomes clear throughout his treatment of the verses that he is aware of their potential to lead Arian interpreters to problematic conclusions.

their master as a result of his provision and care. The knowledge shared between the Father and the Son, however, Theodore explains by paraphrasing Christ: "I know the sameness of nature and of the substance of the Father, being consubstantial with him, and he also knows mine."[28] According to Theodore, whereas the Son knows the Father's essence, the sheep know the shepherd only by his actions, namely, his care and provision of free will, which leads to virtue.

When Theodore turns his attention to 10:17, "For this reason the Father loves me, because I lay down my life in order to take it up again," he deals with the same doctrinal issues as Chrysostom did. However, for Theodore, the words, "For this reason the Father loves me," suggest for Theodore nothing more than that the Son "shows death to be both honorable and solemn as it is pleasing to the Father himself." Theodore does not attribute these words to Christ's humanity, as we saw Chrysostom do above, perhaps because he is concerned to deal with both clauses of the verse together; the words, "I lay down my life in order to take it up again" prove Christ's divinity. Christ's death is not like that of other humans, Theodore claims, for he died "when he wanted to" and soon after that he would live again.[29] Theodore's treatment of this verse is unfortunately very brief, though to his credit, he is operating concisely, just as he claimed he would do in his preface, again exemplifying the exegetical virtue he espouses.[30]

For Theodore, Jesus's words in 10:18, "No one takes it from me, but I lay it down on my own accord. I have power to lay it down, and to take it up again. I have received this command from my Father," justify his treatment of 10:17. For, according to this Antiochene, Jesus's authority over death "transcends human nature." Given this interpretation, the next phrase of 10:18, "I have received this command from my Father," presents what Theodore names "a paradox" (παράδοξον), concerning which he says: "it is a command of the Father, and therefore it is necessary for us to believe it," and therefore Jesus's death took place "how [the Father] wanted it to

---

28. Theodore, *Comm. Jo.* 10:14–15 (Kalantzis, 81). Kalantzis notes that this is only one of three uses of the Nicene term "consubstantial" in the extant Greek fragments. The others occur in his treatment of 16:26–27 and 17:3; see Theodore, *Commentary on the Gospel of John*, 81 n. 66.

29. Theodore, *Comm. Jo.* 10:17 (Kalantzis, 82). If he is concerned that the verse as a whole be explained with respect to either Christ in his humanity or divinity, he does not make this explicit.

30. See *Comm. Jo.* pref. (Conti, 2). See my discussion of this aspect of his interpretive approach in ch. 1.

happen" (*Comm. Jo.* 10:18 [Kalantzis, 82]). Unfortunately, Theodore does not say more than this.

Finally, Theodore treats 10:17–21 as a whole in what seems to be a direct refutation of the position of the Apollinarians, who claimed that while Jesus possessed a human body, his soul was no other than the divine Logos.[31] We do not have Theodore's introductory comments to his discussion, but his defense of Jesus's human soul is probably prompted by the words, "because I lay down my life [τὴν ψυχήν] in order to take it up again" (10:17), a verse that required explanation so that it not be understood as evidence of the Apollinarian position. In fact, the verse might provide an example of a difficult verse, which requires explanation by the precise commentator described by Theodore in his preface.[32] Here he argues that the flesh of Jesus had a soul and that this human soul was "united with the divine Logos (ἐνωθεῖσαν ... τῷ Θεῷ Λόγῳ)." However, Theodore continues, "to say that the body of the divine Logos also had a soul does not suggest the divinity of the soul" (*Comm. Jo.* 10:17–21 [Kalantzis, 82]). Theodore is concerned about the implication of the human Christ's possession of a divine soul, namely, the Logos's subjection to the passions and the corruption of the divine nature. The apostle Peter provides an analogy for him, for when he says in John 13:37, "I will lay down my life [τὴν ψυχήν] for you," there is no difference between his words and the Lord's in 10:17. For, Theodore argues:

> You see, just as Peter, who was a man, composed of body and soul [ὢν ἐκ ψυχῆς καὶ σώματος], said this, so too Christ, being one and not two [εἷς καὶ οὐ δύο], composed of divinity and humanity [ἐκ θεότητος ὢν καὶ ἀνθρωπότητος], says that he lays down his soul, which belongs to him and is part of him [ὡς ἰδίαν ἑαυτοῦ καὶ μέρος ἴδιον] (although he was God in nature, assuming flesh—which had soul—and uniting it to himself) [εἰ καὶ Θεός ἦν τῇ φύσει σάρκα ἀναλαβὼν καὶ ἑνώσας ἑαυτῷ ψυχὴν ἔχουσαν]. (*Comm. Jo.* 10:17–21 [Kalantzis, 83])

---

31. Theodore, *Comm. Jo.* 10:17–21 (Kalantzis, 82–83). For a helpful discussion of Apollinaris's and Theodore's christological positions, see Richard A. Norris's introduction to his translation and edition of the documents pertaining to the christological controversies of the early church (Norris, "Introduction," in *The Christological Controversy*, SECT [Philadelphia: Fortress, 1980], 21–26).

32. As I have already noted, Theodore claims he will deal with difficult verses in his preface.

Thus, Theodore defends the human soul of Jesus and provides us here with a concise classical Antiochene christological statement. Jesus is, as a man, composed of body and soul, even as he is both human and divine, being God in nature, but having "assumed" flesh. His being composed of humanity and divinity does not, however, suggest that he is two; rather he is one. Such a discussion we did not find in Chrysostom's treatment of the verse, probably due to the fact that by the time Theodore composed his commentary, the relationship between the human and divine natures of Christ had become a more pressing matter for the church, due in no small part to the thought of Apollinaris and his followers.

In conclusion to Theodore's treatment of the good shepherd parable, we saw that he too searched for the meaning of the parable primarily within the immediate narrative context of John and elsewhere in the New Testament. As it did for Chrysostom, the parable provided instruction about salvation history, in which the gatekeeper Moses approved of Jesus's observance and interpretation of the law over that of the Pharisees and later, the insurrectionists, Theudas and Judas of Acts. We also saw that Theodore turned to his contemporary church setting very briefly as he instructed his readers concerning the meaning of their discipleship under the shepherd, Christ. Finally, he dealt with the parable's final verses similarly to the way we have seen him and our other authors treat verses of doctrinal import; he changed modes and dealt with these verses as straightforward doctrinal statements. Although Theodore's comments on these verses are briefer than Chrysostom's, they are certainly much more doctrinally complex. While we might like more elaboration, and indeed in some instances we have only fragments of comments that presumably were longer, Theodore clearly thinks that he has dealt with these potential issues sufficiently, and as I have shown throughout this study, he aims to be as concise as possible. We will see that Cyril's comments on these doctrinally significant verses are much more extensive.

Cyril's treatment of the good shepherd parable of John 10 is much longer than those of the Antiochenes; the Alexandrian devotes approximately thirty-eight pages of Greek text to the passage (*In Jo.* 10:1–18 [Maxwell, 55–73]). He, too, sets out to decode the parable's characters and images from the pages of the New Testament, and he also interprets the parable within the context of the drama of salvation history. However, these he does only cursorily, for his primary focus in treating the parable, which he alone describes as explicitly "profitable," is to demonstrate for his readers its "true reality," in which the parable speaks directly about the situation of the church in his own day. This is the major way that his treatment differs from his Antiochene contemporaries. Of course, we do not have enough of Origen's treatment of the passage to be able to claim definitively that this distinction between the two schools holds, although the material we do have points in this direction. I will begin with Cyril's comments about the genre of the passage, and from there I will examine his two major interpretations, followed by his treatment of the doctrinally significant verses in 10:14–15 and 10:17–18.

Like Chrysostom and Theodore, Cyril begins his treatment of the passage by demonstrating his awareness of the genre, but, as I mentioned above, he also adds that the parable is profitable. He begins by saying that Jesus "profitably introduces the parable, hinting somewhat obscurely and in riddles [εἰσκομίζει χρησίμως τὴν παραβολὴν, ἀμυδρότερόν πως καὶ ὡς ἐν αἰνίγμασιν ὑποδηλῶν)]" (*In Jo.* 10:1-5 [Maxwell, 56]). I will show below that Cyril thinks Jesus's symbolic words are profitable not only for Jesus's immediate hearers, but also for Cyril's readers.[33]

Cyril describes in more detail his understanding of how Jesus's symbolic speech in the passage works, as he interprets 10:9:

> As usual, he molds the form of his discourse out of the narrative [ἐξ ἱστορίας διαπλάττει τοῦ λόγου τὸ σχῆμα], so to speak, and shapes it into a spiritual contemplation [συμβαίνειν εἰς θεωρίαν πνευματικήν]. He takes what is to all appearances simple, presenting practically no difficulties for understanding, and he makes it an image of matters that are more obscure [εἰκόνα ποιεῖται τῶν ἀφανεστέρων]. (*In Jo.* 10:9 [Maxwell, 59])

For Cyril, Jesus uses a straightforward image to articulate a profound spiritual reality. Later in his treatment of 10:9, Cyril describes the passage as "the type presented by the narrative [τῆς ἱστορίας ὁ τύπος]" (*In Jo.* 10:9 [Maxwell, 59]). So for Cyril, this is clearly a symbolic passage, which he can describe in different ways; it is a parable, a figure of speech (10:6), an enigma, a (obscure) spiritual contemplation, and a type. As we saw in the previous chapter, he seems not to make a distinction between these terms.

I will now examine how Cyril works to draw out from the parable the spiritual profit it offers. I will begin with his first reading of the parable. Moses and the interpretation of the Scriptures are not in view for Cyril

---

33. Cyril claims that Jesus's words are beneficial to his Jewish contemporaries as he treats John 10:6, 7, 8; see Cyril, *In Jo.* 10:6–8.

as he approaches the parable, as they were for the Antiochenes. Nonetheless, he does briefly provide referents for the various characters and images of the parable from the pages of the New Testament, and for him, Jesus's conflict with the Pharisees and scribes of the Johannine narrative is more squarely in view. The Pharisees are represented by the "thieves and bandits" (10:1), and also by its "hired hand" (10:12–13), and thus Cyril spends a great deal more interpretive energy contrasting Jesus the true shepherd with the false teachers, the Pharisees, as he draws from the parable instruction concerning salvation history (*In Jo.* 10:1, 11–13 [Maxwell, 56, 62–63]). For example, Cyril claims that Jesus "cleverly hints [εὐφυῶς ὑπαινίττεται] that [the Pharisees] will never lead those who are going to believe in him, but the sheep will depart from their teaching and cling to the shepherds appointed by him" (*In Jo.* 10:1–5 [Maxwell, 56]). Cyril develops this further when he comes to 10:16 and claims, like the Antiochenes, that Jesus's "other sheep," which he must also bring into his flock, represent the gentiles. Cyril claims explicitly that with these words Jesus predicts that the gentiles will be gathered into one flock with the believers from Israel, and that he will rule not only the flock of Israel, but also the whole world (*In Jo.* 10:16 [Maxwell, 68]).

For Cyril, Christ, not Moses, is the gatekeeper as well as the shepherd and the gate, or perhaps, he says briefly, "the angel appointed to preside over the churches and to assist the priests for the benefit of the people." Concerning false shepherds, he instructs his readers, the prophet Hosea spoke of leaders who reigned as kings, though not through God's Spirit (Hos 8:4), and concerning true shepherds, we are given examples in the apostles and "the teachers of the holy churches after them," whom Christ called by name (Matt 10:5).[34] Concerning Jesus's words in 10:8, "All who came are thieves and bandits,"[35] Cyril claims that Christ either signifies the lying and deceiving prophets of old, or, he says, "you could take the statement to be about what is written in the Acts of the Apostles," and then he goes on to name Theudas and Judas specifically. Like Chrysostom and Theodore, then, Cyril also has an eye to the figures of Theudas and Judas of Galilee in Acts 5:35–37, whose followers were scattered and slain. Here again, however, Cyril finds in these words a warning to the Pharisees: "He

---

34. Cyril, *In Jo.* 10:1–5 (Maxwell, 56–57). Here already, he alludes to the present leaders of the church in that they are in succession from the apostles.

35. Cyril might be working with a variant text, as is indicated by Pusey's note (+ πρὸ ἐμοῦ Aub).

wants them to be eager to enter through the true gate rather than trying to climb into the sheepfold by another way like plunderers" (*In Jo.* 10:8 [Maxwell, 59]). Likewise, even as Cyril provides the possible referent of "any foreign ruler," such as the Babylonians or the Romans for the hired hands of 10:12, here again it is Jesus's Jewish contemporaries, the Pharisees, who take the blame. For the foreign rulers' allowance of the wolf to steal the flock (10:12) took place within the story of salvation history when the Jewish leaders "shook off their subjection to God and burst the bonds of their ancient allegiance" (*In Jo.* 10:11–13 [Maxwell, 63–64]). Despite Cyril's search of the Scriptures to identify other ways of interpreting the referents of the parable's characters, he keeps the main thread of his interpretation in view: the Jews of Jesus's generation have failed in their role as shepherds of God's people.

In fact, according to Cyril, just as for Chrysostom, the prophet Ezekiel in particular prophesied about the generation of Jewish leaders who proved to be such harmful shepherds of the flock of the people of Israel.[36] His treatment, however, is much more developed than Chrysostom's. As Cyril addresses 10:14, where Jesus says again, "I am the good shepherd," he claims that Jesus spoke in this way to remind the Jews what the prophet Ezekiel had said concerning shepherds, which was "for their great benefit [πρὸς ὠφελείας … πολλῆς]." Cyril then introduces a long quotation, Ezek 34:2–6, by saying, "He says this concerning Christ and those who are charged with leading the flock of the Jews" (*In Jo.* 10:14 [Maxwell, 64–65]). The failures of Israel's shepherds that are laid out in the passage, such as their care for themselves rather than their sheep, their neglect of the weak, the sick, the lost, and the scattered, belong to the Jewish leaders in Jesus's time too, according to Cyril.[37] In Ezekiel's words to the shepherds of old, "Thus says the Lord God, 'Behold, I am against the shepherds, and I will take my sheep out of their hands'" (Ezek 34:10), and again, "I will raise up for them one shepherd, my servant David, and he will shepherd them"

---

36. See, however, Cyril, *In Jo.* 10:11 (Maxwell, 61). Here Cyril briefly mentions that the prophet Isaiah correctly prophesied about the leaders of the Jews in Jesus's day with the words "Woe to those who call evil good and good evil, to those who call sweet bitter and bitter sweet, to those who put light for darkness and darkness for light" (Isa 5:20). Cyril also strings together the following prophetic texts against the Pharisees in particular in this context: Jer 36:24; Hos 7:13, 16. These comments are quite terse, however.

37. Note that Cyril uses the terms "Jew," and "Pharisee" just as interchangeably as does the evangelist, John.

(Ezek 34:23–27), claims Cyril, "God declares quite properly and clearly that the unholy multitude of the Pharisees will be removed from leadership of the Jews, and he openly decrees that after them, Christ, who is the seed of David according to the flesh, will rule over the rational flocks of believers" (*In Jo.* 10:14 [Maxwell, 65]). For Cyril it is quite clear that this prophecy was fulfilled at the time of Christ, and that the Pharisees' mistreatment of the sheep resulted in the transfer of the care of the flock from them to Christ.

I will now examine Cyril's articulation of the significance of Jesus as the good shepherd in his treatment of the parable. It is much more eschatological and universal in tone than the readings provided by the Antiochenes. As he interprets 10:11, in which Jesus claims that the good shepherd "lays down his life for the sheep" (10:11), Cyril provides a complex reflection on the role of Christ the shepherd within the cosmic arch of salvation history, in which Christ redeems all of humanity from the sin that resulted in the primordial expulsion from paradise. He explains that, "The human race had wandered off from love for God and inclined toward sin," and that they had therefore been "banished from the sacred divine sheep pen," that is, from paradise, where the devil tricked them into sin. They fell prey then to the wolves of sin and death.[38] However, Christ the good shepherd "laid down his life for us in the struggle against this pair of wild beasts," declares Cyril. He then goes on to specify how Christ laid down his life: "He endured the cross for us in order to kill death, and he was condemned for us in order to deliver all people from the condemnation for their sin." Whereas, Cyril explains, the devil, "the father of sin," laid us down "like sheep in Hades" (Ps 48:15), the true good shepherd died so as to rescue us from the pit of death, and to prepare us to be added to the flock of the company of heaven, in the "mansions above in the presence of the Father" (John 14:2) (*In Jo.* 10:11–13 [Maxwell, 63]). Jesus's sheep will be tended in this way, he argues. Cyril's interpretation of the significance of Jesus as the good shepherd, while still focused on the place of Jesus's ministry within salvation history, is much more universal and eschatological in tone than those of the Antiochenes.

Cyril's second reading of the parable seems to be his primary concern. In this reading, the parable has direct benefit for the church of Cyril's day

---

38. Cyril, *In Jo.* 10:11–13 (Maxwell, 63). Note that Chrysostom also identified the wolf of the parable with the devil, though he did so by using another New Testament passage that provided a precedent for identifying the devil with an animal, i.e., the lion of 1 Pet 5:8. For Cyril, the wolves are abstract concepts: sin and death.

in that it provides instruction concerning appropriate church leadership. Indeed, of my three post-Nicene authors, Cyril alone articulates explicitly his interpretive movement from the decoding of the parable's characters and images with the use of the New Testament narrative to his application of its meaning to his own contemporary church context, which for him is its true meaning. For example, Jesus's words, "the sheep follow him because they know his voice" and "They will not follow a stranger ... because they do not know his voice" of 10:4–5 prompt Cyril to say, "He says this, extending the meaning of the statement to a more general claim [ἐπὶ τὸ γενικώτερον ἐκπλατύνων τοῦ λόγου τὴν δύναμιν], so that you may understand the true concrete reality [ἵνα πρᾶγμα νοῇς ἀληθές]."[39] Having said this, Cyril goes on to discuss just how these words relate to his own church context:

> For we teach in the churches by bringing forward doctrines from the divinely inspired scriptures and by setting out the evangelical and apostolic word as a kind of spiritual food. Those who believe in Christ and who excel with an unswerving faith listen to these words, but they turn away from the voice of the false shepherds and avoid them like the plague. (*In Jo.* 10:4–5 [Maxwell, 56])

The true concrete reality for Cyril then is the way this passage speaks to his contemporary church setting, in which he has seen Jesus's words about true and false shepherds enacted. In his own churches, those who believe in Christ listen to the doctrines that he and his priestly colleagues teach from the Scriptures.

This emphasis is again expressed clearly in his treatment of 10:9, a context in which he makes another comment about the benefit of the parable. Concerning Jesus's words, "I am the gate. Whoever enters by me will be saved, and will come in and out and find pasture," Cyril claims that there is profit for his own readers to be found in the parable, saying, "when we transfer what is hinted at by the narrative into spiritual profit [μεταβιβάζοντες δὲ τὸ ἐξ αὐτῆς ὑποδηλούμενον εἰς ὠφέλειαν πνευματικήν]." The spiritually profitable teaching provides a warning to those who try to take a position of leadership without God's sanction, and who, Cyril argues, will perish for violating God's judgment. On the other hand, says

---

39. Cyril, *In Jo.* 10:4–5 (Maxwell, 56). Maxwell translates πρᾶγμα ἀληθές as "true point."

5. The Good Shepherd Parable of John 10

Cyril, those who rule because their office was given to them by God will govern the sacred fold with security and grace, and will obtain crowns from above, for they desire to benefit their flock. Thus, Jesus as gate means for Cyril that Jesus actually guards the gate and allows only the one who enters by the will of the Father and the Son.[40] For Cyril then, the safety and security presented by the image is given to leaders whom Christ calls, unlike Chrysostom and Theodore, both of whom envision sheep entering the gate, not other shepherds.[41]

For Cyril, too, 10:14–15 and 10:17–18 provide doctrinal instruction. Like the Antiochenes, once Cyril has discussed who and what the parable refers to, he thinks it necessary to deal with these verses in great detail, claiming that they demand "closer scrutiny" (πικροτέραν ἐφ᾽ ἑαυτῷ τὴν βάσανον), which in this case seems to mean that he will attend to the doctrinal matters presented by the text.[42] He is more explicit then than the Antiochenes about the fact that he is shifting gears as it were, but he deals with verses in the same manner, albeit much more extensively.

I begin with Cyril's treatment of Christ's comparison of his knowledge of the Father with the sheep's knowledge of him in 10:14–15. Just as we saw in the Antiochenes' treatment of these words, Cyril argues that the flock's knowledge of their shepherd is not equal to the mutual knowledge of the Father and Son. He begins by saying, "The Father alone knows his own offspring, and he is known by his offspring alone," just as the evangelist Matthew tells us in 11:27: "For no one knows the Son except the Father, and no one knows the Father except the Son." Cyril adds that although we know and believe that the Father is God, as "the Son is likewise true God," we (the sheep) do not know "what the ineffable nature is in its essence." Cyril explains that the sheep's knowledge of the shepherd in this passage therefore means relationship, by either kinship or nature or by participation in grace and honor (*In Jo.* 10:14–15 [Maxwell, 66]). Like Theodore, then, Cyril makes clear that the sheep do not know Christ's nature fully, and he attempts to describe their knowledge in other terms.

---

40. Cyril, *In Jo.* 10:9; cf. *In Jo.* 10:7.
41. However, we saw above that he provided another referent for the shepherd's pastures in the pastures of paradise.
42. Cyril, *In Jo.* 10:14–15 (Maxwell, 65). Clearly these verses are to be treated differently due to their implications for doctrinal instruction.

Cyril, however, will develop his treatment of these verses even further to discuss the christological implications of the verses and to engage in a reflection on Christ's mediating role between humanity and God the Father. He says: "The Word of God, even in the flesh, is a divine nature; and we are his offspring, even though he is God by nature, because he assumed our very flesh." Therefore, because the Father and the Son are related by nature and because we are also related to him by nature in that he became a human being, "Through him, as through a mediator, we are joined to the Father" (*In Jo.* 10:14–15 [Maxwell, 67]). Thus in Cyril's treatment of these verses, not only does he deal with the potential doctrinal issue of the likening of the sheep's knowledge of Christ to Christ's knowledge of the Father, but he also provides a discussion of the two natures of Christ, of Christ's relationship to the Father, and of the implications of the incarnation.

Like the Antiochenes, Cyril also draws out the doctrinal instruction of Jesus's words in 10:17–18. However, again his discussion is much more extensive. He reflects on the reality enacted by Christ's death and resurrection, and deals with the potential theological difficulty of what is said here concerning the Father's seemingly contingent love for the Son. For Cyril, Jesus's words in 10:17, "For this reason the Father loves me," refer both to his laying down of his life, and to his taking it up again. Furthermore, he argues that the Son would not have remained without love had he not died a sacrificial death, for the Son is loved "always and at all times." However, Cyril explains, Christ did not die like us, but as God, through his death and subsequent resurrection, he "nullified the power of death, and he will make us into a new creation." Thus, when the qualities that inhere in natures are brought to actuality, they are then perceivable, and this is the case in this passage concerning the Father and the Son: when God saw his Son "preserving the exact imprint of the sheer goodness of the Father's nature," by laying down his life in love, he reasonably loved him (*In Jo.* 10:17 [Maxwell, 70]). Cyril concludes his treatment of this verse with the following statement:

> Therefore, although [Christ] is always loved because of his nature, he should also be understood to be loved in the sense that by his love toward us he pleases his Father, since in this very act, the Father is able to see the image of his own nature shining forth in utter clarity with no alteration. (*In Jo.* 10:17 [Maxwell, 71])

Unlike the Antiochenes, then, Cyril uses these potentially problematic words of the passage to offer a well-developed articulation of the eternal love of the Father for the Son.

For Cyril, like the Antiochenes, John 10:18, "No man takes it from me, but I lay it down of myself. I have power to lay it down, and to take it up again," presents Jesus's claim that he is "God by nature." Cyril makes clear that Jesus's death was voluntary, for he has "God-befitting power over this *oikonomia*," that is, over his death and resurrection. Given this interpretation, Jesus's subsequent words, "I have received this command from my Father," require explanation. Cyril explains these words so as to correct anyone who might conclude either that the divine Christ might require permission from the Father to exercise his divine authority over death, or conversely that the Father is "unable to restore the Son's life without the Son's permission," both of which introduce "factions and division into the one divine nature of the Father and the Son." To the contrary, Cyril argues, the Father and the Son think and will the same, for Christ is himself the "counsel of the Father." Cyril continues by claiming, like Chrysostom, that Christ speaks here about the Father's command "as is fitting for the incarnation," but that this should not lead to the conclusion that he is inferior to the Father. Cyril concludes his discussion of this verse in a manner that sounds rather like Chrysostom's notion of condescension: he claims that Jesus uses "human words" to speak about a reality that is beyond our capacity to express for the sake of our understanding, and he urges his readers not to "blame the inconsistency of the meaning," but the "weakness of the words" (*In Jo.* 10:18 [Maxwell, 72]).

In conclusion to Cyril's treatment of the passage, we saw again that his interpretation overlapped a great deal with those of the Antiochenes. For he too searched for the parable's meaning in the immediate narrative context of John's Gospel and elsewhere in Scripture, thus finding there instruction about the place of Christ's ministry within the arc of salvation history. For Cyril, the parable's indictment of the Pharisees plays a greater role within this story than we saw in the Antiochenes' treatments, however. Cyril also articulates the significance of Christ as the good shepherd on more cosmic and universalizing terms than did the Antiochenes; for him, the parable teaches about Christ's role within the redemption of humanity from the original fall from paradise through the incarnation and his death and resurrection. However, perhaps the biggest distinction between his and the Antiochenes' treatments of the parable is to be found in his insistence that the parable speaks directly to the church in his own day concerning who ought to lead the church. We saw only hints of such interpretive moves in the Antiochenes' treatments. Furthermore, in the little we have of Origen's treatment of the passage, we saw that the third-century Alexandrian, too, spent a great deal of time explaining how the parable spoke to his own church setting, whether to the individual Christian member of his church, or on a more corporate level, such as how the passage instructed the church about its relationship to heretics.

Conclusion

In this chapter we saw that all four of the authors, in so far as we can include Origen, provided a fitting interpretation of the good shepherd parable, given its genre. All four authors interpreted the parable word by word and identified whom each of the characters of the parable represented. We saw Origen searching the pages of the New Testament in order to do so, and therefore the parable provided instruction about the role of Jesus's ministry within salvation history. These were features of the other three authors' treatments of the passage as well. However, Origen also associated the parable's characters with persons and groups from within his own church setting, and this was also a central thread of Cyril's treatment of the passage. This second interpretive move we saw much less of within the Antiochenes' treatments of the parable. Here, then, lies the main distinction between the two schools in this example.

6
The Resurrection of Lazarus of John 11

In this chapter I examine one final example of the four authors' exegesis of John, namely, the raising of Lazarus in John 11:1–44. The passage follows Jesus's claims in John 10 that he is "the good shepherd, who lays down his life for his sheep" (10:11–18); in our passage, John gives his readers an example in which Jesus does in fact risk his own life by going back to Judea where the Jews have just tried to stone and arrest him (10:31–39), in order to save the life of his friend, Lazarus (11:7–16). Much of the narrative is dedicated to Jesus's interactions with Lazarus's sisters, Mary and Martha, who are grappling with the death of their brother in light of Jesus's identity and love for them (11:3–6, 20–29), and the authors all highlight their exemplary virtue. Prior to raising Lazarus, Jesus announces, "I am the resurrection and the life" (11:25), and "everyone who lives and believes in me will never die" (11:26), which provides evidence for these authors of Jesus's divinity and occasion to explain the general resurrection at the end of the age. My authors also comment, however, on the Fourth Evangelist's very human description of Jesus as he weeps (11:35) and is "troubled in spirit" over the death of his friend, Lazarus (11:33, 38). Finally, the authors seek to solve the potential doctrinal problem of Jesus's prayer to the Father as he raises Lazarus (11:41–42).

Within their literal treatments of the narrative all four authors find moral exemplars in the narrative's characters: Lazarus's virtuous and faithful sisters, Mary and Martha, and Christ, who provides an example of how best to deal with grief, and for Origen, of exemplary posture in prayer. Theodore even finds Thomas exemplary, for he demonstrates great zeal for Christ in his desire to follow him to Judea in the face of potential hostility from the Jews. All four deal with doctrinal issues at the literal level as well, such as the potential christological problem (or not, in the case of Origen) of Jesus's prayer to the Father in 11:41–42, and in the case of the three post-Nicene authors, Jesus's tears and troubled spirit in 11:33–38.

In their treatment of this passage, the Antiochenes stop here, and do not move beyond the letter in order to draw out the passage's benefits.

The Alexandrians, however, find much more that is useful beyond the letter of the text. For Origen, the death and resurrection of Lazarus provides an image of the process of spiritual death and life that can be witnessed in the lives of church members at various stages in their spiritual journey toward the Father, from the Christian who has fallen away, to the one who is made alive through repentance. The passage at this level also teaches about Jesus's work of removing sin and leading individuals toward virtuous lives. For Cyril, similarly, the raising of Lazarus is a type of Christ's universal redemption of all humanity from sin, in addition to his healing of each individual's mind. Cyril finds an additional benefit in that the nonliteral level of the passage also provides instruction about the sacrament of baptism.

In this chapter, then, the distinction between the two schools is stark: the Antiochenes simply do not move beyond the letter of the narrative in order to provide instruction for the spiritual development of their audiences, whereas, once again, the Alexandrians discern the passage's spiritual benefit both at the level of the narrative and beyond it, at the nonliteral level. Once again, we will see that this distinction has implications for the kinds of benefits that the school members draw out of the passage. That is, the nonliteral level is where one discusses the manner in which the passage relates directly to one's contemporary church setting, such as we see in the Alexandrians' treatments of this passage. For each of them, the raising of Lazarus story speaks about Christ's renewal of the spiritual life either within individual church members or for the entire church. We simply do not find such readings in Antioch, for these authors do not move beyond the letter to discern this kind of instruction.

I will first examine Origen's treatment of the passage, whose comments on this chapter we have in book 28 of his *Commentary on John*, which is approximately twenty-two pages of Greek text (*Comm. Jo.* 28.1–79 [Heine, 292–309]). Unfortunately, we do not have his treatment of 11:1–38, but we do have his comments on 11:39–45, the (admittedly) brief section of the Johannine passage in which Jesus raises Lazarus from the dead. Fortunately, however, these extant comments also include a summary of his understanding of the passage as a whole. Origen deals with these verses on both the literal and nonliteral (in this example, the anagogical) plane, and I will first examine his treatment of the text at the literal level before turning to examine his move to the nonliteral level and the benefits he discovers there.

6. The Resurrection of Lazarus of John 11

However, before turning to Origen's explanation of the literal narrative, I should note that Origen begins his treatment of 11:39–45 with a prayer, as is his custom, and thus he models for his readers what he has argued is necessary for the correct understanding of the Fourth Gospel.[1] "Let us call upon God," he says, "who is perfect [τὸν τέλειον] and the provider of perfection through our perfect high priest Jesus Christ, that he might grant that our mind may discover [εὑρεῖν] the truth concerning what will be investigated [τῶν ἐξετασθησομένων] and their composition [κατασκευὴν αὐτῶν]."[2] After this prayer, Origen sets to work examining the words of 11:39, and indeed, once he has concluded his literal treatment of 11:41, he makes the implicit claim that as a result of his prayer his careful examination of these verses has been assisted by God.[3] He claims that "So many related thoughts have been disclosed [φανέντα] to us on this point in relation to the statement, 'Jesus lifted up his eyes,'" and demonstrates once more for his readers the necessity of seeking God's help in searching the Scriptures (*Comm. Jo.* 28.25 [Heine, 297]).

For Origen there are two kinds of beneficial instruction the passage has to offer at the literal level, which he treats briefly before moving to the nonliteral plane: The characters offer examples to be emulated and there is doctrinal teaching to be gleaned. We will begin with the former.[4] As he deals with 11:41, in which Jesus looks upward after the stone of Lazarus's tomb has been removed and says, "Father, I thank you that you have heard me," Origen indicates, as is his tendency, that he will deal first with the verse at the literal level, which he describes here as "what has been written" (τὰ γεγραμμένα). Concerning "what has been written" in the verse, Origen says, "The statement now being examined teaches us that he changed his thought from his conversation with those below and lifted it up and exalted it, bringing it in prayer to the Father who is over all."[5] It becomes clear that

---

1. Origen, *Comm. Jo.* 28.6 (Heine, 293). See his comments in his preface about the necessity of prayer for proper biblical interpretation in *Comm. Jo.* 1.89; see also my discussion of these comments in ch. 1.

2. Origen, *Comm. Jo.* 28.6 (Heine, 293). I note below that his prayer is seemingly answered in the course of his treatment of these six verses, which he claims at 28.38.

3. There are forty-one lines missing from the manuscript in his treatment of 11:39, so I am unable to use his examination of these words for my purposes here.

4. Origen provides a brief discussion about why his readers should not emulate the unbelief of Lazarus's sister Martha as he deals with 11:39–41, which I shall not examine here; see *Comm. Jo.* 28.14, 17, 22 (Heine, 294–96).

5. Origen, *Comm. Jo.* 28.24 (Heine, 296); cf. *Hom. Ps.* 15 1.3. In his first homily on

Origen finds Christ's manner of prayer to the Father to be exemplary for his readers as he goes on to compare Christ's prayer, particularly the position of his eyes, with the prayer postures and eye positioning of other scriptural figures. Origen proceeds to discuss the question of who (of his readers) ought to be able to imitate Jesus by lifting up his eyes in this manner of prayer, and who is not able to do so. The apostle Paul provides Origen with an example of one who is able to emulate Christ, for Paul prays zealously and "lifts up the eyes of his soul," and thus brings them up from "deeds, memory, thoughts, and reasonings" to "great and heavenly matters." The tax collector of Luke 18:9–14, however, could not bring himself to lift his eyes but prayed, "God be merciful to me, a sinner," thus providing a counterexample.[6] Having provided these scriptural examples of two different postures of prayer, Origen claims, "But let each one judge himself concerning such matters," whether the posture of Jesus or the tax collector applies to oneself (*Comm. Jo.* 28.26–28 [Heine, 297]). He continues by explaining that there are times in one's life where it will be proper to lift up one's eyes and times when it is not, and it is up to each person to judge appropriately.[7] At the literal level, Jesus's posture of prayer in 11:41 has provided an occasion for Origen to instruct his readers not only about Jesus's exemplary posture of prayer, but also about the posture of prayer more generally. Therefore, for Origen, these words uncomplicatedly present Jesus's exemplary prayer to the Father, whereas for my later three authors, as we shall see, Jesus's prayer to the Father requires a great deal of explanation, lest the Son be understood as inferior to the Father.[8]

Origen finds a second kind of benefit at the literal level of the narrative: His discussion of a potential doctrinal issue that arises for him as he interprets 11:43–44. He thinks it necessary to address whether it was the Father or the Son who raised Lazarus. The question arises because while

---

Ps 15, Origen provides a similar discussion of Jesus's prayer to the Father; cf. *Or.* 13.1. Here Origen again makes the same argument and cites John 11:41–42 alongside his high priestly prayer in John 17:1 and instances of Jesus's solitary prayers in the Synoptic Gospels (Mark 1:35; Luke 11:1).

6. Origen, *Comm. Jo.* 28.25–26 (Heine, 296–97); cf. 28.32–34.

7. Origen, *Comm. Jo.* 28.30–38 (Heine, 297–99). Origen finds another exemplary posture of prayer in Susanna in the story of Susannah in the Daniel cycle Susannah (Theodotion Susannah 9:35) in 28.34–45, the prophet David in 28.33.

8. I will demonstrate below that Cyril too thinks Jesus exemplary in his prayer to the Father, but he also feels the need to deal first with the potential issue for Trinitarian doctrine that the Son's prayer to the Father presents.

6. The Resurrection of Lazarus of John 11

Jesus claimed, "but I go that I may awaken him" in 11:11, which Origen suspects is fulfilled when he then says "Lazarus, come forth" in 11:43, Jesus also prays to the Father concerning Lazarus's soul. Origen solves this tension and "makes a distinction [διαφορὰν διδούς]" between the statements "Lazarus is asleep" (11:11) and "Lazarus is dead" (11:14); when Jesus cries, "Lazarus come forth" (11:43), he is simply waking Lazarus, whom he said was asleep in 11:11 (*Comm. Jo.* 28.70 [Heine, 307–8]). In this reading, then, it is the Father who raised him from the dead, and it is Jesus who woke him from sleep.

However, Origen entertains another solution to the problem, which he introduces through a rhetorical opponent who "refutes the apparent distinction [ὁ λύων τὴν ἐν τούτοις δοκοῦσαν εἶναι διαφοράν]," and argues that the resurrection of Lazarus was "the common work of the Son who prayed and the Father who heard." This person, Origen argues, will need to adduce the words Jesus spoke to Martha: "I am the resurrection and the life" (11:25), and also the words, "For as the Father raises the dead and gives life, so also the Son gives life to whom he will" (5:21).[9] In other words, there is evidence within the passage at hand, and in an earlier Johannine passage, to support the hypothetical opponent's position. Origen does not commit himself to one option or the other, however, but seems to leave the decision up to his reader. Given that he writes so much earlier than the Trinitarian and christological controversies that ensue in the fourth and fifth centuries, he is able to leave the question open, a luxury his successors did not have, as we shall see below.

It becomes apparent that Origen has been working with 11:43–44 at the literal level as he discusses these doctrinal matters only once he reaches 11:45, "Many of the Jews who had come with Mary and had seen what Jesus did believed in him." As he turns to deal with the verse, he says, "But hear the words about these people also not only in the literal sense [μὴ μόνον σωματικώτερον]" (*Comm. Jo.* 28.76 [Heine, 309]). Having announced this

---

9. Origen, *Comm. Jo.* 28.71 (Heine 307–8). We do not have Origen's treatment of Jesus's words in 11:25–26, "I am the resurrection and the life," and "those who believe in me ... will never die," words that for him clearly here provide an example of John's "more perfect expressions" about Christ, since it manifests his divinity fully; cf. *Comm. Jo.* 1.22; cf. 1.125, 181, 267–268; 19.6; 32.106; *Princ.* 1.2.4; *Hom. Lev.* 9.11.3; *Hom. Exod.* 12.1.4. In a few instances he uses this verse to clarify other texts containing the word "life": *Comm. Jo.* 13.19 where he interprets the "living water" of John 4; *Comm Rom.* 6.11.3 on Rom 8:1–2, "the law of the Spirit is life"; *Dialogus cum Heraclide* in explanation of Deut 30:15, "see I have set before you life."

shift, he moves to the nonliteral plane to deal with this verse. I will not deal with his treatment of it, as it does not contribute to the overarching nonliteral meaning that Origen finds in the narrative.

Origen makes another explicit shift from the literal to the nonliteral level of the narrative. Once he has finished dealing with 11:41–42, which we examined above, Origen confirms once more here that those comments were "in relation to the literal meaning [πρὸς τὸ ῥητόν]." However, he goes on to make an explicit shift to the nonliteral plane by saying, "On the other hand, the anagogical sense concerning the passage is not difficult in consequence of what we have already explained [ἡ δὲ κατὰ τὸν τόπον ἀναγωγὴ ἐκ τῶν προαποδεδομένων οὐ δυσχερής]" (*Comm. Jo.* 28.48–49 [Heine, 302]).

I will now examine the nonliteral reading Origen provides the passage, to which he devotes most of his attention. Once he has made the shift above the letter, he sets to work relating the various aspects of the story of Lazarus's physical death and resurrection to Lazarus's spiritual death and restoration. For Origen, Lazarus's physical death is representative of Lazarus's sin, which he understands as his death to God, and the physical raising of Lazarus represents the restoration of Lazarus's relationship with God. In this anagogical reading, the crowd standing around saw that someone had become foul-smelling (11:39), which for Origen, was the result of his "sins unto death" (1 John 5:16); Lazarus's return to life was his return to virtue, at which the crowd marveled (*Comm. Jo.* 28.49–50 [Heine, 302]).

As he develops his nonliteral reading, Origen relates the main features of the story of Lazarus to the various stages of church members' journeys toward the Father. The passage teaches about Jesus's work of removing sin and leading individuals toward virtuous lives, and about the movement from spiritual death to spiritual life. For example, as Origen interprets Lazarus's resurrection from the tomb at Jesus's command in 11:43–44, he finds that Lazarus represents those persons within the church who had fallen away, but had now returned to God at the invitation of Christ. Origen says, "there are some Lazaruses even now who, after they have become Jesus's friends, have become sick and died … and later were made alive by Jesus's prayer, and were summoned from the tomb to the things outside it by Jesus with his loud voice" (*Comm. Jo.* 28.54 [Heine, 303]).

There are other members of the church, however, whom Origen finds represented by those outside the tomb, whom Jesus commands to remove Lazarus's bandages (11:44). Concerning this verse Origen claims that even after he receives life at Jesus's command (11:43), Lazarus still possesses "bonds worthy of death from his former sins," about which he can do nothing "until Jesus commands those who are able to loose him and let him go." Those able to free the Lazaruses in the present church are its other members, those who are able to say, "Christ speaks in me" (2 Cor 13:3).[10] Thus, according to Origen the person who has fallen away can return to life by the command of Christ through an invitation by the mature members of the church who abide in Christ. To aid him in this nonliteral interpretation, Origen draws on the words of Heb 6:4–6, for the author of Hebrews (for Origen, this is Paul) discusses the fate of the person who has fallen away "after having been enlightened, after having tasted the heavenly gift, and after having become a partaker of the Holy Spirit." Although this person ought to be considered as though they were in Hades in the land of the dead, there is hope for them when Jesus comes to the tomb asking the Father that his words and voice be full of power, when he cries out with a loud voice, and when he summons his friend to come outside the tomb (or out from the life of the gentiles).[11]

Finally, Origen develops his nonliteral reading further, introducing another way in which the raising of Lazarus represents members in the church, as he turns to provide another interpretation of 11:44. In this case he focuses on John's description of the strips of cloth on Lazarus's hands, feet, and face. For Origen, this provides an image for another kind of person in the contemporary church, namely, the one who is made alive through repentance, but who is still bound by sin.[12] The bandages on Lazarus's hands, feet, and face Origen understands as the bonds of sin. However, Origen explains, Christ's command, "Loose him and let him go,"

---

10. Origen, *Comm. Jo.* 28.54 (Heine, 303). Origen also provides another interpretation of "them" whom Jesus commands to "loose him and let him go" (11:44). He says that Jesus's command "could perhaps even be addressed to angels," citing Matt 4:11, "angels came and ministered to him," and reminds his reader of "the anagogical sense related to the passage"; see *Comm. Jo.* 28.66. (Heine, 306).

11. Origen, *Comm. Jo.* 28.55–56 (Heine, 304). While Origen draws on the words of this verse, he ignores the words, "it is impossible," which introduces the words he has quoted, and thus the (altered) verse from Hebrews authorizes his reading. For the author of Hebrews, it is impossible to restore such a person again, since they are "crucifying again the Son of God and are holding him up to contempt" (Heb 6:5–6).

12. Origen, *Comm. Jo.* 28.57–58 (Heine, 304); cf. Irenaeus, *Haer.* 5.13.1. Irenaeus associated Lazarus's death with the spiritual death of sin, though in a less developed manner than we will see here in Origen's treatment. In particular, Irenaeus associates Lazarus's bandages (11:44) with the bondage of sin.

is so strong that it releases this person's hands and feet, and removes the veil from their face (a probable allusion to 2 Cor 3:14–15), so that this person too might become one who himself reclines with Jesus, as Lazarus does in John 12:2 (*Comm. Jo.* 28.60 [Heine, 305]).

In conclusion to Origen's treatment of the passage, we saw that he dealt with the narrative both literally and nonliterally. As in the previous chapters, the literal narrative provided him with two kinds of instruction: that based on the examples set by the characters of the narrative, and doctrinal teaching. In this case, Christ (and several other scriptural figures) provided an example of appropriate posture in prayer. Concerning doctrine, the raising of Lazarus provided Origen the opportunity to discuss the degree to which the Father and the Son shared equal operations and wills. We saw Origen shift explicitly to the nonliteral level, where the passage provided his readers with instruction concerning the various stages of the individual Christian's journey from the spiritual death of sin to spiritual life, which is marked by communion with God and virtue.

Chrysostom interprets the narrative in three homilies that make up about eighteen columns of Greek text (*Hom. Jo.* 62–64 [Goggin, 165–205]). Chrysostom deals with the passage at the literal level, though he does not claim this explicitly.[13] As is his habit, he treats the passage verse-by-verse, commenting on textual and doctrinal issues, and paraphrasing the speech of the various characters. Again, he dedicates the last section of his homilies to moral exhortation, in this case concerning topics that are (for the most part) connected directly to the passage at hand, namely, dealing faithfully with one's grief.

According to Chrysostom, the literal narrative provides two main kinds of beneficial instruction, just as we saw in Origen's treatment. First, the characters of the story provide models to be followed. Christ's example teaches about the virtue of humility and the appropriate manner of dealing with grief, as do Lazarus's faithful and virtuous sisters. Second, the passage provides doctrinal instruction concerning Jesus's divinity, despite the potential christological issues posed by Jesus's grief over the loss of his friend Lazarus, and of Jesus's prayer to the Father in 11:41–42.

I will begin with the first kind of instruction provided by the literal narrative, namely, the exemplary lives of the narrative's characters, on which Chrysostom spends a great deal of interpretive energy. He introduces what

---

13. See my discussion in the introduction about my choice to characterize his treatment in this way.

is for him the main theme of the passage immediately, claiming that John told the story "in detail [ἕνεκεν ἀναμιμνήσκει]," in order to teach us that we "ought not to complain and bear it hard if those who are exemplary men and friends of God become sick." Therefore, he argues, we should not be "scandalized" by the suffering of those who are pleasing to God, such as Lazarus and his sisters, for it is actually the privilege of those who are dearest to God to suffer (*Hom. Jo.* 62.1 [Goggin, 165–66]). Within this discussion, Chrysostom discusses the examples provided by Lazarus's sisters and Christ, for they dealt appropriately with their grief.

I will first examine Chrysostom's treatment of Lazarus's exemplary sisters, Mary and Martha. For Chrysostom, they are "worthy of admiration," for although they heard Jesus's words, "This sickness is not unto death" (11:4) and then watched their brother die, the sisters maintained their confidence in Christ and did not conclude that he deceived them by claiming that his sickness was not unto death. While we might have expected them to lament or cry upon seeing Christ's late arrival in Bethany, Chrysostom claims, to the contrary, they expressed admiration of him (*Hom. Jo.* 62.1 [Goggin, 167]). Concerning Jesus's exchange with Martha in 11:25–27 specifically, Chrysostom credits her with having "gained enough profit" (ἐκέρδανε) through the power of Christ's words so as to bring her grief to an end. Chrysostom notes that Mary too is praiseworthy here for neither is she "overcome by her strong feeling of grief" in Jesus's presence. He concludes his comments about the exemplary women by saying that "besides being loving, the minds of the women were truly virtuous" (*Hom. Jo.* 62.3 [Goggin, 174]). In fact, Mary in particular is a clear example for Chrysostom of one who "puts the tenets of Christian philosophy into practice," for she was not held back by grief, nor did she wish to make a show of her sorrow, and so she went out to meet Jesus (*Hom. Jo.* 63.1 [Goggin, 179]).

Chrysostom also thinks that Christ's manner of handling his grief in the passage is exemplary for his readers. While Christ showed grief when he wept over his friend Lazarus (11:35), he was not guilty of "weeping without restraint," and thus Christians are to act likewise and "weep, but gently, with decorum, with the fear of God." However, Chrysostom clearly does not think that his parishioners currently know how to deal appropriately with their grief, for he goes on to remonstrate with his hearers, who "make a show of their mourning and lamentation," for the remainder of his homily, which he concludes with an extended discussion of the appropriate manner of expressing the grief that results from the loss of a loved one. The Christian, he argues, who knows about the resurrection, which is the most important blessing of the faith, ought not to weep like the pagans, who "know nothing of the resurrection." Instead of grieving for the Christian brother or sister who has fallen asleep in the Lord, Chrysostom exhorts his parishioners to "grieve, rather, for your sins," which is "the soundest practice of Christian teachings" (*Hom. Jo.* 62.4–5 [Goggin, 174]). The passage's instruction concerning the appropriate manner of dealing with grief as a Christian person is one of its primary benefits at the literal level.

According to Chrysostom, in this passage Christ also provides a model of humility for his readers. For example, as he treats 11:11, where Christ tells his disciples that Lazarus has "fallen asleep" and that they must go to Bethany so that he might wake him, Chrysostom observes that Christ did not add words such as "I go that I might raise him up," for he did not want to be boastful. In fact, Chrysostom claims explicitly that Jesus's humility in the passage provides a lesson for his parishioners: "This was to teach us to always avoid vainglory and that we ought not to make promises too freely" (*Hom. Jo.* 62.1–2 [Goggin, 168–69]). Similarly, concerning 11:42, in which Jesus acknowledges that many have gathered to witness the raising of Lazarus, Chrysostom claims that Jesus says humble things of himself in order to induce his hearers to "reflect on his humility … and instruct his hearers not to say anything great of themselves" (*Hom. Jo.* 64.1 [Goggin, 193]).

The second kind of instruction that Chrysostom finds at the literal level is doctrinal and concerns the humanity and divinity of Christ. For example, as he deals briefly with Jesus's words in 11:4, "This sickness is not unto death, but for the glory of God so that through it the Son of God may be glorified," he claims that with these words, Jesus "spoke of his glory and the Father's as one" (*Hom. Jo.* 62.1 [Goggin, 167]). Not surprisingly, another verse that provides evidence of Jesus's divinity is his "I am" statement in 11:25, "I am the resurrection and the life," and the words of the following verse, "everyone who believes in me … will never die." By this "I am" statement, says Chrysostom, Jesus gives clear evidence of his own authority, and "he made it plain" that he did not need anyone to help him raise Lazarus.[14]

Just as the passage provides evidence of Christ's divinity, according to Chrysostom, so too does it prove that he is fully human. For example, John's portrayal of Jesus in 11:33, "he was troubled in spirit and deeply moved [ἐνεβριμήσατο τῷ πνεύματι καὶ ἐτάραξεν ἑαυτόν]," confirms "the

---

14. Chrysostom, *Hom. Jo.* 62.3 (Goggin, 172–73); cf. 10.28.4 on John 5:21; *Hom. Heb.* 11.2 where John 11:26 is an example of an oath sworn by Jesus as God as Chrysostom interprets Heb 6.

fact of his human nature," and that by the words, "he groaned in spirit [ἐνεβριμήσατο τῷ πνεύματι]," John meant that Jesus "outwardly restrained his troubled feelings."[15] According to Chrysostom, then, Jesus's emotions in these verses demonstrate emphatically his full humanity, and furthermore, that he was in control of these emotions, which he restrained in an exemplary fashion.

The passage also provides doctrinal instruction about the divine Christ's condescension, one of the most prominent themes of Chrysostom's thought, as we have seen in previous chapters. For example, concerning 11:26, which I mentioned above, Chrysostom claims that since Christ is the resurrection and the life, he is not "restricted by place," but he is present everywhere, and thus while he could have raised Lazarus from a distance, that is, without taking four days to get to Bethany, "he condescended" (συγκάτεισιν) to the sisters' wishes and came to them to raise Lazarus (Hom. Jo. 62.3 [Goggin, 173]). Similarly, Chrysostom thinks that Jesus's question in 11:34, "Where have you laid him?" has the potential to lead some to an inappropriate view of Christ, and therefore he argues that the question does not betray Jesus's ignorance, but that with it, he "condescended [συγκαταβαίνει] to their weakness."[16]

The theme of Christ's condescension resurfaces as Chrysostom deals extensively with 11:41–42, in which Jesus is depicted as praying to the Father.[17] For Chrysostom, these words again pose the potential doctrinal problem of Jesus's inferiority to the Father, which he deals with by claiming that Jesus's act of prayer in this passage is again first and foremost the product of "his condescension."[18] The passage itself provides Chrysostom

---

15. Chrysostom, Hom. Jo. 63.1 (Goggin, 181); see also 63.2 where he deals again with the verb ἐνεβριμήσατο in John 11:38, and provides the same interpretation.

16. Chrysostom, Hom. Jo. 63.1 (Goggin, 181). Another way of dealing with this verse is represented by Athanasius in his C. Ar. 3.26. According to Athanasius, John 11:34 was used by the Arians to argue that the Son is not the true wisdom of the Father if he has to ask "where have you laid him?" Athanasius argued in this context that the ignorance ascribed to Jesus must be attributed to the flesh, for the Logos knows everything. He asked the question, "bearing our ignorance," so that he might grant us the grace of knowing his Father. This example of partitive exegesis is another way of dealing with such verses, which Chrysostom himself uses in other instances.

17. Chrysostom devotes nearly an entire homily to these two verses (Chrysostom, Hom. Jo. 64.1–3 [Goggin, 190–200]).

18. Chrysostom, Hom. Jo. 64.1 (Goggin, 192); cf. 80.1 where he comments on Jesus's high priestly prayer in John 17:1.

part of this argument: Jesus prays "for the sake of the crowd standing here," which Chrysostom quotes alongside a similar verse, John 12:30, in which Jesus claims that his Father's voice came down from heaven "not for me did this voice come, but for you" (*Hom. Jo.* 64.1 [Goggin, 192]).

Having argued that the potential doctrinal issue raised by Jesus's prayer in 11:41–42 is effectively explained with recourse to the loving condescension of Christ, Chrysostom provides several supplementary arguments that demonstrate Christ's equality to the Father. The Old Testament in particular is of help here; Chrysostom finds several examples in which God the Father speaks with a "humble tenor" for the sake of humanity. For example, he cites God's question to Adam and Eve, "Where are you?" in Gen 3:9 to argue that God the Father also allowed many such things to be said about himself.[19] Furthermore, Chrysostom argues, despite Jesus's prayer to the Father, the Son is equal to the Father, just as Jesus claims: "I in the Father and the Father in me" and "The Father and I are one" and "He who sees me sees the Father" (John 10:37–38, 30; 12:45). Finally, through the use of a rhetorical opponent, an unnamed heretic, probably an Arian, Chrysostom provides additional argumentation that the divine Christ did not need prayer to raise Lazarus. He goes on to list examples from the gospels in which Jesus performed miracles without prayer, followed by examples in which the apostles call on Christ's name in their prayers before performing miracles.[20]

We have seen that for Chrysostom the story of the raising of Lazarus provides instruction for the church through the examples set by the narrative's characters; Christ, Mary, and Martha model primarily the appropriate manner of dealing with grief over the loss of a loved one. The passage also provides doctrinal teachings concerning Christ's divinity, humanity, his loving condescension to sinful and limited humanity, and his equality with the Father. We will see that Theodore draws out similar instruction for his readers from the passage, and we will turn now to examine his treatment of it.

Theodore also remains at the literal level as he interprets the raising of Lazarus narrative, and his treatment is again shorter than Chrysostom's.[21]

---

19. Chrysostom, *Hom. Jo.* 64.2 (Goggin, 195). He also cites Gen 18:21; 22:12; Ezek 3:11; Deut 5:29; Ps 85:8; 2 Kgdms 18:19; see also *Hom. 1 Cor.* 39 on 1 Cor 15:27.

20. Chrysostom, *Hom. Jo.* 64.2 (Goggin, 195–97). He marshals examples from Mark 1:41; 4:39; 9:24; Matt 9:2.

21. Again, Theodore does not claim to be working at the literal level of the narrative; this is my assessment.

Nearly all of Theodore's comments on John 11 are extant in Greek. We have eleven pages of Greek text in sixteen fragments; the full Syriac translation also consists of eleven pages (*Comm. Jo.* 11:1–55 [Greek: Kalantzis, 86–95; Syriac: Conti, 100–106]). In his verse-by-verse comments, Theodore deals with the verses he deems unclear and with those that have potential doctrinal implications. He claims explicitly that the passage is beneficial, particularly as a result of the Fourth Evangelist's description of Mary and Martha, concerning which we shall say more below.

Like Chrysostom, in his literal treatment of the passage, Theodore highlights the virtue of Lazarus's sisters, and that he too thinks the story teaches about the appropriate manner of dealing with grief, but only through the behavior of Christ. However, as we mentioned above, Theodore also highlights for his readers the positive behavior of the disciple Thomas. Finally, as we saw in Origen's and Chrysostom's treatments, Theodore too finds beneficial doctrinal teachings in the literal narrative, primarily concerning Christ's divinity. However, he too deals at length with 11:41–42, in order to explain the christological implications of Jesus's prayer to the Father.

I will first examine Theodore's comments about the positive behavior of the narrative's characters, beginning with the sisters of Lazarus, Mary and Martha, for indeed, according to Theodore, John "mentions the virtue of the women for our benefit [πρὸς ἡμετέραν ὠφέλειαν]," and John shows "clearly" (σαφῶς) that "he wants to indicate incidentally that the virtue of the women contributes to the education of the readers." He claims that both Mary and Martha were "God-fearing," particularly Mary, for she anointed the Lord with myrrh (John 12:1–8) (*Comm Jo.* 11:1–3 [Kalantzis, 86]). For Theodore, among the myrrh-bearing women, Mary had a "great affinity" to Christ, and was also obedient.[22] Despite this introductory statement, however, Theodore says very little about the behavior of Mary and Martha throughout the remainder of his treatment. After he says briefly concerning 11:3, in which the women send for Jesus once Lazarus becomes ill, that their request demonstrates their faith and respect for him, he says little more on the matter.[23]

Theodore alone of my four authors thinks that Thomas's behavior and words in the passage are to be highlighted for his readers. For Theodore,

---

22. He probably has the story of Mary and Martha from Luke 10:38–42 in view as he makes this comment.

23. Theodore, *Comm Jo.* 11:3 (Kalantzis, 87); cf. *Comm. Jo.* 11:5. Concerning 11:5, he says in passing again that the women "were in accord with virtue."

Thomas exhibits noteworthy love for Christ, which he says as he comments on 11:16, in which Thomas says, "Let us go, that we may die with him."[24] Not only were Thomas's words to the other disciples "logical" according to Theodore, but they were also "sufficient to show what great love he had gained for the Master," despite their betrayal of his weak faith. In fact, for Theodore, Thomas appears as a leader of the disciples in this moment due to his suggestion that it was "better to share in death, than to save themselves and desert their teacher" (*Comm Jo.* 11:16 [Kalantzis, 89]). This positive discussion of Thomas is similar to his positive treatment of the disciples' question concerning the sin of the blind man in 9:2–3, which we discussed in chapter 4; for Theodore, the (saintly) disciples are straightforwardly to be treated in a positive light.

For Theodore, it is Christ who provides a model to be followed in regard to dealing with grief. For example, concerning 11:35, in which Jesus weeps, Theodore claims that even though he knew he was about to raise Lazarus, "he gave us the tears as the boundary of grief, so as not to do anything beyond this." According to Theodore, then, his tears were given as a pedagogical gift to the Christian reader, an interpretation of the verse that is similar to Chrysostom's. Similarly, as he comments on 11:38, in which Jesus is "moved in spirit," Theodore claims that Christ was "moved, as was reasonable" (*Comm. Jo.* 11:35, 38 [Kalantzis, 93]). Unfortunately, he says no more than this. Again, his discussion of this application is much briefer than Chrysostom's, but they are similar to those of his fellow Antiochene.

Theodore too finds the literal narrative to be beneficial in another way, namely, in its doctrinal instruction. For him, the story of the raising of Lazarus teaches primarily about Christ's divinity. For example, concerning 11:4, "This sickness is not unto death, but for the glory of God so that through it the Son of God may be glorified," Theodore claims that the event would contribute to the glory of the Father and the Son, but that "it makes no difference if someone wants to apply [εἰρῆσθαί] what is said of God to Christ himself" (*Comm. Jo.* 11:4 [Kalantzis, 87]). In other words, the two are equal in glory. Jesus's words in 11:25–26, "I am the resurrection and the life ... those who live and believe in me will never die," provide further

---

24. For Chrysostom, in the face of the Jews' hostility, Thomas is "more fearful than the rest," and he instead highlights Jesus's compassion for Thomas's weakness, and Thomas's later redemption; see Chrysostom, *Hom. Jo.* 62.2 (Goggin, 169–70). While Cyril acknowledges Thomas's zeal, he focuses on his cowardice and his failure to recognize Christ's power in his treatment of the verse; see Cyril, *In Jo.* 11:16 (Maxwell, 85).

evidence of Jesus's divinity, for by them, claims Theodore, Jesus argues that he is "the cause of the resurrection," not only of this man, but also of those at the end of the age. Theodore goes on to paraphrase Jesus's words in these verses, claiming that he is saying: "as the Father is so am I; whoever believes in me lives, even though he may die, accepting death with the promise of the blessed hope of future things" (*Comm. Jo.* 11:25–26 [Kalantzis, 90]).

However, Theodore, too, must deal with the potential doctrinal issues presented by 11:33 in which Jesus is deeply moved in spirit when he arrives in Bethany to find Lazarus dead. Unlike Chrysostom, for whom the verse provides proof of Jesus's full humanity, for Theodore, this verse too concerns Jesus's divinity. For Theodore, Jesus's distress "means anger," and this anger he had "as God," for he saw beforehand that the Jews would not believe in him even upon seeing this miracle.[25] Just as we saw in Theodore's treatment of the cleansing of the temple narrative in John 2, for this interpreter, Jesus's godly anger is not a problem, and he turns quickly to 11:34 to address Jesus's question, "Where have you laid him?" According to Theodore, the question does not betray ignorance, an implication of the verse that Chrysostom worried about. In Theodore's view, Jesus "saw from a great distance" that Lazarus had died, but delayed his journey to Bethany so as to avoid boasting, and in order to show that he did the miracle by a certain "order" (*Comm. Jo.* 11:34 [Kalantzis, 93]). Unfortunately, Theodore does not explain further what he means by this, but it suggests something similar to Chrysostom's concept of condescension, and perhaps also that Theodore understands Jesus to perform the miracle in a way that allows for its veracity to be clear to all.

Theodore's recourse to an explanation very much like Chrysostom's notion of Christ's condescension surfaces again as he deals with Jesus's prayer in 11:41–42, though he does not use the term συγκατάβασις. Like Chrysostom, Theodore argues that with his prayer Christ "seems to attribute in some way the miracle to the Father," but as Jesus says in 11:42, such an attribution is "on account of those who were present," in order than none of them would think that his will was "foreign to the Father." So, like Chrysostom, Theodore argues that Jesus's prayer demonstrates his unity of will with the Father. Of course, Theodore explains, it is "not fitting for the God Logos, the creator of all, to receive power to raise him who was dead through prayer," and he did not need the prayers to do so.

---

25. Theodore, *Comm. Jo.* 11:33 (Kalantzis, 92); cf. *Comm. Jo.* 11:38 (Kalantzis, 93).

Theodore uses John 2:19, in which Jesus says, "Destroy this temple and in three days I will raise it up," to argue that Jesus did not even need the power of another to raise his own body, as we saw him argue in chapter 2 above. Therefore, Theodore concludes, Jesus certainly did not need the help of prayer to raise Lazarus.[26] For Theodore, then, Jesus prayed because his hearers needed to see that he was aligned with the Father, with whom they were more familiar.

This concludes my section on Theodore's brief literal treatment of the passage. We have seen that he finds the passage beneficial in its provision of examples for his readers to follow in the characters of the sisters of Lazarus, Thomas, and Christ himself. He too finds doctrinal instruction in the passage, particularly in that it highlights Christ's divinity and unity with the Father, but also Christ's condescension to the needs of the crowds who observed the raising of Lazarus. Like Chrysostom, he does not go beyond the literal level of the passage in order to draw out this beneficial instruction.

Cyril provides his reading of the passage in thirty pages of Greek text (*In Jo.* 11:1–44 [Maxwell, 82–95]). He deals verse by verse with the text and comments on verses and words that require clarity and that pose doctrinal difficulties. He claims explicitly that Jesus's words, his humble example, and the miraculous raising of Lazarus are all beneficial. Unlike the Antiochenes, but like Origen, Cyril deals first with the literal narrative, followed by the nonliteral, which he describes variously as the narrative's type, image, and its inner meaning. These nonliteral meanings too he explicitly describes as beneficial. I will first deal with the benefits he finds at the literal level before turning to examine his explicit shift to the nonliteral plane and the benefits he finds there.

Like the previous three authors, there are two major benefits that Cyril finds in the passage at the literal level. For Cyril, the characters of the narrative, particularly Lazarus's sisters, the disciples, and Christ behave in ways that warrant positive comment. Christ's example in particular teaches the leaders in his own church setting how best to comfort someone who is grieving. This is a slight variation on the interpretations of the Antiochenes, for Cyril finds Christ exemplary for the church leader

---

26. Theodore, *Comm. Jo.* 11:41–42 (Kalantzis, 94). Similarly, Jesus did not need to give a "loud cry" in order to raise Lazarus in 11:43, but this too was for the sake of the onlookers. The onlookers needed to know that Jesus was summoning the soul from far away in order to believe the miracle; see, Theodore, *Comm. Jo.* 11:43 (Kalantzis, 94).

who is comforting the grieving person, rather than for the person grieving. Cyril also finds the passage doctrinally beneficial; the passage teaches about Christ's divinity, and about the relationship between Christ's two natures. I will next examine the explicit indications of Cyril's move beyond the letter of the narrative, and the benefits he draws from the text once he has made this shift. In this example of Cyril's exegesis, it is his explicit shifts to the nonliteral plane that indicate to us that his discovery of moral exemplars and doctrinal teaching have been part of his literal treatment of the narrative. We will see that for Cyril at the nonliteral level, the passage provides instruction about Christ's redemption of all humanity, who were spiritually dead in their sin, in addition to Christ's redemption of the individual Christian's mind, which he calls the passage's inner meaning. He also finds in 11:21–27 a type concerning his contemporary church's sacrament of baptism.

I begin with Cyril's comments about the positive behavior of the characters of the narrative. Cyril claims immediately that Lazarus's sisters, Mary and Martha, are named by the evangelist "intentionally" to demonstrate that they are distinguished in piety, and furthermore that the perfume with which Mary anointed Jesus's feet (John 12:1–8) is mentioned not by chance, but so as to demonstrate her "thirst for Christ."[27] Cyril describes the sisters' words in 11:3, in which they send Christ the message that their brother is sick, as being "full of faith" (*In Jo.* 11:3 [Maxwell, 83]). Concerning Martha in particular, Cyril claims in his treatment of 11:40, that with her faith she healed Lazarus; since he was dead, with her own faith, she made up for what was lacking in his.[28]

For Cyril, all of Jesus's disciples behave positively in this passage, particularly in their attempts to prevent Christ from going to Bethany (11:7–8). This they did, claims Cyril, "because of their love for him." Even though they were "thinking in a human fashion" when they reminded Jesus of the Jews' maliciousness, their intention was good, and in any case, once they gained more understanding, they obeyed Jesus and followed him

---

27. Cyril, *In Jo.* 11:1–2 (Maxwell, 82). Clearly Cyril too has Luke's story of Mary and Martha in view as well as he makes these comments (Luke 10:38–42); cf. *In Jo.* 11:28–29.

28. Cyril, *In Jo.* 11:40 (Maxwell, 91). However, he will go on again to compare Martha and Mary, claiming that "Mary is more intelligent" and thus expresses no doubt, while Martha fell into "the disease of double-mindedness"; see *In Jo.* 11:30 (Maxwell, 92).

to Bethany, conceding that he knew best (*In Jo.* 11:7–8 [Maxwell, 83–84]). According to Cyril, the disciples' behavior in this passage is to be celebrated, rather than ridiculed.

As we saw in the Antiochenes' treatments of the passage, Jesus in particular provides an example to be followed. For Cyril, as we saw in Chrysostom's treatment, he is exemplary in his humility. Cyril claims explicitly that by Christ's words in 11:11, "Our friend Lazarus has fallen asleep," he avoids boasting "for our instruction and benefit [πρὸς ἡμετέραν διδασκαλίαν καὶ ὠφέλειαν]." Instead of saying directly that he must go to Bethany to raise Lazarus from the dead, says Cyril, Jesus utters words that are "obscure and hidden" in order to provide an example of humility for his disciples, and for the contemporary reader in Cyril's day. Similarly, as Cyril interprets 11:14–15, in which Jesus tells his disciples plainly, "Lazarus is dead," followed by, "For your sake, I am glad I was not there, so that you may believe," he argues that Christ's words and attitude are worthy of emulation. According to Cyril, he is not glad due to a "love of glory" but because the situation has become an occasion for faith (*In Jo.* 11:11, 14–15 [Maxwell, 84–85]). Likewise, he finds Jesus's words in 11:23 exemplary as well. When he tells Martha, "Your brother will rise again," Cyril claims that Jesus did not say, "I will raise your brother," because of his "aversion to boasting."[29] In all of these examples, Jesus could have boasted to his hearers by giving them more information about the miracle he was about to perform, but he held back for "our sake," claims Cyril, so that we might learn to avoid boasting.

According to Cyril, Christ is an example in particular for those leading the churches of his present day.[30] For church leaders, he is exemplary in the manner that he deals with Mary's grief in 11:32. In response to her words, "Lord, if you had been here, my brother would not have died," he says nothing to correct her, observes Cyril, but he weeps with her. Thus, he is "an example for us [ἡμέτερον ὑπόγραμμον]," so that when we deal with a mourning person, we do not correct them in their grief (*In Jo.* 11:32 [Maxwell, 89]).

Interestingly, Cyril finds one more way in which Jesus is exemplary, and this in his treatment of Jesus's prayer in 11:41–42. Even though these verses

---

29. Cyril, *In Jo.* 11:23 (Maxwell, 86); cf. *In Jo.* 11:40.

30. Here again we have potential support for Maxwell's theory that Cyril wrote his commentary on John's Gospel for leaders within the church who would be teaching catechism. See my discussion of his theory above.

cause Cyril just as much interpretive anxiety as they did the Antiochenes, he manages to maintain, as did his Alexandrian predecessor, that Christ, by praying to the Father, provides an example for the church.[31] Like the Antiochenes, Cyril claims that Jesus gave "the appearance of prayer" for the sake of the crowd and not because he needed the Father's help to perform the miracle. However, he is still able to say that, "according to the *oikonomia*," Christ gives thanks "as an example to us [πρὸς ὑπογραμμὸν ἡμῶν], honoring the Father" (*In Jo.* 11:41–42 [Maxwell, 92]).

The second kind of benefit Cyril finds in this passage at the literal level is its provision of doctrinal instruction. Several of Jesus's words and deeds instruct Cyril's readers about Christ's divinity. For example, like the Antiochenes, Cyril claims that in 11:4, in which Jesus says, "This illness does not lead to death; rather it is for God's glory, so that the Son of God may be glorified through it," that Jesus speaks as God, foretelling what he will do.[32] Cyril understands Jesus's words here as a clear statement that he is "by nature God."[33] Similarly, when Jesus claims in 11:11 that "Our friend Lazarus has fallen asleep," according to Cyril, these words demonstrate his "God-befitting power," in that death to him is merely sleep (*In Jo.* 11:11 [Maxwell, 84]). Similarly, for Cyril, as we saw in my other three authors' treatments, Jesus's words in 11:25–27 provide further evidence of Christ's divinity, for Christ claims to provide eternal life to all in the general resurrection (*In Jo.* 11:25–27 [Maxwell, 87]).

Like the Antiochenes, according to Cyril, in addition to his divinity, some of Jesus's words and deeds in the episode demonstrate his true humanity and his loving condescension. For example, Cyril claims concerning 11:32, in which Christ comforts Mary in her grief, that with his own weeping Christ "condescends [συγκαταβαίνει] to her and reveals his human nature." Similarly, concerning 11:34, in which Jesus asks those present in Bethany, "Where have you laid him?," Cyril claims that the question does not betray any ignorance on his part, for Jesus knew of Lazarus's death from "another part of the country." Rather, in speaking this way, Christ speaks "in accordance with the *oikonomia* to draw many people to that place with his word"; that is, Christ speaks in his humanity, as an act of

---

31. Cyril, *In Jo.* 11:41–42 (Maxwell, 92); cf. *In Jo.* 6:11 where Jesus prays before multiplying the loaves.

32. Cyril, *In Jo.* 11:4 (Maxwell, 83); cf. *In Jo.* 11:14–15, 43–44 where Jesus says, "Lazarus is dead … let us go to him," and "Lazarus, come out!" respectively.

33. Cyril, *In Jo.*11:4 (Maxwell, 83); cf. *In Jo.* 11:21–24.

condescension to those present.³⁴ As he discusses 11:34, Cyril, like Chrysostom, uses Gen 3:9, in which God asks, "Adam, where are you?" in order to argue that the Father, like the Son, can be found asking a question and feigning ignorance, and thus by Jesus's question, says Cyril, "he is shown to be equal to the Father."³⁵ Similarly, for Cyril Jesus's suffering in 11:36–37 "was proper to the flesh and not the divine nature" (*In Jo.* 11:36–37 [Maxwell, 90]). One final example is Cyril's treatment of 11:41–42. Like the Antiochenes, Cyril argues that with his prayer in 11:41–42, Jesus is "speaking in an earthly fashion as a human being according to the *oikonomia*, not according to the superiority of the divine nature."³⁶ It is not a mark of "inferiority of essence," Cyril argues, "when an equal gives thanks to an equal," but here, as Jesus himself claims, his prayer was "for the sake of the crowd" (11:42).³⁷ Actually, notes Cyril, in a manner that is similar to Origen's comments on the verses, these words gave "the appearance of prayer" for the sake of the crowd, for the "mind of the Trinity … is one" (*In Jo.* 11:41–42 [Maxwell, 92]).

Finally, for Cyril, 11:33, in which Jesus "groaned in his spirit and was deeply moved," provides an opportunity to discuss the interaction between Jesus's divine and human natures. Unlike Chrysostom, who claimed that Jesus's grief displayed his true human nature, and unlike Theodore, who thought it demonstrated his divinity, for Cyril, the verse indicates something more profound. He begins by saying that "Christ is not only God by nature but also human." Therefore, "When grief begins to stir in him and his holy flesh inclines to tears, he does not allow it to indulge those tears without restraint," but "by the power of the Holy Spirit he rebukes his own flesh." In other words, even though the flesh trembles and issues tears, and thus gives it "the appearance of being troubled," Jesus's divine nature teaches the weak flesh and transforms it (ἀναμορφώσῃ), so that all human flesh learns to have feelings "beyond its own nature," feelings that are pleasing to God.³⁸ According to Cyril, in the flesh of Christ's own

---

34. Cyril, *In Jo.* 11:32–34 (Maxwell, 89–90). For a similar understanding of this verse, see *Hom.* 2 of Severian of Gabala on the creation.

35. Cyril, *In Jo.* 11:34 (Maxwell, 90). Tertullian, however, in *Prax.* 16.4, understands Gen 3:9 as evidence of the Son's preincarnational assumption of human affections.

36. Cyril, *In Jo.* 11:41–42 (Maxwell, 92); cf. *In Jo.* 17:1.

37. Cyril, *In Jo.* 11:41–42 (Maxwell, 92). Note that he made a similar argument about Jesus's voluntary death in John 10:18 as he discusses the Father's command to the Son.

38. Cyril, *In Jo.* 11:33 (Maxwell, 89); cf. *In Jo.* 11:38–39; 13:21.

person, the universal human infirmity of being subject to grief is "neutralized" (καταργεῖται), and as a result, all of humanity receives benefit from what first took place in the flesh of Christ (*In Jo.* 11:33 [Maxwell, 89]). Cyril thus goes beyond the Antiochenes' discussions of Christ's grief, by providing his readers with an explanation of the implications of the incarnation for such infirmities as the experience of despair and grief.

I will now examine Cyril's explicit articulation of his shift to the nonliteral level of the passage. It is Jesus's loud cry in 11:43, which he claims is "completely foreign and unusual for Christ the Savior," that indicates to Cyril that Jesus performs the miracle "for the benefit [χρήσιμον] of the hearers," and that it was "a kind of type [τύπον] of the general resurrection of the dead."[39] He continues: "He sets forth what he did for one person as a beautiful image [εἰκόνα καλήν] of what is more general and common to all" (*In Jo.* 11:43 [Maxwell, 94]). Thus Christ indicates by this action, that he will act in the same manner on behalf of all humanity as he heals the one man, Lazarus. It is Christ's (uncharacteristically) loud cry in 11:43 that indicates for Cyril that John intends us to discover the eschatological resurrection of all humanity beyond the letter of the narrative. Cyril draws on the assistance of two Pauline passages to assist him in this argument, both of which discuss the trumpet calls associated with the final resurrection.[40] The first is 1 Cor 15:52, in which Paul says of the general resurrection, "For the trumpet will sound, and the dead shall be raised imperishable," and second is 1 Thess 4:16, "For the Lord himself, with a cry of command, with the archangel's call and with the sound of God's trumpet, will descend from heaven, and the dead in Christ will rise first." Cyril concludes his nonliteral treatment of this verse by saying: "Therefore, as a type of this, the Lord spoke to Lazarus with a loud cry that could be heard from a distance … in order to show us a type of what to expect to happen in the future" (*In Jo.* 11:43 [Maxwell, 94-95). As we have seen in previous chapters then, at the nonliteral level, Cyril finds beneficial instruction concerning salvation history. In this instance the relationship between Jews and gentiles is not his focus as it has been in previous chapters, but here he is concerned with the general resurrection of all in the age to come, which the passage itself indicates (11:25-26).

---

39. Cyril, *In Jo.* 11:43 (Maxwell, 94). Note that Theodore made a similar claim concerning the general resurrection in his interpretation of 11:25-26, but for him such a comment was part of his literal treatment of the passage.

40. Cyril reproduces this discussion in his *Comm. Joel.* 3:13-16.

There are additional benefits to be found in 11:44, in which Jesus says, "Unbind him, and let him go." According to Cyril, Jesus again "profitably [χρησίμως] commanded them to untie him," for this too is "a picture" (δεῖγμα) of the general resurrection, when not only death, but also sin will be destroyed and all people will be set free. Cyril here provides a nonliteral interpretation of this verse that resembles Origen's: Jesus's triumph over Lazarus's physical death represents Jesus's triumph over the spiritual death caused by sin. In addition, for Cyril, the bandages on Lazarus's hands and feet, and the cloth over his face represent the veil of sin by which all people were bound, as he claims, "We had fallen into sin like a kind of veil, and we wrapped its shame around the face of our soul and were bound by the ropes of death." Again, this treatment resembles Origen's, though for Cyril, all of humanity is in the same state of spiritual death; the various classes of believers in Origen's treatment have no place in Cyril's nonliteral reading. At the general resurrection, then, according to Cyril, Christ will free all humanity from "our original evil" and will "remove the veil of shame." According to Cyril, the nonliteral meaning of these verses, namely, Christ's future triumph over the tyranny of sin and the spiritual death that plagues all of humanity, fulfills what was spoken by the prophet Malachi: "You will go out leaping, like calves set free from their bonds."[41]

Cyril's nonliteral treatment goes beyond that of Origen, however, for he provides 11:44 with another nonliteral treatment, which concerns Christ's restoration of the human mind. This Cyril indicates by saying, "Now consider the miracle ... according to its inner meaning [λάμβανε δέ θαῦμα καὶ τὰ ἐντός]." In this particular nonliteral interpretation, Lazarus stands not for all of humanity, but for "our mind," which was also dead like Lazarus. He argues that both "our material flesh and nobler soul" must go to Christ with a confession and a request for help, as did Martha and Mary (11:3). If we do this, Christ will "command the hardness that lies upon our memory to be removed" and cry with the loud voice, "Come out of the distractions of the world," loosing the cords of sin and allowing us to move toward virtue (*In Jo.* 11:44 [Maxwell, 95]). Even if more psychologically developed, this inner meaning of Cyril's reading is similar to Origen's anagogical reading, in which Jesus invites his friend, the Christian individual, first into relationship with God, then toward the life of virtue. Both find in the story Christ's redemption of all humanity from sin, both now at present for the

---

41. Cyril, *In Jo.* 11:44 (Maxwell, 95). Here, then, is another instance in which Cyril's nonliteral treatment of a passage is a fulfillment of Old Testament Scripture.

individuals within their own church settings, but also at the end of the age for all humanity.

Finally, as we have seen in previous chapters, Cyril can treat isolated verses nonliterally, once he has dealt with them first at the literal level. He does so here in his treatment of Jesus's exchange with Martha in 11:21–27, in which Jesus asks her whether she believes that those who believe in him will live forever. After he has dealt with the verses' doctrinal instruction, Cyril claims that in these verses Jesus asks her for "the assent of faith" on behalf of her brother Lazarus, by which he is "establishing a type for the churches in this matter [τὺπον ταῖς ἐκκλησίαις τὸν ἐπὶ τούτῳ θείς]." Here again Cyril uses the term "type" in an ambiguous manner. However, I will take it to refer to something of a prediction concerning his contemporary church practice, for Cyril continues by saying that in the churches, "we say, 'I believe' during the reception of holy baptism ... when a newborn infant is brought either to receive the chrism of the catechumenate or at the consummation of holy baptism, the one who brings the child says 'amen' on its behalf."[42]

In conclusion to Cyril's treatment of the passage we have seen that he works at both levels of the text to draw out its beneficial teaching, as did his predecessor, Origen. As for all three other authors, for Cyril the passage provides practical lessons through the narrative's characters. For Cyril, Mary, Martha, and the disciples demonstrate exemplary faith and piety, whereas Christ exemplifies the virtue of humility, and models the appropriate way for church leaders to deal with a grieving person. For Cyril, as was also true for my other three authors, the story illustrated the doctrines of Christ's divinity and his humanity. We saw that Cyril also found occasion to discuss the relationship between the two natures of Christ much more explicitly than the Antiochenes.

Finally, in a manner similar to Origen, we saw Cyril make an explicit shift to the nonliteral level in order to draw out the beneficial teaching that Christ's raising of Lazarus represented his resurrection of all humanity, both literally at the end of the age, and spiritually, at present. He found the additional benefit of the passage's inner meaning, that is, the narrative's teaching about Christ's healing of the individual person's mind, and finally a type concerning the sacrament of baptism in the contemporary church.

---

42. Cyril, *In Jo.* 11:27 (Maxwell, 88). Cyril continues to explain that the same teaching holds with respect to the situation in which an infirm person cannot confess the faith on his own behalf.

Conclusion

Once again, we have seen in this example of the narrative of the raising of Lazarus that the Alexandrians dealt with the passage at both its literal and nonliteral levels, whereas the Antiochenes remained at the level of the narrative. Again, this had implications for the ways in which these authors derived instruction for the spiritual development of their audiences. All four authors found moral and practical instruction through the characters of the narrative, and doctrinal teaching at the literal level. However, the Antiochenes did not make an explicit move beyond the letter to find the additional beneficial instruction found by the Alexandrians, in which the passage spoke directly about their contemporary church settings, and about Christ's redemption of humanity from the spiritual death caused by sin, at present and at the end of the age.

Conclusion

In this study I have aimed to demonstrate that a critical distinction between the two schools of Antioch and Alexandria lies in the ways the school members found instruction for the spiritual development of their audiences in the biblical text. To demonstrate this, I have focused my analysis on a major exegetical principle shared by all four of these authors: Scripture is inherently beneficial or useful and it is the exegete's duty to draw out the benefits of the text for their audiences. This, in turn, has allowed me to determine the authors' rationales—or perhaps in some cases at least, their rhetorical justification—for providing either a literal or a nonliteral reading of a given text.

We saw in chapter 1 that all four authors introduced the Gospel of John as a beneficial text, primarily because it provided doctrinal instruction concerning the divinity of Christ. However, throughout this study, we have seen that despite their shared understanding of the benefit of the Fourth Gospel, the authors' treatments of specific passages of John provided evidence of important differences between the two schools' exegesis. In each passage I examined we saw that the Antiochenes remained at the level of the literal narrative as they drew out the benefits of the Fourth Gospel for their respective audiences, whereas the Alexandrians found much that was beneficial for their readers at both the literal and the nonliteral levels. Therefore, while I hope to have provided a more nuanced articulation of the distinction between the two schools than the scholars of the traditional position, my study has nevertheless demonstrated that, in one sense, the difference between the two schools is certainly not unrelated to literal and nonliteral exegesis. Consequently, we cannot do away with these categories for our analysis. Indeed, I have demonstrated a direct correlation between the type of reading—either literal or nonliteral—and the kinds of benefits these authors draw out of the text for the spiritual development of their readers and hearers.

We saw that the literal level of the Johannine narrative was indeed a site of overlap between the two schools, for all four authors found the gospel beneficial in its provision of doctrinal instruction, and of moral and practical lessons—often through the examples set by the characters of the narrative—about the life of virtue and serious discipleship. In addition, the literal narrative of John also provided the occasion for instructing their readers and hearers concerning the relationship between Jesus's life and teaching and Old Testament Scripture, and on occasion, it also provided instruction about the place of the gentile church within salvation history. In my view, it is significant that all four of the authors seem to be in agreement that further insight or contemplation (θεωρία) is not required to discern doctrinal and moral instruction in John's narrative.

In addition to the overlap in the authors' treatments of the literal narrative, however, we observed a major difference between the two schools' treatments of John. As mentioned above, in each of our case studies we saw that the Alexandrians consistently moved explicitly beyond the letter to provide a nonliteral reading wherein they drew out further benefit for their readers. Except for Chrysostom's brief shift to the nonliteral plane in his treatment of the narrative of the man born blind, such an explicit move above the letter is simply absent from the Antiochenes' exegesis of our passages of focus. The Alexandrians tended to provide each Johannine passage as a whole with an overarching nonliteral reading in addition to occasional nonliteral treatments of isolated verses. Above the letter, the Alexandrians tended to find benefits for their readers that related directly to the church in their own day, at either the corporate or the individual level.

In fact, one of the most important differences between the two schools that I have demonstrated in this study is that for the Alexandrians each passage of John spoke directly concerning the authors' contemporary church settings, and not infrequently, to the individual Christian's soul or mind. That is, in Alexandrian nonliteral exegesis the biblical text provided teaching concerning Christ's redemptive work in the life of the contemporary corporate body of the church and in the lives of its individual members. We have seen throughout this study that Origen and Cyril frequently found the Gospel of John, at its nonliteral level, to provide instruction for their church settings concerning the church's relationship to the heterodox other, concerning appropriate church leadership, and concerning the present church's sacramental life, including the practice of the veneration of the saints and the rite of holy baptism. In addition, the gospel provided illustrations of Christ's manner of providing discipline and healing to the church body through the removal or punishment of sinful members, and finally, it provided depictions of Christ's visitation and healing of the individual Christian's soul. We saw only one example in which in the Antiochenes' treatments of the passages of John we examined came close to this kind of reading, namely, the good shepherd parable, and this they did only in passing. This difference simply cannot be ignored.

I will conclude with a quotation of Brian E. Daley from a recent encyclopedia entry on Christology in the early church. There he draws a parallel between the two schools' biblical exegesis and their christological positions, saying the following:

> The usual way of understanding their differences is to see the Antiochene theologians maintaining a 'Word-human being' (*Logos-anthropos*) model of the person of Christ, in which the eternal Word or Son of God, fully divine in nature, has taken up a complete human being to be in his 'temple.'... The result is that while God the Son and Jesus are never to be confused into a single subject or agent, they reveal each other in a single common form. Along with this approach to understanding Christ, these authors were also known for their distinctive way of interpreting the message of scripture, in which God is understood to reveal his will and our future through human events, but as God, remains independent of history, transcendent, and uncircumscribed. The Alexandrian school of the late fourth and fifth centuries, on the other hand, took the inspiration for its Christology from Athanasius and for its biblical interpretation from Origen. Jesus, in Cyril of Alexandria's understanding, always remained God the Word, subsisting in the full humanity that he had made his own—a single divine subject acting and suffering in his own soul and flesh. To those spiritually gifted enough to seek the Bible's deeper meaning, the whole canon of scripture told this story, as well as that of the people united with him by faith and the sacraments. The active, personal presence of God in the world, which had reached its climax in Christ and the Church, is the central message of the Gospel.[1]

Daley articulates here what was once a commonly held distinction between the two schools, both in terms of their christological positions and their parallel approaches to Scripture. It has not been my aim in this study to address the distinction between the two schools vis-à-vis Christology,

---

1. Brian E. Daley, "Christ and Christologies," in *The Oxford Handbook of Early Christian Studies*, ed. Susan Ashbrook Harvey and David G. Hunter (Oxford: Oxford University Press, 2008), 886–905, esp. 897.

though I have noted such distinctions as they have arisen within these authors' treatments of John's Gospel. I am more interested here in the way that Daley articulates the distinction between their understandings of Scripture's message, which he describes in terms of transcendence and immanence. In Antioch, as he says, God's will is thought to be revealed through the lives and events described in the text, but God is thought not to be immediately engaged in the ongoing workings of history and the lived lives of human beings. In Alexandria, however, the Bible—especially its "deeper meaning"—tells the story of Christ and his people, the Church, for God is personally active in the world. While I would have liked Daley to have expanded upon these comments, the distinction he draws goes some way to describing what I have articulated in this study concerning the different ways the school members discerned Scripture's benefits for the sake of the spiritual development of their audiences. The Antiochenes, as we have seen, tended to find moral and doctrinal instruction for their audiences based on the lives and events presented by John's Gospel. In the remarkably few instances in which they offered a nonliteral reading of a passage or dealt with a compositional allegory, their readings pertained to the place of Jesus's ministry or of the church within the drama of salvation history, the details of which they found within the pages of Scripture itself. There is here a degree of remove with respect to Scripture's ability to speak to the specific situation of the Christian community and its individual persons. By contrast, the Alexandrians' belief that Scripture provided not only moral and doctrinal instruction but also teaching that related directly to the situation and practice of their contemporary church and its individual members illustrates well the immanence to which Daley refers.

Bibliography

PRIMARY SOURCES

Critical Editions

Cyril of Alexandria. *Commentarium in Isaiam prophetam*. PG 70. Paris, 1862.
———. *Sancti Patris nostri Cyrilli archiepiscopi Alexandrini in D. Joannis Evangelium*. Edited by Philip Edward Pusey. 3 vols. Oxford: Clarendon, 1864.
John Chrysostom. *Expositio in Psalmos*. PG 55. Paris, 1862.
———. *Homiliae in Genesin*. PG 53. Paris, 1863.
———. *Homiliae in Joannem*. PG 59. Paris, 1862.
———. *Homiliae in Matthaeum*. PG 57. Paris, 1862.
Origen. *Commentaire sur le Cantique des Cantiques*. Edited by Luc Brésard, Henri Crouzel, and Marcel Borret. SC 375, 376. Paris: Cerf, 1991, 1992.
———. *Commentaire sur saint Jean*. Edited by Cécile Blanc. SC 120, 157, 222, 290, 385. 5 vols. Paris: Cerf, 1966–1992.
———. *Homilien zu Samuel 1, zum Hohelied und zu den Propheten*. Edited by W. A. Baehrens. GCS. Origenes Werke 8. Leipzig: Hinrichs, 1925.
———. *Homélies sur la Genèse*. Edited by Henri de Lubac and Louis Doutreleau. 2nd ed. SC 7. Paris: Cerf, 2003.
———. *Homélies sur Jérémie 1*. Edited by Pierre Nautin. SC 232. Paris: Cerf, 1976.
———. *Jeremiahomilien; Klageliederkommentar; Erklärung der Samuel- und Königsbücher*. Edited by Erich Klostermann and Pierre Nautin. 2nd ed. GCS 6. Origenes Werke 3. Berlin: Akademie, 1983.
———. *Mattäuserklärung*. Edited by Erich Klostermann, Ernst Benz, and Ursula Treu. 2nd ed. GCS 57. Origenes Werke 11. Berlin: Akademie, 1976.

———. *Die neuen Psalmenhomilien: Eine kritische Edition des Codex Monacensis Graecus 314*. Edited by Lorenzo Perrone. GCS 19. Origenes Werke 13. Berlin: de Gruyter, 2015.

———. *La Philocalie 1-20 sur les Scriptures*. Edited by Marguerite Harl. SC 302. Paris: Cerf, 1983.

———. *Der Römerbriefkommentar des Origenes: Kritische Ausgabe der Übersetzung Rufins*. Edited by Caroline P. Hammond Bammel. Vetus Latina 34. Freiburg: Herder, 1998.

———. *Traité des principes, Livres I–V*. Edited by Henri Crouzel and Manlio Simonetti. SC 252, 253, 268, 269, 312. Paris: Cerf, 1978, 1980, 1984.

———. *Traité des principes (Peri Archon)*. Edited by Marguerite Harl, Gilles Dorrival, and Alain Le Boulluec. CEAug.SA 68. Paris: Études Augustiniennes, 1978.

Theodore of Mopsuestia. *Commentarius in Evangelium Ioannis Apostoli*. Edited by Jacques Marie Vosté. CSCO 115. Leuven: Ex Officina Orientali, 1940.

———. *Essai sur Theodore de Mopsueste*. Edited by Robert Devreesse. ST 141. Vatican City: Biblioteca Apostolica Vaticana, 1949.

Translations

Cyril of Alexandria. *Commentary on the Gospel of John*. Translated by David R. Maxwell. ACT. 2 vols. Downers Grove, IL: InterVarsity Press, 2013, 2015.

———. *Commentary on the Prophet Isaiah 1–14*. Translated by Robert C. Hill. Brookline, MA: Holy Cross, 2008.

Jerome. *Commentary on Isaiah: Including St. Jerome's Translation of Origen's Homilies 1–9 on Isaiah*. Translated by Thomas P. Scheck. ACW 68. New York: Newman Press, 2015.

John Chrysostom. *Homilies on Genesis 1–17*. FC 74. Translated by Robert C. Hill. Washington, DC: Catholic University of America Press, 1985.

———. *Homilies on Genesis 18–45*. Translated by Robert C. Hill. FC 82. Washington, DC: Catholic University of America Press, 1990.

———. *Homilies on Genesis 46–67*. Translated by Robert C. Hill. FC 87. Washington, DC: Catholic University of America Press, 1992.

———. *Commentary on the Psalms*. Translated by Robert C. Hill. 2 vols. Brookline, MA: Holy Cross, 1998.

———. *Commentary on Saint John the Apostle and Evangelist Homilies 1–88.* Translated by Sister Thomas Aquinas Goggin. FC 33, 41. Washington, DC: Catholic University of America Press, 1957, 1959.

———. *Old Testament Homilies: Homilies on Isaiah and Jeremiah.* Translated by Robert C. Hill. 3 vols. Brookline, MA: Holy Cross, 2003.

Origen. *The "Belly-Myther" of Endor: Interpretations of 1 Kingdoms 28 in the Early Church.* Translated by Rowan A. Greer and Margaret M. Mitchell. WGRW 16. Atlanta: Society of Biblical Literature, 2007.

———. *Commentary on the Epistle to the Romans Books 6–10.* Translated by Thomas P. Scheck. FC 104. Washington, DC: Catholic University of America Press, 2002.

———. *Commentary on the Gospel according to John.* Translated by Ronald E. Heine. FC 80, 89. Washington, DC: Catholic University of America Press, 1989, 1993.

———. "Commentary on the Gospel of Matthew." Translated by John Patrick. *ANF* 9:780–1017.

———. *Homilies on Jeremiah; Homily on 1 Kings 28.* Translated by John Clark Smith. FC 97. Washington, DC: Catholic University of American Press, 1998.

———. *Homilies on Luke; Fragments on Luke.* Translated by Joseph T. Lienhard. FC 94. Washington, DC: Catholic University of America Press, 1996.

———. *Homilies on Numbers.* Translated by Thomas P. Scheck. ACT. Downers Grove, IL: InterVarsity Press, 2009.

———. *On First Principles.* Translated by G. W. Butterworth. New York: Harper & Row, 1966.

———. *The Song of Songs Commentary and Homilies.* Translated by R. P. Lawson. ACW 26. Westminster, MD: Newman Press, 1957.

Theodore of Mopsuestia. *Commentary on the Gospel of John.* Translated by George Kalantzis. ECS 7. Strauthfield: Saint Pauls, 2004.

———. *Commentary on the Gospel of John.* Translated by Marco Conti. ACTS. Downers Grove, IL: IVP Academic, 2010.

———. *Commentary on the Minor Pauline Epistles.* Translated by Rowan A. Greer. WGRW 26. Atlanta: Society of Biblical Literature, 2010.

———. *Commentary on Psalms 1–81.* Translated by Robert C. Hill. WGRW 5. Atlanta: Society of Biblical Literature, 2006.

———. *Commentary on the Twelve Prophets.* Translated by Robert C. Hill. FC 108. Washington, DC: Catholic University of America Press, 2004.

SECONDARY SOURCES

Aletti, Jean-Noël. "D'une écriture à l'autre: Analyse structurale d'un passage d'Origène, commentaire sur Jean, livre II, paragraphe 13–21." *RSR* 61 (1973): 27–47.
Allen, Pauline. "John Chrysostom's Homilies on I and II Thessalonians: The Preacher and His Audience." *StPatr* 31 (1997): 3–21.
Attrep, Abe. "The Teacher and His Teachings: Chrysostom's Homiletic Approach as Seen in Commentaries on the Gospel of John." *SVTQ* 38 (1994): 293–301.
Auerbach, Erich. *Scenes from the Drama of European Literature*. Minneapolis: University of Minnesota Press, 1984.
Azar, Michael G. *Exegeting the Jews: The Early Reception of the Johannine "Jews."* Bible in Ancient Christianity 10. Leiden: Brill, 2016.
Blowers, Paul. "Interpreting Scripture." Pages 618–36 in *Constantine to c. 600*. Vol. 2 of *The Cambridge History of Christianity*. Edited by Augustine Casiday and Fredrick W. Norris. 9 vols. Cambridge: Cambridge University Press, 2007.
Boulnois, Marie-Odile. *Le paradoxe trinitaire chez Cyrille d'Alexandrie: Herméneutique, analyses philosophiques et argumentation théologique*. CEAug.SA 143. Paris: Études Augustiniennes, 1994.
Broek, Roelof van den. "The Christian 'School' of Alexandria in the Second and Third Centuries." Pages 39–47 in *Centres of Learning: Learning and Location in Pre-Modern Europe and the Middle East*. Edited by Jan Willem Drijvers and Alasdair A. MacDonald. Brill's Studies in Intellectual History 61. Leiden: Brill, 1995.
Brooke, A. E. *The Commentary of Origen on S. John's Gospel*. 2 vols. Cambridge: Cambridge University Press, 1896, 1939.
Brown, Raymond E. *The Community of the Beloved Disciple*. New York: Paulist, 1979.
Cameron, Averil. *Christianity and the Rhetoric of Empire: The Development of Christian Discourse*. Sather Classical Lectures 55. Berkeley: University of California Press, 1991.
Clark, Elizabeth A. *Reading Renunciation: Asceticism and Scripture in Early Christianity*. Princeton: Princeton University Press, 1999.
Crawford, Matthew R. *Cyril of Alexandria's Trinitarian Theology of Scripture*. OECS. Oxford: Oxford University Press, 2014.
Cribiore, Raffaella. *The School of Libanius in Late Antique Antioch*. Princeton: Princeton University Press, 2007.

Crouzel, Henri. "Le Contenu spirituel des dénominations du Christ selon le Livre I du *Commentaire sur Jean* d'Origène." Pages 131–50 in *Origeniana Secunda: Second colloque internationale des etudes, Bari 20–23 septembre 1977*. Edited by Henri Crouzel and Antonio Quacquareli. QVetChr 15. Rome: dell'Ateneo, 1980.

———. "La Distinction de la 'typologie' et de 'l'allegorie'." *BLE* 65 (1964): 161–74.

Daley, Brian E. "Christ and Christologies." Pages 886–905 in *The Oxford Handbook of Early Christian Studies*. Edited by Susan Ashbrook Harvey and David G. Hunter. Oxford: Oxford University Press, 2008.

Daniélou, Jean. *Origène*. Paris: La Table Ronde, 1948.

Dawson, David. *Allegorical Readers and Cultural Revision in Ancient Alexandria*. Berkley: University of California Press, 1992.

Dively-Lauro, Elizabeth Ann. *The Soul and Spirit of Scripture within Origen's Exegesis*. BAC 3. Leiden: Brill, 2005.

Farag, Louis M. *St. Cyril of Alexandria, A New Testament Exegete: His Commentary on the Gospel of John*. Gorgias Dissertations 29. Piscataway, NJ: Gorgias, 2007.

Froehlich, Karlfried. *Biblical Interpretation in the Early Church*. SECT. Philadelphia: Fortress, 1980.

Früchtel, E. "Ἀρχή und das erste Buch des Johanneskommentars des Origenes." *StPatr* 14 (1976): 122–44.

Grant, Robert M. *The Earliest Lives of Jesus*. New York: Harper, 1961.

Grant, Robert M., and David Tracy. *A Short History of the Interpretation of the Bible*. 2nd ed. Philadelphia: Fortress, 1984.

Greer, Rowan A. *Theodore of Mopsuestia: Exegete and Theologian*. Westminster: Faith Press, 1961.

Guinot, J.-N. "La frontière entre allégorie et typologie: École alexandrine, école antiochienne." *RSR* 99 (2011): 207–28.

———. "L'école exégétique d'Antioche et ses relations avec Origène." Pages 1149–66 in vol. 2 of *Origeniana Octava: Origène e la tradizione Alessandrina; Papers of the 8th International Origen Congress 2003, Pisa 27–31 August 2001*. Edited by Lorenzo Perrone. BETL 164. 2 vols. Leuven: Peeters, 2003.

Hanson, R. P. C. *Allegory and Event: A Study of the Sources and Significance of Origen's Interpretation of Scripture*. Richmond: John Knox, 1959.

Harl, Marguerite. *Le déchiffrement du sens: Études sur l'herméneutique chrétienne d'Origène à Grégoire de Nysse*. Paris: Études Augustiniennes, 1993.

Harnack, Adolf von. *Lehrbuch der Dogmengeschichte*. Tübingen: Mohr, 1883.

Heine, Ronald E. "The Introduction to Origen's *Commentary on John* Compared with the Introductions to the Ancient Philosophical Commentaries on Aristotle." Pages 3–12 in *Origeniana Sexta: Origène et la Bible; Actes du Colloquium Origenianum Sextum, Chantilly, 30 août–3 septembre 1993*. Edited by Gilles Dorival and Alain Le Boulluec. BETL 118. Leuven: Peeters, 1995.

———. *Origen: Scholarship in Service of the Church*. Christian Theology in Context. Oxford: Oxford University Press, 2010.

———. "Stoic Logic as Handmaid to Exegesis and Theology in Origen's Commentary on the Gospel of John." *JTS* 44 (1993): 90–117.

Hill, C. E. "The Gospel of John." Pages 602–13 in *The Oxford Handbook of Early Christian Biblical Interpretation*. Edited by Paul M. Blowers and Peter W. Martens. Oxford: Oxford University Press, 2019.

Hill, Robert C. *Reading the Old Testament in Antioch*. BAC 5. Leiden: Brill, 2005.

Jacobsen, Anders-Christian. *Christ—The Teacher of Salvation: A Study on Origen's Christology and Soteriology*. Adamantiana 6. Münster: Aschendorff, 2015.

Kalantzis, George. "*Duo Filii* and the *Homo Assumptus* in the Christology of Theodore of Mopsuestia: The Greek Fragments of the Commentary on John." *ETL* 78 (2002): 57–78.

Kannengiesser, Charles. "Allegorism." Pages 248–55 in *Handbook of Patristic Exegesis: The Bible in Ancient Christianity*. BAC 1. Leiden: Brill, 2004.

Keefer, Kyle. *The Branches of the Gospel of John: The Reception of the Gospel of John in the Early Church*. LNTS 332. New York: T&T Clark, 2006.

Kelly, J. N. D. "The Bible and the Latin Fathers." Pages 41–56 in *The Church's Use of the Bible: Past and Present*. Edited by Dennis Eric Nineham. London: SPCK, 1963.

———. *Early Christian Doctrines*. 5th ed. New York: A&C Black, 1977.

Koen, Lars. "Partitive Exegesis in Cyril of Alexandria's Commentary on the Gospel according to St. John." *StPatr* 25 (1993): 115–21.

———. *The Saving Passion: Incarnational and Soteriological Thought in Cyril of Alexandria's Commentary on the Gospel according to St. John*. Philadelphia: Coronet, 1991.

Lubac, Henri de. "Typologie et allegorisme." *RSR* 34 (1947): 180–226.

MaCaulay, William. "The Nature of Christ in Origen's 'Commentary on John.'" *SJT* 19 (1966): 176–87.
McLeod, Frederick G. "The Christology in Theodore of Mopsuestia's *Commentary on the Gospel of John*." *JTS* 73 (2012): 115–38.
———. *The Image of God in the Antiochene Tradition*. Washington, DC: Catholic University of America Press, 1999.
———. *The Roles of Christ's Humanity in Salvation: Insights from Theodore of Mopsuestia*. Washington, DC: Catholic University of America Press, 2005.
Margerie, Bertrand de. "Saint John Chrysostom, Doctor of Biblical 'Condescension.'" Pages 189–212 in *The Greek Fathers*. Vol. 1 of *An Introduction to the History of Exegesis*. Petersham, MA: Saint Bede's Publications, 1993.
Martens, Peter W. *Adrian's Introduction to the Divine Scriptures: An Antiochene Handbook for Scriptural Interpretation*. Oxford: Oxford University Press, 2017.
———. *Origen and Scripture: The Contours of the Exegetical Life*. OECS. Oxford: Oxford University Press, 2012.
———. "Revisiting the Allegory/Typology Distinction: The Case of Origen." *JECS* 16 (2008): 283–317.
Mayer, Wendy. "John Chrysostom and His Audiences: Distinguishing Different Congregations at Antioch and Constantinople." *StPatr* 31 (1997): 70–75.
McGuckin, John A. "Structural Design and Apologetic Intent in Origen's *Commentary on John*." Pages 441–57 in *Origeniana Sexta: Origène et la Bible; Actes du Colloquium Origenianum Sextum, Chantilly, 30 août–3 septembre 1993*. Edited by Gilles Dorival and Alain Le Boulluec. BETL 118. Leuven: Leuven University Press, 1995.
Meyer, Marvin, ed. *The Nag Hammadi Scriptures*. New York: HarperOne, 2008.
Mitchell, Margaret M. *The Heavenly Trumpet: John Chrysostom and the Art of Pauline Interpretation*. Louisville: Westminster John Knox, 2002.
———. "John Chrysostom." Pages 571–77 in *Dictionary of Major Biblical Interpreters*. Edited by Donald McKim. Downers Grove, IL: InterVarsity Press, 2007.
———. *Paul, the Corinthians and the Birth of Christian Hermeneutics*. Cambridge: Cambridge University Press, 2010.
Nassif, Bradley. "'Spiritual Exegesis' in the School of Antioch." Pages 343–77 in *New Perspectives on Historical Theology: Essays in Memory*

of John Meyendorff. Edited by Bradley Nassif. Grand Rapids: Eerdmans, 1996.
Nautin, Pierre. *Origène, sa vie, son œuvre*. CAnt 1. Paris: Beauchesne, 1977.
Neuschäfer, Bernhard. *Origenes als Philologe*. SBA 18. 2 vols. Basel: Reinhardt, 1987.
Norris, Richard A. *The Christological Controversy*. SECT. Philadelphia: Fortress, 1980.
Oden, Thomas C., and Christopher A. Hall. "Introduction to Mark." Pages xxi–xxxv in *Mark*. ACCS New Testament 2. Downers Grove, IL: InterVarsity Press, 1998.
O'Keefe, John J. "Theodoret's Unique Contribution to the Antiochene Exegetical Tradition: Questioning Traditional Scholarly Categories." Pages 191–203 in *The Harp of Prophecy: Early Christian Interpretation of the Psalms*. Edited by Brian E. Daley and Paul R. Kolbet. CJAn 20. Notre Dame: University of Notre Dame Press, 2015.
O'Keefe, John. J., and R. R. Reno. *Sanctified Vision: An Introduction to Early Christian Interpretation of the Bible*. Baltimore: Johns Hopkins University Press, 2005.
Ondrey, Hauna T. *The Minor Prophets as Christian Scripture in the Commentaries of Theodore of Mopsuestia and Cyril of Alexandria*. OECS. Oxford: Oxford University Press, 2018.
Pazzini, Domenico. *Il prologo di Giovanni in Cirillo di Alessandria*. StBi 116. Brescia: Paideia, 1997.
Pepin, Jean. *Mythe et allégorie: Les origines grecques et les contestations judéo-chrétiennes*. 2nd ed. Paris: Aubier, 1976.
Poffet, Jean-Michel. *La Méthode exégétique d'Héracléon et d'Origène commentateurs de Jn 4: Jésus, la Samaritaine et les Samaritains*. Paradosis 28. Fribourg: Éditions Universitaires, 1985.
Pollard, T. E. "The Exegesis of John 10.30 in the Early Trinitarian Controversies" *NTS* 3 (1956–1957): 334–48.
———. *Johannine Christology and the Early Church*. SNTSMS 13. Cambridge: Cambridge University Press, 1970.
Quasten, Johannes. *The Golden Age of Greek Patristic Literature from the Council of Nicaea to the Council of Chalcedon*. Vol. 3 of *Patrology*. Westminster, MD: Newman Press, 1960.
Reinhartz, Adele. *The Word in the World: The Cosmological Tale in the Fourth Gospel*. SBLMS 45. Atlanta: Society of Biblical Literature, 1992.
Rowe, J. N. "Origen's Subordinationism as Illustrated in His Commentary on St. John's Gospel." *StPatr* 11 (1972): 222–28.

Russell, Norman. *Cyril of Alexandria*. ECF. New York: Routledge, 2000.
Shuve, Karl. "Entering the Story: Origen's Dramatic Approach to Scripture in the *Homilies on Jeremiah*." *StPatr* 46 (2010): 235–40.
Simonetti, Manlio. *Biblical Interpretation in the Early Church: An Historical Introduction to Patristic Exegesis*. Translated by John A. Hughes. Edinburgh: T&T Clark, 1994.
———. *Lettera e/o allegoria: Un contributo alla storia dell'esegesi patristica*. Rome: Institutum Patristicum Augustinianum, 1985.
Torjesen, Karen Jo. *Hermeneutical Procedure and Theological Method in Origen's Exegesis*. PTS 28. Berlin: de Gruyter, 1985.
Trigg, Joseph W. Introduction to *Allegory and Event: A Study of the Sources and Significance of Origen's Interpretation of Scripture*, by R. P. C. Hanson. Repr., Louisville: Westminster John Knox, 2002.
———. "Origen and Cyril of Alexandria: Continuities and Discontinuities in Their Approach to the Gospel of John." Pages 955–65 in vol. 2 of *Origeniana Octava: Origène e la tradizione Alessandrina; Papers of the Eighth International Origen Congress 2003, Pisa 27–31 August 2001*. Edited by Lorenzo Perrone. BETL 164. 2 vols. Leuven: Peeters, 2003.
Wallace-Hadrill, D. S. *Christian Antioch: A Study of Early Christian Thought in the East*. Cambridge: Cambridge University Press, 1982.
Ward, Clifton H. "'Symbolic Interpretation Is Most Useful': Clement of Alexandria's Scriptural Imagination." *JECS* 25 (2017): 531–60.
Westerholm, Stephen, and Martin Westerholm. *Reading Sacred Scripture: Voices from the History of Biblical Interpretation*. Grand Rapids: Eerdmans, 2016.
Widdicombe, Peter. "Knowing God: Origen and the Example of the Beloved Disciple." *StPatr* 31 (1997): 554–58.
———. "Origen." Pages 316–29 in *The Blackwell Companion to Paul*. Edited by Stephen Westerholm. Blackwell Companions to Religion. Malden, MA: Blackwell, 2011.
———. "The Patristic Reception of the Gospel of Matthew: The Commentary of Jerome and the Sermons of John Chrysostom." Pages 105–19 in *Mark and Matthew II: Comparative Readings; Reception and Cultural Hermeneutics*. Edited by Eve-Marie Becker and Anders Runesson. WUNT 304. Tübingen: Mohr Siebeck, 2013.
Wiles, Maurice F. *The Divine Apostle: The Interpretation of St. Paul's Epistles in the Early Church*. Cambridge: Cambridge University Press, 1967.
———. *The Spiritual Gospel: The Interpretation of the Fourth Gospel in the Early Church*. Cambridge: Cambridge University Press, 1960.

Wilson Nightingale, Andrea. *Spectacles of Truth in Classical Greek Philosophy: Theoria in Its Cultural Context*. Cambridge: Cambridge University Press, 2004.

Young, Frances M. *Biblical Exegesis and the Formation of Christian Culture*. Cambridge: Cambridge University Press, 1997.

———. "The Fourth Century Reaction against Allegory." *StPatr* 30 (1997): 120–25.

———. "The Rhetorical Schools and Their Influence on Patristic Exegesis." Pages 182–99 in *The Making of Orthodoxy: Essays in Honour of Henry Chadwick*. Edited by Rowan Williams. Cambridge: Cambridge University Press, 1989.

———. "Towards a Christian *paideia*." Pages 484–500 in *Origins to Constantine*. Vol. 1 of *The Cambridge History of Christianity*. Edited by Frances M. Young and Margaret M. Mitchell. 9 vols. Cambridge: Cambridge University Press, 2006.

———. "Typology." Pages 29–48 in *Crossing the Boundaries: Essays in Biblical Interpretation in Honour of David D. Goulder*. Edited by Stanley Porter, Paul Joyce, and David E. Orton. BibInt 8. Leiden: Brill, 1994.

Zaharopoulos, Dimitri. *Theodore of Mopsuestia on the Bible: A Study of His Old Testament Exegesis*. New York: Paulist, 1989.

Ancient Sources Index

Septuagint

Genesis
1	146
1:1	68
1:26	62
2:7	117
2:8	60, 146
3:9	33–35
9	202, 210
15:16	32
16–18	156
18:21	34
22	202
22:12	117
49:8	202
49:10	104
	104, 117

Exodus
12	117
34:5–7	155

Leviticus
10:14–15	48

Numbers
12:10	31
14	167
21:8	156
21:9	117
24:7–9	62
24:17–19	104
33:1–49	104
	31

Deuteronomy
5:29	202
13:15	195
18:15	117
33:7	104

2 Kingdoms
18:19	202

3 Kingdoms
21	156

1 Maccabees
2:24–25	90

Psalms
3	60, 90
3:8	35
9:8	35
15	61–62
22	194
22:1–2	165
32:10–11	168
36	80
36–38	31
45	31
48:15	60
50:13–14	185
66:4	159
68	159
68:10	90
68:24	89–90, 93
73:1	93
85:8	168
109:7	202
	117

Proverbs		7:16	184
5:16–17	62	8:4	183
19	62		
		New Testament	
Ecclesiastes			
10:9–10	74	Matthew	
		4:11	197
Song of Songs	31, 48, 166, 168	4:21–22	55
1:2	48	5:3	172–73
1:7	165–66, 168	5:8	48, 172–73
		5:7	172–73
Isaiah		6:19	166
1:11–14	94	8:11	94, 112
5:20	184	9:2	202
6:9–10	144, 157	10:5	183
6:10	143	11:27	102, 187
11:12–13	74	13:37–43	119
12:3	134	14	17
35:5–6	157	15:9	170
43:20–21	133	16:19	55
		17:1–13	112
Jeremiah	31	19:16	116
6:11	156	20:20–23	55
12:10–12	92	21:1–11	147
17	167	21:3	91
17:11	167	21:43	84
36:24	184	24:28	92
38:12	133	27:45–48	85
Ezekiel		Mark	
3:11	202	1:1	47
13:1–19	143	1:19–20	55
18	156	1:35	194
18:2	155	1:41	202
34	163	3:17	55
34:2	171	4:39	202
34:2–6	184	9:24	202
34:10	184	10:38–39	55
34:23–27	184–85		
		Luke	
Susanna		1:1–2	70
9:35	194	1:3–4	56
		10:29–37	166
Hosea		10:38–42	203, 207
7:13	184	11:1	194

Ancient Sources Index

16:19–31	34	4:6	97–99, 114, 117, 125–26, 134–36
18:9–14	194	4:7	97, 106
		4:8	114
John		4:9	97, 121–22
1	6–7	4:10–14	27, 120, 124, 133, 135
1–13	6	4:10–15	97
1:1	47, 64	4:11–14	122
1:1–2	5, 70	4:12	114
1:1–18	32, 44, 46	4:13–14	105, 125
1:15	36	4:14	133
1:18	48	4:16	114
1:46	55	4:16–18	108
2	6–7, 41, 50–51, 80, 85–86, 91–92, 117, 136, 142, 164, 205	4:16–26	97
		4:20	105
2:12–13	78	4:21	109, 118, 159
2:13–14	81	4:21–24	118, 122, 128
2:14	78	4:22	98–100, 105, 113, 116, 121, 123, 125, 127–28, 130, 135–36
2:14–15	90		
2:14–16	77, 94	4:23–24	123, 159
2:14–22	77	4:24	100–103, 113, 117, 123, 127–28, 135, 161
2:15	94		
2:15–16	85, 91	4:25	102, 104, 117, 122
2:15–17	92	4:26	122, 129–30
2:16	78–79, 83, 91	4:26–27	103
2:17	82, 89–90, 93	4:27	130–31
2:18	77, 87, 89, 94	4:28	110, 129–31
2:18–19	87	4:28–29	97, 103, 115–16
2:19	27, 77, 78, 81–83, 85–89, 92, 164, 206	4:28–30	97
		4:31–32	131
2:19–21	86	4:32	98, 128
2:20	92–93	4:34	98, 128–29, 135
2:21	82, 88, 92	4:35	111, 119, 124, 132
2:21–22	77, 86	4:35–38	20, 27, 98, 105, 110, 118, 123, 125, 132, 167
2:22	93		
2:23	86	4:36	112, 124
3:14	62	4:36–37	111
4	5–7, 41, 45, 97, 99–110, 112–13, 120–22, 131, 137, 164, 167–68, 195	4:38	124, 133
		4:39–42	97
4:1	118	4:40–41	110
4:1–5	134	5:21	100, 195
4:1–12	99	5:39–47	169–70
4:3–4	118	5:49	104
4:3–6	97	6	64
4:4–5	98, 118, 134, 136	6:9–10	141
4:4–42	97	7:38–39	120

John (cont.)

8	6–7, 139
8:12	46, 139
8:31	37
8:37–53	5
9	41–42, 140–41, 143–44, 148, 151, 156
9:1	139
9:1–3	149
9:1–9	147
9:1–42	171
9:2	149
9:2–3	149, 151–52, 154, 204
9:3	146, 150, 156
9:4	37, 139–40, 144, 146, 152
9:4–5	143, 150, 152–53
9:6	139, 150
9:6–7	16, 139–40, 144–48, 151, 158–62
9:7	139, 142
9:8–34	139
9:10	158
9:12	147
9:14	139
9:15	154
9:15–22	147
9:24	157
9:24–33	145, 147
9:26–32	150
9:28	154, 159
9:28–31	154
9:34	145, 158–59
9:35	146, 160
9:35–41	147
9:36	154
9:37	151, 156–57
9:37–38	150
9:38	159
9:38–41	145
9:40	175–76
9:41	143
10	41, 117, 130, 164–66, 168–69, 181, 191
10:1	85, 166, 170, 176, 183
10:1–3	172
10:1–15	171
10:1–18	27
10:1–19	163
10:4–5	186
10:5	170
10:6	163, 182
10:7	177, 182
10:8	166, 170, 177, 182, 183
10:9	46, 165, 168, 171, 182, 186
10:10	166
10:11	46, 173, 185
10:11–18	191
10:12	170, 184
10:12–13	170, 177, 183
10:14	184
10:14–15	173, 175, 178, 182, 187
10:14–18	163–64, 169
10:15	173
10:16	167, 171–72, 178, 183
10:17	174, 179–80, 188–89
10:17–18	173–75, 178, 182, 187–88
10:17–21	180–81
10:18	174, 179, 210
10:26	167
10:27	165
10:30	202
10:31–39	191
10:37–38	202
11	6–7, 41, 202–3
11:1–38	192
11:1–44	191–214
11:3	203, 207, 212
11:3–6	191
11:4	199–200, 204, 209
11:5	203
11:7–8	207–8
11:7–16	191
11:11	195, 200, 208–9
11:14	195
11:14–15	208
11:16	203–4
11:20–29	191
11:21–27	207, 213
11:23	208
11:25	46, 191, 195, 200

11:25–26	41, 195, 204–5, 211	Acts	
11:25–27	199, 209	4:13	55
11:26	191, 200–201	5	170
11:32	208–9	5:34–36	170
11:33	191, 200–201, 205, 210–11	5:35–37	183
11:34	201, 205, 209–10	5:36–37	177
11:35	191, 199, 204		
11:36–37	210	Romans	
11:38	191, 201, 204	1:9	117–18
11:39	193, 196	3:27–31	103
11:39–41	193	6:4	82
11:39–45	192, 193	6:5	82
11:40	207	8:1–2	195
11:41	193–94	10:10	48
11:41–42	191, 194, 196, 198, 201–3, 205–6, 208–10	11	167
		12:1	118
11:42	200, 205, 210	15:3	90
11:43	195–96, 206, 211		
11:43–44	194–96	1 Corinthians	
11:44	196–98, 212–13	2:1–16	22
11:45	195	2:16	52, 107
12:1–8	203, 207	3:17	91
12:2	198	6:12	107
12:30	202	6:19	92
12:45	202	10:4	148
13	6–7, 41, 48	10:11	111
13:23	4, 47–48, 55, 63	12:27	82
13:23–25	47–49, 51, 55, 69	13:8–12	22–23
13:23–26	69	13:12	22–23
13:25	47	15:27	202
13:31–32	5	15:52	211
13:37	180		
14:2	185	2 Corinthians	
14:6	46	3:12–18	22
14:28	103	3:14–15	198
15:15	56	3:18	22
16:26–27	179	4:7	46
17:1	194, 201	12:1–5	22
17:3	179	12:4	107
19	51	13:3	197
19:26	4		
19:26–27	51	Galatians	34
20:2	4	2:20	52, 82
21:7	4, 55	4:23–24	34
21:20	4, 55	4:24	34

Galatians (cont.)
  5:6   172

Ephesians
  2:21   82
  3:9   112

Philippians
  2:5–8   130

Colossians
  2:3   48

1 Thessalonians
  4–5   22
  4:16   211

1 Timothy
  6:20   110

Hebrews
  1:10   45
  4:8   61
  6:4–6   197
  6:5–6   196

1 Peter
  2:5   82
  5:8   171, 185

1 John
  5:16   196

Revelation
  10:4   107

Early Christian Writings

Athanasius, *Orationes contra Arianos*
  3.26   201

Clement of Alexandria, *Hypotyposes*   4, 57

Cyprian, *Epistulae*
  63.8   107

Cyril of Alexandria
  Commentarius in Amos
    2:8   91
    8:9   74
    9:13–15   74
  Commentarius in Habacuc
    3:2   92, 197
  *Commentarius in epistulam
    ad Hebraeos*
    1:1   70
  Commentarius in Isaiam
    pref.   36, 70, 72, 74
    11:12–13   74
    21.3–4   36–37
    26:17–18   70
    29:11–12   70
    43.9   70
  Commentarius in Joelem
    2:28–29   70
    3:13–16   211
  Commentarius in Michaeam
    7:11–15   74
    7:14–15   36
  Commentarius in Zachariam
    3:1   36–37, 74
    8:3   128
    8:8   128
    9:9   128
    11:3   128
  De dogmatum solutione
    1–2   127
  *De recta fide ad Theodosium
    Imperatorem*
    32   192
  Epistula ad Calosyrium
    2–3   127
  Epistula ad Valerian
    50.3   127
  Epistulae
    6.6   89
  Homiliae in Lucam
    38   71–72

48	71–72	9:1–41	150
78	71	9:2–3	155–56
In Joannem	8	9:4	37, 152
1.pref.	56, 68–73, 128	9:4–5	153
1:1	70, 72	9:5	153
1:9	72	9:6–7	158–61
1:15	36	9:10	158
2:14	92, 94–95	9:15	154
2:14–22	90	9:24	157
2:16	91	9:27	154
2:17	93	9:28	154, 158–59
2:18	94	9:29	157
2:19–20	78, 93	9:31	154
2:21–22	92	9:34	154, 159
2:22	93	9:35	160
4:1–5	134	9:36	154
4:1–42	125	9:37	156–57
4:6	126, 135	9:38	128, 159
4:7–9	126	9:39	154
4:10–11	130, 133	10:1	183
4:12–13	129	10:1–5	182–83
4:14–15	130, 134	10:1–18	181–82
4:17–19	126, 129	10:4–5	186
4:22	127, 130	10:6–8	182
4:23	118	10:7	187
4:24	127–28	10:8	183–84
4:26	129–30	10:9	182, 186–87
4:27	131	10:11	184
4:28	129–30	10:11–13	183–85
4:29	130	10:14	184–85
4:31–32	131	10:14–15	187–88
4:32–34	98	10:16	183
4:34	128, 131	10:17	188–89
4:35	132–33	10:18	189
4:36–37	133	11:1–2	207
4:38	133	11:1–44	206
5:37–38	71–72	11:3	207
6:12–13	74	11:4	209
7:8	128	11:7–8	207–8
7:38–39	133	11:11	208–9
7:39	70	11:14–15	208
8:31	37, 74	11:16	204
8:46	128	11:23	208
9	69	11:25–27	209
9:1	158	11:27	213

Cyril of Alexandria, In Joannem (cont.)

11:28–29	207
11:30	207
11:32	208
11:32–34	209–10
11:33	210–11
11:34	210
11:36–37	210
11:38–39	210
11:40	207–8
11:41–42	208–10
11:43	211
11:44	212–13
13	72–73
13:21	210
14:20	71, 72
14:21	70
15:3	128
15:9–10	72
16:12–13	70
16:23–24	70
17:1	210
17:24	70
20:1–9	70

Responsio ad Tiberium

2	127
10	127

Diodore of Tarsus
  On the Difference between Theoria
    and Allegoria 9
  Commentarius in Psalmos
    pref. 9, 25, 35

Eusebius
  Demonstratio evangelica
    6.18.48–49 107
  Historia ecclesiastica
    6.3.8 2
    6.14.7 4, 57
    6.18.1 7

Eustathius
  De engastrimytho contra Origenem 9, 21

Irenaeus, Adversus haereses

3.2.1	57
3.17.2	107
3.22.2	126
4.22.2	126
5.13.1	197
5.15.3	160

Jerome, Commentariorum in Matthaeum
  pref. 57

John Chrysostom
  Adversus Judaeos
    5 117
  Commentarium in Galatas
    4:24 35
  Commentarius in Isaiam
    5.3 61
  Commentarius in Psalmos

6:1	58
8:5	33, 62
9:8	33, 61–62
9:11	33
11	62
45.pref	60
45:1	55–56
47:4	55
49:3–4	56
112:4	33, 62
113:7	33, 62

  Homiliae in Acta apostolorum

1	56
3	56
55	59

  Homiliae in epistulam I ad Corinthios
    39 202
  Homiliae in epistulam i ad Thessalonicenses
    8 56
  Homiliae in epistulam ad Hebraeos

1	56
11	117, 200

  Homiliae in Genesim
    2 56

4	55–56, 59	28	147
7	55–56	37	119
8	55	63	116
12	55	78	85
13	33–34, 58, 60–61	*Homiliae in Psalmos*	
21	59	110	55, 58
22	56	146	56
29	32–33	*Homiliae in Romanos*	
36	61	pref.	59
37	75	2	117
44	115	*De laudibus sancti Pauli apostoli*	
58	32	1–7	59
Homiliae in Isaiam		*De Lazaro*	
2	32–33, 55–56, 59	3	32, 34
6	61	*De prophetarum obscuritate*	
Homiliae in Joannem	7, 44, 55	1	23, 34, 57
1	55–60, 160	2	32, 62
2	56–59		
23	84–89	Julian, *Oratorio contra Galilaeos*	
27	61	62.253b–254b	15
31	114–15, 117–18	64.262c	15
31–34	113		
32	113, 115, 120	Origen	
33	114, 116–18	*Commentarii in evangelium Joannis*	
34	98, 116, 119–20	6–7, 44, 109, 164, 166, 168	
46	148	1.1	52–53
48	146	1.1–89 (= pref.)	45, 51
50	120	1.10	53
56	145–46	1.12	53
56–59	144	1.12–14	46
57	144–45, 147–48	1.13	46–47
58	32, 145–47	1.14	45
59	85, 145, 149, 169–73	1.15	45
59–60	169	1.17	45
60	170–74	1.20	45–46
62	198–201, 204	1.21–22	46
62–64	198	1.22	46–47, 64, 195
63	199, 200–201	1.23	51–52
64	201–2	1.24	46, 52
80	201	1.28	49–50
Homiliae in Lucam		1.30	106
1	59	1.32–34	49
Homiliae in Matthaeum	55	1.33–34	45
1	56–57, 59	1.36–37	45
5	56	1.39	45

Origen, Commentarii ... Joannis (cont.)

1.45	53	12	99
1.46	53–54, 81	13	99, 109–10
1.60	45	13.1–363	99
1.60–61	106	13.6	105–6
1.63	51	13.6–7	106
1.68	106	13.15–16	108
1.80	46	13.16	107
1.89	52–54, 181, 193	13.19	107–8, 195
1.118	165	13.23–24	106
1.125	195	13.23–42	106
1.162–168	143	13.26	106
1.180	143	13.27–29	107
1.181	195	13.30	107–8
1.267–268	195	13.31	107
6	165	13.32–35	107
10.15	50–51	13.35	107
10.18–19	50	10.35–36	142
10.19	79	13.37	107–8
10.19–20	79	13.39	106, 165, 167–68
10.20	79	13.42	107
10.21–23	165	13.43	108
10.129	79–80	13.48	108
10.119–323	78	13.51	108–9
10.130	81	13.81	105
10.131	81	13.84	105
10.133	81	13.98	108
10.134–36	81	13.101	100, 105
10.138	83–84	13.101–118	99
10.140	84	13.102	100
10.141–42	83	13.106–107	100
10.145	80	13.109–110	103
10.148	80	13.123–153	101
10.214	78–79	13.124–125	101
10.216	78–79	13.130	101
10.226	81–82	13.131	101
10.228	81–82	13.132–139	101
10.228–229	82	13.136	101
10.230	82	13.140–146	101
10.231–232	82	13.143	101
10.239	82	13.144	102
10.242	82	13.146	102–3
10.263	82	13.147	102
10.263–287	82	13.148	102
10.266	81	13.150	102
		13.151	103

13.151–153	102–3	28.48–49	196
13.154–163	104	28.49–50	196
13.161–162	104	28.54	196–97
13.162	102	28.55–56	197
13.166–167	103	28.57–58	197
13.169	103	28.60	197–98
13.173	104	28.66	197
13.174	104	28.70	195
13.175	110	28.71	195
13.181	110	28.76	195–96
13.203–249	98	32.106	195
13.250	110–11	32.263	47–48, 51
13.250–326	110	32.264	48
13.259	111	32.276	48
13.269	111	32.278	48
13.270	111	frag. 36	107
13.279	111	*Commentarius in Canticum*	42, 164
13.280	111	pref.	106
13.284	111	1.2.2	48
13.297	111	1.2.3	48
13.298	111	1.2.4	48
13.305	112	1.2.20	48
13.308	112	2.4.1	165
13.309–310	112	2.4.3	165
13.314–319	112	2.4.4	165–66
13.320–321	112	2.4.5	165
13.340	110	2.4.11	166
13.343	110	2.4.13	165
19.6	195	2.4.23	166
20.26	142	2.4.24	165
21–27	140	2.4.24–26	166
28.1–79	192	2.8	45
28.6	193	*Commentarius in evangelium*	
28.14	193	*Matthaei*	
28.17	193	10.14	166
28.22	193	frag. 139	52
28.24	193	*Commentarius in Romanos*	167
28.25	193	1.4–7	45
28.25–26	194	6.11.13	195
28.26–28	194	6.12.6	100
28.30–38	194	7.17.4	53
28.32–34	194	8.5.6	107
28.33	194	8.7.3	167
28.34–45	194	8.8.13	52
28.38	193	1.18	31, 53

Origen (cont.)
  Contra Celsum
    1.44   49
    2.69   142
    6.70   101
  De oratione
    13   194
    15   107
  De pascha
    1.13   48
  De principiis   11, 51
    pref. 9   101
    1.1.1–2   101
    1.2   46, 53
    1.2.4   195
    1.8   52
    4   30, 49, 54, 60, 79, 110
    4.1.7   46, 53
    4.2.1–6   106
    4.2.3   46, 52, 81
    4.2.4   54
    4.2.4–6   142
    4.2.5   54
    4.2.7   50, 53
    4.2.7–8   46
    4.2.8–9   30, 46
    4.2.9   51
    4.3.1   54
    4.3.5   52–54
    4.3.6   100
    4.3.9   100
    4.4.1   79
    6.2.8   30
    6.2.9   30, 31
    6.2.4–6   30–31
  Diologus cum Heraclide   195
  Epistula ad Gregorium Thaumaturgum
    3 [= Philoc. 13.4] 52–53, 169
  Homiliae in Canticum
    1   31, 47–48
  Homiliae in Exodum
    4   102
    5   52
    12   195
  Homiliae in Ezechielem
    2   49, 143
    3   53
    6   48
    13   102, 107
    14   45
  Homiliae in Genesim
    7   106
    10   106
    11   106
    12   107
  Homiliae in Isaiam   42
    6   140–43
    7   107
  Hom. Jer.
    1   31
    5   23
    9   49
    13   141–42
    15   141–42
    17   167
    19   46
    frag. 2.1   31
  Homiliae in Josuam
    20   31
  Homiliae in Leviticum
    1   48, 52
    4   49
    9   195
    13   51
  Homiliae in Lucam
    1   46
    7   142
    34   166
    frag. 223   48
  Homiliae in Numeros   167
    1   102
    2   31
    6   167
    11   31
    12   106–7
    26   49, 52
    27   31
  Homiliae in Psalmos   168
    3   31

15	193	4:36	124
36	31	4:38	124
73	168	6:27	125
77	31, 83, 165–66, 168	9:1–2	149
Homiliae in Samuelum		9:1–3	149
5	31	9:1–9	148
Philocalia		9:1–41	148
2.4	49	9:6	150
10.2	31	9:12	148
12.2	31	9:15–22	148
13.4 [= *Ep. Greg.* 3]	52, 53, 169	9:24–33	148
		9:32	150
Severian, *Homilae*		9:34	150
2	210	9:35–41	148
		9:35–36	150
Socrates, *Historia ecclesiastica*		9:39	150
6.3	2	10	175–76
6.3.1–7	15	10:1–6	176–77
		10:1–9	176–77
Tertullian		10:1–18	175
Adversus Praxean	79	10:7	178
16.4	210	10:7–8	177
De baptismo		10:7–9	177
1	160	10:12–13	177
		10:14–15	178–79
Theodore of Mopsuestia		10:16	178
Commentarii in evangelium		10:17	179–81
Joannis	7–8	10:18	89, 179–80
pref.	34, 63–66, 87, 176, 179	11:1–3	203
2:17	89	11:1–55	202–3
2:19	87–88	11:3	203
2:19–21	88–89	11:4	204
2:21	87	11:5	203
4:1–42	121	11:16	204
4:9	122	11:25–26	204–205
4:10	122	11:33	205
4:10–14	124–25	11:34	205
4:11–14	122	11:35	204
4:21	118	11:38	204–5
4:21–25	122	11:41–42	205–6
4:23	123	11:42	89
4:24	123	11:43	206
4:26–29	122	*Commentarii in Jonam*	
4:32–34	98	pref.	65, 67
4:35–38	124		

Theodore of Mopsuestia (cont.)
  Commentarius in Aggaeum
    2:1–5   66
  Commentarius in epistulam ad Galatas   34
    4:23–24   67–68
    4:24   9, 34–35
  Commentarius in epistulam ad Philippenses
    2:8   89
    3:3   123
  Commentarius in Michaeam
    4:1–3   123
    5:5–6   9
  Commentarius in Nahum
    1:1   66
    3:8   9
  Commentarius in Osee
    pref.   65
    3:2   64
  Commentarius in Psalmos
    1.pref   66–68
    3:7   35–36
  Commentarius in Malachiam
    1:11   128
    3:2–4   123
  Commentarius in Zachariam
    9:9   67–68
  Homiliae ad catechumenos
    10   124

Theodoret, *Historia ecclesiastica*
  5.27   15

Greco-Roman Literature

Alexander, *In Aristotelis metaphysica commentaria*   29

Ammonius, *In Porphyrii isagogen sive quinque voces*   29

Cicero, *De inventione rhetorica*
  2.41.119   29

Plato, *Respublica*
  382d   29

General Index

allegorical explanation 61, 132
allegory
  anagogy 99
  compositional 27, 218
  interpretive 27
  language 61
  narrative coherence 15–16
  spiritual meaning 99, 108
  typology 12–13, 16–18, 24–25, 67–68
Ambrose, Origen's patron 7
anagogy 79, 82, 105, 110, 192, 196–97, 212
  allegory 99
  spiritual meaning 99
  symbol 79
  typology 79, 82–83
Antiochene school. See also exegetical schools
  Christology 8, 217
Apollinarianism 180–81
Arianism 8
Arians 7, 8, 75, 88, 126–27, 178, 201–2
asketerion 1–2
baptism 151, 159–61, 213
Basilides 167
beloved disciple 4, 47–48, 55, 69. See also disciples; discipleship
benefits 3, 28; see also usefulness of Scripture
  baptism 151, 159–60, 161, 213
  contemporary church 81–84, 126, 134–36, 156–57, 167–69, 172–73, 175, 177–78, 185–87, 189–90
  discipleship 90, 93

benefits (*cont.*)
  exemplar 99, 103–4, 112–16, 121–22, 125, 129–31, 135, 144–46, 149–54, 161, 192–94, 198–200, 202–4, 206–9, 213
  Father-Son relationship 85–86, 91
  heterodox other 105–10
  Holy Spirit 120–22, 124–26, 133–35
  Jesus
    and OT 86, 89–90, 92–93, 99, 104–6, 112, 114, 117, 121, 151, 157, 161
    condescension 173–74, 189, 201–2, 205–6, 209–10
    divinity 85, 90–92, 95, 144–48, 150, 173–74, 200, 204–5, 207, 209, 213
    humanity 116–17, 121–23, 126–27, 200–201, 209–10
    mediation 188
    redemptive death 179, 188–89
    two natures 92, 135, 140, 156–57, 188, 207, 210–11, 213
    unity with Father 128–29, 146–48, 173–74, 194–95
  knowledge 173, 178–79, 187–88
  nature of God 99–102, 117, 121, 123, 127–28
  refutation of heresy 86–89, 99–102, 108–10, 126–28, 154–57, 180–81
  resurrection 81–83, 85–88, 188–89, 211–13
  salvation history 81, 83–84, 86–87, 93–95, 105, 110–114, 118–21, 123–26, 132–36

-243-

benefits (cont.)
  spiritual development   83–84, 105, 107–8, 112, 142–44, 164–66, 168, 196–98
  worship   117, 123, 127–28
Candidus   110
Christology. *See also* Jesus Christ
  Antiochene   8, 217
  exegetical schools   217–18
  Gospel of John   4
church. *See* contemporary church; salvation history
clarification of obscurity   20
Clark, Elizabeth   20–21
cleansing of temple   41, 50, 51, 77–96, 99, 121, 142
  benefits
    contemporary church   81–84
    discipleship   90, 93
    Father-Son relationship   85–86, 91
    individual souls   83–84
    Jesus and OT   86, 89–90, 92–93
    divinity   85, 90–92, 95
    two natures   92
    refutation of heresy   86, 88–89
    resurrection   81–83, 85–88
    salvation history   81, 83–84, 86–87, 93–95
  Cyril of Alexandria   77–78, 90–96
  exegetical schools   77–78, 96
  John Chrysostom   77–78, 84–86, 96
  literal reading   77–81, 84–93, 95–96
  nonliteral reading   77–79, 81–84, 90, 93–96
  Origen   77–78, 78–84, 96, 99
  Theodore of Mopsuestia   77–78, 86–90, 96, 121, 205
  typology   79, 81–83
  usefulness of Scripture   78–81, 87
commentary on John   7–8.
  Heracleon 5, 7, 73, 78–79, 88, 99–100, 102–3, 109
  Origen   6–7, 109
condescension
  Cyril of Alexandria   189, 209–10

condescension (cont.)
  exegetical principle   58
  Jesus   173–74, 189, 201–2, 205–6, 209–10
  John Chrysostom   58, 173–74, 201–2
  Theodore of Mopsuestia   205–6
contemplation   10, 16, 24–25, 52, 69, 90, 107, 182, 216
contemporary church
  as temple   81–83
  Cyril of Alexandria   126, 134–36, 156–57, 185–87, 189–90
  John Chrysostom   169, 172–73, 175
  Origen   81–84, 167–68
  Theodore of Mopsuestia   177–78
Cyril of Alexandria
  benefits
    baptism   151, 159–61, 213
    contemporary church   126, 134–36, 156–57, 185–87, 189–90
    discipleship   90, 93
    exemplar   125, 129–31, 135, 152–54, 161, 206–9, 213
    Father-Son relationship   91
    Holy Spirit   125–26, 133–35
    Jesus and OT   90, 92–93, 151, 157, 161
    condescension   189, 209–10
    divinity   90–92, 95, 207, 209–10, 213
    humanity   209–10
    mediation   188
    redemptive death   188–89
    two natures   92, 135, 140, 156–57, 188, 207, 210–11, 213
    unity with Father   128–29
    knowledge   187–88
    nature of God   127–28
    refutation of heresy   126–28, 154–57
    resurrection   188–89, 211–13
    salvation history   93–95, 126, 132–36, 151, 158–59, 161, 182–85
    worship   127–28

Cyril of Alexandria (cont.)
   cleansing of temple   77–78, 90–96
   ideal interpreter   71–73, 160
   Lazarus   206–13
   man born blind   150–61
   parable of good shepherd   163–64, 181–90
   parable of the harvest   125, 132–33, 135
   refutation of Jewish error   158–56
   Samaritan woman at well   125–37
   typology   182
      cleansing of temple   90, 94–95, 99
      Lazarus   192, 206–7
      man born blind   151, 158–60, 162
      parable of good shepherd   182
      Samaritan woman at well   125, 127–28, 130–31, 134–35
   usefulness of Scripture   36–38, 131–32, 150–51
   veneration of OT saints   134–35
Daley, Brian E.   217–18
Daniélou, Jean   13
definitions: reading levels   24–27
Diodore of Tarsus   1, 15, 19, 25, 34, 60
   asketerion   1–2
   Jesus's two natures   127
disciples   56, 86, 89–90, 111, 114–15, 130, 133, 152, 200, 204
   exemplar   149–51, 154, 161, 206–9, 213
   precision   93
discipleship. *See also* spiritual development
   benefit   37–39, 90, 93, 216
   man born blind   139, 144–46, 149, 154
   Samaritan woman at well   114–16
   Thomas   191, 203–4, 206
divine inspiration. *See* inspiration
divinity. *See also* Jesus Christ: divinity
   Cyril of Alexandria   90–92, 95, 207, 209–10, 213
   John Chrysostom   85, 144–48, 173–74, 200, 202

divinity (cont.)
   Theodore of Mopsuestia   150, 204–5
   usefulness of Scripture   43
doctrinal instruction. *See* benefits
eagerness   60, 75
enigma   23, 133
   and symbolic words   182
   and type   125, 134–35
equality with Father. *See* Jesus Christ: divinity
evangelists
   precision   52, 59, 66, 70, 75
exegesis/biblical interpretation   11–12, 19
   Jewish   10
exegetical principles
   allegorical explanation   61, 132
   clarification of obscurity   20
   clarity   23, 28–29
   condescension   58
   gospel interpretation   141–42
   interpretation by Scripture   60–61
   literal and nonliteral meaning   62–63, 73–74
   narrative sequence   67–68
   narrative similarity   67
   nonliteral interpretation   61–62, 67
   precision   19, 57
      biblical authors   55
      evangelists   52, 59, 66, 70, 75
      ideal interpreter   52, 57, 59–60, 65, 72–73, 75, 180
   purpose   57
   unity of Scripture   60
   usefulness of Scripture. *See* usefulness of Scripture
   varied meaning   66–67
exegetical schools   1–3, 13, 16, 28–29, 42
   Alexandrian   2
   Antiochene   2, 10, 18–20
   definition   2
   distinctives   38–40, 215–18
      approach to Scripture   28–29, 39–40, 42–76, 217
      Christology   217–18
      cleansing of temple   77–78, 96

exegetical schools: distinctives (cont.)
   ideal interpreter   75
   Lazarus   191–92, 214
   man born blind   139–40, 161–62
   parable of good shepherd   163–64, 190
   Samaritan woman at well   97–99, 136–37
   usefulness of Scripture   29–40
  Greco-Roman   1–2, 10, 15
  scholarship   8–24
exemplar
  disciples of Christ   39, 84, 93, 95–96, 113, 139, 149–51, 154–55, 161, 206–8, 213
  Jesus
   Cyril of Alexandria   125, 129–31, 135, 206–9, 213
   John Chrysostom   113–14, 121, 198–200, 202
   Origen   99, 103, 112, 193–94
   Theodore of Mopsuestia   204
  man born blind   144–46, 150–51, 153–54, 161
  Mary and Martha   198–99, 201–3, 206–7, 213
  Samaritan woman at well   99, 103–4, 112–16, 121–22, 125, 129–30, 135
  Thomas   191, 203–4, 206
Ezekiel, prophecy   163, 171, 184–85
Father-Son relationship   85–86, 91
  Cyril of Alexandria   91
  John Chrysostom   85–86
figure of speech   27, 111, 119, 163, 169, 182
form
  and image   182
  and type   127–28, 128
Froehlich, Karlfried   9–10, 13–14
Galilee   94, 97–98, 118, 177, 183, 191
Gnosticism   49, 106, 108–9
gnostics   7, 49, 99, 110, 116, 155
good shepherd   *see* parable of good shepherd

Gospel of John   3–6
  and Synoptics   56–57, 74, 79–80
  beneficial nature   43, 59–50, 57–59, 65, 74
  Christology   4
  composition   43, 47–48, 55, 63–65, 79
  doctrine   75–76
  ideal interpreter   43–44, 51–53, 59–60, 65, 71–73, 75, 80–81, 160, 176, 193
  imagery   3, 74
  inspiration   49, 51, 56–57, 64–65, 70
  interpretive principles   40, 44–45, 53–55, 60–63, 66–68
  mysteries   76
  preeminence   48–49, 74
  typology   53–54
gospels.
  interpretive principles   141–42
  typology   50–51
Heracleon
  refutation   7, 72–73, 109–10
  commentary on John   5, 7, 73, 78–79, 88, 99–100, 102–3, 109
  divine nature   102–3
  John 4   5, 99–100
  heterodox other
  Samaritan woman at well   105–10
  Samaritans   100, 105, 110, 112
hidden things   79, 81
Holy Spirit
  Cyril of Alexandria   125–26, 133–35
  John Chrysostom   120–21
  Theodore of Mopsuestia   121–22, 124–25
humanity   116–17, 121–23, 126–27, 200–201, 209–10. *See also* Jesus Christ: humanity
humility   17, 114, 130, 198, 200, 208, 213
iconic reading
  symbolic reading   16
ideal hearer. *See* ideal interpreter
ideal interpreter   40, 43–44
  attentiveness   59–60, 71–73, 75
  Cyril of Alexandria   71–73, 160

ideal interpreter (cont.)
    doctrinal knowledge   72–73
    eagerness   59–60, 75
    exegetical schools   75
    faith   72–73
    inspiration   59
    intentions   72–73
    John Chrysostom   59–60
    Levitical class   52–53, 71, 75
    prayer   65, 193
    Origen   51–53, 80–81, 81, 193
    precision   52, 59–60, 65, 72–73, 75, 180
    Theodore of Mopsuestia   65, 176
    virtue   44, 51–52, 59–60, 80–81, 179
ideal reader. *See* ideal interpreter
image
    and form   182
    and type   142, 158–60, 182
    cleansing of temple   92, 142
    Gospel of John   3, 74
    Lazarus   192, 197, 206, 211
    of God   103, 117
    of the Father   188
    parable of good shepherd   163–66, 168–69, 172, 175, 178, 181–83, 186–87
    parable of harvest   132
    Samaritan woman at well   103, 108, 117, 119
    usefulness of Scripture   139, 158–60
incarnation   11, 45, 50, 58, 124, 128, 133, 188–89, 211
individual and church   142–43
individual soul. *See* spiritual development
inspiration
    ideal interpreter   59
    Gospel of John   49, 51, 56–57, 64–65, 70
    usefulness of Scripture   33, 36, 38, 43
    virtue   55
interpretive principles. *See also* exegetical principles
    Gospel of John   40, 44–45, 53–55, 60–63, 66–68

interpretive principles (cont.)
    gospels   141–42
Jesus and OT
    Cyril of Alexandria   90, 92–93, 151, 157, 161
    John Chrysostom   114, 117, 121
    Origen   99, 104–6, 112
    Theodore of Mopsuestia   86, 89–90
Jesus Christ
    and Moses   176
    anger   77, 80, 85, 90, 91, 205
    condescension
        Cyril of Alexandria   189, 209–10
        John Chrysostom   173–74, 189, 201–2, 205
        Theodore of Mopsuestia   205–6
    divinity
        Cyril of Alexandria   90–92, 95, 207, 209–10, 213
        John Chrysostom   85, 144–48, 173–74, 200, 202
        Theodore of Mopsuestia   150, 204–5
        usefulness of Scripture   43
    equality with Father. *See* divinity
    exemplar
        Cyril of Alexandria   125, 129, 130–31, 135, 206–9, 213
        John Chrysostom   113–14, 121, 198–200, 202
        Origen   99, 103, 112, 193–94
        Theodore of Mopsuestia   204
    humanity
        Cyril of Alexandria   209–10
        John Chrysostom   116–17, 121, 200–201
        Theodore of Mopsuestia   122–23, 126–27
    humility   17, 114, 130, 198, 200, 208, 213
    incarnation   11, 45, 50, 58, 124, 128, 133, 188–89, 211
    Jew   116
    mediation   188
    redemptive death   179, 188–89
        Cyril of Alexandria   188–89

Jesus Christ (cont.)
- resurrection   77
  - Origen   81–83
  - John Chrysostom   85–86
  - Cyril of Alexandria   188–89
  - Theodore of Mopsuestia   87–88
- two natures
  - Cyril of Alexandria   92, 135, 140, 156–57, 188, 207, 210–11, 213
  - Diodore of Tarsus   127
- type   9, 61, 62–63
- unity with Father
  - Cyril of Alexandria   128–29
  - John Chrysostom   146, 148, 173–74
  - Origen   194–95

Jewish leaders. *See* Pharisees

Jews. *See also* Judaism
- antiexemplar   115, 143
- as church   105, 112
- Gospel of John   6
- Gospel of Matthew   56
- in temple   79–95
- Jesus's self-identification   116, 125, 127
- receptiveness   56, 114–15, 118, 195
- salvation history   78, 79–95, 96–136, 159, 167, 172, 178, 184–85, 211
- versus Jesus   87, 126, 169–70, 191, 204–5, 207
- versus man born blind   139, 150, 154–57
- versus Samaritans   97, 99–100, 112–13, 117–18

John Chrysostom
- benefits
  - contemporary church   169, 172–73, 175
  - exemplar   113–16, 121, 144–46, 198–200, 202
  - Father-Son relationship   85, 86
  - Holy Spirit   120–21
  - Jesus and OT   114, 117, 121
  - condescension   173–74, 189, 201–2, 205

John Chrysostom: benefits (cont.)
- divinity   85, 144–48, 173–74, 200, 202
- humanity   116–17, 121, 200–201
- unity with Father   146, 148, 173–74
- knowledge   173
- nature of God   117, 121
- resurrection   85–86
- salvation history   114, 118–21, 169–72, 175
- worship   117
- cleansing of temple   77–78, 84–86, 96
- condescension   58, 173–74, 201–2
- Gospel of John
  - and Synoptics   56–57
  - beneficial nature   57–59
  - composition   55
  - inspiration   56
  - interpretive principles   60–63
  - ideal interpreter   59–60
- Lazarus   198–202
- literal reading   77–78, 84–86, 96–99, 113–21, 136–37, 144–46, 163–64, 169–75, 190, 191–92, 198–202, 214
- man born blind   144–48
- nonliteral reading   144, 146–48
- parable of good shepherd   163–64, 169–175, 190
- parable of the harvest   118–20
- Samaritan woman at well   113–21, 136–37
- typology   17, 61–63
- usefulness of Scripture   32–34, 38, 84–85, 86, 113, 144, 147

journey to God/Father. *See* spiritual development

Judaism. *See also* Jews; Pharisees
- exegesis/biblical interpretation   10
- temple   81–83
- Torah   122
- worship   84, 87, 95–96, 116–18, 123, 127–28, 159

Judas, insurrectionist   170–71, 175, 177, 181, 183

Judea   98, 118, 134, 191
knowledge
  Cyril of Alexandria   187–88
  John Chrysostom   173
  Theodore of Mopsuestia   178–79
law, spiritual meaning   103
Lazarus   41, 191–214
  benefits
    baptism   213
    exemplar   192–94, 198–200, 202–
      4, 206–9, 213
    condescension   201–2, 205–6,
      209–10
    divinity   200–202, 204–5, 207,
      209–10, 213
    humanity   200, 209–10
    two natures   207, 210–11, 213
    unity with Father   194–95
    resurrection   211–13, 213
    spiritual development   196–98
  Cyril of Alexandria 191–92, 206–13,
    214
  exegetical schools   191–92, 214
  John Chrysostom   191–92, 198–202,
    214
  literal reading 191–96, 198–211, 213,
    214
  nonliteral reading   192, 195–98, 206,
    211–14
  Origen   191–98, 214
  Theodore of Mopsuestia   191–92,
    202–6, 214
Levitical class
  ideal interpreter   52–53, 71, 75
Libanius   1, 15
literal and nonliteral meaning   62–63,
  73–74
literal reading. See also nonliteral reading
  cleansing of temple
    Cyril of Alexandria   90–93
    exegetical schools   77–78, 96
    John Chrysostom   84–86
    Origen   79–80
    Theodore of Mopsuestia   86–90
  definition   24–27

literal reading (cont.)
  difficulty   79–80
  exegetical schools   77–78, 96–99,
    136–37, 139–40, 161–62, 190–92,
    214
  Lazarus
    Cyril of Alexandria   202–11
    exegetical schools   191–92, 214
    John Chrysostom   198–202
    Origen   192–96
    Theodore of Mopsuestia   202–6
  man born blind
    Cyril of Alexandria   150–57
    exegetical schools 139–40, 161–62
    John Chrysostom   144–46
    Origen   140–42
    Theodore of Mopsuestia   148–50
  parable of good shepherd
    Cyril of Alexandria   181–90
    exegetical schools   163–64, 190
    John Chrysostom   169–75
    Origen   164–68
    Theodore of Mopsuestia   175–81
  Samaritan woman at well   99–104,
    112–36
    Cyril of Alexandria   125–36
    exegetical schools   97–99, 136–37
    John Chrysostom   113–21
    Origen   99–104, 112
    Theodore of Mopsuestia   121–25
  Theodore of Mopsuestia   77–78, 86–
    90, 96–99, 121–25, 136–37, 148–
    50, 163–64, 202–6, 214
Lubac, Henri de   12–13
man born blind   41, 139–62, 204
  benefits
    baptism   151, 159–61
    contemporary church   156–57
    exemplar   144–46, 149–54, 161
    gospel interpretation   141–42
    individual and church   142–43
    individual souls   142–44
    Jesus and OT   151, 157, 161
    divinity   144–48, 150
    two natures   156–57, 161

man born blind: benefits (cont.)
   unity with Father   146, 148
   refutation of heresy   154, 155–57
   salvation history   142–43, 151, 158–59, 161
  Cyril of Alexandria   139–40, 150–62
  exegetical schools   139–40, 161–62
  John Chrysostom   139–40, 144–48, 161–62
  literal reading   139–40, 144–46, 148–57, 161–62
  nonliteral reading   139–44, 146–48, 150–51, 153, 158–62
  Origen   139–44, 161–62
  Theodore of Mopsuestia   139–40, 148–50, 161–62
  usefulness of Scripture   144, 147, 149–51
Marcion   116, 167
Martens, Peter   18–20
Mary and Martha as exemplars
  Cyril of Alexandria   206–7, 213
  John Chrysostom   198–99, 202
  Theodore of Mopsuestia   203, 206
Mary, mother of Jesus   51, 195
meaning. *See* literal and nonliteral meaning; spiritual meaning; varied meaning
mediation, Jesus   188
metaphor
  interpretation   27
  reading level   27
Mitchell, Margaret   21–23, 29
Moses
  as gatekeeper   163, 169–70, 175, 175–77, 181–83
  Israel   167
  Jesus   62, 104, 154, 176
  prophets   98, 111–13
  rock struck by   148
  writings   117
narrative coherence   15–16
narrative sequence   67–68
narrative similarity   67
nature of God
  Cyril of Alexandria   127–28

nature of God (cont.)
  John Chrysostom   117, 121
  Origen   99–102
  Theodore of Mopsuestia   123
nonliteral reading. *See also* literal reading
  cleansing of temple
    Cyril of Alexandria   90, 93–95
    exegetical schools   77–78, 96
    Origen   81–84
  definition   24–27
  exegetical schools   77–78, 96, 97–99, 136–37, 139–40, 161–62, 191–92, 214
  Lazarus
    Cyril of Alexandria   211–13
    exegetical schools   191–92, 214
    Origen   192, 195–98
  man born blind
    Cyril of Alexandria   150–51, 153, 158–61
    John Chrysostom   144, 146–48
    exegetical schools   139–40, 161–62
    Origen   141–44
  parable of good shepherd   165–66, 168
    exegetical schools   163–64, 190
    Origen   165–66, 168
  Samaritan woman at well   99–102, 104–12, 112–13
    Cyril of Alexandria   125–26, 134–36
    exegetical schools   97–99, 136–37
    Origen   99–102, 104–113
Old Testament typology   39
Origen
  benefits
    contemporary church   81–84, 167–68
    exemplar   99, 103–4, 112, 192–94, 198
    gospel interpretation   141–42
    heterodox other   105–10
    individual and church   142–43
    Jesus and OT   99, 104–6, 112
    Jesus's unity with Father   194–95

Origen: benefits (cont.)
    nature of God   99–102
    refutation of heresy   99–102,
        108–10
    resurrection   81–83
    salvation history   81, 83–84, 105,
        110–13, 142–43, 166–67
    spiritual development   83–84, 105,
        107–8, 112, 142–44, 164–66,
        168, 196–98
cleansing of temple   77–84, 96, 99
gospel nature   45–47
Gospel of John
    and Synoptics   79–80
    beneficial nature   59–50
    composition   47–48, 79
    ideal interpreter   51–53, 80–81,
        193
    interpretive principles   53–55
    preeminence   48–49
ideal interpreter   51–53, 80–81 193
Lazarus   192–98
literal reading   77–81, 96–105, 112,
    136–37, 140–42, 163–68, 190–96,
    214
    difficulty   79–80
man born blind   140–44
parable of good shepherd   163–68, 190
parable of the harvest   105, 110–13
Samaritan woman at well   99–113,
    136–37
Synoptic problem   79–80
typology   50–51, 53–54
    cleansing of temple   79, 81–83
    man born blind   142
    Samaritan woman at well   103, 128
usefulness of Scripture   28–32, 38,
    51, 78–81, 106–7, 132
parable
    symbolic words   182
    type   182
    intepretation   27
    reading level   27
parable of good shepherd   41–42, 163–
    90, 217

parable of good shepherd (cont.)
    benefits
        contemporary church   167–69,
            172–73, 175, 177–78, 185–87,
            189–90
        condescension   173–74, 189
        divinity   173–74
        mediation   188
        redemptive death   179, 188–89
        unity with Father   173–74
        knowledge   173, 178–79, 187–88
        refutation of heresy   180–81
        salvation history   166–67, 169–72,
            175–78, 182–85
        spiritual development   164–68
    Cyril of Alexandria   163–64, 181–90,
        190
    exegetical schools   163–64, 190
    John Chrysostom 163–64, 169–75, 190
    literal reading   163–90
    nonliteral reading   165–66, 168
    Origen   163–64, 164–68, 190
    referents
        contemporary   166, 167–69, 172–
            73, 175
        NT   166–72, 175–78, 181–84
    Theodore of Mopsuestia   163–64,
        175–81, 190
parable of harvest
    Chrysostom   118–20
    Cyril   125, 132–33, 135
    exegetical schools   98–99
    Origen   105, 110–13
    Theodore of Mopsuestia   121, 123–24
parabolic action   87
parabolic description   92
Passover   77–78, 111
Pharisees   41, 139, 163
    Cyril of Alexandria   154, 158–59,
        182–85, 189
    John Chrysostom   144–46, 170–71,
        174–76
    Origen   143–44, 166
    Theodore of Mopsuestia   149, 150,
        177, 181

precision
  biblical authors 55
  disciples 93
  evangelists 52, 59, 66, 70, 75
  exegetical principle 19, 57
  ideal interpreter 52, 59–60, 65, 72–73, 75, 180
  Mosaic law 176
reading. *See also* literal reading; nonliteral reading
  exegetical schools 215–16
  level
    definition 24
    literal 24–27, 215–18
    nonliteral 24–27, 215–18
    metaphor 27
    parable 27
  rationale 147–48, 151–52, 215
redemptive death 179, 188–89
refutation
  Heracleon 7, 72–73, 109–10
  heresy
    Cyril of Alexandria 126, 126–28, 154–57
    Origen 99–102, 108–10
    Theodore of Mopsuestia 86, 88–89, 180–81
  Jewish error 158–56
resurrection 11
  Cyril of Alexandria 188–89, 211–13
  general 78, 81–83, 86, 191, 211–13
  Jesus 77, 81–83, 85–88, 188–89
  John Chrysostom 85–86
  Lazarus 41, 191–214
  Origen 81–83
  Theodore of Mopsuestia 87–88
salvation history 32, 34, 36, 38–39, 42, 77–78, 98–99, 140, 163
  Cyril of Alexandria 93–95, 126, 132–36, 151, 158–59, 161, 182–85, 211
  John Chrysostom 114, 118–21, 169–72, 175
  Origen 81, 83–84, 105, 110–13, 142–43, 166–67

salvation history (cont.)
  Theodore of Mopsuestia 86, 87, 121, 123–25, 175–78
Samaria 97–98, 114, 118, 134
Samaritan woman at well 41, 97–137
  apostle 104, 116, 139
  benefits
    contemporary church 126, 134–36
    exemplar 99, 103–4, 112–16, 121–22, 125, 129–31, 135
    heterodox other 105–10
    Holy Spirit 120–22, 124–26, 133–35
  Jesus and OT 99, 104–6, 112, 114, 117, 121
  humanity 116–17, 121–23, 126–27
  unity with Father 128–29
  nature of God 99–102, 117, 121, 123, 127–28
  refutation of heresy 99–102, 108–10, 126–28
  salvation history 105, 110–14, 118–21, 123–26, 132–36
  spiritual development 105, 107–8, 112
  worship 117, 123, 127–28
  Cyril of Alexandria 97–99, 125–36, 136–37
  exegetical schools 97–99, 136–37
  exemplar 99, 103–4, 112–116, 121–22, 125, 129–30, 135
  heterodox other 105–10
  John Chrysostom 97–99, 113–21, 136–37
  literal reading 97–104, 112–21, 121–37
  nonliteral reading 97–102, 104–12, 125–26, 134–37
  Origen 97–113, 136–37
  Theodore of Mopsuestia 97–99, 121–25, 136–37
  usefulness of Scripture 106–7, 113, 131–32
Samaritans
  heterodox other 100, 105, 110, 112

General Index

Samaritans (cont.)
  messianic expectations   104, 117
  receptiveness   119, 122–24, 132
  versus Jews   97, 99–100, 112–13, 117–18
  worship   116–18
sequence. *See* narrative sequence
sign   77, 83, 87, 89, 94, 151, 158
signification   94, 119, 129, 183
soul. *See* spiritual development
spiritual development   83–84, 105, 107–8, 112, 142–44, 164–66, 168, 196–98
spiritual meaning
  law   103
  allegory   99, 108
  anagogy   99
  contemplation   16
Sychar   110
symbol   27, 79, 83
symbolic action   87
symbolic reading   16, 47, 83
  iconic reading   16
symbolic representation   39
symbolic words   3, 27, 61,
  cleansing of temple   77–78, 81–82, 85–86, 88, 90, 93, 96
  man born blind   150, 152–53
  parable of good shepherd   164, 169, 175, 182
  Samaritan woman at well   98, 110, 112–13, 118, 120–21, 123–25, 128, 132–33
Synoptic problem   79–80
temple. *See also* cleansing of temple; Judaism
  as contemporary church   81–83
  end of cult   84, 87, 95–96, 116–18, 123
Theodore of Mopsuestia
  benefits
    contemporary church   177–78
    exemplar   121–22, 125, 149–51, 203–4, 206
    Holy Spirit   121–22, 124–25
    Jesus and OT   86, 89–90
    condescension   205–6

Theodore of Mopsuestia: benefits (cont.)
    divinity   150, 204–5
    humanity   122–23, 126–27
    redemptive death   179
    knowledge   178–79
    nature of God   123
    refutation of heresy   86, 88–89, 180–81
    resurrection   87–88
    salvation history   86–87, 121, 123–25, 175–78
    worship   123
  cleansing of temple   77–78, 86–90, 96, 121, 205
  Gospel of John
    beneficial nature   65
    composition   63–65
    ideal interpreter   65
    interpretive principles   66–68
  ideal interpreter   65, 176
  Lazarus   202–6
  man born blind   148–50
  parable of good shepherd   163–64, 175–181, 190
  parable of the harvest   121, 123–24
  Samaritan woman at well   121–25, 136–37
  typology   67–68
  usefulness of Scripture   28–29, 34–36, 38, 87, 148–49
Theudas, insurrectionist   170–71, 175, 177, 181, 183
Thomas, disciple
  exemplar   191, 203–4, 206
Torjesen, Karen Jo   12, 31
Trinity   210
  controversies   4, 195
  doctrine   91, 116, 194
  heresy   36
  inspiration   49, 56, 57
  knowledge   160
  Nicene   7–8, 91, 179
  subordinationist   103
two natures, Jesus. *See* Jesus Christ: two natures

254   Interpreting the Gospel of John in Antioch and Alexandria

type 9, 94, 128, 182
   contemplation 90, 96, 182
   enigma 125, 134–35, 182
   example 130–31, 135
   form 127–28, 128
   image 142, 158–60, 182
   cleansing of temple 90, 94–95
   Jacob's well 99, 134–35
   Jesus's actions 134–35, 142, 159–160, 211, 213
   Jewish worship 103, 127–28
   law 103
   Lazarus 192, 206–7, 211, 213
   man born blind 142, 151, 158–160, 162
   of Christ 9, 61–63
   parable of good shepherd 182
   Pharisees 159
   resurrection of Jesus 82–83
   Samaritan woman at well 125, 134–35
   spiritual worship 128, 159
   temple 79, 81–82
typology 9–10, 16
   allegory 12–13, 16–18, 24–25, 67–68
   anagogy 82–83
   cleansing of temple 79, 81–83, 90, 94–95, 99
   Gospel of John 53–54
   gospels 50–51
   John Chrysostom 17, 61–63
   Lazarus 192, 206–7
   man born blind 142, 151, 158–160, 162
   Old Testament 39
   parable of good shepherd 182
   Samaritan woman at well 103, 125, 127–28, 130–31, 134–35
   Theodore of Mopsuestia 67–68
unity of Scripture 60
unity with Father 128–29, 146, 148, 173–74, 194–95
usefulness of Scripture 3, 21, 51, 144, 147, 150–51, 158, 215
   analytical category 28

usefulness of Scripture (cont.)
   Cyril of Alexandria 36–38, 131–32, 150–51
   exegetical principle 28–30
   exegetical schools 28–29, 38–40
   inspiration 33, 36, 38, 43
   Jesus's divinity 43
   John Chrysostom 32–34, 38, 84–86, 113, 144, 147
   Origen 29–32, 38, 51, 78–81, 106–7, 132
   reading levels 38–40
   Theodore of Mopsuestia 34–36, 38, 87, 149
Valentinian. *See* Ambrose; Heracleon
Valentinus 167
varied meaning 66–67
veneration of OT saints 134–35
virtue 212, 216. *See also* discipleship
   disciples 39, 84, 113, 150
   evangelists 59
   ideal interpreter 44, 51–52, 59–60, 80–81, 179
   inspired author 46, 55
   Jesus 139, 198, 213
   Jesus as means to 177–79, 192
   John the Evangelist 55, 59, 64
   Lazarus 191, 196
   Mary and Martha 191, 198–99, 203
   Samaritan woman at well 113, 115, 121–22, 125
   worship 123, 127–28
woman at well. *See* Samaritan woman at well
woman of Samaria. *See* Samaritan woman at well
worship 83, 123, 127–28. *See also* temple cult
   bodily versus spiritual 116–18, 127–28, 133, 159
   Cyril of Alexandria 127–28
   Jesus 98–100, 117, 121, 123, 127, 136
   Jewish 116, 127–28
   John Chrysostom 117
   Origen 98–100

worship (cont.)
  Theodore of Mopsuestia   123
Young, Frances   6, 9, 14–18, 20, 25

www.ingramcontent.com/pod-product-compliance
Lightning Source LLC
Chambersburg PA
CBHW021351300426
44114CB00012B/1170